C0-AMY-549

Briefly,
ABOUT THE BOOK

James Connolly, Irish Socialist Republican
and greatest of all Irish labour leaders,
was shot – strapped to a chair because his
wounds forbade him to stand – by a British
firing squad on May 12, 1916. Although several biographies of Connolly exist this is
the first to tell in detail the story of
his political life and public activity.
From 1889 to 1916 Connolly was politically
involved in three countries: in Scotland
he was one of the pioneers of the modern
labour movement; in Ireland he founded
the Irish Socialist Republican Party and
whilst in the U.S.A. he became a founding
member of the I.W.W. – the "Industrial
Workers of the World". Upon his return to
Ireland in 1910 he played a leading role
in the struggles of the Irish working class,
which culminated in the Easter Rising of
1916 .... In preparing this biography
to produce an authoritative account of the
C. Desmond Greaves had access to many
unpublished sources which enabled him
man and the movements he helped to shape.

INTERNATIONAL PUBLISHERS
381 Park Avenue South
NEW YORK, N.Y. 10016

THE LIFE AND TIMES
of
JAMES CONNOLLY
by
C. DESMOND GREAVES

THE LIFE
AND TIMES
of
JAMES
CONNOLLY

by

C. DESMOND
GREAVES

International Publishers
New York

063726⌐ 82712

First published by Lawrence & Wishart, London, 1961
This edition is published simultaneously by
International Publishers, New York, Lawrence & Wishart,
London, and Seven Seas Books, Berlin, 1971
Second impression 1976

Copyright (c) C. Desmond Greaves, 1961
ISBN 0-7178-0330-9
Cover Design by Lothar Reher
Printed in the German Democratic Republic

CONTENTS

Preface   9

I Childhood 1868–1882   11

II Youth 1882–1889   26

III Able Apprentice 1889–1894   44

IV Local Leader 1894–1896   56

V Dublin and the I.S.R.P. 1896–1897   72

VI Polemics and Set-backs 1897–1898   93

VII The Workers' Republic 1898–1899   106

VIII International Socialism 1900–1902   126

IX The Socialist Labour Party 1902–1903   146

X America 1903–1905   168

XI The Industrial Workers of the World 1905–1908   189

XII The Harp 1908   214

XIII Preparing for Return 1908–1910   229

XIV The Socialist Party of Ireland 1910–1911   246

XV Belfast Organiser 1911–1912   264

XVI Counter-revolution 1912–1913   284

XVII The Great Lock-out 1913   305

XVIII Partition 1913–1914   340

XIX Imperialist War 1914–1915   351

XX Maturing Revolution 1915–1916   371

XXI The Dread Abyss   394

Epilogue   425

Bibliography   432

Index   440

0637267 82712

PREFACE

This book is the story of James Connolly's political life and public activity. It is not the story of his personal affairs or inner emotions, something of which has been published by his daughter in her *Portrait of a Rebel Father*.

Apart from existing biographies, articles in periodicals, newspapers and other primary sources, efforts have been made to consult Connolly's surviving associates, who have in most cases proved helpful in the extreme. The bulk of Connolly's correspondence has not been available, but it is unlikely that its ultimate publication will materially alter the conclusions drawn.

So many individuals have assisted with reminiscences and material that it is impossible to thank them all by name. There are some however to whom special thanks are due, particularly to Mr. H. A. Scott in Edinburgh, Mrs. Ina Connolly-Heron in Dublin, and Mr. Levinson of New York City who placed his unpublished *Life of Connolly* unconditionally at my disposal. I should like also specially to acknowledge the help given by Mr. Jack Mullery of Liverpool, whose death during the period when the MS. was being prepared prevented his reading the chapters on the I.S.R.P.

I can do no more than mention the American newspapers which inserted my advertisements free of charge, and their readers who replied, the many hundreds on this side of the Atlantic who replied to correspondence, and the helpful officials of the National Library of Ireland, the British Museum at Colindale, the Edinburgh Public Library, the Monaghan County Library at Clones and the Marx Memorial Library in London.

I shall be grateful to readers who can supply additional facts or point out possible errors. Every effort has been made to check all details from original sources and, generally speaking, surmises of probabilities are clearly indicated as such. But there are cases where one authority must be preferred to another. Needless to say any criticism based on a scientific approach will be more than welcome.

C. D. G.

London, June 1960

I

CHILDHOOD

When Edinburgh first became the capital of Scotland, it consisted of a row of wooden houses perched on the heights of Castle Hill. As the city grew, buildings extended eastwards along the declining ridge of High Street.

To the south is a large natural basin where terminated the roads from the Highlands and the west. Goods too heavy for bulk transport up the stony paths to the town were unloaded here and, in course of time, here were established the principal markets of the city, beginning with the Grassmarket by the "West Port" and extending along Cowgate, parallel to High Street, but nearly a hundred feet below it.

Feudal Edinburgh displayed class distinction topographically—the nobility straddled on the pig's back, and the merchants and artisans almost like H. G. Wells's morlocks, who did all the work but were condemned to live underground. The two tiers of the Old Town were made independent by the inter-connection of adjacent ridges by three viaducts. North Bridge linked Castle Hill with Calton Hill, spanning the formerly populous area now occupied by Waverly Station. South Bridge linked High Street with the higher ground of Chambers Street. Finally, King George IV Bridge crossed Cowgate at the west end, linking Castle Hill with Grayfriars. Once the bridges were complete, gentlemen could commingle without passing through the plebeian areas; at the same time wheeled traffic could freely traverse the upper level, and the reason for the stratification disappeared.

Well into the nineteenth century, Grassmarket remained Edinburgh's commercial gateway to the country. Hither trundled wagons of farm produce, hay-carts for the city stables, accompanied by herds of Highland cattle and poultry. Here were established the inns farmers stayed at, and the Corn Exchange where they did business with the city merchants. Around these settled the artisans who made harness, clogs and farm implements. Here, consequently, grew up the first elements of a wage-earning class, ostlers, grooms, porters and odd-job men, journeymen, artificers, and an assortment of vagabonds and social castaways, inhabiting the rough lodging-houses of the West Port.

The rapid development of industry and commerce in Scotland at the beginning of the nineteenth century created Edinburgh as we know it. The upper tier of the old town still housed many of the moderately comfortable professional class. But the newly-rich merchants were satisfied with nothing less than a new town altogether, which, beginning with Princes Street and working northwards, they erected in the space of a generation. Its wide imposing streets and roomy squares increasingly drew the middle class across the line of what is now the railway. It might be possible for Walter Scott to be born in the Cowgate while David Hume inhabited High Street. Fifty years later the entire lower tier was given over to the proletariat, which had even begun to seep upwards, especially through the dark wynds which lead into High Street and Lawnmarket.

Population expanded rapidly. The new town was to be built. Canals, docks, coalmines and, later, railways were constructed. Large-scale commercial farming developed in the counties of Berwick and Selkirk. Commerce with the textile areas of Glasgow and the west brought increasing wealth and business to the capital. Adequate labour could only be supplied by immigration, whose direction was predetermined.

To south and east were mines, farms, docks and ships. North-west was a Highland peasantry destituted by repeated clearances. West was Ireland, in a state of chronic agrarian crisis with recurrent famines, arising from a system of land ownership of which it was said there was no known disadvantage which it did not possess. Immigrants therefore came through the West Port of the Grassmarket seeking unskilled work around the markets, or farmers in need of hourly labourers for the harvest.

The tenement system was early established. Tall buildings grouped round a central close were let out room by room to as many families as could be crowded into them. Sanitation was primitive. Each family had a bucket which was deposited at nightfall in the close, to be collected after dark and its contents sold to the farmers. This was a perquisite of the factors, or landlord's agents. Later the municipality took over the service and employed "manure carters" or "nightsoil workers".

Edinburgh was thus a focal point of interchange between town and country, though further industrial development destroyed their "natural" relationship, with sewers and incinerators on the one side and artificial fertilisers on the other.

Irish immigrants began to come in substantial numbers for the building of the new town and, from that time on, one project after another held the new arrivals. They landed at the Broomielaw in Glasgow, but at harvest time scarcely one remained in the city by nightfall, all having hit the road for Edinburgh. Most were hired by farmers in the Grassmarket, and would work from south to north as the crops ripened, starting at Berwick and reaching as far as Perth. Some avoided the whisky-shops and confidence tricksters and returned to Ireland for the winter, carrying a year's respite for their rackrented holdings. Others found employment to tide them through the winter in Scotland and began to loosen their hold on agricultural life.

In this way an Irish colony established itself in the city. Its centre was the Cowgate, where some of its more fortunate members found openings in the clothing trade. Just as farmers bought implements and hired labourers in the same Grassmarket where they sold stock and produce, so the Irish farm labourers, arriving to sell their muscle-power, bought the cast-off clothing of artisans and farmers, or such as had made its way down from the gentry, in store-rooms which were mostly owned by Irish people established a few years.

The most depressed section of the people was not Irish but Scots. Thanks to stronger physique and rural upbringing the Irish had access to employment unavailable to the worst placed native labourers. The natural camaraderie of those who had made good in Edinburgh was of service to the newcomers, and joined the Irish in a freemasonry which was reinforced by a wide use of the Gaelic language. Looked down on by the skilled trades, they were regarded with bitter jealousy by the poorest labourers who occasionally adopted violent means of showing their feelings.

Profiting from their contact with a migratory population, a section of the Irish became petty pawnbrokers, then local dealers, and finally established a substantial trade exporting second-hand clothes to Ireland, a trade whose counterpart in London was largely in Jewish hands. In the thirties three-quarters of the two hundred and fifty second-hand clothes dealers of the Grassmarket area were Irish, and migratory labourers turned hawker peddled fish, fruit, cheese, sweetmeats, cheap jewellery, handkerchiefs and halfpenny tapes. They carted coal from local pits and sold it on the streets. In due time a section of these entrepreneurs rose still higher in the social scale and acquired the small businessman's outlook. On the other hand, among those who sought steady employment, a high proportion of the porters at the market, nearly all the one hundred and twelve scavengers, and all the forty-five lamplighters, were Irish.

Anti-Irish feeling, with a sectarian tinge, had much in common with modern anti-semitism. Two lives were lost when the tents of provision sellers at Musselburgh races were searched for Irishmen after a minor dispute. On another occasion local labourers invaded the Cowgate area and assaulted every Irishman they could find, wrecking the shops of the second-hand clothes sellers, and smashing the doors and windows of Irish houses.

The effect was to drive the Irish close together in the ghetto of "little Ireland" and to increase the overcrowding of its teeming warrens. To some extent class-consciousness was postponed. But regional consciousness was proportionately diminished. Two streams of emigration had converged on Edinburgh, the first from Donegal, Derry and Tyrone, the second, somewhat later developing, from Monaghan and the west. While not entirely distinct, the two streams were subjected to different experiences *en route* and emerged in Edinburgh as competitors.

There was particularly strong feeling between the Monaghan men who were mostly labourers and the Donegal men who had secured the more favoured positions.

These divisions further declined in importance as Scots and Irish workers were led to combine against the employers. Scotland has held a strong current of radical tradition, favourable to Irish national aspirations, since the time of the United Irishmen. This was reinforced when joint meetings of Chartists and Repealers were held in Edinburgh in the days of Feargus O'Connor.

Fresh immigrants kept the knowledge of Ireland green. The hostility of the more backward Scots workers made the children Irish even if they had no wish to be so. The freedom from national prejudice which characterised the radicals drew the Irish towards the left, a process accelerated when after the vast influx of the famine years came the political refugees of 1848.

The lower tier of the old town then presented an amazing spectacle. In this melting pot of occupations and origins, overcrowding, filth, squalor, poverty, drunkenness and disease were illuminated by flashes of philanthropy, heroism and revolt.

Against poverty, charitable institutions organised relief work. The temperance movement tackled the drunkenness which arose from intolerable conditions of existence. Missions combined social work with religious teaching, and the task of uplifting their less fortunate brethren fell naturally to the dealers who were rising in the social scale and who became at once pillars of the Church and political chiefs of the Irish community. As time went on Irish nationalism exfoliated a Whiggish crest, though its adherents belonged overwhelmingly to the working class.

On October 20, 1856, two twenty-three-year-old members of this Irish community, John Connolly and Mary McGinn, who lived at 6, Kingstables, a street branching from Grassmarket right under the shoulder of Castle Hill, presented themselves at the house of their parish priest and were married according to the rites of the Catholic Church. The ceremony took place at 17, Brown Square, now part of Chambers Street, and the priest was Alexander O'Donnell, of St. Patricks, Cowgate. The two witnesses, Myles Clarke and Mary Carthy, being illiterate, signed with a cross.

John described himself as an agricultural labourer; but from the fact that the couple were in the same house six years later it seems he was then ready to finish with the harvest and become a townsman. Mary was a domestic servant. Each had lost one parent, John his father, also a farm-labourer called John (or Owen), and Mary her mother, Maria McGinn whose maiden name was Burns. The two surviving parents were Mary Connolly (born Markie) and James McGinn, also a labourer.

Nothing is known of the origin of the Connolly family except that John Connolly was born somewhere in Ireland and had some knowledge of Gaelic. But the McGinn family is better documented thanks to the circumstance that one of Mary's brothers was married in Glasgow in 1855, the one year when the Registrar demanded particulars of birthplace. Both James McGinn and his bride, Bridget Boyle, were born in Co. Monaghan. They were married at St. Andrews Chapel, Great Clyde Street, and lived at 71, Stockwell Street. Both they and Bridget's two brothers, Owen Boyle and Thomas Boyle, who witnessed the marriage, were then illiterate. Subsequently James became a boatyard worker in Glasgow and a gasworker in Dundee, where Owen Boyle also settled, opening a business as a hawker in St. Mary Street, Lochee Road.

Two years after his marriage to Mary McGinn, John Connolly entered the service of the Edinburgh Corporation as a manure carter. His duties would be to remove soil and dung at night when the streets were free from traffic, and at times possibly to cart ashes on a Saturday and sweep up what was spilt on the following morning.

The work was arduous and ill-paid. Discontent grew to a head in 1861. During an exceptionally hard winter marked by severe unemployment the sufferings of the working class were intense. As prosperity returned to the seasonal trades, wage demands were lodged. The building trades struck in March, and on August 13 took place the famed and almost legendary manure carters' strike. The scavengers presented a letter to the Town Clerk reporting a general meeting at which it was resolved that since all other classes of operatives had received wage increases, they themselves demanded a rate of 15s. a week to take effect on Wednesday, August 14. They demanded an answer by 10 a.m. of that day, and received it. The streets and buildings committee met specially to consider and grant their application. This strike had an invaluable effect on the morale of unskilled workers.

A few months after the strike, Connolly's first son John was born. But following the birth, which took place on January 31, 1862, Mary Connolly fell sick with chronic bronchitis from which she suffered until her death thirty years later.

The family then moved to Campbell's Close, Cowgate, where Thomas Connolly was born on April 27, 1866.

The youngest son, James, was born in yet another lodging, 107, Cowgate, on June 5, 1868. The site of the house is now covered by part of the Heriot-Watt technical college. James followed his brothers to school at St. Patrick's, a few hundred yards east along Cowgate.

Shortly after James's birth the family moved into Carubbers Close off High Street. This was topographically, and in those days possibly socially also, "up in the world".

John Connolly had been promoted to the rank of lamp-lighter shortly before the move, but apparently did not hold the better position long. By 1881 he was again a carter and the family lived in extreme poverty, back again in King-stables, but this time at No. 2a. Following the custom among the unskilled workers, the eldest son spent a few years in "blind alley" occupations, but as soon as he was in a position to claim the age of eighteen, enlisted in the King's Liverpool Regiment (2nd Battalion) and was despatched to India in September, 1877. He was not yet sixteen. It may have been to facilitate the falsification of his age that he assumed the name of John Reid.

Thomas, the second son, was more fortunate. He secured

17

work as a compositor's labourer, tradition has it in the office of the *Edinburgh Evening News*. Little definite is known about him. He is believed to have learned the trade and emigrated. James's first verifiable job was in a bakery when he was twelve years old, but it is stated that he had already spent a year in the same office as Thomas. He must therefore have started work at the age of ten or eleven. The law placed the onus of "providing education in the Three R's" on the parents. The elder John's confident signature in the marriage register indicates his ability to accept it. But poverty had certainly denied him the means. To this period belong, without a doubt, James's reminiscences of reading by the light of embers, whose charred sticks served him as pencils. From this doubtless came his slight squint. His slight bow-leggedness may have been due to a trace of rickets. He worked as a printer's "devil"—the boy who washed inky rollers, fetched adult workers' beer or tea, filled cans of oil or ink and acted as the general factotum and butt of all pleasantries. When the Factory Inspector made his periodical visit, James was hastily summoned from his multifarious duties and planted on a high stool behind a case of type. But the manœuvre was discovered and he had to be dismissed.

The duration of James's next employment, in a bakery, is uncertain, but may have been two years. According to Ryan, whose information was derived from Leslie, contemporary and intimate of the elder brother John, his health broke down under the strain, and he then secured work in a mosaic tiling factory. This was presumably Messrs. Hawley's in Frederick Street, but could scarcely be described as a factory. It was rather a depot for supplying marbles and chimney pieces, the firm acting as agents for manufacturers in Staffordshire. A certain air of elegance seems to have attached to the establishment, for one of its advertisements stated that "ladies" were "taught mosaic". The work here would be lighter. But since Connolly was at the bakery until the spring of 1881, and left Edinburgh the following year, he cannot have spent more than a year at it. The firm may have been failing. It ceased to advertise in 1885. But that its interest in

James Connolly would cease the moment younger boys became available is a certainty.

Thus at the age of fourteen Connolly faced the common dilemma of children of the labouring class. He must "take the shilling" or starve. From indications in his writings he was possibly already politically conscious and a "nationalist of the extreme type". He "devoured the publications of the Land League", founded in 1879 in Mayo, but now with a supporting organisation throughout Britain.

These were days of crisis and struggle, the centre of which was the agrarian agitation. Physical force Fenians joined hands with militant Parliamentarians when Parnell led the greatest conjunction of Irish national forces in modern times. At Westminster the watchword was "obstruction"; in Ireland "boycott". New methods of struggle had been devised to meet new needs, and the Land League came to comprise practically the entire adult tenantry of Ireland. Grandmasters of Orange lodges spoke from the same platform as Michael Davitt, and because the land agitation had a counterpart in Britain, from Scotland as far south as Lancashire, it was sympathetically appreciated by British workers who still regarded the landlord rather than the capitalist as their principal enemy.

Whatever the precise foundation for the family tradition that Connolly was taught Irish nationalism by a Fenian uncle who enlisted under the name of MacBride and retained it after settling in Edinburgh, in these days he could scarcely have escaped it. The jailing of the Land League leaders in 1881 was followed by a manifesto calling for a general withholding of rent. Ribbonism (violent reprisals organised by secret agrarian societies) or, as the Government described it, "agrarian crime" reached record proportions. The land question dominated all else, and the Irish community in Britain followed with breathless interest Parnell's tactical success at Kilmainham, when the Government was compelled to ask his terms for calling off the land war, and the sudden destruction of his advantage by the Phoenix Park murders a few days later.

There was nothing in a nationalist background to prevent James following his brother into the army. In 1900, during his campaign against enlistment for the South African War, Connolly still had to meet the objections of sincere nationalists who cited the Fenian precedent of joining up in order to "learn the use of arms". An article in *The United Irishman* in November 1900, possibly written by Connolly, described how the Fenians joined the King's Liverpool Regiment with subversive intent. In 1867 all rifles were held in the depot, and again in 1881 their nipples were removed in order to render them useless.

When, therefore, James Connolly joined the first battalion of the King's Liverpool Regiment at the age of fourteen, he was committing no act of apostasy, but following the custom of his day. The regiment counted as an Irish one. The uniform was dark green and the badge an Irish harp surmounted with a crown. The band played Irish airs during marches, and on such ceremonial occasions as St. Patrick's Day there were Church Parades to hear Mass. The battalion was moved to Cork in July 1882, and it was thus as a raw militiaman that Connolly first set eyes on Ireland, where he was to remain for nearly seven years.

Most accounts of Connolly's early years differ substantially from that given here, and it is of some importance to know the origin of the major inaccuracies. The correct birthday (June 5, 1868) and place (107, Cowgate, Edinburgh) are recorded in the register of births, and a simple comparison with the registration of Connolly's marriage establishes that the entry relates to the right man.

The post-dating of the birth originated in a notice signed by Mark Deering (though said to have been written by Murtagh Lyng) in the *Weekly People* before Connolly's first visit to the U.S.A. in 1902. Connolly was lecturing in Manchester when it was written and was both amused and irritated when he saw it. His comment that the date given for his birth (1869) was a year out led his friends to prefer 1870.

The same writer lightly invented a birthplace "near

Clones", and once his successors accepted it the chronology of Connolly's life was thrown into confusion. For example, Connolly's statement that he lived twenty years among the Irish exiles in Britain is confirmed when we know those years were 1868–82 and 1889–96. If, on the other hand, we believe he spent his first ten years in Ireland, but know that he was at work in Edinburgh at the age of twelve and quit Scotland in 1896, we have to assume that he was in Britain between 1882 and 1889, and even then there are not enough years to make up the twenty, still less when 1870 is taken as the year of his birth.

All attempts to identify the supposed locality "near Clones" have completely failed. They have been numerous and often repeated after some new scrap of evidence seemed to have appeared. In the *Irish Press* on April 28, 1941, Seamus O'Mordha mentioned Anlore, two miles east of Clones, but later rejected it in favour of Bochoill about six miles away. He stated that there were still a few people who remembered Connolly's parents, who were labourers. This would assume a recollection stretching back over sixty-one years, not impossible, or necessarily improbable. But whether, in view of the fact that Connolly is the second commonest name in Monaghan, and James by no means a rarity, it is possible to identify one particular James Connolly across those years of disturbance and emigration is another matter.

The possibility of Anlore came to the fore again when in 1954 the Clones Urban Council considered the possibility of a memorial to Connolly in the town. Careful investigations were conducted, in which the present author was concerned, and every spot mentioned in the literature was visited without result. It was difficult to avoid the conclusion that James Connolly the socialist leader had been confused with another James Connolly, a ribbonman who was hanged around the year 1806, and whose fame is still sung in the rhyme:

> "In famous Anlore,
> James Connolly was born."

There is no more support for the other suggested district in Co. Monaghan, Ballybay. This is first mentioned in Robert Lynd's preface to Nora Connolly's *Portrait of a Rebel Father* and owes its origin to a short story written by Connolly in his first *Workers' Republic* and entitled "A Night in the Mendicity". For some reason, possibly by reference to Monaghan, this was considered to be autobiographical. A reference to a cabin "where the road from Keady strikes over the hills into the town of Ballybay" gave rise to the belief that Connolly was describing his birthplace. But the story is offered as pure fiction and its purpose is to illustrate the disintegration of the peasantry and the degradations which accompany absorption into the proletariat. Keady is situated at a considerably greater elevation than Ballybay and no spot answering Connolly's description seems to exist.

Robert Lynd first met Connolly around 1897 and could have known nothing of Connolly's early life. The obituaries written in 1916 give no help. *The Irish Times* first cited Cork, but later substituted Monaghan. *The Cork Examiner* mentioned Scotland, then changed it to "the North of Ireland". Other newspapers suggested Liverpool (probably confusing Connolly with Larkin) and Glasgow, where he was known to have lived. *The Scotsman,* possibly basing itself on information supplied by Leslie, said that "when a young man" Connolly "came to Edinburgh with his parents". On the other hand, H. W. Lee, historian of the Social-Democratic Federation, states that Connolly was born in Edinburgh, but incorrectly substitutes Grassmarket for Cowgate.

Gerald O'Connor, T. A. Jackson and some others refer to a tradition that Connolly's grandfather or great-uncle was hanged for his part in the 1798 rising. O'Connor derived his information from Thomas Lyng who met Connolly in 1896; T. A. Jackson from Con O'Lyhane who met him a year or two later. The date of Connolly's father's birth makes such possibilities somewhat remote.

Once the false chronology was accepted and the periods of Connolly's life were transposed there seemed to follow logically what was in reality a fantastic edifice of specula-

82712

tion. The famine year of 1880 was adopted for a supposed migration to Edinburgh. Descriptions of country life in Co. Monaghan were adduced to fill in the missing details of childhood. Quinlan described Connolly's father leading an exodus from the district, breaking the journey in Belfast, crossing to Glasgow and undertaking potato-picking till enough money was earned to take them all to Edinburgh where they were welcomed by James's uncle, an old Fenian. Old Monaghan people in New York and Massachusetts were said to remember him. But, like those who have seen ghosts, the people with long memories never come forward in person. Quinlan may indeed have gathered from Connolly some reminiscences of his parents; the error was in placing these events in 1880. If Connolly's parents emigrated as a result of a famine, it was the great famine of 1846–7, and not the lesser one of 1880. In his attempt to reconstruct the past, Quinlan telescoped two generations. But fact and date remain the belly and spine of history. The historian should as soon lose one of these as a maiden her virginity. The sooner the legend of Connolly's Monaghan birthplace and the diaspora of 1880 is discarded the better.

Consequences for a later period follow from the Monaghan legend. If imagination must fill out the non-existent childhood in Ireland, it must also invent a youth in Britain. The question was bound to be asked, if Connolly was in Monaghan till 1880, and worked in Edinburgh till 1882, where was he between then and the date of his marriage in 1890?

"Connolly left Edinburgh at the age of eighteen", says Ryan, and became in turn "tramp, navvy and pedlar, spending a roving and eventful life in different parts of Britain". But he records Connolly's extreme reticence on this period. According to this chronology Connolly would reach the age of eighteen in 1888 and would thus rove and peddle for some eighteen months before marrying and settling down. But on the same basis there is a gap between 1884 and 1888, in addition to which there are the additional two years due to the error in the year of birth.

That Connolly did work as a pedlar is known. William O'Brien refers to it in an article in *The Irishman*, but Carolan who peddled with him gave the date as 1900–1. Nora Connolly also relates it to the Dublin period, long after he was married.

As to navvying, R. M. Fox, basing himself on Quinlan's reminiscences written in 1931, develops a picture of the itinerant labourer which owes more to Patrick McGill than to Connolly. Quinlan, incidentally, could not have clearly distinguished the different periods of Connolly's life, for he refers to Connolly living in Newcastle, "labouring in the vineyard" contemporaneously with the residence there of the two Healy brothers. These were there from 1871 to 1878 when, according to Quinlan, Connolly was in Monaghan. Apart from one poem, "The Legacy", no more autobiographical than the "Night in the Mendicity", there is nothing further adducible in support of the "tramp-navvy-pedlar" theory, and Connolly's old associates in Edinburgh derided it. They spoke of deliberately misleading visitors from Dublin out of concern to protect Connolly's reputation. They believed that to admit that he had served in the British forces would discredit him, oblivious of the fact that were this so almost every family in Ireland would be discredited.

The fact of Connolly's army service is attested in several ways. His adoption of a pseudonym rules out direct documentary proof. But there is ample evidence from the statements of contemporaries in Edinburgh, oblique references in his correspondence, his own statements to such friends as Mullery, the authority of Larkin, the surprising knowledge of Cobh he showed in an emergency in 1911, and finally his military proficiency. The evidence is part personal testimony, part inferential, but provides an intelligible coherent picture leaving little of importance to be explained. Connolly spent seven years in America. If he was right in saying that he spent twenty years among the exiles in Britain, then he must have spent twenty-one years in Ireland. These are known to have included 1896–1903, and 1911–16. It has been shown that the missing seven years cannot be placed between 1870 and 1880, so they must fall between 1882 and 1889. If Connolly was in Ireland then, as he must have been on his own statement, what was he doing? There is no alternative to set against the fact that the first battalion of the King's Liverpool Regiment was in Ireland from precisely July 1882 to February 1889. Those who reject this must tell us what else he was doing.

1 Mullett said "Spike Island," but the King's Liverpool Regiment had no men there on the day the records were made up; possibly there may have been a small detachment sent to Spike Island to relieve the Oxfords, but more likely the two stations, which are in very close proximity, were confused.

II
YOUTH

Very few details of Connolly's army life are known. He told Mullery of spending the night on guard, at Haulbowline[1] in Cork Harbour, when Myles Joyce was executed for his part in the Maamtrasna massacre. There is no doubt that Joyce was innocent, and had he been able to speak or understand English he might have been acquitted. Connolly spent the whole night thinking about the impending execution, all his sympathy going out to the men convicted of "agrarian crime". The case had dragged on since July and had excited public interest only less than the Phoenix Park murders.

The battalion remained in Cork until September 1884 when it was transferred to The Curragh of Kildare, two companies being sent to Castlebar, Co. Mayo, until the following March when they joined the others at The Curragh. These may possibly have been the Haulbowline companies, which seem to have been at Youghal since the spring of 1883. If so, Connolly was never stationed in Cork City with the majority of the regiment, and reached The Curragh after periods in Youghal and Castlebar.

Quinlan speaks of Connolly's thirst for Irish nationalist literature and mentions that Connolly told him of sending to Dublin for copies of *Penny Readings*. These were thirty-two-page miscellanies containing popular historical material, poems, speeches from the dock and more current items. They were published from 1884 onwards each month, by the Sullivans, editors of *The Nation*. The picture of Connolly in Edinburgh scraping together his coppers to order from Dublin what was readily available at his doorstep does not carry conviction. If, however, he was at The Curragh during the

---

[1] Mullery said "Spike Island" but the King's Liverpool Regiment had no men there on the day the records were made up: possibly there may have been a small detachment sent to Spike Island to relieve the Oxfords, but more likely the two stations, which are in very close proximity, were confused.

period of publication (1884–7) this account is perfectly comprehensible.

The battalion was rapidly built up during the stay at The Curragh, and had more than doubled in strength when in October 1885 it was moved to Dublin and distributed between Ship Street barracks and the Linen Hall, with a detachment at the Pigeon House fort. The following June, somewhat reduced by transfer to Warrington and Bengal, its entire strength was concentrated at Beggars Bush.

It was in Dublin that Connolly met his future wife, Lillie Reynolds, during an evening trip to Dun Laoghaire, then Kingstown. Connolly strolled from Beggars Bush to near Merrion Square for the tram. The trams used then to stop wherever they were hailed. On this occasion both he and a young woman of his own age, fair, small and refined in an unassuming way, were left behind by an impatient driver and entered into conversation. Their friendship ripened quickly and by the end of 1888 they had decided upon marriage.

"I love Dublin", Connolly said years afterwards. It was at this time that he came to love it. For three years he had observed the spirit of rural Ireland. In Dublin he was present for the Jubilee celebrations, and must have seen, or at least known of, the black flags and unemployed demonstrations. He had feasted on the literature of the Land League and now his mind was being prepared for the advance from nationalism to socialism. At this very time came the first breath of softness into a life of unrelieved asperity.

No contact with the Dublin socialists can be traced. Yet a few years later he was advising Keir Hardie on how to present the socialist case in Dublin. Possibly he was present at open-air meetings. It would seem incredible that a young man whose total knowledge of Ireland was derived during the first ten years of childhood in the hills of Co. Monaghan would feel competent to advise the leader of the I.L.P. on how to address a public meeting in the capital. The Monaghan legend creates this kind of difficulty throughout the course of Connolly's life. But that he could offer such advice meant that Dublin working-class activity had forced itself upon his attention.

For working-class Irish people the advance from nationalism to socialism was the logical outcome of the struggles of the eighteen-eighties. In the struggle against the landlords the boycott expressed the principle of solidarity and the germ of the sympathetic strike. Knowledge that in Britain socialists alone supported Irish national demands was penetrating into Ireland, and Connolly must have heard of it from his brother John who was now back in Edinburgh.

His residence in Ireland corresponded with the most progressive phases of the land agitation. Again and again throughout his life he returned to the Land League as a model of plebeian solidarity. But his own development was sharply accelerated by a sudden personal crisis.

In February 1889 his father suffered an accident which left him all but totally incapacitated. He was discharged from Edinburgh Corporation as unfit for further service. Later the Inspector relented, and found him "light" work as caretaker of the Public Convenience in the Haymarket. For this the Council decided to pay him 7s. 6d. a week "during pleasure", though his previous wage had been 19s. 6d. He was still so engaged as late as December 1891.

The young man must have felt sharp anxiety over his father and chronically sick mother. Then came the threat of parting from his fiancée. The battalion was ordered to Aldershot. He had only about four months to serve, but decided on a precipitate parting from Her Majesty, and arranged to meet Lillie in Perth. As a result of the transfer there seems to have been some confusion in the records of the battalion, and the next muster was not held until after he could be judged to have been discharged. Connolly never knew this, and told his friend Mullery of his surprise at never being apprehended.

The reason for the rendezvous at Perth is obscure. Possibly Peter Boyle of 139, South Street was a distant relative, and found Connolly his accommodation with Mrs. Reilly at No. 129 in the same street. It was from there he wrote to

Lillie an undated letter apologising for being unable to meet her and offering himself some pity for "having fallen so low in the social scale". His next letter was written in Dundee on April 7, but seems to have been delayed in the post, since he followed it with a reply to Lillie's anxious demand for acknowledgement of one of hers.

What seems most likely is that on arrival in Perth he decided to "lie low" until he found civilian clothes, but that some accident took place which disturbed his plans and compelled him to seek the assistance of his mother's brother-in-law, Owen Boyle of Dundee. In the first letter to Perth he thanked Lillie for her generous contribution to the "distressed fund". He explained that it was "want of cash and the necessary habiliments" which prevented him from meeting her. But he hoped to do so before she left Perth. He had secured work in another man's place, but this was purely temporary. "I could get plenty of work in England," he added, "but you know England might be unhealthy for me–you understand." He made some point of his hesitation in writing. "For the first time in my life I feel extremely diffident about writing a letter. Usually I feel a sneaking self-confidence in the possession of what I know to be a pretty firm grasp of the English language for one in my position."

And he added inconsequently at the end that "only across the street from here a man murdered his wife".[1]

The final letter expressed surprise that she had not received his last, and explained once more that he had received her letter and secured work. He had also received the socks she had knitted him, and his landlady had commented "the lass who sent you those didn't make a fool of you".

She had complained that she "could not warm to the Perth people". He replied that Scots people were pious hypocritical

[1] The murder was reported on April 1, 1889, a circumstance which is of importance in confirming the date of Connolly's letters. Only one of the three bears the year, and was originally written "1888" but superimposed on it is what might be a 7 or a 9. This also confirms the place. Connolly gave no number in St. Mary Street, but the numeration of the street was such that the murderer (a grocer named Redmond), living at No. 24, was exactly opposite No. 9.

sharks, but pure gold when good. The remainder of the letter is of interest as the first documentation of Connolly's interest in social questions. He told his fiancée that Dundee contained more Irish people per head of population than any other place in Britain, and that they came from every county in Ireland. Women worked while husbands were unemployed. According to the census there were eleven women working for every two men.

That Connolly came by this information so soon after his arrival is probably explained by the presence in Dundee of his brother John who had become a close friend of John Leslie of the Social-Democratic Federation. Leslie himself spoke in Dundee on April 1, and it may be that this was the occasion Leslie spoke of in 1916, when he welcomed James Connolly into the movement. That this was the approximate time is shown by an appreciation of Connolly published in the Edinburgh *Socialist* on his departure for America in 1903. It refers to his *fifteen years* activity in the socialist movement. And in May 1914 he himself referred to his twenty-five years membership.

Connolly arrived in Dundee at a time when all eyes were turned on the Socialists who were in the midst of their great free speech campaign. The two branches of the S.D.F. had begun to hold open-air meetings early in the season of 1889, selecting Barrack Park for the afternoon at 3.30 p.m., with shorter meetings in High Street at 1 p.m. and 6 p.m. At 7 p.m. they repaired to their Hall at 44, Overgate, where they also met each Wednesday. The meetings proved too successful for the liking of the authorities and at the end of March the magistrates issued proclamations forbidding public meetings in certain districts without their sanction. The districts, needless to say, were those where socialist meetings were customarily held.

The S.D.F. decided to take up the challenge, and a gathering estimated by the local press at 20,000 strong heard Robertson and Hutcheson make protests in Albert Square, just outside the proclaimed area. The speakers then led the crowd to High Street, where they began to speak and were promptly arrested. An indignation meeting held immediately afterwards does not appear to have been interfered with. The police were trying their strength.

On the following Sunday, April 1, several meetings were held to which speakers came from Glasgow and Edinburgh, among them Leslie and Bruce Glasier. The day's activity culminated in a great protest meeting in Barrack Park, and a few weeks later the magistrates climbed down. Meetings were resumed in High Street. The unity achieved in this campaign between the S.D.F. and the Socialist League was one of the factors contributing towards the amalgamation of the two organisations in Scotland, under Leslie's leadership, in the following October. Thereafter the S.D.F. Hall in the Overgate was a centre of constant activity. These were the opening days of the "New Unionism" and one section after another of the unskilled workers was invited to the Hall and encouraged to organise. The tremendous part played by the early socialists in this work has not been sufficiently recognised.

Lillie had meanwhile established herself in London, but the marriage was arranged to take place in Perth. First it was necessary to secure a dispensation from the Bishop of Dunkeld to enable James to marry a Protestant. Lillie Reynolds came of a Wicklow family. Her father had died when she was young, and her mother had a struggle to bring up four children unaided in their little house in Rathmines. When she was old enough Lillie entered domestic service with the Wilsons, a family of substantial stockbrokers who belonged to the social club connected with the local church. The family was of Unionist sympathies, but preserved the recollection of an ancestor hanged for his part in the Rising of 1798.

The dispensation obtained, Connolly published the banns in Edinburgh and arranged accommodation for Lillie in Perth where she must reside for three weeks. He forwarded her Perth address to the Bishop so that the priest could call on her and receive assurances that any children of the marriage would be reared in the Catholic faith, and that she would not interfere with her husband in the practice of his religion. James permitted himself a sly pleasantry on the latter point. If she required further advice, Mrs. Angus would give it her.

At the last moment Lillie proposed to remain a further week in London and Connolly wrote to her in some perturbation. "If we get married next week I shall be unable to go to Dundee as I promised, as my fellow-workmen on the job are preparing for a strike at the end of this month, for a reduction of the hours of labour. As my brother and I are ringleaders in the matter it is necessary we should be on the ground. If we were not we should be looked upon as blacklegs, which the Lord forbid."

How this matter was settled is not known. The marriage took place at St. James's Church, Perth, on April 13, Connolly describing himself as a carter. He had joined the staff of the Edinburgh Cleansing Department and the young couple proudly took occupation of a home of their own at 22, West Port, almost on the corner of the Grassmarket. So opened the Edinburgh years which Lillie Connolly always referred to as the happiest of their lives.

The decision to settle in Edinburgh did not mean that James now had a permanent job. There were two grades of carter employed by the Corporation, one permanent, the other temporary. In addition it seems that during holiday periods, snowstorms and other emergencies, work was let out on contract, and the periodical attempts to augment contractors' staff at the expense of the Corporation men caused recurring friction.

John Connolly, the father, had been on the permanent staff. But neither of the sons took his place. John seems to have been given temporary status from which no doubt in time he could graduate to the more privileged position, while James's position seems to have been less secure. James, however, was a good worker, a non-drinker, non-smoker and a "steady man" unlike his more flamboyant brother, and thus appears to have had regular employment even on the casual basis.

It is not known how long the father enjoyed his 7s. 6d.

a week. The officials salved their consciences by employing the son in his stead. But John could not long have assisted him. A year later he married Elizabeth Aitchison, daughter of another manure carter, and went to live at 8, Kingstables Road. Mary Connolly died of acute bronchitis the following May, at 15 Alisons Close, Cowgate. Thereafter the old man pottered round the tenements, sat on his haunches at street corners talking with the unemployed, and from time to time attended the socialist meetings. He was gentle, kindly and intelligent, with wit and a shrewd smile, but not a man of deep political convictions.

Connolly entered active political life just in time to witness the disappearance of the world in which he had been brought up. The character of that world, its hopes and possibilities, and why it suffered such a strange and sudden mutation, are crucial for the understanding of his development. The hitherto accepted pillars of society, the landlord and the industrialist, gave way before the investor. The twin colossi of revolt, Parnellism backed by land agitation, and non-political (radical) trade unionism, lost their pre-eminence simultaneously. Modern times came in.

Britain had ceased to be the workshop of the world at the same time as the basis of agricultural rent was undermined by cheap grain from virgin lands. Hence throughout the eighties British capitalism faced industrial depression and agrarian crisis simultaneously, with the constant tendency for the two consequent streams of discontent to merge. A policy corresponding to the economic realities of the new age must be introduced even if powerful interests were sacrificed. This policy involved the reorganisation of agriculture and the abandonment of free trade. British land went down to grass. And since the world was no longer an open market, Britain must seize and hold as much of it as she could, and make that her market, trade following the flag.

To sacrifice British agriculture was one thing. To sacrifice Irish agriculture meant a revolution. Either Ireland must be separated, in which case the landlord would not survive any-

33

way, or he must make way in the interest of the Union, and be compensated. In the struggles of the eighties these issues were fought out. Matters were not mature enough for the most progressive solution—socialism in England and a free Ireland. Instead came imperialism. The profits of empire were to perfume and spice British capitalism—and incidentally finance the bloodless liquidation of the Irish landlords. These were progressively bought out through a series of Land Acts skilfully designed to split the remaining tenantry. An increasing element of reformism entered the land agitation, while the revolutionary impact of Home Rule was blunted though its slogans remained the same.

The buying out of the landlords before the advent of national independence prevented a democratic solution of the land question. It evacuated the landlord garrison, but into the vacuum stepped financial interests. Instead of a provincial estate, Ireland became a financial colony. Formerly a British administration saw that tenants paid their rent and helped to evict them if they did not. Under the emasculated Home Rule Bill of 1893, an Irish administration wholly subordinate to Westminster would see that Ireland as a whole paid her interest. And who better qualified to form such an administration than the landlords who had invested their compensation in partnership with the larger commercial and industrial capitalists? The palm of reaction in Ireland was being passed from landlord to rentier, and the split in the Irish Nationalist Party, which led to the death of Parnell, was a struggle over the content of Home Rule in which reaction proved victorious.

By contrast, the labour movement grew immeasurably stronger. So many strikes are recorded during the year Connolly was in Dundee that it is impossible to distinguish between them. The "New Unionism" seized the imagination of the working class, carrying all before it. And from 1890 onwards, the British working class, as a class, asserted its demands in concert with the workers of the whole world.

Connolly entered politics when Parnellism was at its height, and the labour movement was surging forward. At that time the most progressive outcome seemed possible. Such an outcome depended on the two currents of progressive struggle forming a firm alliance. Throughout the eighties this had seemed possible, and here is the origin of Connolly's constant preoccupation with the relations between nationalism and socialism, since the socialists, the most advanced section of the labour movement, were the first to urge freedom for Ireland.

Connolly always spoke with admiration of the work of the British socialists for Irish independence. "The Land League," he wrote in *Labour in Irish History*, "had at the outset to make way against the opposition of all the official Home Rule press, and in Great Britain, among the Irish exiles, to depend entirely upon the championship of poor labourers and English and Scottish socialists."

The growth of socialism during the eighties was at the same time a growth of the alliance between British socialism and Irish nationalism. From the very start the two movements were intertwined, socialism being represented by the Social-Democratic Federation (S.D.F.) and Irish nationalism by the British section of the Irish Land League, to which was linked the Scottish Land League in the Highlands.

The Socialist League which Connolly joined in Dundee, was a breakaway from the S.D.F. Both drew inspiration from Marx, though neither had, to use Engels's phrase, "fermented themselves clear". They were not unitary parties, but loose informal unions of quasi-independent socialist clubs. While their leaders were opposed, many of the rank and file held joint membership.

On the Irish question clear statements had been made by the founders of scientific socialism. They stood for the complete separation of Ireland from Britain, an agrarian revolution, and tariffs to protect Irish industrial development. The S.D.F. journal *Justice* supported Home Rule in the movement's hey-day. "Only in Dublin can the Irish people control their laws. Let the two agitations go side by side." This was not quite the same as Marx's demand that the English socialists should put the Irish question in the *forefront* of *their* agitation. But it was much appreciated.

3*

In 1884, the Avelings and William Morris broke with Hyndman, founder of the S.D.F., and founded the Socialist League.

William Morris did not at first understand the national question. He told the Irish in *Commonweal*: "Your revolutionary struggles will be abortive or lead to mere disappointment unless you accept as your watchword 'wage-earners of the world unite'." But after visiting Dublin in 1886 and being all but howled down for the gaffe of referring to O'Connell Street as Sackville Street, he wisely drew the conclusion that "until the Irish get Home Rule they will listen to nothing else".

Thereafter *Commonweal* handled the Irish question admirably, and Sketchley's articles written in 1887 called for unconditional support for Ireland's national and agrarian demands.

"The union was accomplished by corruption, treason, rapine and murder," said Sketchley. "It has been maintained and is now by the same means. The so-called Imperial Parliament never possessed and does not now possess any legitimate right to rule or govern the people of Ireland. Every attempt to govern people against the will of the people is treason, is an act of rebellion against the people. It is not a question of majorities or minorities, but the principle of equal liberty for every people, of right, of justice, of independence."

No wonder that as coercion increased and was extended to the socialist movement in Britain, the Irish in Britain more and more rallied to its banner.

This was even more so in Scotland than in England. The heart of Scottish socialism was Edinburgh. Notwithstanding Glasgow's superiority in the numbers and industrial concentration of its working class, at this time the Clyde lagged behind the capital. Indeed, within the County of Edinburgh, it was the mercantile City rather than industrial Leith which led the way, a fact which Connolly puzzled over. The reason may have been partly that Edinburgh was the centre of such vestiges of Scottish national organisation as survived the union of 1707, and also that the University was a haven for continental refugees. Political responsibility acts as a forcing house; theory as a fertiliser.

Apart from the intellectuals, socialism won more influence at the outset among the unskilled than the skilled workers. A large proportion of these were Irish and, of those who joined the S.D.F., many had been members of the Land League.

Two strangely contrasted refugees, Andreas Scheu and Léo Meillet, were mainly responsible for building up the Edinburgh S.D.F. Scheu was an Austrian journalist, forceful and forthright, possessed of immense energy and capacity for work, a militant atheist who scorned subterfuge and answered a woman who asked had he been to church with a withering "Not this morning, ma'am". Meillet was a greater influence on Connolly. He had been mayor of a Commune in Paris. It was he who in 1889 told Edinburgh's first meeting to commemorate the Commune that "without the shedding of blood there is no social salvation". As a speaker he had the finer quality. He began quietly but gradually worked up to a passion, dazzling his hearers with the play of wit and epigram. If a previous speaker had made his point badly he would take what was good from it, purge it of inessentials, and so develop it without claiming possession that the originator would see his own idea transfigured with sharpness and lucidity. These two drew around them a group of supporters which included the Rev. W. Glasse, subsequently translator of the "Internationale", and together they formed the University Socialist Society.

The proletarian element in the Edinburgh branch was composed of workers from the Scottish Land League, notably Robert Banner and John Lincoln MacMahon, who had founded a "Republican Club". They affiliated to the S.D.F. and later all three organisations merged to become the Scottish Land and Labour League. Scheu and MacMahon (born in Ireland of the Monaghan Clan, and given the proud name of Lincoln by a republican father) held the first open-air meetings at East Meadows, which came to be called the "devil's half-acre". When MacMahon left for Leeds, Scheu sought new sites, for example Drummond Street on the edge of "Little Ireland". When the split took place, the Edinburgh section affiliated to the Socialist League, but the Federation established another branch which began to attract the Irish through holding its meetings in the East Meadows.

The two organisations were furthest apart in 1885 immediately after the split. But from February 1887, when they held a joint meeting to support the strike of the Scottish miners, their co-operation steadily increased. They were both represented at the anti-coercion meeting at the Good Templar Hall, when John Leslie took the chair. Members of both organisations participated in the classes for the study of Marx's *Capital* which began under Socialist League auspices in April of the same year. The tutor, the Rev. W. Glasse, translated from the German. But very soon the Moore and Aveling translation published by Sonnenschein became generally available and the classes were expanded into open-air lectures during the summer and resumed next autumn in a shed in Park Street. Local tradition has it that Connolly attended some of these classes, and so acquired his close familiarity with Marx's works. They were continued over several years and it is quite possible that Connolly did attend in 1890 or 1891.

In 1888 both the S.D.F. and the Scottish Land and Labour League appear to have been using the East Meadows, though not in competition, when there appeared, or reappeared, one Job Bone, an ardent Protestant with considerable vocal powers. His hatred of Catholicism was equalled only by his determination to make socialist meetings impossible. The two organisations co-operated in marathon meetings which ran from 3 p.m. till 10 p.m.

The routing of Job Bone was accomplished with the aid of a native of Little Ireland, John Leslie, a former scholar of St. Patrick's School. For his first speech in the Meadows he chose as his subject "the Irish famine". He became a popular speaker at the Irish National League, which had recruited nine-tenths of the membership of the Young Men's Catholic Institute. When a delegate conference of Scottish Socialist Societies met at the end of 1888 to establish the Scottish Socialist Federation, Leslie became the first secretary. It was decided to "work alongside" Keir Hardie's Independent Labour Party,[1] and try to "imbue it with socialist principles". Leslie joined the new party, and later became its Edinburgh secretary.

Born in Edinburgh of a Scottish father and an Irish mother, Leslie regarded himself as an Irishman. There is however no basis for Quinlan's fanciful story that he was from Waterford and ten years secretary of a ribbon lodge. Perhaps Quinlan fell foul of the long memories of Irish exiles who cherished their ancestors' exploits as their own.

Leslie was a fluent and witty speaker, an omnivorous reader and a capable and pointed writer in poetry as well as prose. More flamboyant than Connolly, he had a touch of the bohemian of later days, which sprang from a gifted and artistic nature hemmed in by poverty and lacking the training or the discipline fully to express itself. He rapidly became the embodiment of socialist influence among the Edinburgh Irish.

The S.D.F. won so much support that it could hold meetings in the Grassmarket itself, where every window held an Irish face and even the most apathetic would at least listen. Unity of these forces grew during the period of the crofter trials in 1888 and could not be shaken even by the Papal rescript, as an incident will show.

In August 1888 the Archbishop of Edinburgh deposed

[1] Keir Hardie advocated the establishment of an independent "Labour Party" and set up preparatory committees for the purpose. After the "Scottish Labour Party" was founded some of its constituent bodies retained the old descriptive title for local purposes. Thus the Edinburgh group which sent James Connolly to the fifth conference of the Scottish Labour Party in Glasgow seems always to have been known in Edinburgh as the "Independent Labour Party". This title became general only after the foundation of the British I.L.P. in 1894.

Mr. Flanagan from presidency of the Young Man's Catholic Institute. He had been a member for twenty-three years, but had expressed his support, in his capacity as a leader of the Irish National League, for the "Plan of Campaign" against which the rescript was directed. A furore followed in which the entire nationalist press took his part, and *The Nation* was full of the arguments which Connolly used years later and developed in *Labour, Nationality and Religion*.

"The result has been to enhance his worth," said *The Nation* and added, "an Irishman may even be an active worker for social reform", which was a concession from *The Nation*.

Then followed a sentence which will have a familiar ring to those who have read Connolly's writings in *The Harp*: "They will be all the better Irishmen and none the worse Catholics for keeping their eye open to the truth."

When John Deasey, M.P., spoke in Edinburgh, Flanagan took the chair and stuck to his guns. The hall rang with cheers when Deasey declared: "In Edinburgh something similar to Dublin Castle rule seems to have sprung up, not in Edinburgh Castle but in a more remote place."

The upshot was that, as has frequently happened in Irish history, some of the faithful absented themselves from their devotions. They did not abandon the faith but protested against what they considered a misuse of the altar. They still required the services of the church for personal purposes. Hence arose the custom of journeying into the next diocese (Dunkeld) for such purposes as marriage. His contemporaries in Edinburgh gave this explanation of Connolly's decision to marry in Perth.

When Parnell proclaimed his victory over *The Times*, which had attempted to link him with "terrorist" actions, there was universal jubilation among Irish and British workers alike. Never was there such a pregnant conjunction of progressive forces. Parnell received the freedom of Edinburgh and it was announced that the Irish National League, despite the clerical frowns which had been cast on Flanagan, had reached the highest membership in its existence. But the old guard of Liberals had no heart for the popular movement. They intended to betray Parnell and were quietly biding their time.

Within a few weeks of his victory Parnell was named co-respondent in a divorce suit filed by Captain O'Shea, and a cloud no bigger than a man's hand swelled into a violent tempest.

Technically successful, the suit completely failed to show Parnell in the bad light that was intended. For personal reasons Parnell decided not to defend it. But it was too much to hope that Gladstone would let his opportunity slip. It was his long awaited chance to free himself from the Irish party. He threatened to abandon Home Rule unless Parnell was deposed from the leadership. The engines of nonconformist conscience were turned full steam astern. Catholic priests who had unhesitatingly defied the Papal rescript vied with one another in the condemnation of Ireland's hero. At the bidding of an English statesman the Irish party broke into impotent factions. Their only alternative would have been to seek a close accord with Labour. Parnell himself finally did this. From the end of 1890 he fought on bravely, but his health proved unequal to the strain. He died in October 1891, just after he had rallied the Dublin workers to his side and was looking forward to restoring unity to the Irish national cause.

When Gladstone betrayed Parnell the chief casualty was the alliance of progressive forces. Mass support for the Liberal party was twofold, the skilled workers (promised reforms, but not all at once) and the Irish (who would get land and freedom provided they were patient). The leaders of Liberalism were adept at preserving these two sources of influence while preventing their coalescence. Had they combined they could have dispensed with the Liberals. The overthrow of Parnell was intended to preserve Liberalism from such a contingency. But in point of fact such a blow was dealt its mass basis that it remained out of office with but one brief interlude for fifteen years. Its feet were firmly planted on the path to ultimate suicide.

Gladstone stood by Home Rule, but emasculated it. During his last brief spell as Prime Minister he introduced a second Bill which was so much less radical than the first that it died as much from contempt as from opposition.

But the former "uncrowned King of Ireland" was the subject of a bitter and protracted feud in which the contestants rejected all rational analysis. Everybody must be either for or against Parnell. From the grave he dominated the party which had rejected him, and every sect and faction within it.

In this situation the German *Neue Zeit* correctly forecast the twofold result: the Tories would be strengthened at one pole, the socialists at the other. Many Irish people left the national movement in disgust. Socially-conscious members of the I.N.L. threw themselves increasingly into the new trade unionism, the I.L.P. and the socialist societies. In Ireland the ensuing years marked the birth of those political organisations which, though formally altered, still hold the field today.

Those Irish in Britain who already understood something of radical doctrines moved over rapidly to socialism. But a barrier had been created between them and the less advanced elements. To these nationalism was still embodied in Parliamentary factions angling for Liberal recognition. The more conservative forces in the Irish National League re-established their control. There were no more joint campaigns with the socialists. The seeds of destruction were sown within the Irish National League itself.

Connolly's feelings, as he witnessed the wrecking of the movement on which he had placed his hopes from childhood, can be judged from the relevant pages of *Labour in Irish History*. Indeed his classic is a commentary on this page of history, just as *Labour, Nationality and Religion* draws on the rescript and the Flanagan case.

The split which developed between the Irish Nationalists and the Socialists was exploited to the full by reactionary interests. The *Pall Mall Gazette* wrote:

"It will be curious if the old struggle between Church and State reopens in a new form. If the Socialists capture the state machine in any country, the Catholic Church may again be the protagonist of individual liberty."

In the new Home Rule-Liberal alliance the Irish were very much the subordinate partner. Every progressive or militant element was eliminated in the interests of "unity". As Connolly wrote, "the solid phalanx of Irish voters was again and again hurled against the men who had fought and endured suffering, ostracism and abuse for Ireland at a time when the Liberal Government was packing Irish jails with unconvicted Irish men and women."

Such was the new situation. From this background sprang the problem whose challenge Connolly took up. In those Edinburgh days he took up the study of scientific socialism. He was a constant attender at Leslie's meetings. Hindered by a slight stammer, he would occasionally devastate interrupters with the intensity of his invective.

His first daughter Mona was born in St. Mary Street at the East End of Cowgate, but shortly afterwards he moved to 6, Lawnmarket, the westward continuation of High Street. This was on the upper level, as was also his next lodging at 6, Lothian Street. In this pleasant salubrious area, near the Meadows, surrounded by bookshops and colleges, his second daughter Nora was born.

Here the Edinburgh socialists foregathered, where there was always a stick of furniture and a cup of tea. Though Lillie was not interested in politics she enjoyed company and, except immediately before the birth of a child, the house was never free from socialist meetings. Indeed, James deliberately took a tenement large enough to accommodate them. In the three years from 1889 to 1892 he matured politically. But before he could take up the challenge of the time he must serve another four years of apprenticeship.

ABLE APPRENTICE

The routine of socialist activity into which James Connolly was drawn consisted of three weekly meetings of which the most important was the public meeting each Sunday. This was held in the East Meadows in summer, but during the winter various halls were engaged.

For a time the Scottish Socialist Federation hired the Trades Hall, later moving to the Moulders Hall. Edinburgh Trades Council was slow to feel the draught of the new unionism. Though Ben Tillett was busy on Leith Docks in 1889 and the carters were organising at the same time, the trades viewed the new ideas of political action which accompanied these developments with profound suspicion. Even the eight-hour-day agitation did not attract them. It was the Scottish Socialist Federation which organised the demonstration on this issue in May 1890 and the Trades Council did not participate.

Instead the Council invited as a speaker one O'Connell, a "Labour" candidate in London who proclaimed himself opposed to the eight-hour day. He was also opposed to Home Rule, disestablishment of the Church, and municipal workshops (or in modern parlance direct labour). But whereas in 1890 only six of their number had voted for the acceptance of the affiliation of the Labour Federation (a loose organisation of the S.S.F. and I.L.P.[1] branches for electoral purposes) the next year ten supported it. Very slowly the new ideas penetrated. The old guard wanted no political action at all. A number were moving in the direction of urging the Liberal Party to accept "Labour men" as candidates. Those who believed in an independent pledge-bound Labour party were considered wild revolutionaries scarcely to be distinguished from the Socialists.

The public explanation of socialist ideas was therefore

[1] See note on page 39

essential. The majority of the people had only the haziest notion what socialism was. Nevertheless scarcely a week went by without some professor writing in the local newspapers an expert article proving its impossibility. As Connolly noted in an article in *Justice,* at first the press adopted an attitude of "contemptuous toleration" or "fulsome patronage" but by 1893 this changed to "bitter undisguised hatred and determined opposition". The able propagandist was at a premium. The midweek meeting was devoted to a lecture by one of the members and usually by John Leslie. In 1892 when the S.S.F. started meeting at Connolly's flat in Lothian Street, the occasional Friday "business meeting" was replaced by a regular circle for "reading and discussion".

Socialist literature was still in its infancy. Marx's *Capital* and the *Communist Manifesto* were available, but above the heads of some of the members. They wanted a mental picture of the new society. The writings of Morris and Bellamy's *Looking Backward* helped in this. But even the work of non-socialist radicals and opponents of socialism was pressed into service. Schaffle's two "refutations" of socialism, *The Quintessence of Socialism* and *The Impossibility of Social Democracy,* were advertised in both *Commonweal* and *Justice.* Schaffle was an Austrian finance Minister who studied socialism with a view to refuting it and gave a comparatively balanced account of its teachings, though he believed that the "labour theory of value" implied paying people with labour tickets according to the number of hours worked. This and much similar material was avidly consumed by groups of men thirsting for something "about socialism".

The growth of the Independent Labour Party was spectacular. Unlike the S.S.F. it demanded no appreciaton of scientific principles. But it did reflect the growing demand of the working class for an independent voice in the policy decisions which affected them. There was a tacit division of labour between the two organisations and much joint membership. While the S.S.F. preached and taught, the I.L.P. prepared the way for an electoral organisation and won increasing influence in the trade union movement, especially when the

45

trade recession of 1893 caused hardship and discontent and drew the different elements of the labour movement closer together.

Thus, only two years after they had sponsored O'Connell, the Trades Council agreed to participate in a joint eight-hours demonstration committee under whose auspices a demonstration was held on May 6. The suggestion had come in a letter from John Leslie, secretary of the I.L.P., at the end of March, but was followed by another, a week later, from John Connolly, secretary of the S.S.F. The I.L.P. also used to meet in James's flat, so it is likely that both were drawn up in his presence. The procession started from Bruntsfield Links and marched through the streets to Queen's Park where a resolution demanding the eight-hour day was passed at three platforms—the platforms of the participating organisations. One of the speakers was John Connolly.

The demonstration was considered a great success and the Trades Council busied itself with defraying the expenses, though with rather bad grace. At the meeting on June 13, delegate Mallinson asked if it were true that John Connolly[1] had been dismissed because of his action on May Day. The Trades Council thought this extremely unlikely but agreed to enquire. Two weeks later they learned that John Connolly had indeed been dismissed and that his case was being considered by the Cleaning and Lighting Committee. The Trades Council thereupon passed a resolution:

"That the action of the Cleaning and Lighting Committee of the Town Council in refusing to consider the communication of the Trades Council on the Connolly dismissal case is an infringement of the principle of arbitration."

The Town Clerk had referred the Trades Council's letter to the Committee together with two others, one from John Connolly himself, and the other from the secretary of the demonstration general committee.

The Cleaning and Lighting Committee held an enquiry to

[1] The erroneous statement that this was James originated in *Forward*, of January 23, 1915 and is due to D. Lowe.

which Connolly brought witnesses. But whereas Inspector McKay was present while Connolly's witnesses gave their evidence, each man had to retire as soon as his evidence was completed. On July 3 the Cleaning and Lighting Committee found that Connolly's complaint was not substantiated and recommended the Magistrates and Council to take no action. Only Councillor Watson dissented and the Council accepted the Committee's recommendation.

The Trades Council considered the matter further at their meeting in August and were:

"Unanimously of the opinion that the Cleaning and Lighting Committee investigation is to say the least unsatisfactory but owing to the difficulties surrounding the case are unable to recommend any further action being taken."

The difficulties were summarised in another sentence:

"The men best able to give direct proof were liable to the same treatment Connolly received."

It was as a result of John's having to seek work elsewhere that James became secretary of the Scottish Socialist Federation. With James's accession came a marked change in the branch reports which appeared in *Justice*. John's reports had been flamboyant and euphuistic. The peculiarly passionate logic of James's mind appeared in his very first report, which was probably his earliest published writing.

From the start he took his job seriously. He wanted his reports to be word perfect, and pored over them, consulting Lillie in matters of grammar, spelling and punctuation.

According to his first report, the S.S.F. had decided to send a delegate to the International Conference at Zurich. The delegate was to have a free hand in all matters but one. He must vote against the admission of the Anarchists. This issue was a bone of contention with some of the branches of the I.L.P. There was bitter feeling among the S.S.F. against the Anarchists who had broken up the Socialist League and forced the S.S.F. to function as an independent organisation increasingly drawn towards the S.D.F.

The other subject was his idea of conducting a speakers' class, and he invited "suggestions as to the best manner in which such a class should be conducted". Connolly learned to speak after an apprenticeship during which he acted as chairman for John Leslie. It was customary, then as now, for the neophyte to carry the platform and learn the art of oratory standing on high before an empty street.

In another report included in the "Scottish Notes" of *Justice* for August 12, 1893 Connolly announced the intention of the S.S.F. to seek a footing in Leith.

"The population of Edinburgh is largely composed of snobs, flunkeys, mashers, lawyers, students, middle-class pensioners and dividend-hunters. Even the working-class portion of the population seemed to have imbibed the snobbish would-be-respectable spirit of their 'betters' and look with aversion upon every movement running counter to conventional ideas. But it has won, hands down, and is now becoming respectable. More, it is now recognised as an important factor in the public life of the community, a disturbing element which must be taken into account in all the calculations of the political caucuses.

"Leith on the other hand is pre-eminently an industrial centre. The overwhelming majority of its population belong to the disinherited class, and having its due proportion of sweaters, slave-drivers, rack-renting slum landlords, shipping-federation agents, and parasites of every description, might therefore have been reasonably expected to develop socialistic sentiments much more readily than the Modern Athens."

Connolly's practical business-like approach stood out plainly even in these early contributions. Equally striking is his combination of Irish and British tradition in the phrase "rack-renting slum landlords" which he afterwards used in many a famous passage.

In his next notes[1] Connolly castigated Paisley, the Vice-

---

[1] There is the possibility that these notes were either by John or, perhaps, a joint effort.

President of the Glasgow Trades Council, for remaining a member of the Co-operative Society while admitting and condemning its practice of paying less than trade union rates in order to raise dividends. He poured scorn on the Master Bottlemakers' Association for refusing to meet strikers from Portobello, Alloa and Glasgow on the grounds that there were foreigners among their number. "It was all very well," he wrote, "to employ a foreigner at starvation wages and so cut down the wages of the native–but to treat with the foreigner.... Why it was preposterous!"

During the winter of 1893–4 the Edinburgh Socialists grew intensely interested in the Irish Question. The fact that a new situation existed in Irish politics, both within Ireland and in their application to Britain, could not be missed.

Existing literature had become out of date almost overnight. Sketchley's *Irish Question*, written in the hey-day of the democratic alliance, contained nothing to meet the new situation. *Justice* was completely disorientated and became increasingly contemptuous of the Irish struggle.

The S.D.F. had had close links with Parnell's lieutenant Michael Davitt, who had founded his *Labour World* in September as organ of the "Irish Democratic Labour Federation" and three months later swung it uncompromisingly against Parnell, thus disorganising the working-class forces at the crucial time. As the Irish workers returned to their former allegiance *Labour World* lost its democratic basis and before a year was out ceased publication. Davitt left for the U.S.A.

The *Labour Leader* remained friendly. Hardie was a man of the heart and responsive to sentiments around him. He knew already how Irish nationalism could be used against Labour candidates, even before the fall of Parnell. Jim Connell, who had composed "The Red Flag" to the air of "The White Cockade" in 1889, stood as Labour candidate in Finsbury in September 1890 and was bitterly attacked both by the Liberals and by T. P. O'Connor's *Star*.

Despite Hardie's caution, when in the municipal elections of 1893 the I.L.P. opposed the Liberals with Edinburgh's first Labour candidate, the full strength of the National League was placed behind the Liberal. This was a sign to Leslie that a complete reassessment of the position was necessary. Only five years after he had been acclaimed as the defender of Irish Nationalism he was being condemned as a traitor to Liberalism. He gave a series of lectures on Ireland to the S.S.F. and, in the course of discussion, hammered out a new line of thought. Beginning in March 1894 he published in *Justice* his "Passing thoughts on the Irish Question". The articles were collected and issued as a pamphlet, called *The present position of the Irish Question.*

Leslie's articles were written with an eye to the inaugural Conference of the Irish T.U.C. which was to follow the May Day demonstration in Dublin. His argument therefore led up to the conclusion that the time was ripe for the establishment of an independent working-class party in Ireland. This would make possible, through the achievement of socialism in Ireland, not only the industrialisation of the country without the "brutal and heartless exploitation of the working class", but the healing of the feud of centuries between Britain and Ireland. "The mastery of man over man, of class over class, of nation over nation," said Leslie, "springs from the hell-born system of exploitation which has cursed both countries alike."

This thesis was developed with a wealth of historical detail and argued with a passion and imagination only possible in a poet and a man of genius. He took his text from Charles Lever's *Tom Burke* which he considered a micrograph of how "the greatest movement in Irish History reached its anticlimax in what is termed with fine irony Mr. Gladstone's 'Home Rule Bill'. Lever's character, 'Darby the Blast', when the great movement for Irish Freedom was crumbling in ruins around him, in the hour of wisdom learned too late, hurled his curse at the heads of the 'Gintlemen', the Gintlemen 'who ever and always betrayed us'."

Speaking as an Irish wage-worker, Leslie did not believe that "the Alpha and Omega of the Irish Question" consisted "in the hoisting of the green and gold banner above the Old

Parliament House of Dublin". Ireland was not a beautiful abstraction of the poet's mind. "Ireland means all the people enclosed within its four seas, the Irish People one and indivisible—only that and nothing more."

Taking up a position occupied by Davitt he blamed the "Kilmainham Treaty" of 1881, under which Parnell agreed to discourage the agrarian movement in return for the release of political prisoners, for diverting the land struggle into a purely political channel. For the old cry of the land for the people "was substituted the single plank 'Home Rule'." The first would go to the root of the question; the second left the class issue of property ownership untouched.

Leslie justified his argument by quoting extensively from James Fintan Lalor, "the man who first pointed out the class nature of the Irish movement and who laid down as the essential basis of a successful insurrectionary movement in Ireland: resistance by any and every method to eviction, the retention of the harvest, and the non-payment of rent."

The Land League had adopted, though in modified form, two of these demands—and Gladstone "never did a cleverer piece of work in his life than in inducing Parnell to drop them". An opportunity to "lay in the dust the whole structure of English administration in Ireland" was lost, even though Parnell "entered upon that astonishing and dazzling career of political success and Parliamentary triumphs in which he proved himself a born leader of men and an astute political chief such as the Irish people never had before". Despite his mistakes, Leslie thought him a "Titan strangled by pygmies" and bitterly reproached Davitt for betraying him.

Leslie summed up the results of the fall of Parnell in simple and telling words: "Parnell is sound asleep in Glasnevin and Gladstone is wide awake, very wide awake indeed, in Hawarden. Home Rule has become a dissolving view; the Irish party is split into half a dozen sections each warring on the other; the economic conditions of the country are upon the point of again becoming disturbed and no one seems to know it."

Leslie then dealt with the part of clericalism in bringing

about the downfall of Parnell. Despite the fact that the Fenians were "for the transfer of government from London to Dublin; but the transfer of not a single acre from the thief to the owners", they had been denounced from the altar in famous terms. "Hell is not hot enough," it was thundered, "nor eternity long enough to punish the wretches who are endeavouring to root Continental Socialism in the soil of Holy Ireland."

Here Leslie realised he was entering highly disputed territory. "If there are any who expect," he warned, "that I am setting out to prove that the Irish are an ignorant and a priest-ridden people, they may as well not read what is to follow."

He distinguished between the policy of the Church and that of individual priests who do not determine policy. "The priesthood is drawn from the people, and shares to a large extent the sympathies and desires of the people." He considered, however, that the high policy of the Church as an organisation was to place its own interests above all others, *ad majorem Dei gloriam.* Ever since the penal laws had fallen into desuetude the Catholic Church had been the most potent instrument in preserving the connection between England and Ireland because, on the avowed open confession of the Church itself, its great aim, the object nearest its heart, was the reconversion of England.

Leslie did not condemn it for cherishing this aim. He simply invited Irishmen and Socialists to note that it was not the same thing as the aim of Irish independence or socialism.

"I well remember the odd sensation I felt when I first heard it propounded that God in his inscrutable wisdom and methods had intended and used the Irish race to carry Catholicism to the ends of the earth. . . . Now I do not say there is anything wrong in this, I do not deny the possibility of it, certainly I will not attempt to deny the inscrutability of it, but I do say that the Irishman who accepts this teaching cannot any longer lay the misfortunes of his country upon the shoulders of the English Government."

The "crowd of roaring reverend bigots from Belfast, barristers from Dublin and Orange Lords and Militia officers" who had swarmed all over England denouncing the Home Rule Bill as opening the door to the "Scarlet Woman" and a "general prelude to the cutting of Protestant throats" knew perfectly well that the Catholic Church was an instrument for preserving the connection, but used the anti-popery cry as a means of keeping Irish democracy split into two parts. Indeed, some colour was lent to the fears of northern Protestants by the "pernicious nonsense and humbug spouted by blatant 'champions of the faith' in the South, whose Catholicism is the only quality they possess." To support his case on the position of the Church, Leslie then quoted from Mitchel, Plowden and Doheny to show its position at each critical turn of Irish history, and concluded by attributing the Kilmainham Treaty itself to the intervention of the Archbishop of Cashel.

In his final article, on the outlook, Leslie developed a thesis well known to readers of Connolly's *Labour in Irish History,* namely that the progress of Ireland depends on the independent organisation of the working class.

> "It is none other than the wage-earners of town and country who have fought the Irish fights since '48 and who have furnished nine-tenths of the martyrs and victims of the fight without reaping any of the advantages that may have followed from it. The workers of the towns constituted the strength of Fenianism; the labourers of the country were the fighting force of the Land League. . . . Is it too much to ask of the workmen of town and country to come together and . . . try to find an answer to the question why they who produce all the wealth of their native land should be precisely the most trampled and despised class in it?"

He then outlined his suggestion for the foundation of a working-class party whose object would be to attain what John Boyle O'Reilly in his later days conceived, "a nation whose wealth and greatness will not be measured in pounds sterling but by the amount of free and healthy and happy and cultivated human life contained within its shores."

"But," warned Leslie, "deal firmly with the 'gintlemen'. One experience such as the Land League ought to be enough."

These brief and summary extracts will convey some notion of Leslie's wide reading and breadth of ideas. Sketchley had made plain the attitude of British socialism towards a progressive Irish movement demanding land and national independence. Leslie took the analysis a stage further. He showed that in the new era there were two trends in Irish nationalism. The dominant one was that of the 'gintlemen', while the other, that of the common people, still lacked organised expression. Therefore neither uncritical acceptance of nationalist demands irrespective of class content, nor impatiently brushing them aside, was demanded. A new yardstick was adopted. Instead of considering "Ireland" in the abstract, Leslie proposed judging by the criterion of "the Irish people". His analysis added another dimension to the Irish struggle as it was generally understood, that of a class struggle within Ireland.

His articles appeared at a time when the Irish movement was reeling in confusion and the British labour movement was beginning to desert it. He saw that what had replaced the alliance of the British progressives with an *independent* Irish national movement, was a reactionary compromise between British capitalism and a section of the Irish capitalists, in which the Irish were *dependent*. His hope was that those of the Irish people who still retained their independence should bravely raise the banner of socialism in Ireland, and that the British movement, in supporting Irish independence, should primarily support *them*.

Leslie was also a poet. From 1893 on, *Justice* published his poems almost weekly. In part they followed on the trail blazed by Jim Connell. But Leslie's intellect was keener, his style free from sentimentalism and emotional clichés; his translation of the "Internationale" is said to have been preferable to that of Dr. Glasse but to have failed to commend it-self generally from containing the word 'hell'. His poem on the death of Engels is probably his finest work.

That curious intensity of expression which many have noted in Connolly, giving a prophetic ring to prosaic state-ments, was present to an equal degree in Leslie. There were still in those days people who had "seen Shelley plain" and remembered Freiligrath. The poet of the people was not the oddity he afterwards became, but a recognised member of the political movement. The poetry and prose of political life had not yet completely separated themselves. Perhaps it is to be regretted that Leslie now chose the poetic path. *The present position of the Irish question* was his only political work. Standing alone, it would be a great achievement; that it was James Connolly's starting point gives it a special historical importance.

LOCAL LEADER

Thanks to the liberating effect of Leslie's work, James Connolly could stride forward with new confidence. His new rooms at 21, South College Street became a hive of socialist industry. More and more the work of the S.S.F., even of the Central branch of the I.L.P., came to revolve around him. He began to develop as a speaker. On the first occasion he spoke, Lillie stood beside the platform waiting for him to begin. When the fateful moment came her heart failed her and she fled, not stopping till she had regained South College Street.

This may have been on the awkward occasion of Saturday, May 13, 1894 when the Central Division of the I.L.P. was contemplating a Parliamentary candidate and Messrs. Swan and Grady had proposed and seconded Councillor Beever of Halifax. A meeting was arranged to support his candidature and Keir Hardie was advertised to speak at East Meadows. Some hundreds waited in the rain and there was an ominous silence when Connolly mounted the platform to apologise for Hardie's absence. He had been notified of the time and place, Connolly explained, but had failed to arrive. Then came a characteristic touch. Connolly promised that an apology would appear in the *Labour Leader* for this breach of faith. And the *Labour Leader* did in fact go to the length of publishing the complaint, though no explanation was given.

Councillor Beever did not secure adoption. Shortly afterwards a special meeting of the Labour Party was held in the Moulders Hall at which Connolly, on behalf of the Central Division of the I.L.P. announced that William Small, a miners' agent from Blantyre, had been selected. Already known to the Edinburgh Socialists at the Meadows and Queens Park, Mr. Small, unfortunately, fell foul of his fellow-officials in the miners' union on account of some misdemeanours and no further steps were taken.

Meanwhile the trade depression showed no sign of lifting. A miners' strike was impending and the working class was in an increasingly militant mood. Connolly's work in Leith began to bear fruit in a large branch of the I.L.P. which acknowledged its indebtedness to the S.S.F.'s propaganda on the Links. The S.S.F. formed a women's branch which also met at 21, South College Street, and as the "Clarion" ideas spread into the movement, there was founded a Socialist rambling club which made its first excursion to Dalkeith, and a cycling club, both of which combined recreation with propaganda.

Socialists were full of optimism. The I.L.P. campaigned against the City Council's plan to assist the North British Railway financially in its North Bridge scheme, and plans were laid for the municipal elections in the autumn. Progress was reported every day. Barriers were down and the counter-campaign not yet organised. Such heroic days occur in the lives of all organisations. The rivalry between the S.S.F. and the I.L.P. was kept in check by joint membership, common aims and the goodwill of men like Dickenson, who began to publish his *Edinburgh and Leith Labour Chronicle* in October, 1894, and gave full publicity to the S.S.F. On its front page Connolly read the words of Camille Desmoulins, which he quoted so often in the next thirty years:

"The great appear great because we are on our knees. Let us rise."

At the time, the S.S.F. and the I.L.P. had their differences, for example, when Keir Hardie gave the S.S.F. a date in October 1894, and the I.L.P. claimed him. The S.S.F. "generously waived their claim" and the meeting took place in the largest hall in the Central division. The I.L.P. decided that year to contest five or six seats and even secured some assistance from the Trades Council, much to the indignation of those who still favoured the Liberal party.

The S.S.F. decided to offer James Connolly, not as "independent Labour" but as a "Socialist" candidate. The reason for his candidature was not, as has been stated, his brother's victimisation, which was now no longer an issue and was mentioned in none of the election literature. There was an agreement that the S.S.F. should fight St. Giles. They expressed a preference for Canongate, which they regarded as the key. The I.L.P. had declared their intention of contesting it, and caused much dissatisfaction when they failed to do so. The S.S.F. having decided, the question of a suitable candidate arose, and two obvious possibilities at once presented themselves, Leslie and Connolly. Both had lived in the parish for many years and Connolly had been born there. Both were Irish and of Catholic background. Leslie was better known, but Connolly was in the ascendant. He had made rapid strides as a public speaker and had surpassed first his brother John and then Leslie himself. From the standpoint of the S.S.F. the issue was probably decided by Connolly's possession of a house and an address and that minimum of economic stability which, for all his intellectual gifts, Leslie usually lacked.

From Connolly's standpoint there was much risk. It has been said that in order to contest the election he was obliged to resign his employment. This was not legally necessary even for the permanent staff. But if he took time off to fight his campaign he would run the danger of not being re-engaged. There seems to have been a vague proposition to employ him in some capacity in the local labour movement, but it came to nothing. He explained his decision to stand as arising from the Liberals making compacts with the Tories to divide the City seats between the two parties. "I refused," he said, "until I saw Liberal and Tory hand in glove to retain the Liberal in St. Cuthberts and the Tory in George's Square." He doubtless thought the situation favourable to transferring the Irish allegiance from Liberal to Labour, and so rebuilding the front that had been broken.

During the election campaign and for some time afterwards Connolly contributed a monthly article to the *Labour Chronicle* under the pseudonym "R. Ascal" ("rascal") in which local and national issues are discussed with sharp insight and playful wit. But he always returned to the Irish question.

His first article presented the situation in these terms:

"The intelligent and hard-headed elector and the shrewd and practical-minded voter have returned to Edinburgh. Rumour has it that they have already been heard of in St. Cuthberts Ward where Mr. Thomas Blaikie stands as I.L.P. candidate against Lord Provost Russell ... they are at present the most important persons in the British Empire until 8 o'clock on the evening of the polling for the municipal elections. After that ... their place will be taken by our other old friends the mob, the lower classes, the great unwashed, the residuum, and other such great names the organs of the classes are so fond of applying to the masses."

The first move in the election campaign was Councillor Forbes-MacKay's notice of motion demanding waterproof coats and leggings for city employees. Connolly remarked that the proposal was referred to a committee which would report *after* the election. Next day the first candidate in St. Giles presented himself, a Mr. Gardiner, who had figured as one of Mr. Goschen's Committee when that gentleman had won East Edinburgh by placarding the town with anti-Catholic manifestoes. Mr. Gardiner now claimed support "as a Catholic and as an Irishman". On September 8 the *Evening News* had asked editorially: "In view of the distracted and demoralised state of the Irish parties, would it not be as well to strike Home Rule out of the Liberal programme?" On October 2, the day before Gardiner's announcement was made, it announced that "Irishmen should be told plainly that the country will not stand another Home Rule campaign". But when Mitchell, the retiring Liberal, decided to seek re-election, the *News* took it as a matter of course that Gardiner would stand down.

Gardiner declined, but the Liberals had little reason to fear him. *The Edinburgh Catholic Herald* was much more afraid of the I.L.P. and seized upon some foolish utterance of a Labour candidate in Newcastle, to the effect that the Irish would get Home Rule when they knew how to behave themselves, to denounce "I.L.P. insolence" from every news stand. Liberal insolence, as Connolly observed, was let pass unnoticed.

Connolly was not adopted as Socialist candidate until October 22, a week before nomination day. With David Dornan in the chair, two hundred met at the Free Tron Hall to hear him state his programme. He was against the Fountain Bridge improvement scheme, for the water scheme and the amalgamation of Edinburgh parishes. His principal plank was housing. He demanded the end of one-roomed houses in St. Giles. New houses should be built at rents based on building costs and upkeep only. There should be taxation of unlet property to keep rents down, and while high-salaried officials should receive no pensions, city employees should have a superannuation scheme.

At first the Liberals were contemptuous of the Socialists whom they described as "a few noisy fanatics". Mr. Gardiner hoity-toitily described Connolly as a "young man of no business ability advocating ideas repugnant to all right-thinking men". Even the *Scotsman* reported his meetings in a tone of good-humoured curiosity. But his election campaign went with such a swing that they grew alarmed. Five hundred attended the first indoor meeting after his adoption. Pavements were chalked white with his name by enthusiastic supporters. He held an open air meeting for the carters at Kingstables Road, and since his chairman was too tongue-tied to speak, allowed him to preside silently while he addressed his fellow-employees from a cart.

The success of Connolly's campaign brought a new candidate into the field, the Conservative MacLaren. "Why did the Tories not oppose Mr. Mitchell before Mr. Connolly was in the field?" asked R. Ascal, and answered his own question: "Because they knew that Mr. Mitchell was as great a Tory as any one they could bring forward." They opposed him in order to strengthen his hands by a display of Tory opposition.

In this the unfortunate Mr. Gardiner was the principal loser, for the Irish National League held a special meeting at the Moulders Hall, presided over by Mr. Francis McAweeny, who declared: "There is not the least doubt that Mr. Gardiner and Mr. Connolly are serving the Unionist interest by what they are doing."

Connolly's appeal to the Irish was a direct attack on the two capitalist parties as "two sections of one party—the party of property". "Perhaps they will learn," he told them, "how foolish it is to denounce tyranny in Ireland and then to vote for tyrants and instruments of tyrants at their own door. Perhaps they will see that the landlord who grinds his peasants on a Connemara estate, and the landlord who rack-rents them in a Cowgate slum, are brethren in fact and deed. Perhaps they will realise that the Irish worker who starves in an Irish cabin and the Scots worker who is poisoned in an Edinburgh garret are brothers with one hope and destiny. Perhaps they will see that the same Liberal Government which supplies police to Irish landlords to aid them in the work of exterminating their Irish peasantry, also imports police into Scotland to aid Scots mine owners in their work of starving the Scottish miners."

But though Connolly's outdoor meetings were large and enthusiastic he had difficulties from which his opponents were free. Quite apart from the political conduct of the campaign, which went on the principle of "catch as catch can", the S.S.F. was denied the use of church halls and was up against the peculiar stumbling block that many of its supporters were not on the voters' roll. The publication of a new electoral list was the signal for every debt-collector's tout to make a beeline for the slums. Hence those whose livelihood was most precarious preferred to sacrifice their rights as householders and as citizens for the sake of a room and a chair. This circumstance told heavily against Labour candidates whose supporters chose to be voteless "lodgers".

The ill-grace with which the established parties accepted the intrusion of Labour is illustrated by the fate of Blaikie, who had been selected to oppose the Lord Provost in St. Cuthberts. Nominations closed at 4.30 p.m. on Tuesday, October 30. Due to inexperience, the I.L.P. were unaware of this rule and only discovered it around noon on nomination day. A nomination paper was hastily secured and completed, but the candidate, who must sign it, was at work. He was hastily sent for. At ten minutes past four it was returned to the Royal Exchange, but the candidate did not arrive until the Town Clerk started to read the nominations. It was customary to accept fresh nominations even at this late hour. Then the blow fell. Blaikie had come straight from work and had no pen. Neither had his nominator. Not a man in the crowded Exchange could be found to offer the loan of a pen to enable him to sign his nomination paper. The Town Clerk accepted the paper unsigned "for what it was worth" and failed to include Blaikie's name on the list.

Connolly was proposed by John Swan of Blackfriar's Street, and seconded by Walter Coutts of Society (now part of Chambers Street), and provided himself with five assentors named Pat Fitzpatrick, Michael Malone, J. P. Monaghan, David Dornan and William Robertson. Mr. Mitchell was announced as the tried representative of the people and Connolly as "the man who would put down swellocracy". Then the slanders began. Connolly had appealed to the Irish to reject the "crew of hucksters who have seized the National League". They in turn fought him in the interests of "faith and country". The Liberal ladies used the fact that he was a Catholic against him. The I.N.L. proclaimed him to be an atheist in disguise. Pillars of the church were planted at S.S.F. halls to "spot" Irish and Catholic voters, and after the poll the count showed that Connolly had come third. Mitchell received 1,056 votes, McLaren 497, Connolly 263 and Gardiner 54. The Irish vote in St. Giles was 700, the Liberal 1,000 and there were 150 women voters. Granted the dealers had voted Tory, the National League had handed the Liberals 400 Irish votes, and Connolly had held five-sixths of what remained.

In his analysis of the results Connolly made the most of

the increase in the total Socialist and Labour vote. He had achieved one-seventh of the poll.

"The official Liberals," wrote Connolly, "were able to obtain a majority of only four to one over a party the most revolutionary and the most recent in public life, with no electioneering organisation, and with a candidate known to earn his bread by following an occupation most necessary in our city life, but nevertheless universally despised by the public opinion of aristocratic Edinburgh."

Had there been no Unionist, and had the advanced working-class voters been left free to choose between the revolutionary Social-Democrat and the orthodox Liberal, Connolly thought, the result would have been highly satisfactory for socialism. But hundreds of men had cast their votes for Mitchell as the candidate most likely to defeat the Tory.

He concluded: "They will now have twelve months in which to meditate on the difference between the Liberal Tweedledee and the Tory Tweedledum, and after having so meditated they are invited to record the result of their studies at the polling booth on the first Tuesday of November 1895, if not before."

Connolly made little of his victory over Gardiner, though it could, in the light of subsequent history, show that neither in alliance with the Liberals, nor in attempted isolation, could the Irish nationalists ever again exert influence in Britain. The Labour alliance had become a necessity. He did, however, explain his insistence on standing as "Socialist" candidate. He wrote:

"The return of a Socialist candidate does not mean the immediate realisation of even the programme of palliatives commonly set before the electors. Nay, such programmes are in themselves a mere secondary consideration of little weight, indeed, apart from the spirit in which they will be interpreted. The election of a Socialist to any public body is only valuable in so far as it is the return of a disturber of the political peace."

He regarded reforms and the struggle for reform as subordinate to the larger aims of socialism. But such a struggle was an essential part of achieving socialism, and with this in view he announced a further electoral effort in the newly instituted Poor Law elections next year.

Connolly's circumstances now changed abruptly. Throughout November there was much organising activity among the labourers. The women's branch of the S.S.F. continued to flourish and the Clarion Scouts were founded at the Moulders Hall. But unemployment increased sharply once again with the opening of what proved one of the hardest winters of the century. It was customary for the City Cleansing Department to hire extra men and horses from contractors each year. Inspector McKay decided this winter to meet the increased work by means of overtime. He engaged no extra men and, despite the fair wage clause adopted by the Council, he compelled his regular carters to work ten and eleven hours a day without receiving the statutory overtime rate.

Connolly found himself unwanted by the Council and without recourse to the private contractors. As a casual employee he had no means of reply. He therefore attempted to make himself independent in order to pursue unhindered his main, his socialist work, and in February found a small shop, now demolished, at 73, Buccleuch Street where he set up as a cobbler. Unfortunately his skill was not equal to the venture. At one of his meetings two schoolgirls had asked to join the S.S.F. "Does your father approve?" asked Connolly. Strangely enough the father, a professor of languages, did so. It was he who addressed most of Connolly's election envelopes. One of the girls, who became the suffragette, Anna Munro, recalled that she collected all the family footwear and took it to Connolly's shop for repair. Not a pair could be worn again!

It was also unfortunate that this attempt coincided with the winter of 1895 with its interminable frost and snow, hyperborean temperatures and blistering winds, which froze the Thames beneath magnificent aurorae. Buccleuch Street is a fair step from the Cowgate on a summer's day on the way to the Meadows; climbing over heaped snow in a biting wind it seemed the pole of inaccessibility. The cobbler's shop did not prosper for yet another reason. Connolly was more interested in politics than business. It occurred to him to announce the availability of tickets for meetings at his shop long before he thought of mentioning that he mended boots. When he did think of advertising, however, he brought all his wit and originality to play. The I.L.P. seemed full of cobblers. Most people possessed some of the implements of the trade, or they were cheaply acquired. It became the victimised man's retreat. The *Labour Chronicle* advertised several small shops, but Connolly's advertisement stood out over all. It read:

> "Socialists support one another. Connolly, 73, Buccleuch St. repairs the worn-out understandings of the brethren at standard rates. Ladies boots 1/6, gents 2/6."

The "Rascal" continued to write in the *Chronicle* till February, and preparations were made for the Poor Law elections in April. Parish Councils were to be set up covering larger areas than then existed, and the Poor Law was to come under its first democratic administration in 300 years. The S.S.F. once more offered James Connolly for St. Giles's ward and hoped for better success, since this time there was no Liberal vote to split. Connolly intended to stigmatise "the folly of handing over the care of the poor to those who have made them poor". On March 8, the eight I.L.P. candidates and Connolly attended a social evening to launch the campaign. Owing to the cold weather, open-air meetings were virtually impossible: chalk was of little use; and the poll was exceptionally small. But Connolly's opponents were taking no chances. His opponent was no less than Monsignor Grady of St. Patrick's Rectory, who "knew the St. Giles poor and wanted to help them". He asked the electors not to support him merely because he was a priest. After all, he was a ratepayer. But against his 523 votes, Connolly could muster only 169. A third candidate polled 480.

The routine of socialist activity was nevertheless maintained. Keir Hardie spoke in Leith in February and the Trades Council was induced to join the I.L.P. in a demonstration on the unemployment issue. This took place on February 23, when it was said that "even the gas seemed to feel cold and went back into the pipes". The plight of the unemployed was desperate. A deputation from the Women Workers Federation, the Trades Council and the I.L.P. waited on the Town Council and demanded the provision of work. After the demonstration a concert was given in the Operetta House for the purpose of raising relief funds. Leith announced the opening of two soup kitchens, the provision of free dinners and work at stone-breaking. The master builders of Edinburgh had agreed to a reduction of hours just before the great frost commenced. On the arrival of the frost they withdrew their offer. The weather had thrown all discontents together, hence the initiative of the Trades Council.

But these labours seemed to exhaust its energy. Noting that a number of trades had not paid their share of the expenses of last year's effort, and with some heart-burnings on the subject of socialism after the expense of the Poor Law election, the Trades Council decided not to proceed with a May Day demonstration in 1895. After some hesitation the I.L.P. and S.S.F. decided for the first time to hold a meeting on May 1, rather than on the nearest Sunday. Although the expected speaker, Cunningham-Grahame, fell out at the last moment, Bruce Glasier was summoned from Glasgow and addressed three thousand on the East Meadows in a cutting wind. As well as the usual resolution calling for an eight-hour day there was another on the subject of war, which read:

"That as war is a barbarous mode of settling international disputes, is detrimental to progress and injurious to industry, this meeting of workers protests against it in the name of our common humanity, and as a step towards its abolition demands that in future the question of peace or war shall only be decided by the direct vote of the whole people."

In May, James Connolly once more became secretary of the S.S.F., which shortly became the Edinburgh Branch of the S.D.F. New rooms were found at 65, Nicholson Street. The cobbler's shop had proved a failure. With the sardonic remark that he was going out to buy a mirror to watch himself starve to death, Connolly had got up, gone out and locked the door behind him. He now took charge of the new clubroom and did what he could with what he could get.

There is little doubt that Keir Hardie would have wished the S.S.F. to join with the I.L.P. He had been highly impressed with the young orator and organiser on his visits to Edinburgh and Leith, and when a by-election took place in one of the local divisions sent a copy of the manifesto to Connolly asking him to have it printed and distributed so that the I.L.P. would be in evidence. Hardie suggested that rather than his own the signature of the local district committee of the party should be affixed. Connolly laid the letter before them and informed them that he had sent the order to a printer. He had imagined there would be no objection, since he was a member of the Socialist Election Committee for Parliamentary Purposes. But to his surprise he found he had invited a storm. The Committee refused to co-operate in any way and wrote to Keir Hardie sharply reproving him for communicating with Connolly. Connolly, for his part, went down to the division and spoke there for three hours on "pure" and "practical" socialism. Connolly was becoming more than a local leader now, and was experiencing the jealousy of lesser men for the first time.

Following the failure of the cobbler's business, in mid-June Connolly began to think more seriously of full-time work as a political propagandist or organiser. Currie, who wrote the S.S.F. notes in *Justice*, explained how after fighting the two elections Connolly "found it impossible to get employment in his native town. If he has to leave the district it will be a great loss." He was a fluent speaker with a good strong voice which seemed to have been specially created for outdoor propaganda. He had a thorough knowledge of his subject and his untiring zeal and perseverance had made him "a

5*

martyr whose martyrdom would have been saved if certain men had been honourable enough to fulfil an obligation entered into, or at least give some reason for non-fulfilment. Connolly has more than sufficient time on his hands and if any branch of the S.D.F. or I.L.P. is wishful to have an efficient and capable lecturer or organiser, letters addressed to James Connolly, 65, Nicholson Street, will always find one."

A month later appeared an advertisement in the *Labour Leader* to the effect that James Connolly, S.S.F. and I.L.P., was open to book dates for lectures. Terms would be provided by Dan Irving, S.D.F. Club, St. James Hall, Burnley.

There seems to be no record of any of the engagements Connolly received. But there is a probability that he would be invited to Glasgow and Fife. The *Labour Chronicle* contains one or two reports from surrounding districts which may have been prompted by him, though proof is wanting. Certainly his main activity in the next six months was the building up of the S.S.F. (after September, the S.D.F.) to an unprecedented level of prestige.

In the autumn the Operetta House was engaged for a series of lectures which were delivered by such celebrities as Eleanor Marx, Edward Aveling, Dan Irving, the Rev. Bruce Wallace, H. M. Hyndman, Peter Curran, Ben Tillett and Harry Quelch. The Operetta House held one thousand five hundred persons. "There never were such days," said one of the Socialists, comparing them with those of the Moulders Hall and the shack in Park Street. The I.L.P., for its part, brought George Lansbury and Tom Mann, and the result was that Connolly came to know personally the leading figures in the labour movement of the day.

The *Edinburgh Labour Chronicle* was discontinued when Dickenson died of tuberculosis in December; a vote of respect to his memory was proposed by Connolly and seconded by Blakely at the meeting addressed by Pete Curran. The pledge to support socialism, which was voted at Hyndman's meeting, was also proposed by Connolly and seconded by Léo Meillet. For the first time in Edinburgh history the

Trades Council was officially represented at a Socialist gathering.

But Connolly's situation became desperate. It was characteristic of him that at a time when the S.D.F. must have been financially at its most successful he should plough back every gain into increasing the scale of its propaganda, even while he himself approached destitution. At the same time it was clear that he could not remain in Edinburgh and, according to John Leslie, he considered emigration to Chile, from which he was dissuaded with some difficulty.

It has been stated that he had already obtained his passport and that the Chilean Government had offered the passage and a grant of land and tools. On the other hand, elsewhere it is stated that he contemplated founding a socialist colony in Chile. It seems unlikely that a townsman born and bred would contemplate farming so lightly. How little investigation of the circumstances had been done by those who made these statements is shown by the fact that the British passport office has no record of any application from Connolly at this time, because *no passport was necessary,* nor has the Chilean Consulate any record of the supposed transaction. It would seem most reasonable to accept Leslie's statement at its face value. Connolly was contemplating emigration and was dissuaded from it on Leslie's promise to write a special appeal in *Justice* seeking employment from the labour movement or some member of it.

"Here is a man among men," wrote Leslie. "I am not much given to flattery, as those who know me are aware, yet I may say that very few men have I met deserving of greater love and respect than James Connolly. I know something of Socialist propaganda and have done a little in that way myself, and I also know the movement in Edinburgh to its centre, and I say that no man has done more for the movement than Connolly, if they have done as much. Certainly nobody has dared one half what he has dared in the assertion of his principles. Of his ability I need only say, as one who has had some opportunity of judging, he is the most able propagandist in every sense of the word that Scotland has turned out. And because of it, and for his intrepidity, he is today on the verge of destitution and out of work. And we all know what this means for the unskilled workman, as Connolly is. Now this should not be—most emphatically should not be . . . Connolly's case is scarcely an encouragement for others to go and do likewise. Leaving the Edinburgh Socialists to digest the matter, is there no comrade in Glasgow, Dundee, or anywhere else who could secure a situation for one of the best and most self-sacrificing men in the movement? Connolly is, I have said, an unskilled labourer, a life-long total abstainer, sound in wind and limb (Christ in Heaven! how often have I nearly burst a blood vessel as these questions were asked of myself!). Married, with a young family, and as his necessities are therefore very great, so he may be had cheap."

There was a response from a source which must have delighted Connolly as much as the visit of an angel from heaven —from Dublin, the city of his youthful enthusiasms and happy courtship. The Dublin Socialist Club invited him to become its paid organiser.

During the negotiations and preparations for his departure, he spoke every Sunday at the S.D.F. clubroom at Nicholson Street, and began the summer lectures on the Meadows on April 4. Then, early in May, he left for Ireland. His brother John agreed to accommodate the S.S.F. at 6, Drummond Street and resumed (for a time) the notes in *Justice*. Leslie left for Falkirk; Mathieson, a schoolteacher from Argyll, became secretary. "All the pioneers of Socialism in Edinburgh have now left," *Justice* complained, and by a coincidence the "Old Town" never again led the way. As Connolly had foreseen, the banner passed to Leith, and in years to come even the "speaker's corner" crossed the railway into the New Town. After his return to Edinburgh, Leslie gave up the attempt to win back the Irish support, and slowly slum clearance and rebuilding dissipated the old revolutionary centre.

Two months before he sailed, Connolly's third daughter, Aideen, was born. She was given the first Irish name in the family.

The expenses of the migration to Dublin were met by a subscription raised by John Leslie and others. Connolly took with him his precious library of books on socialism and Irish history, an array of blue-books and white-papers, and a sheaf of cuttings of the 1889 London dock strike, collected in Dundee.

DUBLIN AND THE I.S.R.P.

On his arrival in Dublin, Connolly found a one-room tenement for himself and his family at 76, Charlemont Street, and at once held discussions with the Dublin socialists. The group which had invited him was neither homogeneous nor experienced, but none the less reflected the special conditions of Dublin, which was like no other European capital. Two circumstances dominated Dublin's economic life: first the Union, which held industry under the continuous pressure of unrestricted British competition; and second the agrarian crisis in the country, which sent a steady stream of migrants into competition with the unskilled workers. From the first came the political support worker gave capitalist as a provider of employment; from the second the intense craft loyalty of the skilled trades which forbade his employing outsiders to the point where jobs almost acquired a right of entail.

Socialist organisation in Dublin was continuous from the eighteen-forties but suffered repeated set-backs, partly through the difficulty of evolving correct tactics for a movement within an oppressed nation, but also from the prevalence of unemployment and the ease of victimisation. It was strongest in the days of the International Workingmen's Association, when Marx's support for the Fenians indicated the primacy of the democratic struggle. In the seventies Bakuninism gained a temporary influence, to be eclipsed when the Dublin socialists affiliated to the S.D.F.–but only at the price of the British connection. From then onward Irish socialism was essentially provincial, restricted to trade union politics, and ignoring alike the national and agrarian questions which were the purview of the Nationalist party.

The Parnell split, destroying the hegemony of the Parliamentarians, released many new forces and opened the way for an independent working-class party which would be more than a sect. Within a few years were founded the Gaelic

League, the Celtic literary societies, the Irish T.U.C. and Connolly's Irish Socialist Republican Party.

After attending the inaugural congress of the Irish T.U.C., Keir Hardie had been struck with the possibility of transferring the allegiance of the Irish in Britain from the Liberal to the Independent Labour Party. Connolly wrote to him urging him to put Leslie's proposition into effect, and he returned to Ireland later in 1894. The I.L.P. at first seemed to take Dublin by storm. It absorbed the rump of the S.D.F. (the Dublin Socialist Union), took premises in Bachelor's Walk, established branches in Belfast and Waterford, and on May Day 1895 brought many thousands to Phoenix Park accompanied by fourteen bands.

But the movement ebbed with equal rapidity. In Belfast it fell at the hands of Orange bigotry. In Waterford it became involved in the post-Parnellian faction fights. And in Dublin unemployment and the threat of victimisation reduced its numbers to a handful. With a feeling that the I.L.P. was after all a cul-de-sac, the members reverted to the old name; but instead of the old S.D.F. men, Fitzpatrick and Canty, the leading lights were now I.L.P. supporters such as Dorman and the Lyng brothers.

Until Connolly's arrival, Dorman manned the Custom House steps for a weekly outdoor meeting. He is described as a kindly lovable character, and a pleasant though not profound speaker. He was a retired naval officer whose socialism was largely humanitarian. In contrast, the Lyngs were typical Dublinmen, young, talkative and bursting with energy. But they were without political experience. Connolly immediately set to work convincing them that the failure of socialism in Ireland arose from the false internationalism which identified it with England.

He did not have his way without a struggle, and Gerald O'Connor, who had it from T. J. Lyng, described how he challenged the leaders, "pulverised them in debate, preached socialism unblushingly to them, shattered their little organisation, and from the fragments he founded a small Irish Socialist Republican Party".

Unlike his younger brother, T. J. Lyng was not an unqualified admirer of Connolly. But there is doubtless a grain of truth in the story. Connolly's background was that of the S.D.F., with all its faults a teacher of class struggle. The I.L.P. accepted socialism but did not recognise the conflict of classes as the force impelling to it. There must have been some sharp reorientation before the party's manifesto was published in September.

The first meeting was held on May 29, 1896, in the snug of a public house in Thomas Street, where Connolly, with five other total abstainers out of an attendance of eight, sipped lemonade. The motion to establish the party was proposed by Dorman and seconded by T. J. Lyng, and Connolly was appointed secretary with the prospect of £1 a week when he could get it.

Years later he summarised its purpose in these terms:

"The I.S.R.P. was founded in Dublin by a few workingmen whom the writer had succeeded in interesting in his proposition that the two currents of revolutionary thought in Ireland, the socialist and the national, were not antagonistic but complementary, and that the Irish socialist was in reality the best patriot, but in order to convince the Irish people of that fact he must first learn to look inward upon Ireland for his justification, rest his arguments upon the facts of Irish history, and be a champion against the subjection of Ireland and all that it implies. That the Irish question was at bottom an economic question, and that the economic struggle must first be able to function nationally before it could function internationally, and as socialists were opposed to all oppression, so should they ever be foremost in the daily battle against all its manifestations, social and political."

The underlying assumption was not new. But the words "socialists must be foremost" implied a struggle for leadership which had been set aside since the days of the First International. Reaffirming an old Marxian principle, Connolly foreshadowed a new one. Now that finance-capital dominated the highly developed countries and drove them to overseas expansion, he was the first to suggest new tactics, and glimpsed the truth that, in a world divided into oppressed and oppressor nations, the classical national question of Ireland and Central Europe had fused with the newer "colonial question" beyond the seas.

In his first public statement on behalf of the new party, he wrote:

> "The struggle for Irish freedom has two aspects; it is national and it is social. The national ideal can never be realised until Ireland stands forth before the world as a nation, free and independent. It is social and economic because no matter what the form of government may be, as long as one class owns as private property the land and instruments of labour from which mankind derive their substance, that class will always have it in their power to plunder and enslave the remainder of their fellow-creatures."

He drew the moral that "the failure of other so-called 'leaders' to grasp the two-fold character of the 'Irish Question' is the real explanation of that paralysis which at constantly recurring intervals falls like a blight on Irish politics."

The inaugural manifesto was headed "Irish Socialist Republican Party", under which came Desmoulins' aphorism: "The great appear great because we are on our knees: let us rise." Then followed the text of the manifesto:

OBJECT

Establishment of an Irish Socialist Republic based upon the public ownership by the Irish people of the land and instruments of production, distribution and exchange. Agriculture to be administered as a public function, under boards of management elected by the agricultural population and responsible to them and to the nation at large. All other forms of Labour necessary to the well-being of the community to be conducted on the same principles.

PROGRAMME

As a means of organising the forces of the Democracy in preparation for any struggle which may precede the realisation of our ideal, or paving the way for its realisation, or restricting the tide of migration by providing employment at home, and finally of palliating the evils of our present social system, we work by political means to secure the following measures:

1. Nationalisation of railways and canals.
2. Abolition of private banks and money-lending institutions and establishment of state banks, under popularly elected boards of directors, issuing loans at cost.
3. Establishment at public expense of rural depots for the most improved agricultural machinery, to be lent out to the agricultural population at a rent covering cost and the management alone.
4. Graduated income tax on all incomes over £400 per annum in order to provide funds for pensions to the aged infirm and widows and orphans.
5. Legislative restriction of hours of labour to 48 per week and establishment of a minimum wage.
6. Free maintenance for all children.
7. Gradual extension of the principle of public ownership and supply to all the necessaries of life.
8. Public control and management of National Schools by boards elected by popular ballot for that purpose alone.
9. Free education up to the highest university grades.
10. Universal suffrage.

THE IRISH SOCIALIST REPUBLICAN PARTY HOLDS:

That the agricultural and industrial system of a free people, like their political opinion, ought to be an accurate reflex of the democratic principle by the people for the people, solely in the interests of the people.

That the private ownership by a class of the land and instruments of production, distribution and exchange is opposed to this vital principle of justice, and is the fundamental basis of all oppression, national, political and social.

That the subjection of one nation to another, as of Ireland to the authority of the British Crown, is a barrier to the free political and economic development of the subjected nation, and can only serve the interests of the exploiting classes of both nations.

That, therefore, the national and economic freedom of the Irish people must be sought in the same direction, viz. the establishment of an Irish Socialist Republic, and the consequent conversion of the means of production, distribution and exchange into the common property of society, to be held and controlled by a democratic state in the interests of the entire community.

That the conquest by the Social Democracy of political power in Parliament, and on all public bodies in Ireland, is the readiest and most effective means whereby the revolutionary forces may be organised and disciplined to attain that end.

Branches wanted everywhere. Enquiries invited. Entrance fee 6d. Minimum weekly subscription 1d.

Offices: 67, Middle Abbey Street, Dublin.   1896

It is only necessary to read through this manifesto to see that it is not based on the outlook of the I.L.P. The object was socialism, and the programme to be worked for by "political means" was partly a palliative, partly a means of organising the popular forces for a struggle which, it is implicit in the wording, might be by "other means". The objects refer to the people and "public" ownership. But the final section excludes the capitalist and landlord classes from the category of the "people".

Both the phraseology, as in references to the "Democracy", and the immediate programme show the direct influence of the inaugural manifesto of the Democratic Federation of 1883, *Socialism made plain*.

Hyndman's manifesto demanded nationalisation of railways, establishment of national banks, tax on incomes of over £300 per annum, an eight-hour day, free compulsory education and universal suffrage. Those demands which are absent from the S.D.F. Manifesto and present in that of the I.S.R.P., relate to purely Irish questions. Those peculiar to the S.D.F., such as abolition of the House of Lords, are special to Britain. The I.S.R.P. demanded an independent Republic. The S.D.F. had followed the current policy of the Irish movement and asked merely for legislative independence. On one issue alone, the English movement's classical blind spot, was there opposition—on the question of the colonies. The S.D.F. applied the principle of "legislative independence" (Home Rule) to "colonies and dependencies", while the I.S.R.P. declared that the subjection of one nation to another was a barrier to progress in both nations.

The programme of the I.S.R.P. was thus more advanced than that of the most advanced party in Britain. It may have lacked the sharp analysis of tasks and tactics characterising Lenin's draft for the Russian Social-Democratic Labour Party, which was drawn up almost simultaneously. But to proclaim, at a time when the socialists of oppressed nations were frequently taken to task for their "nationalism", that the struggle for national independence is an inseparable part of the struggle for socialism, entitles Connolly to a foremost place as a political thinker.

In asserting working-class leadership of the national struggle, he defined in Ireland what was subsequently recognised as a general tendency during the epoch of imperialism, namely for a section of the capitalist class of a subject nation to compound with the oppressors. But it was not for many years that he appreciated that not all the capitalists will necessarily do this.

He redefined the national and labour interests in Ireland, identifying the first with republicanism, the second with socialism. In so doing he rejected alike the post-Parnellian Home Rule factions and the Liberal-Labour politicians linked with them in the "Union of Hearts". The apparent antagonism between Labour and Nationalism was a product of their compromising leadership which had distorted both national and social aims. An independent working-class party was required, not only to free the Irish workers from bourgeois entanglements, but to establish an alternative centre round which all that was most progressive in Ireland could be rallied.

Connolly's first move after the formal establishment of the I.S.R.P. was to begin open-air meetings on a scale Dublin had never before seen. Advertisements were inserted in the *Telegraph* and *Herald* announcing the first for June 7. They ran:

> "Irish Socialist Republic. Great Public meeting in favour of the above will be held at Custom House on Sunday next 5 p.m. Mr. Jas. Connolly, late of Edinburgh, and others will address the meeting. Mr. Alexander Blane,[1] ex-M.P. will preside."

Thereafter, meetings were held each week. By the end of June two more regular stances were occupied, at Phoenix Park on Sundays at 6 p.m. and at St. James's Fountain each Tuesday at 8 p.m. After a meeting at the Fountain was broken up with cabbage stalks and cries of "You're not an Irishman", the Custom House meeting, brought forward to 3 p.m., then postponed to 3.30 each Sunday, continued until October, when bad weather and Dorman's departure for the south closed the season.

When Connolly arrived in Dublin the building trade had been at a standstill since May 1. Since his £1 a week was not forthcoming, life was very hard until September, when the Corporation succeeded in breaking through Government obstruction of a new main drainage scheme. Connolly then worked as a labourer, and his daughter Nora has written touchingly of how the last family treasures were sold or pawned to buy food and clothing which he needed before he could start.

---

[1] Blane was a prominent Parnellite who lost his seat after the split.

The strike, which ended when the carpenters settled without consulting the labourers, whose union thereupon disaffiliated from the Trades Council, had been vigorously denounced by Mr. T. Harrington, M.P., as an anti-Irish manœuvre dictated from London. He accused the respectable Trades Council of "showing countenance to anti-Parnellite knaves". The I.S.R.P. wrote to the Trades Council suggesting that a joint committee should be set up to oppose him with a Labour candidate at the next election. Momentarily looking up from their consideration of the Guinness label and preferential employment of Dublin men on the drainage scheme, they agreed to throw their full weight against Harrington, while rejecting the joint committee.

To the Trades Council Harrington was an individual M.P. who had blotted his copy-book. They continued their practice of joining with the Liberal-Labour nationalists to hear the annual "Harrington lectures", bacchanals of mental confusion that outraged even the Fabians. Connolly took up the ideological gauntlet with a series of lectures at the Foresters Hall, and encouraged the Fabians to do likewise. But anxious lest there should be cleansing with dirty soap, in December he addressed the Fabians on "Why we are revolutionist", and argued for an independent working-class party.

The trade union movement was too strongly dominated by the skilled trades to yield easily to the new thinking. Connolly's recruits were mostly younger than himself: the three Lyngs, the elder O'Briens, Thomas and Daniel, were in their early twenties; William, who joined later, was a boy in his 'teens. Carolan joined during the winter, and Mullery the apprentice tailor, though not a member, was in daily contact with Connolly, who passed his shop every day he climbed the stairs to his office in 67, Abbey Street, whence the old *Irish Press* had been issued. Youth attracted youth. Tom Lyng was the most active member; a contemporary newspaper commented that the I.S.R.P. had more syllables than members, and consisted of "a Scotto-Hibernian and a long boy" (a reference to Lyng's six feet). These were the days when you knew a socialist from the length of his hair. Bradshawe, a young clerk, and Tom O'Brien wore this insignia. Daniel O'Brien tried it, but since his hair grew straight up instead of down he had to abandon the attempt. Both youth and the touch of bohemianism repelled the trade union movement.

But these presented no obstacle to the Gaelic, literary and Fenian nationalists. These were also young people, seeking new guidance in the twilight of the nationalist party. Maud Gonne, aristocrat, whose romantic nationalism had been repelled by the prosaic humbug and anti-feminism of the "Union of Hearts", had thrown herself into the movement for the amnesty of the remaining Fenian prisoners. Alice Milligan had founded the *Shan Van Vocht*[1] in Belfast in 1886. Her paper became the main literary expression of the Young Ireland societies, behind which, as in the amnesty movement, could be discerned the shadowy influence of the Irish Republican Brotherhood (the surviving Fenian organisation). A great victory was won when John Daly of Limerick was released on September 1. Energy and idealism were in the field, and Connolly thought he could supply a policy.

Throughout the months of unemployment he was reading in the National Library and extracting the writings of James Fintan Lalor. The notion of publishing excerpts from *The Rights of Ireland* and the *Faith of a Felon* may have come from the republican Fred Ryan. Connolly attended his lecture on "The Social Side of the Irish Question" on July 31, together with the two Lyng brothers, Tom and Murtagh. Ryan argued that the ideas of Lalor provided the remedy for Ireland's difficulties. Connolly spoke in the discussion, and after the meeting set to work producing Lalor's writings as a pamphlet, with an introduction by himself. He sent a copy to the *Shan Van Vocht*, which gave a favourable review.

With a view to further influencing the literary republican groupings, which were numerous and divided by mutual jealousies, Connolly now produced his first major political essay, "Ireland for the Irish", which appeared in the *Labour*

---

[1] "Poor old woman", poetic name for Ireland.

Leader in three instalments during October. His main *attack* was directed against the British Government, his main *criticism* against the Home Rule factions whom it was his intention to isolate.

He began with a quotation from John Stuart Mill to the effect that feudal ownership replaced common property in land only with the conquest of Ireland and had never been recognised by the moral sentiment of the people.

Developing this idea, he wrote:

"The Irish question has in fact a much deeper source than a mere difference of opinion on forms of Government. Its real origin and inner meaning lay in the circumstance that the two nations held fundamentally different ideas on the vital question of property in land."

Quoting Morgan's opinion that "primitive communism" was the first stage of all civilised societies, he argued that this form survived longer and blossomed more copiously in Ireland than in the other countries of Europe.

"The English Government were also astute enough to perceive that the political or national subjection of Ireland was entirely valueless to the conquerors while the politically subjected nation remained in possession of economic freedom."

For this reason they declared the public clan lands to be the private property of the chief, who must hold them in feoff for the Crown. Primitive communism was thus replaced by a form of feudalism.

The Irish people, ran Connolly's argument, refused to accept the change until after the break-up of the Kilkenny confederation in 1649, when the clans were dispersed. Then the demand for the restoration of the common ownership of land fell into abeyance in face of the need first to recover political freedom. That freedom was still to be won back two and a half centuries later; meanwhile the new system held the field and the old demands went by the board. The Irish "middle-class" stepped into the breach and secured its own economic position by ruthless exploitation within the framework of British institutions, while preserving its political influence by "lip-service to Irish nationality".

Home Rule was, as then proposed, merely a device to place this class at the head of a local Parliament with no real power, for the better exploitation of the Irish people. It was "simply a mockery of Irish National aspirations".

Connolly scornfully dismissed the "Home Rule" utopia of an industrialised Ireland successfully competing against the older capitalist countries in a world afflicted with over-production and periodic slumps. The Irish could only succeed by becoming the "lowest blacklegs in Europe".

The alternative conception of a peasant proprietary without further development of industry he thought even more utopian. New methods were being introduced into agriculture on a world scale. Modern machinery, which alone made possible production at a competitive price, demanded great capital outlay. "The days of small farmers, like small capitalists, are gone," Connolly declared; and since, in any case, the present "owners" of the land had little historical title to it, and it was "manifestly impossible to reinstate the Irish people on the lands from which they have been driven", the only solution was land nationalisation. The community as a whole would receive collectively what had been stolen from their forebears individually.

In the last section Connolly described the final result of the monopolisation of land and industry by the landlord and capitalist classes. The workers, "deprived of everything by which they can maintain life", were "compelled to seek their livelihood by the sale of their capacity for work, their labour power". They must sell it or starve.

As a remedy for such evils, "Home Rule" was a glaring absurdity. What was needed was a "revolutionary change in the structure of society", an Irish socialist republic, not an "industrial hell" created "under the specious pretext of 'developing our resources'". This involved complete separation from the English Crown, but "no antagonism towards the British people".

"The interests of labour all the world over are identical, it is true, but it is also true that each country had better work out its own salvation on lines most congenial to its own people. No Irish revolutionist worth his salt would refuse to lend a hand to the Social Democracy of England in the effort to uproot the social system of which the British Empire is the crown and apex, and in like manner, no English Social Democrat fails to recognise clearly that the crash which would betoken the fall of the ruling classes in Ireland would sound the tocsin for the revolt of the disinherited in England."

Connolly concluded with an explanation of the immediate programme of the I.S.R.P., once again presenting reform as a means of organising the forces of democracy for revolution.

Some of the formulations in "Ireland for the Irish" follow so closely the thought of Marx (in his correspondence with Engels in the winter of 1869–70) that it is natural to ask whether there was any likely channel of influence. So far as is known, Connolly never met Engels. But he did meet Marx's daughter Eleanor and her husband, Edward Aveling, in Edinburgh on more than one occasion. Eleanor had visited Ireland and had sent Connolly a letter of congratulation when the announcement of the I.S.R.P. appeared in *Justice*. It is certainly possible that she explained her father's view to both Connolly and Leslie.

Having made his general position clear in the *Labour Leader*, Connolly turned his attention to persuading the democratic nationalist movement to adopt it. From January 1897 onwards, largely as a development of the amnesty movement, committees sprang up throughout Ireland for the purpose of commemorating the rising of 1798. This movement, like the literary and Irish language movements, was distinct from and opposed to the parliamentary factions, but was not avowedly republican.

In an article entitled "Nationalism and Socialism" published in *Shan Van Vocht* with editorial disclaimer, Connolly argued that:

"Traditions may and frequently do provide materials for a glorious martyrdom, but can never be strong enough to ride the storm of a successful revolution. If the national movement of our own day is not merely to re-enact the old sad tragedies of our past history, it must show itself capable of rising to the exigencies of the moment. It must demonstrate to the people of Ireland that our nationalism is not merely a morbid idealising of the past, but is also capable of formulating a distinct and definite answer to the problems of the present and a political and economic creed capable of adjustment to the wants of the future."

For this purpose he urged that "all earnest nationalists" should declare their aim to be a republic, but "not a capitalist monarchy with an elected head" as in France, nor the plutocracy of the United States, but a republic that would be a "beacon-light to the oppressed of every land".

The objection that to take this stand would alienate middle-class and aristocratic support, he brushed aside. If the only way to conciliate the "classes" was by promising them that the victorious "masses" would not interfere with their privileges, it was better not to conciliate them at all. The masses would in any case refuse their support on any such basis. Indeed, that freedom so achieved would prove illusory and spurious Connolly explained in a striking passage which today echoes with prophecy:

"If you remove the English army tomorrow and hoist the green flag over Dublin Castle, unless you set about the organisation of the socialist republic, your efforts would be in vain. England would still rule you. She would rule you through her capitalists, through her landlords, through her financiers, through the whole array of commercial and industrialist institutions she has planted in this country and watered with the tears of our mothers and the blood of our martyrs. England would still rule you to your ruin, even while your lips offered hypocritical homage at the shrine of that Freedom whose cause you betrayed."

Not only was this fighting talk which went straight to the

heart of the youth, it was original political thinking of the profoundest kind. Those sections of imperial opinion who were toying with Home Rule regarded it as a means of holding Ireland economically and strategically while granting the appearance of self-government. The reliance they had formerly placed on the landed aristocracy was being transferred to the capitalist class, and especially its mercantile sections.

Alice Milligan was so impressed that she took advantage of the fact that her young brother, an eighteen-year-old law student at Queen's University, Belfast, was visiting Dublin for an examination, to discover more of the I.S.R.P. of which, before Connolly's article reached her, she had never heard. Ernest Milligan found him living in one room with his young family, which had been augmented by a new baby, Ina,[1] whose name was chosen by Lillie.

Milligan described Connolly as of medium height, thick-set in build and "though terribly earnest in conversation" endowed with a rich sense of humour. The young man was a member of the Gaelic League and had hitherto embraced the vague liberal nationalism of Mazzini. Connolly's socialism at once disturbed and fascinated him. "Politics are based on the stomach," Connolly told him, "and economic causes have moulded history." At a meeting in Foster Place, which had now been adopted in preference to the Custom House, he met members of Connolly's party and was lent *Progress and Poverty*,[2] *Merrie England*,[3] *Looking Backward*,[4] *Unto this Last*,[5] and *Labours of the People*.[6] Recalling the discussions he had with Connolly, nearly half a century afterwards, Milligan was still impressed by Connolly's insistence that he should also read the case against socialism. Connolly lent him Schäffle's *Quintessence of Socialism*. With it was the "counter-book", the title of which Milligan gave as *The Impossibility of Social Democracy*, but which was most likely Chatterton's pamphlet The *Practicability of Socialism*, an answer to Schäffle published in 1896 and advertised in *Justice*.

---

[1] Written "Agna" in Nora Connolly's reminiscences.
[2] George. [3] Blatchford. [4] Bellamy. [5] Ruskin. [6] Charles Booth.

Milligan joined the I.S.R.P. and set about organising a branch in Belfast. An advertisement was inserted in Blatchford's *Clarion,* and sufficient replies were received to launch the "Belfast Socialist Society". Once again the response was from the youth. Three students, Robert Lynd, Samuel Porter and James Winder Good, joined at the outset. The meetings were held at the Typographical Hall, College Street, and among the members were Rice, Galliland and a young brushmaker called Monaghan. The new branch, however, had some difficulty in assimilating Connolly's militant republicanism.

Connolly also found support in Cork. In the *Shan Van Vocht* of March 12 appeared an article by another young man, Con O'Lyhane of Cork. He had graduated from technical school with honours in Irish and Chemistry and was newly installed in a clerical post. He strongly supported Connolly's refusal to participate in worship of the past, and urged the '98 Commemoration Committees to make their objective the rededicating of the nation to the *aims* of the United Irishmen.

Connolly meanwhile pushed ahead with educational meetings in Dublin. The methods of work of the I.S.R.P. were based on those of the Edinburgh S.D.F. All members were drawn into giving lectures. Tom O'Brien spoke on the Land League, Daniel O'Brien on Wolfe Tone, and E. W. Stewart, one of the older members, was followed by Alexander Blane and Alice Milligan as guest speakers. At the end of March 1897, outdoor meetings were resumed and the *Labour Leader* and *Shan Van Vocht* articles were collected and republished as a pamphlet under the title, *Erin's Hope, the End and the Means.*

Throughout 1897 the national movement expanded rapidly. The Amnesty Association held a demonstration in Phoenix Park in May, Fitzpatrick and Skelly representing the Trades Council. But influencing the Commemoration movement, apart from individuals like Fred Ryan and the young P. T. Daly, was beyond the resources of the I.S.R.P. Connolly decided to undertake the republication of the most important extracts from the actual writings of the United Irishmen. At the same time, with characteristic flexibility, he solved the difficult problem of fully and officially participating without dispersing his own forces by founding the "Rank and File '98 Club", with T. J. O'Brien as secretary. The new club forwarded a £1 subscription to the Dublin Executive Committee, which was readily accepted. The "Rank and File '98 Club" was to be the centre from which to disseminate a knowledge of the true aims of the United Irishmen. Jack Mullery, the tailor, was one of the first members.

Preparations were being made for Queen Victoria's Diamond Jubilee. The I.S.R.P. made preparations as well, and during the celebrations carried out one of the most spectacular campaigns of its existence. Early in May a Republican Manifesto was distributed at its open air meetings, which were enlivened by the display of cartoons on the same subject. Ten years previously the Dublin unemployed had adopted the black flag as their symbol of defiance. Now John Daly wrote to the newspapers proposing similar gestures in 1897. The I.S.R.P. improved on the proposal with rare imagination, finding an enthusiastic ally in Maud Gonne.

Returning from Paris to London she had been approached by Keir Hardie to organise a counter-demonstration in London. She declined the "astute Scotsman's" invitation on the grounds that the English should do their own fighting, and continued her journey to Dublin. She readily agreed to address the I.S.R.P. meeting in Foster Place, which was to be held on June 21 under the slogan of "Down with Monarchy: long live the Republic!" Jubilee day was June 22.

Maud Gonne, "the most beautiful woman in Ireland", was the daughter of an Irish father and an English mother, brought up in the most aristocratic surroundings, presented at Court, and educated with lavish care. In early youth she was seized by the romance of the Land League, and on her return from Russia in 1892 offered her services to Davitt. Disappointed in that quarter she proceeded to Dublin, where she attended the "Contemporary Club" whose secretary was Oldham, the Barrington lecturer, then a student. A frequenter of his meetings was the veteran Fenian John O'Leary, whom Yeats regarded as the embodiment of "Romantic Ireland". From the Contemporary Club it was but a step to the Celtic Literary Society, where she met William Rooney and Alice Milligan's circle. Her opposition to the Parnellite faction was sealed when Harrington informed her that women were not admitted to membership of the National League. Slowly she found her place. W. B. Yeats introduced her to the National Library where Connolly, at the other end of the social scale, sat studying during his long spells of unemployment. She came to respect him more than anybody, though never understanding his social philosophy. What they possessed in common was a willingness for action and supreme physical courage.

She joined with Connolly in preparing the Jubilee demonstrations. To counter the loyal displays in Grafton Street and elsewhere, she secured a window in Parnell (then Rutland) Square from which lantern slides could be thrown on a large screen. This must be done late, since the Jubilee fell on the longest day. To dim the bright lights installed for the occasion it was arranged with Corporation workers that electrical faults would occur at the most appropriate points. Daniel O'Brien made a large black coffin on which were inscribed the words "British Empire", and to lead the procession which was to accompany it through the streets Connolly secured the services of a workers' band (probably the United Labourers) whose instruments would lose nothing by replacement, if the police destroyed them. Maud Gonne then set to work turning out black flags which were embroidered with the facts of the famines and evictions which had marked Victoria's reign, taken from a manifesto prepared by Connolly.

The convention of the '98 Commemoration Committee had been timed for Jubilee day. It was in session when the sound of the Labourers' band was heard. John O'Leary suspended the sitting so as to allow delegates to join the procession. A rickety handcart had been draped in the semblance of a hearse and was being pushed by a member of the I.S.R.P.

Maud Gonne and W. B. Yeats joined the procession and quickly distributed their black flags. They all moved solemnly down Dame Street to the sound of the Dead March.

As soon as the police realised what was happening, reinforcements were rushed from the Castle. Baton charges began to disperse the dense throng of spectators. Connolly, at the head, had reached O'Connell Bridge when the fighting became exceptionally fierce. It became clear that the procession could not cross the bridge. With a flash of inspiration, he ordered the coffin to be thrown into the Liffey and the whole crowd took up in chorus his valedictory words, "Here goes the coffin of the British Empire. To Hell with the British Empire!" Connolly was arrested and spent the night at the Bridewell. Maud Gonne sent him his breakfast, paid his fine when he appeared in court, and he was released.

Connolly's arrest did not halt the demonstrations. When dark fell, the city was unlit. The great public illuminations were invisible. But a large crowd gathered round Maud Gonne's magic lantern in Parnell Square. Even when rumours of events across O'Connell Bridge had attracted the younger men to a possible scene of excitement, a large crowd of women, children and old people remained to watch. These were baton-charged by the police and one old woman was killed. The indignant crowd hurried to O'Connell Street and smashed every window which contained Jubilee decorations.

The myth of loyal Dublin was destroyed. The demonstrations had the headlines in newspapers of all lands.

Though less spectacular, demonstrations took place in other Irish cities. The most important were in Limerick, where John Daly's black flag flew from the window of his house in Thomas Street, while another was suspended across the river at Thomond Gate. In Cork, Con O'Lyhane and his friends stormed the fire station and tore down the Union Jack from the municipal flagstaff. A black flag was hoisted in its place, and the booty was divided, the fragments of the captured British flag being treasured for years. A black flag flew from the window of the Cork National Society. Though the *Cork Constitution* might ascribe all this activity to the work of a "Dillonite Society", Mr. Dillon's polite parliamentary reprobations of Mr. Balfour's "Loyal Address" excited nobody outside St. James's Palace. The Home Rule Party was forgotten in the midst of the movement of the people. It was Connolly's first great victory.

Two months later the British Government obligingly risked another passage of arms when the Duke and Duchess of York visited Dublin. No effort was spared to recover the ground lost at the time of the Jubilee. Second-hand bunting was dispensed at £1 a lot to loyal shopkeepers, and great efforts were made to induce Dublin's numerous "pensioners, constabulary, police and civil servants" to express their support.

The I.S.R.P. was holding meetings in Foster Place, and now announced a special meeting on the evening Their Highnesses were to arrive. The purpose was not to protest against the new invasion of Dublin, but to commemorate the landing of the French at Killala. All '98 Committees were invited to give their support.

The speakers reached Foster Place only to find it occupied by police who ordered them to disperse and used some force. Under protest they walked to the I.S.R.P. rooms in Abbey Street, where a huge crowd was addressed by Stewart, Lyng and McDonnell. This meeting was also broken up and forty R.I.C. men stood guard outside the premises until early on Thursday morning.

Connolly announced that the suppressed meeting would take place on the following Sunday, and two special banners were prepared. One was a red flag showing a royal crown transfixed on a pike, with the legend *Finis Tyranniae*. The other was green, with a sunburst, and inscribed "Truth, freedom and justice in Ireland". A battle royal followed the unfurling at Foster Place. But after a series of baton charges, once more the meeting was broken up. And again Connolly marched his men to Abbey Street, where the police repeated the performance. A third attempt at a meeting, at the Custom House, was even more brutally attacked. Many socialists were injured. No arrests were made. The meetings were perfectly legal. But Connolly's advertisements of the meetings had specifically invited the representatives of foreign newspapers to attend. The world heard Dublin was disloyal. Not one Home Rule journal even protested against the police brutality. But all Dublin was talking about the band of rebels who had wiped the false smile from the face of royalty and shown behind it the reality of imperialism.

POLEMICS AND SET-BACKS

Connolly may now have believed that the Home Rulers were sufficiently discredited, and the alliance between the Socialists and democratic Nationalists sufficiently cemented, to make possible a challenge on a wider field. He proposed the foundation of a genuinely nationalist party, to contest elections and give the Irish people representation in the House of Commons.

He developed this idea in an article in Maud Gonne's *Irlande Libre* and in the *Shan Van Vocht.*

In the Paris journal he began by declaring that he took his stand on scientific socialism as taught by Karl Marx. The Irish struggle had occupied itself with political emancipation to the neglect of the property question. The I.S.R.P. gave place to nobody in the political struggle for Ireland's emancipation but refused to hide its hostility to the "purely bourgeois parties which at present direct Irish politics". The struggle to free Ireland was based not merely on history but on present needs. During seven hundred years the British people had "no political existence". The great majority in England had been disfranchised and terrorised. The I.S.R.P. did not regard the English workers with hatred. The worst that could be charged to them was criminal apathy. He asked the support of the French workers for the dual programme of Ireland's independence from Britain and Irish socialists' independence from capitalist parties.

In the *Shan Van Vocht* he began by pointing out that Irish workers received lower wages than British. No less than 78 per cent of them earned less than £1 a week. This he attributed partly to the overcrowded state of the labour market in Ireland, but also to the workers' acceptance of the political leadership of their economic oppressors.

In an independent state, the election of a Socialist majority would mean that the "state power—created by the proper-tied classes for their own class purposes—would serve the new social order as a weapon in its fight against such adherents of the privileged orders as strove to resist the gradual extinction of their rule". This was impossible in a dependent country. But that did not mean that the election of a socialist majority was not necessary in Ireland. It was even more necessary. It would amount to the declaration of a state of moral insurrection which might prove the precursor of a military insurrection. In the meantime, before such a socialist majority had arrived, or before the creation of an independent state where it could rule, the socialists should participate in Parliament. At the least they could do everything the existing parliamentarians could claim. And in addition they could call "attention to the evils inherent in that social system of which the British Empire is but the highest political expression". Connolly believed that the alternative was to leave the parliamentary factions unchallenged, as a permanent barrier between the Irish people and the outside world.

An editorial followed which professed full sympathy with Connolly's views on labour and social questions. So far Alice Milligan had moved. But she was "absolutely opposed" to his proposal for "an Irish republican party at Westminster". The principal objection was the oath of allegiance. She stood with John Mitchel, who had refused to take his seat. But she was willing to allow the matter to be debated.

A number of letters followed, and Connolly replied in October. He criticised MacManus, who had objected that the majority of the Irish people were republicans who would not wish for representation in the Westminster parliament. On the contrary, genuine revolutionists were extremely rare. And to illustrate the results of leaving the Home Rulers undisturbed he quoted from speeches. Redmond had told an audience at Cambridge that "separation from England was undesirable and impossible". Alfred Webb had said the Indians "knew their duty to their sovereign and were loyal". The *Freeman's Journal* as recently as August 18 had declared that "Irish people are willing to accept the Monarchy provided that national self-government is conceded". Quoting from Parnellite and anti-Parnellite alike, he established that a vote for either faction was a vote for the British connection. An alternative policy must be urged in both Britain and Ireland.

They were unconvinced. Alice Milligan rejected the notion that "Irish republicans should become politicians". "In advocating the formation of a democratic party in Parliament they are taking the broad road that leads to destruction," said the *Shan Van Vocht*, and added the terrible warning that "such a party would inevitably be in alliance with the English Labour Party".

Connolly had not clearly distinguished between democratic and socialist programmes and failed to carry the Republicans with him. Yet refusing to challenge the Home Rule factions in their chosen sphere of Parliament was to acquiesce in their political predominance, and the Republicans learned something of this to their cost later.

In the meantime Connolly had left Charlemont Street and found another one-room tenement at 54, Pimlico; on the same landing was William Farrell, of the United Labourers. The landlady was a Protestant who stood somewhat aloof from her tenants except on certain ceremonial occasions. Every time a child was born she presented the parents with a chicken and a pint of whisky. She paid no particular attention to the agitator on her premises. He and his family were quiet, and though the neighbours were at times mystified by his comings and goings, they liked him and asked no questions till his fame as a speaker caught up with him. Just before leaving for a short visit to Edinburgh in October 1897, he was stopped on the way home and agreed to speak to the tenants of some buildings in the Coombe area. They had received notice to quit on refusing to pay a rent increase demanded under the pretext of some trifling improvements. His wife looked round her tiny overfull room with misgivings. "Was that wise?" she asked. But she did not prevent his addressing the indignation meeting in Gray Square on October 22.

In Edinburgh he noted a rapprochement between the

S.D.F. and the I.L.P. Discussions were taking place on the subject of fusion, and the Edinburgh branches were favouring this course. The S.D.F. had worn better during the difficult middle nineties and was exercising an attraction on the looser organisation. But clarity existed on neither policy nor tactics. The tradition of Liberal-Labour politics was still strong. The failure to break decisively with the Liberals meant failure to distinguish clearly the rôle of their allies, the Home Rulers. In favour of Home Rule, the I.L.P. and even some of the S.D.F. boggled at Connolly's militant republicanism.

One correspondent in the *Labour Leader* informed Connolly that "many English Socialists" considered the I.S.R.P. agitation for Irish independence "a mere chauvinism", and as such calculated to "perpetuate national rivalries and race hatreds".

Connolly answered his critic in January 1898. He mildly reproved the "confusion of thought", rebutted the charge of jingoism and declared that "under a socialist system every nation will be the supreme arbiter of its own destinies, national and international; will be forced into no alliance against its will, but will have its independence guaranteed and its freedom respected by the enlightened self-interest of the social democracy of the world."

Then in stronger vein he struck at the root of the matter:

"The statement that our ideals cannot be realised except by the paths of violent revolution is not so much an argument against our propaganda as an indictment of the invincible ignorance and unconquerable national egotism of the British electorate, and as such concerns the English Socialists more than the Irish ones.

"The attitude of the orthodox Home Ruler is also subject to much misunderstanding among English Socialists. Seeing that the Home Ruler disavows all desire for separation, our English comrades are prone to draw unfavourable comparisons between him and the Socialist republican. But the Home Ruler stops short at Home Rule, not because he is cosmopolitan or a believer in human brotherhood, but because he is so little of a Democrat that to him the British Empire is an ideal system everywhere except in Ireland, and the sole aim of his political activity is to reproduce in Ireland all the political and social manifestations which accompany capitalist supremacy in Great Britain."

This was Connolly's first passage of arms with the doctrine which attempts to justify imperialism on the specious ground that it unites nations. The small countries must not revolt. All must be left to the social revolution in Britain. After the British workers have got power they will graciously "grant" or "give" the others freedom (within the Empire, of course). Meanwhile the British workers should strive to improve their conditions preparatory to revolution. But the subject peoples, having no independent initiative, need not be encouraged to do the same, least of all to demand independence.

Connolly fought this trend vehemently, passionately and uncompromisingly. It arose from the fact that imperialism was able to make a section of the British workers its political accomplices in the exploitation of the Empire. By making a show of yielding to their economic demands while exacting as a price compliance in external policy, the employing class fostered a "labour aristocracy" which, insofar as these tactics deceived them, spread confusion through the entire movement. If the failure of his efforts to create a democratic opposition to the Home Rule factions in Ireland hindered his work with the British labour movement, equally the development of "social-chauvinism" in England hindered his efforts to foster Labour-Republican unity in Ireland.

It was under such conditions that the Home Rulers were able to regain the initiative temporarily. The factions had held aloof from the 1798 controversy because the "United Irishmen" had been republican and "unconstitutional" and had sought complete separation from England. But as committees multiplied and popular support grew, they perceived as a danger what Alice Milligan was blind to as an opportunity. They feared an alternative leadership for the Irish people. Suspect from their belated conversion, they were adroit enough to choose Belfast for their attack. There the need for defence against Orange sectarianism had blurred distinctions of principle between Catholics and created a soil favourable to the collaboration of classes.

Uniting in September 1897 for the first time since 1890, the Home Rulers called a meeting of members of '98 clubs in the St. Mary's Hall. There it was proposed to elect a committee and organize a demonstration on October 4 to be addressed by Dillon, Harrington and O'Brien. Joseph Devlin, incredible demagogue and "man of influence" who "did things for people", was there to carry the meeting. Opposition was offered by Alice Milligan, who objected to acting without agreement with the Executive in Dublin. But the appeal of a Protestant republican fell on deaf ears in the presence of the leaders of Catholic sectarianism. The demonstration was proceeded with.

The action of the Home Rule party created a sharp division in the Commemoration movement. Under the guise of greater unity they were contriving a split. Some wished to welcome them as newly converted fellow-Irishmen, others to reject them as constitutionalists and monarchists manœuvring for popularity. Expert intriguers, they followed up their initial success with "a word here, and a word there". They understood the petty bourgeois weakness for a "decent fellow" and played on social snobberies. Some were flattered by their recognition; others feared to appear factious at a time of national rededication. W. B. Yeats, a Protestant who was not a Republican, urged on Connolly and Maud Gonne a "Union of Classes" and an invitation to "loyalists" to participate. Connolly's working-class horse-sense saw through the trickery from the start. The I.S.R.P. decided to broaden the basis of its "'98 Club" by "opening it to the general public", and Connolly addressed a meeting called for this purpose at 87, Marlborough Street on December 14. All Republicans were invited. Taking their cue from the I.S.R.P. a second time, the Fabians announced a '98 Club after being addressed by Connolly on "Revolutionary Politics". The Fabian club met in the Drapers Hall.

Thereafter the I.S.R.P. meeting would begin at 7 p.m. and was followed by the '98 Club meeting at about 8.30. A new element was incidentally introduced into I.S.R.P. life. The singing of patriotic and revolutionary songs enlivened the meetings and attracted increased attendances. At a special meeting of the club on December 21, with Connolly presiding, Dolan proposed and T. J. O'Brien seconded a resolution which was passed unanimously. It supported the Executive Committee in its decision to exclude members of the parliamentary party from any official or controlling influence in the commemoration proceedings. A host of controversies surrounded the personality of each and none of them had ever declared support for democratic principles.

Connolly might be in a position to attract some of the "rank and file". But the factions were able to take the general offensive, and agitated for control of the entire movement. In January 1898, following a split in the Executive Committee, a "Centennial Association" was announced with T. D. Sullivan in command and all the factionists represented. The "Rank-and-file club" thereupon disaffiliated and continued as an independent organisation. It still met on Sunday evenings, but its members gradually became assimilated into the I.S.R.P. The new Association was exploring fields of renegacy yet undreamed of. At the end of March, soon after the Rank-and-file club had commemorated Robert Emmet, the Association's platform was decorated with Joe Devlin, Mr. Nannetti, William Martin Murphy, Dublin's biggest capitalist who made no secret of his royalism, Harrington, and representatives of the clergy. To add insult to injury, Harrington referred to the originators of the movement as "some dissidents" who had endeavoured to exclude the "trusted representatives of the people". In April the "dissidents" capitulated and the Centennial Association absorbed the rump of the Centenary Committee. The victory of the parliamentarians was complete.

7*

It was the need to counter the threat of Labour-Republican unity and to stifle the independent initiative of the workers and lower middle class which led the factions to sink their differences, and from this point onwards reunification into a single Home Rule party was a certainty, though it required two years to resolve the question of leadership.

From April till August, when the centenary fell due, Maud Gonne co-operated sadly with the new body. W. B. Yeats and Mark Ryan, who had signed a dignified protest in February, followed her example with flagging interest. She turned her activities to the west. About the same time, Con O'Lyhane in Cork founded the Wolfe Tone Literary Society, which attempted to perform the functions of the Rank-and-file club in the southern capital. O'Leary remained national president but was a prisoner of the Home Rulers. It was an apt commentary on the degeneration of a promising movement that the Home Rule newspaper should note with great satisfaction "the great impetus to Irish industry from the '98 movement which was already benefiting Labour". The ideals of the shopkeeper could not entirely win the day. But when August 15 came, Maud Gonne was so disgusted at the tame but grandiose speechifying that she refused to take part in the proceedings. The fish had gone bad from the head downwards and the memorial still awaits completion.

Connolly had many an argument with her, much to W. B. Yeats's disgust. Yeats had no head for politics and often took the measure of Connolly's tongue. Afterwards Maud Gonne admitted that Connolly had been right and co-operated with him more closely than ever.

The astute manœuvre of the Home Rule factions temporarily halted the progress of democratic nationalism. Once the parliamentarians returned to the saddle the mass movement languished and Ireland was quiet for eighteen months. But there had been other results. The link between the I.S.R.P. and the younger nationalists was strengthened, and the correctness of Connolly's analysis, so strikingly proved, confirmed both the prestige of his party and its Marxist orientation. Connolly summarised I.S.R.P. progress in the

Labour Leader. The struggle for the republican principle had found entrance "into the most remote parts of the country" and its influence had been so far acknowledged abroad that sixty thousand leaflets had been issued by the Socialist Labour Party of America, embodying its appeal to the American Irish to support that party in the municipal elections. This would be the occasion when Daniel De Leon stood as candidate for the 16th Assembly District of New York City.

In eighteen months, Connolly reflected with justifiable pride, the I.S.R.P. had sprung from "obscurity to public recognition, and even approval". He proposed to follow up the contact made with the Irish in America with an appeal to Irishmen abroad to take up Associate Membership at 1s. a year. The first to avail himself of this opportunity was Edward Aveling. From America came a response which was later to draw Connolly across the Atlantic, and temporarily divert him from his chosen path of development.

Connolly only once more contributed to the *Shan Van Vocht*, and that was to correct a contributor who had denied Munster any part in the rising of 1798. Above all he felt the time was favourable for the consolidation of his own party and its development as a fighting force. His own poverty and almost continuous unemployment meant nothing to him. Propaganda was pursued unremittingly. The new members were encouraged to speak. Educational work was intensified and indoor lectures on the *Communist Manifesto* and "Revolutionary Socialism" proceeded to their logical culmination on March 12, when Connolly lectured on the Paris Commune.

Immediately after delivering this commemoration lecture, Connolly was called away from Dublin for his first and only experience of the agrarian struggle. The weather in 1879 had been disastrous for the potato crop. There was drought during the growing season, followed by a merciless August. In Kerry the rainfall for the month was 7·5″ against the ten year average of 4·85″. The yield of potatoes at Kenmare was less than half a ton per acre against the average of four tons.

Blight was rampant while, to make matters worse, the floods made bogs inaccessible and added to the potato famine a fuel famine.

The small farmers were faced with disaster. At Sneem the potato crop was a total loss. At Cahirciveen a widow whose rent was £6 12s. 6d. lifted three baskets which were worthless either as food or as seed. Though her income from her butter was only £6 for the entire year, the landlord claimed every penny she had and left her to starve. An old man of eighty-one sent his daughter on a sixteen mile tramp for the sake of 2s. outdoor relief. Sneem and Cahirciveen were the two worst affected areas in a distress which afflicted all Kerry. In those districts where there was a better-off peasantry, the small farmers revived the agitational methods of their fathers and Captain Moonlight was resurrected in Castle Island and elsewhere.

The situation in Mayo was equally serious. Famine fever broke out in Crossmolina. But apart from vague promises of free seed next season for those who lived to see it, the Government took no action. Landlords evicted starving tenants for non-payment of rent, while the railway companies issued special advertisements to the effect that "Emigrants will be booked to Queenstown". There is no reason to doubt that British policy was to afford succour only to those who could not be induced to leave the country. The land acts were based on further clearing of the estate of Ireland, as T. A. Jackson acutely pointed out. Relief must not hinder the good work of depopulation.

Public protest meetings began in Co. Mayo. Popular, witty and eccentric Father Henry started the campaign at Kiltimagh, together with Thomas Roughnean and William O'Hora, P. and J. Durcan started the agitation at Curry. Kerry followed closely behind. Sneem Dispensary Committee sent resolutions to the Lord Lieutenant demanding relief works. But it became increasingly obvious that the farmers must depend on charitable funds. Relief Committees were established in the cities. That in Manchester was to serve the west, Dublin was to look after the south.

Maud Gonne visited Mayo in January and busied herself urging relief till it became clear that the Government would do nothing. She returned to Dublin and saw Connolly, who told her of reports he had received from Kerry. They were both oppressed by the precedent of 1847 and resolved that the fatal error of that year must not be repeated. Then the tenants had paid their rents, watched the landlords export the healthy cattle and plentiful grain, and died from starvation through lack of potatoes. Together they drafted a manifesto. Connolly provided quotations from the Fathers of the Church after a visit to the National Library. He seems to have drawn his references from Nitti's *Catholic Socialism*.

The manifesto was entitled *The Rights of Life and the Rights of Property*. It included extracts from the writings of Pope Clement I, Gregory the Great, Cardinal Manning and St. Thomas Aquinas.

"Fellow-countrymen," it ran, "at the present juncture, when the shadow of famine is already blighting the lives of so many amongst us, we desire to offer a few words of calm advice.

"In 1847, our people died by thousands of starvation, though every ship leaving an Irish port was laden with food in abundance. The Irish people might have seized that food, cattle, corn and all manner of provisions before it reached the seaports, have prevented famine and saved their country from ruin, but did not do so, believing such action to be sinful, and dreading to peril their souls to save their bodies. In this belief we know now they were entirely mistaken. The very highest authorities on the doctrine of the church agree that no *human* law can stand between starving people and their right to food, including their right to take that food whenever they find it, openly or secretly, with or without the owner's permission."

Maud Gonne gave Connolly £25 to enable him to print the manifesto. She then left for Mayo, arranging that he should despatch copies after her before he himself left for Kerry. The story of her agitation in Belmullet, Foxford and

Ballina is told in her memoirs *The Servant of the Queen.* Connolly's leaflet was distributed and, after stormy demonstrations, relief work was granted on a substantial scale.

Connolly himself left Dublin in mid-March, with an assignment to report the famine for Daniel De Leon's *Weekly People.* He began his tour at Kenmare and worked round the peninsula to Cahirciveen, interviewing, questioning and recording. It was on this trip that he called at Derrynane and inspected Daniel O'Connell's blunderbuss which was carried by the Liberator while a volunteer against the United Irishmen. Connolly spent three weeks in Kerry, ample time to study the extent of the famine, its causes, and the measures of resistance that were being taken. He found that his leaflets taught a lesson that was already learned. The landlords' monopoly had been broken, and the local authorities were less under their control. The clergy had also moved with the times, especially after the year which prepared the commemoration of Ireland's greatest struggle for freedom.

For Connolly, Kerry was but one more illustration of the depth of betrayal of the parliamentary leaders, and the disastrous emasculation of the Commemoration movement. The poison of constitutionalism had been injected just at the time when the countryside could have been fanned into revolt, not perhaps to free Ireland, but to strengthen immeasurably the forces preparing for it. Connolly returned to Dublin in mid-April and delivered two lectures at Foster Place on April 24 and May 1. Once more he demanded "liberty, truth and justice". In the audience was a young Kerryman, afterwards famous under the name of "Sceilg".[1] He joined with Connolly in condemning the heartlessness of the Government, but was so upset by the socialism he heard that he began to heckle. Connolly recognised him as a genuine republican and Gaelic enthusiast, and adopted the unusual course of inviting his interrupter on to the platform, where unity against imperialism was once more restored.

Connolly's articles appeared in June. His explanation of

[1] J. J. O'Kelly

the causes of the famine is of interest. It was not the existence of an "alien government", nor landlordism except to a minor degree. It was the failure of the system of small farming, and the restricted mental horizon of the peasants who could have prevented the blight if they had but been prepared to co-operate. In these circumstances state action was required to avert the disaster. The Home Rule party was not averse to it, but to their Liberal allies it was anathema. Hence the post-Parnellian factions staged a demonstration and left it at that. Connolly concluded with the wry comment that the British M.P.s paid their own hard cash for their seats and sat in them quietly, but the Irish members were paid by their supporters and were adept at creating a good harmless scene.

VII
THE WORKERS' REPUBLIC

The capture of the Commemoration movement by the Home Rule factions, and their failure to make an issue of the famine, confirmed Connolly in an important resolve. The I.S.R.P. must have its own newspaper. Only then could it break through the silence or opposition of the Home Rule press. The spring and early summer of 1898 were spent in preparation for issuing the *Workers' Republic*.

The stress of open-air propaganda was shifted in the direction of current events, though general education was not neglected. Speakers still addressed their audiences on "the coming social revolution", "Socialism and disarmament" and "the coming European war". The reformists of the Centennial Committee were never allowed to forget they were commemorating a revolutionary. Connolly lectured them thoroughly on "Socialism and the '98 celebrations". And the Rank-and-file Committee organised a visit to the grave of Wolfe Tone at Bodenstown where Connolly made the oration. As the commemorators pursued their dull and inglorious course, the I.S.R.P. gave the Dublin workers its views on contemporary matters, the future of the tramway system, the rise in the cost of bread, old-age pensions, the Spanish-American war, and the Italian insurrection.

Socialism was staking out its full claim. The interrupter who urged the virtues of sobriety was given a lecture on "Socialism and the Temperance Movement". The older trades were offered "Dublin Trade Unionism and Socialism". Gradually it became apparent that there was no aspect of life without its socialist commentary.

By July preliminary arrangements for the issue of the paper had been completed. Connolly therefore left for Scotland to seek financial support for his venture. Since losing his seat in West Ham, Keir Hardie had been producing the *Labour Leader* in Glasgow. This was Connolly's first port of call, and he secured from Hardie a loan of £50.

From Glasgow he went to Edinburgh. His daughter Nora, then convalescing from a serious illness, has described the trip. She recalls her grandfather, John Connolly, as a tall man with a curly red beard. He lived alone (in Lawnmarket), and she remembers his loosening her laces to enable her to walk up the steep hill from Princes Street. He decided she "needed fattening" and cooked collops with which he offered her bread plastered over with generous thicknesses of butter. She could not eat. But her father arrived in the nick of time and cut her bread without butter, much to the grandfather's disgust. Then he took her away to stay with his sister-in-law, Margaret Reynolds, while he attended to the business of his visit.

Connolly's public meetings were as usual a success. There were changes, however, which he noted. The centre had shifted from the Old Town to Leith, where George Yates, who had been active in Dublin until he was victimised about the time of the anti-Jubilee demonstration, had built up a flourishing branch. Connolly had a great regard for this brilliant young man, but was not convinced of his ability to see a thing through. He chaffed him for his over-optimism and told him he would believe the promise of the Leith branch when it survived another quarterly meeting.

There were changes in personnel too. Leslie was now Scottish District organiser of the S.D.F. and started his two weeks' campaign in Edinburgh as soon as Connolly left. Meillet had returned to Paris. A number of the old members were still active, but around Yates and John Robertson, with whom Connolly stayed,[1] a group of young left-wingers was forming, afterwards to constitute the "unholy Scotch current". They had come under the influence of Daniel De Leon's *What Means This Strike?*, published in February 1898.

Throughout the S.D.F. there was a growing dissatisfaction with Hyndman's leadership. Strong signs of developing chauvinism were apparent and De Leon had sent a letter to *Justice* admonishing Hyndman on the subject of "War and

[1] On occasions he stayed also with Coburn and Jeanneret.

Imperialism". Theodore Rothstein also protested at the anti-semitism which was creeping into its columns in connection with the Dreyfus case. Hyndman had observed the new function of finance as an integral component of modern capital, but was identifying finance-capital with Jewry. The slow blunting of socialist principle evinced in multiplying instances was particularly repellent to the younger and most active members of the S.D.F., for example Cotton in Oxford, jailed for his struggle for free speech, and Jackson and Newell in London. Quelch, editor of *Justice,* in part sympathised with them, but was financially dependent on Hyndman. Nor was he assisted by the crude political tactics and theoretical confusion of the left. Connolly was later to play a leading part in the struggle which was developing. For the moment he had other things on his mind. In two years he had moved far from Edinburgh, had developed both politically and intellectually, and was full of plans for the future.

He proposed to bring out his first number the day before the foundation stone of the '98 Memorial was laid in Dublin. On the very day when republicanism was to be buried with tears and panegyrics, it was to pop up again in Foster Place, more vigorous and challenging than ever. A small printer was found to undertake the job. P. T. Daly, later secretary of the Dublin Trades Council, was employed there and set much of the type. An advertisement in *Justice* ran:

IRISHMEN ATTEND!

NEW IRISH WEEKLY.   ONE PENNY.

THE
WORKERS' REPUBLIC

A literary champion of Irish Democracy, advocates an Irish Republic, the abolition of landlordism, wage-slavery, the cooperative organisation of industry under Irish representative governing bodies. Every Friday, 1st issue August 12th. Ask your newsagent.

It was offered to the world on Sunday August 14, when Connolly spoke on "Wolfe Tone and the Irish Social Revolution". It was at this meeting that Connolly and O'Lyhane met for the first time. The inaugural number threw down the gage to those who had "united the centennial movement with the bogus organisation engineered by Mr. Tim Harrington". It accused them of distorting the meaning of "United Irish" to mean a "union of class and creed", and scoffed at the idea of a "revolutionary party that would take no account of social injustice". What, it asked, was the "feasibility of uniting in one movement underpaid labourers and over-paid masters?" On the day of the commemoration Tom Lyng was busy from dawn to dusk selling the new paper to the crowds that had come into Dublin.

This issue contained a poem by John Leslie entitled "Wolfe Tone", and Connolly drove the issue home by adding "Apostles of freedom are ever idolised when dead but crucified when living". Tone was a Democrat and his "social ideas were such that he would have been a rebel even had he been an Englishman. His principles could only be realised in a socialist republic."

In another article he declared war on religious sectarianism. The American Irish were distinguishing themselves in the war against Spain. While the Home Rulers were prating about "Faith and the Fatherland", which linked national demands with a particular religious belief and served the purpose of dividing the workers, Catholic Irishmen were fighting Catholic Spaniards, and Protestant workers were on strike in Belfast against Protestant employers.

He then stated the principle upon which the paper was founded. It was:

"To *unite* the workers and to bury in one common grave the religious hatreds, the provincial jealousies, and the mutual distrusts upon which oppression has so long depended for security."

The *Workers' Republic* had only eight pages, but it could both comment on current events and relate these to general principles in educational articles. These were, so to speak, congealed from speeches in Foster Place. Connolly elaborated such theses as the capitalist origin of modern war, which he attributed to the struggle for markets, the inevitable instability of a peasant proprietary, and the need for political action by trade unionists.

The files of the *Workers' Republic* contain examples of Connolly's application of scientific socialism to the most diverse subjects. On October 1 he made his first attempt to grapple with the difficult question of the Irish language. The eighteen-nineties had seen the rapid growth of the Irish language movement, and one result of the loose link between the Gaelic League and the '98 Commemoration movement was the beginning of the bilingual designation of streets in Irish cities. The literary movement in English drew heavily on ancient Gaelic sources, and Dr. Douglas Hyde's *Early Gaelic Literature,* published in 1895, was widely read. It is not generally known outside Ireland that Gaelic was the majority language in Ireland until the time of the famine, though English was making inroads. Dr. Hyde ascribed the decline of Irish to political causes, its proscription in courts, camps and colleges since the seventeenth century, and its eclipse in the mid-nineteenth to the extreme difference between English and Irish which discouraged bilingualism. The Gaelic Leaguers were enthusiastic in defending Europe's third classical language against the absurd charge that it possessed no literature, but in so doing they laid an undue stress on the things of the past.

Connolly's first judgement of the Gaelic movement was cautious, even sceptical. He saw in the replacement of Irish by English an illustration of Marx's dictum that "capitalism creates a world after its own image", but a few years later he enlarged his conception by attributing the spread of English to the Irish mercantile class during the industrial revolution and afterwards. Not till he was in America, ten years later, did he give his mature opinion, which was that the suppression of one tongue by another was an illustration of imperialism, and that defence of a people's mother tongue was an integral part of the defence of its soil. After his return to Ireland he set about learning Irish himself. But now, in 1898, his reply to the Gaelic enthusiast was "You cannot teach starving men Gaelic", and therefore those who wished to preserve or restore the language must stand for a socialist republic.

Connolly had in mind establishing a national Irish weekly comparable to *Justice* or the *Leader*, and during the first weeks prospects seemed bright. The open-air activity of the I.S.R.P. ensured a regular sale at meetings in Dublin. In Belfast, Milligan found a wholesaler who would distribute the paper to shops. The Belfast Socialists, however, mistrusted the new paper's nationalist flavour. Nor did they rally round when a Catholic Bishop condemned it, and the wholesaler was constrained to discontinue. For a while Milligan distributed it himself to shops in key positions, for example Queen's Bridge, Old Lodge Road, Ormean Avenue and Donegall Street. But opportunities in Dublin also declined with the year, and at the end of October it suspended publication.

The abeyance of the *Workers' Republic* was a serious loss to the I.S.R.P. in its first election campaign. On October 12, "burgesses" favourable to labour representation were invited to a meeting at 61, Pimlico. The response does not seem to have justified a candidate in Merchants Quay ward. But on the 22nd, after E. W. Stewart had lectured at Marlborough Street on "Municipal Socialism", he was adopted as I.S.R.P. candidate for North Rock ward. W. H. Bradshawe, business manager of the *Workers' Republic,* became election agent.

The elections of January 1899 were the first to be held under the Irish Local Government Act, one of a series of Conservative measures designed to "kill Home Rule with kindness" (other methods not being excluded). The network of variously appointed boards (of which it was said Ireland "had more than would make its coffin") and elected and semi-elected committees with overlapping functions, was replaced by County, Urban and Rural District Councils. Dublin, Belfast, Cork, Derry, Limerick and Waterford were constituted County Boroughs. Financial and administrative powers held previously by Grand Juries (appointed and subject to a property qualification), Poor Law Boards (partly elected, partly ex officio), Dispensary Committees and Town Commissioners, were transferred to the new councils which were voted for by a newly created category of "local government electors" consisting of Parliamentary electors "plus peers and women". The new local government system was the administrative counterpart of the new land system. It aimed at creating a vested interest in the connection with England by securing a share of government patronage for the middle classes.

The democratisation of the system of election raised high hopes among the working class. Labour Electoral Associations sprang up throughout Ireland. Some were linked to trades councils or clubs; others to Davitt's Land and Labour Leagues; and others were purely *ad hoc* bodies. They brought with them all the preconceptions and misconceptions of the period since Parnell. But they registered almost uniform success. Limerick City returned a "Labour" Council and John Daly was elected Mayor. In Waterford the showing was almost as favourable: L. C. Strange became Mayor.

In Dublin, the I.S.R.P. candidate was defeated. This was largely because the party lacked financial resources. Its election propaganda was confined to open air meetings at Spenser Dock, which the *Evening Telegraph* refused to advertise on the ground that Stewart's leading opponent, Tim Harrington, had been described as a "mugwump".

Immediately after the election, Connolly visited Cork. At 21, Grattan Street, with Mr. J. Jones in the chair, what the *Cork Constitution* described as a "fairly large" audience gathered to hear him. His subject was "Labour and the Irish Revolution". Connolly declared that the class which ground the Irish workers down economically would never lead them to national victory. "We should have done with this middle class leadership," he told them, which meant "middle-class patriotism" and "middle-class compromise". It remained for the Irish workers "to give to patriotism a purer and a nobler significance, and by organising, to shatter for ever the system which condemned the people to misery".

The Cork meeting took place on February 14, 1899. Back in Dublin, Connolly conducted energetic Marxist education. Already he had encouraged his colleagues with a lecture on the "technical terms of scientific socialism". Now Bradshawe introduced discussions on "Class Struggle" and "Are we Utopians?" T. J. O'Brien spoke on "Old and New Socialism—Robert Owen and Karl Marx". It was this constant theoretical training which gave the I.S.R.P. its toughness and ability to react to situations. Nor did it hesitate to tackle problems then newly exercising the labour movement. The distinctive feature of the opening epoch of imperialism, "the growth of monopoly", was discussed in Foster Place just as the new era was proclaiming its advent in the trumpets of the Boer War.

The *Workers' Republic* was re-issued on Friday May 12, 1899. Connolly had realised that it was impracticable to carry the burden of commercial printing while dependent on voluntary distribution. He decided to be a "printer's devil" again, and spent some months procuring a small hand press, a case or two of type, an imposing surface and a few accessories. He was the editor, contributors, composing room staff, and, except when he could get help, machine room staff as well. Each new issue would now appear only when its predecessor had sold out. Leaflets and pamphlets were produced in the same size and worked off with a topical outer sheet. The paper appeared most regularly when Connolly was unemployed. A pound or two was scraped together to keep him going. He wittily summarised the two systems of publication; the first series was "so weekly that it almost died", and the second appeared "whenever it was strong enough to get out". The title was designed and cut from linoleum by Carolan, who, being unemployed, helped Connolly with the printing.

Leading the fight against the Boer War, the I.S.R.P. entered its great days. With branches in Dublin and Cork, and groups of supporters in Belfast, Limerick,[1] Dundalk,

---

[1] The Dublin members were critical of Dorman for his inactivity in Limerick, but this was unfair.

Waterford and Portadown, a newspaper and an appreciable pamphlet literature based on Irish conditions and needs, it had become a political force. At the same time its numbers did not exceed a hundred, and it held no regular delegate conventions. This circumstance, possibly, explains the failure to hold the outlying groups of sympathisers and integrate them into a national party with a single policy. The party's connections with the trade union movement were slight. Those of its members who were trade unionists were compelled to live a double political life—trade unionists on week days, socialists on Sunday. Where there was no regular socialist activity Sunday became doubly a day of rest. The socialist became a trade unionist pure and simple. The success of the Labour Electoral Association increased the centrifugal tendency. Thus at the very time when the I.S.R.P. was conducting some of its most spectacular campaigns in Dublin it was losing influence in every other centre but Cork. This must be borne in mind in order to understand what followed.

From the very first Connolly realised the importance of the Transvaal crisis. Before the outbreak of war, both at Phoenix Park and Foster Place from June onward, he strove to bring its significance home to Dublin workers. The meeting held by the I.S.R.P. in Foster Place on August 27, 1899, was the first public protest to take place anywhere.

In the *Workers' Republic* of the preceding week, Connolly had traced the war to its origin in the purpose "of enabling an unscrupulous gang of capitalists to get into their hands the immense riches of the diamond fields".

"Such a war," he continued, "will undoubtedly take rank as one of the most iniquitous wars of the century ... No better corroboration of the truth of the socialist maxim that the modern state is but a committee of rich men administering affairs in the interest of the upper class. . . . There is no pretence that the war will benefit the English people."

He went on to point out that British troops were being transferred from Ireland to the Transvaal, because the Government relied on the Home Rule Party and the R.I.C. to keep the country quiet.

"But if the working class of Ireland were only united, and understood their power sufficiently well, and had shaken off their backs the Home Rule-Unionist twin brethren, keeping us apart that their class may rob us, they would see in this complication a chance for making a long step forward towards better conditions of life and, seeing it, act upon it in a manner that would ensure the absence from the Transvaal of a considerable portion of the British Army."

In other words, England's difficulty ought to be Ireland's opportunity.

He advised the "Irish working-class democracy" to work peacefully while they might, but keep before them the fact that the capitalist class was a "beast of prey" not to be "moralised, converted or conciliated".

It is clear that Connolly looked forward to the possibility of a revolutionary situation in which Ireland might win freedom and set foot on the road to socialism. Peaceful means were preferred and maintained while possible, but if the enemy adopted forceful methods, these must not be rejected as a reply. This was of course the classical position of scientific socialism.

On the other hand Connolly completely rejected the notion of making "physical force" a political principle, distinct from the aims for which it was used. Ireland, he wrote in July 1899, was remarkable in possessing a "physical force" party "whose members are united on no one point, and agree upon no single principle, except upon the use of physical force as the sole means of settling the dispute between the people of this country and the governing power of Britain."

The alternate failure of "constitutionalism" and "insurrectionism" in Irish history, he argued, arose from the fact that "neither method is ever likely to be successful until . . . a perfect agreement on *the end to be attained*" is arrived at. The '98 Commemoration had been started by physical force men who stood for "national independence as understood by Wolfe Tone", yet "in less than twelve months they elect on their governing committee men notorious for their royalist proclivities". Physical force (a means) was being made the test of advanced nationalism, instead of the social system (the end). Connolly concluded:

> "Socialists believe that the question of force is of very minor importance; the really important question is of the principles upon which is based the movement that may or may not need the use of force to realise its object."

Maud Gonne was invited to attend the first meeting, and sent a message of support. The authorities had not yet adapted themselves to the new position and the police did not interfere when Bradshawe moved a resolution condemning Britain's "criminal aggression" and urging the Irish in the Transvaal to take up arms against Her Majesty's Forces. Maud Gonne's letter proposing protest meetings all over Ireland was read to the accompaniment of loud cheers.

The lead of the I.S.R.P. was taken up. The Boer War provided an opportunity for anti-imperialists to shake themselves free of the Home Rule Party. Maud Gonne had founded a women's nationalist organisation called *Inghinidhe na h'Eireann,* which now conducted propaganda against war and enlistment. Bold spirits in Trinity College organised a "pro-Boer Society" and held stormy meetings at which the windows of their rooms were smashed. Trade unions began to take an interest. But the literary centre of advanced nationalism was no longer the spirited *Shan Van Vocht* but the *United Irishman,* edited by Arthur Griffith, a young journalist recently returned from South Africa.

Griffith subsequently became world-famous. At this time he was poor, unknown and unmistakably sincere. His outlook was that of the shopkeeper rather than the intellectual, and though he attended literary functions and became very friendly with William Rooney, ideas did not interest him. His one passion, Irish nationality, pursued with miser-like singleness of purpose, was unphilosophic and ill-defined. The Irish Republican Brotherhood (I.R.B.) helped to finance his paper, but he was no Republican. He advocated a dual monarchy after the model of Austria-Hungary. Far from being anti-imperialist, he desired an "Anglo-Irish Empire" in which Britain and Ireland would jointly exploit the lesser breeds. The equality of the African and Asiatic peoples he expressly denied. In his paper he was not above referring to "Anglo-Jews" and "Niggers", and he completely failed to distinguish between capitalist and worker in Britain or in Ireland. He threw all his weight on the side of the Boers. But, unlike Alice Milligan, he obstructed the spread of progressive ideas. He listened to Connolly's open-air meetings with a glum face. The small-trading class he represented was jealous of the big cross-Channel mercantile interests, but wanted to share the pickings, not abolish them. At times it could grow rebellious and even anti-clerical. Arthur Griffith could do both. But fear of the working class arose from the feeling that the concessions trade union action was wringing from big business, which could afford them, would ruin the small employer. Griffith was very sparing of publicity for Connolly's activities, but Connolly was thankful for what he received. The story of a long intimate connection between Connolly and Griffith is completely apocryphal.

Diverse national and working-class elements were gathered into a loose "Irish Transvaal Committee", which held several meetings during the autumn. The most famous of them took place just before Christmas, on the occasion of Mr. Joseph Chamberlain's receiving an honorary degree at Trinity College. Both Michael Davitt and William Redmond had consented to speak at Beresford Place, together with Councillor Nannetti and Councillor Cox. At the last moment police posters appeared on the hoardings announcing that the meeting was proclaimed. The only speakers to appear at Abbey Street were Connolly, Maud Gonne and John O'Leary, who set off to Beresford Place in a brake. Pat O'Brien, M. P., joined them later, explaining that he was deputising for Michael Davitt.

Maud Gonne noted that Connolly climbed beside the driver, though there was room behind. As they turned the corner of Abbey Street the officer in charge of a police cordon ordered them back. The driver hesitated and the police at once pulled him from his box. In an instant Connolly had the reins in his hands and drove through the cordon, scattering police and people as the brake swayed amid loud cheers.

At Beresford Place a huge crowd was assembled. "We've not much time," said Connolly. O'Leary called for silence and Maud Gonne read the resolution. It was passed by acclamation. Hardly had the applause died down when the mounted police arrived. They dispersed the crowd and, seizing the reins, led the brake into Store Street police barracks. Then followed an act of pure comedy.

"We can't keep them here," said the superintendent who was holding puzzled consultations with his subordinates. What was he to do with O'Leary, Connolly, Maud Gonne and a Home Rule M.P.? Finally an Inspector approached Connolly in his capacity as driver and said severely:

"You can't stay here."

"We don't want to," said Connolly.

The gates were opened and Connolly turned out to freedom. But it was made clear that any attempt to go to Beresford Place would lead to arrest. Such being the case, he drove along Abbey Street and across O'Connell Bridge. The interrupted meeting was resumed in Foster Place. Cheering crowds rapidly assembled and Maud Gonne announced that the resolution passed in Beresford Place would be read out. As Connolly disputed matters with protesting foot police, O'Brien called for three cheers for the Boers, after which the mounteds arrived and made a charge. Used to horses, the Dublin crowd simply gave way in front of them and re-formed behind. But gradually the brake was separated from the audience and there was little more to be done than to arrange for an indoor meeting which took place the same night. It was later found that the police had raided the I.S.R.P. premises and smashed the press that printed the *Workers' Republic.*

After Christmas the I.S.R.P. plunged into the municipal election campaign, once more contesting North Dock Ward. They first announced E. W. Stewart as candidate, but, on his withdrawing about the middle of January offered Tom Lyng in his place. The anti-enlistment campaign was in full swing and Connolly had difficulty in dissuading his enthusiastic supporters from inserting a clause denying the right of employment to ex-soldiers. "I'll resign if you put that in," he said. Labour throughout Ireland suffered a resounding defeat, in which Connolly thought the I.S.R.P. shared. In Dublin, said the *Freeman's Journal,* it received a "knock-out blow". The reason had already been given by Connolly in the previous September:

> "From the entry of the Labour Party into the Municipal Council to the present day their course has been marked by dissension, squabbling and recrimination. No single important move in the interest of the worker was even mooted, the most solemn pledges were incontinently broken, and where the workers looked for inspiration and leadership, they have received nothing but discouragement and disgust ... The Labour Lord Mayor of the Dublin Labour Party declared that he would represent no class or section and thus announced beforehand that those responsible for his nomination only sought to use the name of Labour as a cover for the intrigues of a clique ... we did not expect that the splendid class spirit shown by the Dublin workers at the late election would through the arrogance and weakness of their elected representatives be of no practical advantage to them as a class."

The working class declared unmistakably what it thought of them. Ten years later Connolly defended the tactics of the I.S.R.P. in supporting the Labour Electoral Associations at the outset while criticising their subsequent failures. It was important not to repudiate the spontaneous surge of working-class feeling which led to their formation. But it was equally important to give a distinct lead after the Labour Councillors had attached themselves to one or other of the Home Rule factions and local cliques. The misfortune was that the I.S.R.P. was still not influential enough to do this effectively.

The result of the Labour debacle was felt outside Ireland. It shook Keir Hardie's faith in Irish Labour. The Home Rule factions had completed their negotiations, and at the end of January 1900 merged into a single parliamentary party at Westminster. They merged their organisations to form the United Irish League. John Redmond became leader.

Hardie was also influenced by a report brought from Ireland by Bruce Glasier. It affected his prospects of winning the strong Irish constituency of Merthyr Tydfil. In a scathing attack, the one time Socialist Leaguer described Connolly as stampeding with a mob through the streets, "brandishing the Boer flag and shouting for an Irish Republic and for the defeat of Britain in the Transvaal". "How I envied him his self-indulgence and irresponsibility," Glasier went on. "How straight and broad, but ah! how exhilarating seemed the path along which he was careering with the policemen at his heels."

Glasier's article was written in Blatchford's *Clarion* in March. In a reply in *Justice*, Connolly published the conversation he had had with Bruce Glasier in November 1899 (Glasier had not been present at the meeting in December, and had written up his supercilious account from newspaper reports). Glasier was touring Ireland lecturing for the Fabian Society, but denied he was a Fabian. Asked why, then, was he lecturing on Fabianism and advocating Fabian policy, Glasier replied: "You see, I'm paid by the Fabians and must do what I'm paid for."

"Ireland has not," wrote Connolly, "until last year received much attention from the Fabian gentry. The Irish worker had not the municipal franchise, therefore Fabian gas and water schemes would have been lost on him. But as soon as he obtained the franchise and manifested the desire to use it in a true class spirit, the cry went up for the Fabian missionaries. In order to prevent the Irish working class from breaking off entirely from the bourgeois parties and from developing a revolutionary tendency, the Fabians sent their lecturer to Ireland, to induce the Irish working class to confine themselves to the work of municipalising, and to fritter away their energies and break their hearts on the petty squabbles of local administration, to the entire neglect of the essential work of capturing the political power necessary for social reconstruction."

Glasier, whom Connolly remembered as a "revolutionary socialist" for whom the S.D.F. was too moderate, then as an "I.L.P.er for whom the S.D.F. was too extreme", had been teaching that in municipal enterprises not the worker but the "community" was "exploited" for the extraction of profit. He considered the working class "conservative", and thought the greatest prospect of reforms came from "generous-minded members of the upper or middle classes".

The current of opportunism within the British labour movement had been greatly strengthened by the wave of frenzied chauvinism which accompanied the outbreak of the war. Blatchford, editor of the *Clarion*, openly boasted that he "remained pro-British". The Fabian Society's support for the war led to the resignation of J. MacDonald, Pete Curran, Mrs. Pankhurst and others. The fact that men claiming Labour allegiance could support a war of unprovoked aggression revolted others besides Connolly. It was Bruce Glasier's adherence to the Fabians in these circumstances that accounted for the asperity revealed in what was for the time being a brief passage of arms between two tendencies later to do battle on a world scale. Glasier was anxious to blunt the edge of principle. The I.S.R.P. would have none of him. Hearing that John Daly was participating in the arrangement of his lectures in Limerick, Stewart wrote repudiating him, an action which Glasier never forgave. Connolly had indeed done more. He urged Dorman to stage a counter-demonstration and reacted very coolly to his failure to do so.

Meanwhile the efforts of the Transvaal Committee, *Inghinidhe na h'Eireann* and the I.S.R.P. had brought recruiting to a virtual standstill, despite unemployment. Connolly told Mullery that he feared his outspoken exposures in the

Republican press of the conditions of serving soldiers might direct official attention to him. But he was prepared to take the risk. The Government decided to send Queen Victoria to Ireland in the hope of reawakening loyal sentiments and translating them into soldiers. Before Her Britannic Majesty's royal person was risked in a capital so sunk in sedition, the Duke of York was despatched on a preliminary tour. That visit cost the Lord Mayor his coach, which was attacked by indignant crowds.

Nevertheless it was decided to venture the old lady for the sake of the young men. There were rumours of knighthoods. The decorating trades would boom. Patronage would be forthcoming for the right people, and Dublin was not all Ireland. Recruits might be forthcoming from the country districts. Security measures were taken. Special ships brought fifteen thousand of Harland and Wolfe's employees from Belfast to help line the route for her arrival. School children were given a holiday for the same purpose and a great "treat" was announced by the Lord Lieutenant. Guinness employees were given a "Queen's Holiday" and an extra shilling in their pay packet, and a huge stand was erected for them to cheer from. Nothing was neglected that could arouse enthusiasm, but with little success.

Connolly issued a manifesto which ran:

"Monarchy is a survival of the tyranny imposed by the hand of greed and treachery in the darkest and most ignorant days of our history.... The Socialist demands that the only birthright necessary to qualify for public office should be the birthright of our common humanity, we deny all allegiance to the institution of royalty.... The mind accustomed to political kings can easily be reconciled to social kings—capitalist kings of the workshop, the mill, the railway, the ship and the docks."

Maud Gonne arranged a "counter-treat" for the children, which was attended by many thousands and seriously affected the success of the Lord Lieutenant's. The Transvaal Committee held torchlight demonstrations which were broken up by the police. As the first assembled outside the committee's office at 32, Abbey Street, the police charged with batons. Dispersing the procession they picked out three editors who were standing on the steps, and felled to the ground Connolly, Griffith and O'Leary Curtis of the *Weekly Independent*. A second procession starting from Capel Street was ambushed at Green Street by 200 policemen, who gave no exemption to age or sex. When the I.S.R.P. members of this procession returned to Abbey Street to get their bicycles, a third charge was ordered by Inspector Lynam, who had been responsible for the Parnell Square charge during the Jubilee celebrations. Throughout the month Victoria remained in Ireland there was a continuous tumult of protest.

At the height of the turmoil Connolly was called away to Edinburgh. His father had suffered a cerebral haemorrhage on April 3 and was lying in the Royal Infirmary, where he died seventeen days later. Connolly registered the death, remained for the funeral, and hurried back to Dublin.

As British arms suffered repeated defeats, Connolly hoped the struggle against the war might end in a revolutionary crisis, in which it would be possible to free Ireland. He was encouraged by the struggle of the "Boxers" in China to think that such a possibility might occur in connection with a revolt in India. But this prospect faded. There were riots between British and Irish troops on Salisbury Plain, and outbreaks of "soldier-baiting" in Cork. But unemployment was growing rapidly. The employers and government launched a systematic attack on working-class conditions and civil liberties. At the same time the reunification of the Home Rule party restored public confidence in parliamentary action. Those who still disparaged it were provided with a "middle-of-the road" alternative by Arthur Griffith. This amounted to boycotting parliament while exploiting the opportunities of the Local Government Act, with the ultimate perspective of governing Ireland through abstentionist M.P.s and local authorities, while accepting the British connection. The debate over physical force and parliamentary action was replaced by one equally sterile between parliamentary action and Griffith's policy, to which he later gave the name of Sinn Fein. In October 1900 he founded *Cumann na nGaedheal*, thereby shutting off sections of the middle class alike from working-class politics and the older republicanism. Irish Labour's defeat in the municipal elections, and British Labour's rapproachement with the parliamentary party, helped to limit the possibilities of the I.S.R.P. The forces against imperialism were growing, but it proved impossible to unite them. Hence the shift of Connolly's attention and interest which, as a logical conclusion, later led him to America.

The I.S.R.P. fought a valiant rearguard action in defence of civil liberty. While the *Workers' Republic* was suspended the *United Irishman* had been the sole opposition organ. In mid-April 1900 its publication of Maud Gonne's article "The Famine Queen" led to the seizure of an entire issue. Police interference intensified and Doyle's printing shop was frequently invaded. The *Workers' Republic* resumed publication on May 11, 1900 as a ½d. weekly, despite the protests of printers who now accused Connolly of depriving them of employment by producing it with voluntary labour. He replied that by the same token he robbed the barbers by shaving himself. To his readers he said:

> "Let the soundness of the doctrine preached compensate for the lack of excellence in the printing . . . and we promise that uncorrupted by the promises of politicians, as unterrified by threats of Castle police, we shall continue to hold aloft the banner of the Socialist Republic."

The general attack on civil liberties was conceived with some cunning. It began by attempts to prevent the Salvation Army from holding parades at Abbey Street on grounds of obstruction. It was expected that a Catholic city would show no sympathy for a small Protestant sect. Unfortunately for the Castle, the Salvationists held their ground with public support, and won. Attempts to camouflage reaction failed.

After an unpublished issue of the *United Irishman* was seized, Connolly began an open-air campaign for civil liberty. In a series of meetings at Foster Place, the I.S.R.P.

demanded freedom of the press and the control and curtailment of police functions. The result was a temporary halt to the worst excesses. The campaign for democracy was followed by one in favour of the striking Dublin dock workers, threatened by the importation of blacklegs from Scotland. The "Leather v. Craig" decision in Belfast meant that employers could now sue unions for losses incurred as a result of strikes. The implied tort involved in a strike encouraged the police to intervene, especially in provincial towns. The "Khaki election" which returned the Conservatives to power in the midst of a wave of unparalleled jingoism was followed by the total proclamation of public meetings in Dublin. Seething discontent among the workers and unemployed was held down by increasing repression. For the next period Connolly's attention was turned towards the labour movement and its problems.

INTERNATIONAL SOCIALISM

In taking up the cudgels against Glasier's shamefaced Fabianism, Connolly announced his position in a political contest of world-wide importance. Two trends had now become visible in the labour movement. They cut across the formal divisions of parties, for the time being, as one after another showed symptoms of internal strife. The soil which nourished the dispute was the success of imperialist policy in harnessing backward countries to the service of western capitalism. As the new slaves took the load, pressure on the old could, if necessary, be eased. In Ireland both land and local government reform rested on this principle.

But it was by no means obvious at the time. Capitalism's new lease of life might be that of a vampire finding a fresh victim. But the circumstances surrounding the discovery obscured it. There were new social developments inseparable from the age of monopolies which were not obviously related to it. The huge combines of the twentieth century had more to lose from industrial stoppages than the small masters they replaced. Industrial organisation of new complexity demanded corresponding social organisation, and this was facilitated by tapping new sources of unpaid labour. But since these were many miles away, in far-away countries of which the British workers knew nothing, few noticed the connection. Under such conditions the trusts, amalgamations, public utilities and cartels of imperialist countries could appear, or at least represent themselves, as creators of wealth. Seeing the new wealth in the hands of their rulers, the working class did not always probe too closely how it was come by. Throughout Europe there was talk of killing socialism by ingeniously contrived reforms.

The division in the socialist parties was in essence between those who were prepared to integrate the labour movement into the framework of imperialism, and those who still demanded socialism and allowed reform only a subordinate part. Hence the antithesis, "revolutionism" or "reformism".

It was in France that the issue was most sharply posed. Here, memories of proletarian revolution lived on. Parisians would never forget the Commune. When, under the plea that he would be able to assist Dreyfus, the Socialist deputy Millerand entered a government which included General Galliffet, "butcher of the Commune", the French Socialist Party was all but crippled by the intense war of factions that ensued. Lafargue and Guesde denounced Millerand as a traitor. Jaurès sprang to his defence. The issue was not resolved by the time the International Socialist Congress met in Paris in 1900, and it formed the main topic there. Moreover, the international scope of the question was at once recognised.

The I.S.R.P. appointed three delegates, but only two appear to have attended, Stewart and Lyng. Connolly was probably unable to attend for economic reasons. This was the first international congress ever to recognise Irish nationhood. Even Arthur Griffith, three months later, could scarce forbear a cheer.

The battle-royal over Millerand raged for hours, during which the French "right" chanted "*Vive la République*" while the "left" interrupted with "*Vive la Commune*". In the end the leading theoretician of the International, Karl Kautsky, was induced to frame a compromise resolution which avoided the question of whether Millerand was right or wrong to enter a reactionary capitalist government, but criticised him for not obtaining the sanction of his party first. A "centrist" position was found. Individual sin was castigated, collective sin was condoned. The British, Germans and Austrians plumped for Kautsky. The Polish, Italian and American delegations were divided. Only Ireland and Bulgaria voted unanimously against. Ireland was thus planted firmly on the "left" of the International, for "revolutionism" against "reformism".

But not on the "ultra-left". One of the most eloquent opponents of Millerand and Kautsky was the Polish socialist, Rosa Luxemburg. In the debate on the credentials of delegates, which was long and bitter, she objected strongly to Poland's being regarded as a separate nation. The importance of her contribution lies in the fact that, thanks to her spirited opposition to the Kautsky resolution, her position was widely accepted as the "revolutionary" answer to the "reformism" of nationalism, a judgement which Connolly had to combat again and again.

On what she said then, history has already made its comments. She declared:

"On the one hand are purely international socialists who accept annexation and who want to walk hand in hand with their brothers of all countries, without occupying themselves with the unfortunate partition between Russia, Germany and Austria. It is this section which I and my friends have the honour to represent. On the other hand there are socialists who cling to a utopian and fantastic plan for the reconstitution of Poland. This dangerous utopia, this nationalist heresy, is exactly what we struggle against, convinced that the proletariat is not in a position to change capitalist political geography, nor to reconstruct bourgeois states, but that it must organise itself on existing political foundations, historically created, so as to bring about the conquest of socialist power and the social republic, which alone will be able to liberate the proletariat of the whole world."

She was received with deafening applause. She had proclaimed the doctrine of working-class revolution. But she had failed to appreciate the part in retarding that revolution which was played by the annexations which she accepted. She failed to appreciate the assistance that could be given it by those who fought imperialism merely to "reconstruct bourgeois states". Just as she omitted to observe that the working class in freeing itself frees all other oppressed classes, so she unwittingly rejected the aid these classes could give the proletariat. She stood for world revolution, but rejected the conditions which would make it possible.

In Dublin the delegation made their report. Almost immediately afterwards Stewart, who now represented the shop assistants on the Dublin Trades Council, had occasion for a tussle with the local Millerandists. The Home Rule Party had promised safe rural seats to "Liberal-Labour" candidates Nannetti and Simms. When the council received no reply to their letter forwarding the names, they feared they were being cheated. The entire council was embroiled in indignant recrimination, in the course of which one delegate suggested that Mr. William Martin Murphy should be pressed as a candidate, since he was one of the largest and best employers of labour "not only in Ireland, but the world over". Stewart put up a stout resistance and urged that "Labour should not be absorbed in other parties".

In a later discussion he suggested that Labour policy on public boards should be the opposite of that of the "middle-class representatives". They should demand the giving of "as much employment as possible" and ask for wages and conditions of a superior standard. The ability of the I.S.R.P. to influence the labour movement from within was then increased by MacLoughlin's election to the Trades Council by the Tailors. In response to a letter by Murtagh Lyng, secretary of the I.S.R.P., the council endorsed his candidature in North City ward, on the express grounds that he was supported by the Tailors' Union.

Connolly reissued the *Workers' Republic* after a short intermission in October 1900, and for a time secured a distribution through newsagents. Unemployment in Dublin was now reaching desperate proportions and his wages from the I.S.R.P. were being paid with decreasing regularity. At Christmas he brought home two shillings. The family had no Christmas dinner and no presents. Yet even under these difficulties Connolly continued his work of combating reformism.

In the *Workers' Republic* he published the essays of which some were reprinted in 1901 in a pamphlet called *The New Evangel*. Here he explained the difference between "state monopoly" and "socialism", and pointed out that many of the reformist ideas which were spreading arose from a failure to distinguish these two. While not denying that municipal enterprise, railway nationalisation, and state investment in public works were signs that the "overweening belief in the all-sufficiency of private enterprise" had been discarded, he argued that "to call such demands socialistic is in the highest degree misleading".

> "State ownership and control is not necessarily socialism—if it were, then the army, the navy, the police, the judges, the jailors, the informers, and the hangmen, would all be socialist functionaries, as they are all state officials—but the ownership by the state of all the land and materials for labour, combined with the co-operative control by the workers[1] of such land and materials would be socialism. . . . Schemes of state and municipal ownership if unaccompanied by this co-operative principle, are but schemes for the perfecting of the mechanism of capitalist government . . . an immense gulf separates the 'nationalising' proposals of the middle class from the 'socialising' demands of the revolutionary working class.
>
> "To the cry of the middle-class reformers, 'Make this or that the property of the government', we reply, 'Yes, in proportion as the workers are ready to make the government their property'."

He opened another essay by remarking that the man in the street is apt to be astonished at the "implacable hostility shown by the socialist parties towards the political parties hitherto identified with the agitation for political reform . . . why the socialist party . . . should seek the downfall of political reform parties with a zest and eagerness which the most bigoted conservative could never hope to excel". His explanation was that whereas conservative parties would "survive as long as there was something to conserve", the old reform parties were "shedding their members at both ends"[2] because of the futility of their attempt to "blend the principles of progress and reaction". Socialists uniformly sought "the dis-

---

[1] This is Connolly's first step of transition to De Leonism, since the criterion for judging the state is placed outside it—the state is placed above classes because its *character* is ignored.

[2] This also is a De Leonist conception, distinct from the Marxist one of dislodging one reactionary section after another.

comfiture of the Liberal and Home Rule parties" in order to hasten the day when the political battlefield might be left clear for the only parties possessing a logical reason for existence.

This challenge was issued at the time Keir Hardie had become most busy conciliating the Liberal and Home Rule Parties. Hardie had accepted Glasier's view of the Irish scene, and his *Labour Leader* grew ever more fulsome in its praise of Redmond's followers. The T.D. Sullivan memorial was hailed with enthusiasm. A "great friend of Labour" was discovered in Kendall O'Brien, M.P. for mid-Tipperary. By May 1901, Hardie was extolling John Dillon, and in September toured Killarney "under the personal guidance of Mr. John Murphy, M.P., the talented and energetic member for the Division of Kerry", of whom he wrote "although not a member of the Land and Labour League, Mr. Murphy is yet full of a passionate desire to serve the poor". Connolly continued to hold Hardie in personal regard, but their political association ceased.

The I.S.R.P. held occasional outdoor meetings during the winter of 1901, but Connolly had two reasons for advertising his availability for engagements in Britain from June onwards. One was financial. The other was the desire to combat reformism in Britain.

Justice published his advertisement, and the leader of the S.D.F. in Lancashire, Dan Irving, arranged the tour. The intention was no doubt to provide one continuous lecture tour, but this does not seem to have been possible. Opposition to the Kautsky resolution had become the touchstone of revolutionism in Britain. The S.D.F. branches were at variance. The position of the Irish being known, the Executive did not conceal their misgivings about the visitor. Their disapproval signified nothing in Scotland, but restricted him in the broader pastures of England. The Salford, Oxford, Reading and North London branches welcomed him. The Birmingham and Southampton branches held up their hands in horror. The remainder maintained the silence of neutrality.

Connolly had removed any doubt which may have existed on the subject of his own personal position in a letter to *Justice*, sent early in May, but held over until May 25. *Justice* had stated that "the presence of Millerand in the French Cabinet is an injury to Socialism all over the world" and "an international scandal". Connolly reminded *Justice* that the S.D.F. had voted against the "Guesde-Ferri" resolution at Paris which would have "prevented the scandal".

He continued:

"The great difficulty in the way now ... arises out of the circumstance that the Kautsky resolution declared the acceptance and retention of such a position as that of Millerand to be merely a matter of tactics and not of principles.... Millerand could still logically claim to be considered a good socialist differing only in tactics from the socialists of the world, who agreed with him in principle. I would like to know how you are going to get out of the difficulty in which you have placed yourself, except by repudiating the Kautsky resolution and accepting the definite and uncompromising resolution proposed against it, viz. that the revolutionary proletariat should, through its delegates, accept no government position which it cannot conquer through its own strength at the ballot box."

Connolly concluded by saying that the stand taken up at Paris was contrary to all the traditions of the S.D.F., and that it was noteworthy that since Millerand had entered the cabinet no less than twelve strikes had been broken by the use of the military.

"What good Millerand may have done is claimed for the credit of the bourgeois republican government: what evil the cabinet has done reflects back on the reputation of the Socialist party. Heads they win, tails we lose."

The editor of *Justice* reconciled the two positions the S.D.F. had taken up by saying that the Kautsky resolution had condemned Millerand's participation in the government under the conditions which actually obtained at the moment, and invited Connolly to reread the resolution. But the editor did not reread his own article and admit that he was criticising Millerand on grounds which were in no way connected with the Kautsky resolution. His reply caused much dissatisfaction.

The Scottish part of Connolly's tour began in Glasgow, where he addressed the May Day meeting on Glasgow Green, under the auspices of the S.D.F. The Trades Council had decided not to demonstrate that year. He concluded his week's propaganda with a meeting in Jail Square, after which he appears to have returned to Dublin for a short interval. His tour was resumed at Falkirk at the beginning of June. Prominent among the members he found William Mathieson, whose recoil from reformism had now led him to embrace De Leon's teachings. Connolly's meetings were acclaimed. The membership increased, among a working population made responsive to socialism through a general slackness of trade. One of his hearers wrote:

> "He possesses an attribute comparatively rare among socialist lecturers, that of being at the same time simple and perfectly intelligible to the ordinary man, and also perfectly accurate and rigid in his adherence to scientific verity."

Despite bad weather and opposition from the Temperance Party, he held several effective meetings in Aberdeen, went on to Leith where once again he suffered from the weather, and then travelled south into England.

Dan Irving had arranged that the South Salford S.D.F. should share the expenses of the week's campaign with the West Salford I.L.P. Both organisations were in the doldrums, with empty meeting rooms and no activity. Connolly's arrival turned their attention away from their internal difficulties and convinced them that those who have something to tell the people must force it upon their attention. He spoke at street corners every night of the week and concluded with a rally which brought in an influx of new members. "Comrade Connolly's visit put new life into the branch", wrote C. W. Fraser, and a return visit was arranged for September.

Connolly seems to have made Salford the starting point of his second tour, and spent the interval in Dublin.

Meanwhile, the S.D.F. Conference took place in Birmingham. Mathieson led the opposition to the Kautsky resolution and was ably seconded by Len Cotton of Oxford. Yates, representing Leith but living in Glasgow, criticised the editorial policy of *Justice*, complaining that the left wing were denied adequate space. He demanded that the paper (which was Hyndman's personal property) should be brought under the control of the party. After the conference the issues continued to be debated in the branches. Most of Scotland was for Mathieson and Yates, though John Leslie did not join them. He was expelled from the Edinburgh branch, which then severed its connection with the local Labour Representation Committee. The recoil from reformism was leading to "ultra-leftism", particularly on those issues which even revolutionaries must tackle with patience. The Executive Committee refused to accept Leslie's expulsion, but solved the problem by establishing an "Edinburgh East" branch which contained the "fakirs" (pronounced "faker") as opposed to the "clear-cuts" of the old town. Aberdeen, Falkirk, Leith and Glasgow declared for the "clear-cuts"; only Dundee for the "fakirs". These terms were imported from the U.S.A.

Once again in Salford, Connolly found his converts among the "clear-cuts". This was especially so among a group of Irishmen who worked at the old Pendleton pit, reputedly the hottest and hardest in England. After his first visit these constituted themselves a branch of the I.S.R.P. and arranged their first public meeting on his return. The chairman, John Keegan, was unable to attend, and William O'Dowd presided, making it clear in his opening remarks that the branch of the party had been started with a view to challenging Home Rule policies within Britain. This was to be Connolly's reply to Keir Hardie—the "fakirs" could follow Redmond, the "clear-cuts" must follow the I.S.R.P. At the same time Connolly made it clear in his own speech that the new organisation must not compete with either I.L.P. or S.D.F. In order to prevent this, it would be confined exclusively to those of

Irish birth or descent–whether that restriction would exclude many of the residents of Pendleton was, of course, another matter.

"The Home Rule Parties of the past," said Connolly, "like their successor today, were always the open enemies or the treacherous friends of the working class, but the revolutionary parties have always been in favour of full political and social freedom. I hope that every Irish worker will join, and be as zealous in co-operating with the militant revolutionary class at home in working for the full emancipation of their class and country, as the Irish of Great Britain have been in helping the middle-class movement of Home Rule."

During the meeting, at which many members were enrolled, Connolly gave an account of the I.S.R.P. in Ireland, mentioning the strong branches and big following in Dublin and Cork.

Among those who listened in Salford was the future Labour M.P. Joseph O'Toole, who recorded that "Connolly was one of the most convincing speakers I ever heard in my life, a man with a great passion for the cause of the labouring classes, and probably a greater passion for the cause of Ireland". At a spot in Trafford Road, now railed off and covered with grass by the democrats of Salford Corporation in order to prevent socialist propaganda, Connolly explained that:

"The term revolution did not necessarily mean bloodshed or violent social upheaval. The revolution spoken of by the Socialist Party meant such an organic change in any system of thought or action as would replace an old and outworn system and, by a newer and better system, accomplish more satisfactory results.

"The necessity for the revolution in England was demonstrated by the fact that the industrial supremacy of this country was fast disappearing" (the more so since British capitalists were establishing factories in India and Japan).

After a visit to Reading, where he held large but uneventful meetings and made no new members for the S.D.F., he joined Len Cotton at Oxford, where the struggle was consistently difficult owing to the high spirits of the students and the true blue conservatism of the local authority. Three years previously, about the time Mancunians were struggling for free speech at Boggart Hole Clough, Len Cotton had been jailed for a month after addressing an open-air meeting, and socialist propaganda was only permitted when Hyndman, Quelch and others from London kept up a weekly defiance which finally wore down the opposition.

Tolerated by the police, the socialists were left to the mercy of the students who were also tolerated by the police. Trouble began at Connolly's first meeting at St. Giles. A combination of aristocratic students and plebeian down-and-outs gathered round the platform and began to sing and shout, afterwards throwing stones at Connolly and threatening to tear down the red flag. The meeting was abandoned after something over an hour and the crowd followed Connolly and Cotton down Cornmarket Street, where they made an attempt to seize the platform and flagpole.

Cotton had the platform, Connolly had the pole, which was seven feet high and as thick as a broom handle. Cotton was impressed at Connolly's physical strength. He broke the pole across his knees, as if it were a match, and set about the nearest hoodlums, four of whom he laid out. The police intervened. The socialists were separated and in the mêlée lost sight of Connolly. He appeared again at dusk. He had been searching the streets for his hat, which had been knocked off in the fracas. Further meetings were held, but were so stormy that it was impossible to take collections. This meant that Connolly did not receive his expenses and the Oxford Branch issued a public appeal for donations.

In London he fared better. The North London Socialist Club held meetings at Finsbury Park and Highbury Corner. A branch of the S.D.F., it attracted a varied membership. Frank Newell, who attended one of his meetings, recalls his account of the worsening economic prospects of the traditional Irish immigrants who had for years gone to the Eastern Counties for harvest work. "They used to be waylaid by farmers wanting to give them a job," Connolly declared, but since the introduction of machinery on the land, "they were now waylaid by the farmer's dog, wanting to give them a bite."

On the controversial issue of reform or revolution he said: "If the workers ask for the capitalist baker's shop, he will throw the loaves at them to keep them out." When an I.L.P. man named Cook asked why he called his socialist party "Republican", he delighted the Marxists present with: "I cannot imagine a socialist party being in favour of a monarchy."

It was now mid-October, and becoming too dark for open-air evening meetings. Connolly therefore returned to Dublin, where he held one Sunday meeting at Foster Place before autumn closed in. He had been elected to the Dublin Trades Council by the United Labourers' Union, which had reaffiliated, and chose as his subject "Politics of Trade Unionism". What he said is unrecorded, but probably followed closely De Leon's criticism of the "pure and simple" trade unionism which avoided politics altogether. This criticism did not, however, betoken support for the so-called "dual unions". The United Labourers supported his nomination as Labour candidate in the Wood Quay ward and he was formally adopted at a meeting at 71, Francis Street on Wednesday, November 13. MacLoughlin, less fortunate with his trade union, was adopted as a Socialist candidate in North City ward, which Stewart contested for Alderman. "If I don't die fighting for Ireland," said Connolly, "I'll leave people behind who will."

As usual, Connolly's campaign consisted for the most part of open-air meetings, the stance favoured being in New Street. His election agent was Brannigan, and when the poll took place he secured 431 votes against the successful candidate's 1,424. MacLoughlin polled 371 against 530, while Stewart received 267 against his opponent's 751. The support of the Trades Council did not save Connolly from a campaign of slander and vilification. Sermons were preached, in which it was said that he was an anti-Christ and that no Catholic must vote for him under pain of excommunication. To those who replied that his children went to a Catholic school, it was said that this was to camouflage his atheistic beliefs. The outgoing councillor contrived to have the poll held in a schoolroom attached to a Catholic church, so that all voters would be reminded of their duty by the priest as they passed. In the circumstances his vote was a remarkable achievement. The Builders' Labourers Union marked it by inviting him to become secretary, but he declined.

Support on the Trades Council continued to grow. A new adherent was P. T. Daly, who represented the printers. Stewart, Connolly and MacLoughlin gave their fullest support to Daly's proposals for "Town Tenant Relief", which were extraordinarily advanced for the time. Daly demanded:

1. The taxation of land values.
2. Rating of unoccupied houses.
3. Rent tribunals to fix fair rents, accessible to all tenants.
4. Fixity of tenure whilst obeying tribunals' findings.
5. Compulsory registration of all tenement houses.

These demands were adopted by the Trades Council, winning the support of even such tradesmen of the old school as Leahy and G. L. Richardson. Trade union politics were in the air. The struggle for an Act to nullify the Taff Vale decision was engaging attention. Connolly's demand that the Corporation should carry out its building work by direct labour was readily accepted by the Trades Council. So effective was the work of the I.S.R.P. members that in April 1902 Stewart and P. T. Daly were sent as delegates to the Cork T.U.C. meeting, while Stewart and MacLoughlin were elected to the Council's executive committee.

While Connolly was away during the summer, P. T. Daly's association with the socialists drew him steadily to the left. But Stewart's outlook began to assimilate something of the non-political trade unionism of the older men. At the T.U.C.

he challenged the credentials of the Cork Trades Council on an inter-trade union dispute. While still active he became more orthodox, and in September 1902 was elected president of the Trades Council.

During the election campaign in January the *Workers' Republic* had been suspended, but the publishing committee was concerned to have it reissued for the summer propaganda. An appeal was issued for donations to replace the foolscap imperial hand press by a more efficient and rapid machine, which was obtained.

A by-election in Dewsbury involved the I.S.R.P. in a dispute with the I.L.P. and S.D.F. The S.D.F. decided to contest the seat, selecting as candidate the editor of *Justice*, Quelch. The Dublin *Evening Telegraph* at first declared for Quelch, and in his election address Connolly pointed out the inconsistency of the Home Rulers' supporting Smillie in North-East Lanark and Quelch in Dewsbury, while they opposed Connolly so bitterly in Dublin. The I.S.R.P. issued a manifesto to English Socialists, appealing to them not to give support to the Home Rule Party. Such support might bring them a few Irish votes, but it held back the day when Irish socialists would stand alongside them in the common struggle. *Justice* made no reference to the manifesto, Quelch subsequently explaining that he had never seen it. This Connolly did not believe. He was ironically amused when the Convention of the United Irish League repudiated the advice of the *Evening Telegraph* and advised Irish electors to vote for Runciman, the Liberal, on the grounds that Quelch could never win.

What had happened in the meantime is somewhat obscure. Its outward sign was a declaration from the I.L.P. that Quelch was showing "irresponsibility and bad faith" by standing for election. Keir Hardie declared that he had "alienated the trade union vote, and handed the Irish over to Runciman". Quelch's rejoinder was to accuse Hardie of a secret pact with the Liberals, under which the I.L.P. would keep out of Dewsbury in return for the Liberals' standing down in Bradford.

Recriminations continued over a period, but the differences were patched up and, if a trifle half-heartedly, the I.L.P. supported Quelch. Dan Irving was election agent. When the *Workers' Republic* reappeared in March, Connolly accused *Justice* of suppressing his appeal to English socialists "on obvious grounds of opportunism", and added that "but for the loss to the socialist cause, he would have been glad Quelch lost". Quelch probably did not know that the *Evening Telegraph* had at first supported him, and claimed that the Home Rulers had opposed him all the time. His explanation did not satisfy the I.S.R.P. It was decided to appeal to the international movement. Their manifesto was translated into French and German, appeared in *Vorwärts* and *Le Petit Sou,* and was published by Daniel De Leon in the *Weekly People.* After some further exchanges it ultimately appeared in *Justice.*

Connolly crossed to Scotland at the end of April 1902 and addressed the May Day meeting held by the S.D.F. in Edinburgh. The I.L.P. and Trades Council were anxious for a united demonstration on Saturday, May 3, but the S.D.F. declined to participate and organised their own for the Thursday. They claimed to attract four times as many people. How many more again a united demonstration might have attracted was not considered. Into the fight against opportunism an excess was creeping. Concern for the spiritual integrity of the party sometimes outweighed the desire to lead and leaven the whole.

This sectishness had its theoretical centre in America. De Leon's *Reform or Revolution,* consisting of an address delivered in Boston in January 1896, declared that "reform is invariably a catspaw" and denied all value to demands less than the whole. His address at New Bedford two years later was reprinted under the title *What Means This Strike?* and consisted of a sharp criticism of "pure and simple, or British trade unionism", together with the demand for political trade unionism. But his method of achieving his objective was not by transforming existing organisations through mass leadership; this he called "boring from within" and dismissed as a sterile tactic. He founded a distinct socialist trade union movement, which he hoped would grow and displace the old established American Federation of Labour. Members of his party must not hold office in "pure and simple" trade unions.

Attempts by the Scottish branches to introduce a similar rule into the S.D.F. were scornfully dismissed by Quelch. But the "unholy Scotch current" was not to be dammed. The members started to collect funds for the foundation of a newspaper which would give fuller expression to their views, in the meantime sending their contributions to the New York *People*. The sales of *Justice* in Scotland declined, as they carried out their intention to "flood the country with S.L.P." The Finsbury Park branch of the S.D.F. was dissolved for supporting Friedberg in sending to the *Weekly People* a letter on the I.S.R.P. Manifesto which *Justice* had refused to print.

De Leon believed that the United States was destined to lead the world proletariat. Defending and popularising the principles of Marx, he regarded himself in some way as the successor of Marx, bringing to a brilliant and forceful gift of exposition an extreme rigidity and tactlessness. His vigour, forthrightness and sparkle captivated the young Marxists. His sectish jealousy and refusal to abate one tittle of anything gave them the example they wanted, while driving them further than they needed to go. The ultra-leftism in the American Socialist Labour Party linked itself with the dogmatic tradition of the British Social-Democratic Federation. This was regrettable, but one fact remained. The London leadership was prepared to blunt the edge of revolutionary socialism; the "unholy Scotch" wished to resharpen it. This was the crux of the matter, not the manœuvres of the one, nor the crudities of the other. But the splitting of the movement could and should have been avoided.

Before leaving for Scotland, Connolly had been invited to visit America by the S.L.P., which had republished his pamphlet *Erin's Hope* in February. His own trade union, the United Labourers of Ireland, was anxious for him to go and was prepared to assist financially. They wished to secure first-hand information about the conditions of workers in America, which for the Home Rule Party was a land of milk and honey, a paradise for the Irish worker, and a great furnisher of funds to their party chest. In Scotland Connolly received further encouragement for the trip. He spent a week in Aberdeen, and once more visited Falkirk, where a vigorous republican manifesto on the coronation of Edward VII was issued. It was one of the crimes charged against Hyndman by Yates, the following year, that the S.D.F. had published a manifesto beginning with the word "Sire", and saying "this great and growing popularity of the king is not undeserved".

On his way back to Dublin, Connolly once more spent a week with his friends in Salford. The I.S.R.P. branch had not flourished, but the I.L.P. and S.D.F. had continued their co-operation, and both favoured the "clear-cuts". Connolly, of course, never identified himself with the refusal to struggle for reforms or the boycott of other sections of the labour movement. He had trouble with De Leon over this later on. As in Dublin he had urged republicanism on the '98 commemorators, and revolutionism on the Fabians, so now he preached "clear-cut" policy to the socialists but not a complete isolation from all the impurities of the sinful world. In Aberdeen one of his speeches was devoted to urging that the trams should be run on Sundays. In Salford he gave socialist education to S.D.F. and I.L.P. alike.

One of his lectures on "The Growth of Industrial Trusts" has been preserved in as accurate a reproduction as was possible when an open-air meeting was covered by the local newspaper reporter. In those days before the wide use of shorthand, reporters relied on their memory; they gave better general pictures, since they used their brains, but the figures were sometimes wrong. Despite this, after making such corrections as changing back pounds into dollars, and "twice as much" into "half as much again" (Connolly's hosts described him poring over books and papers all day in preparation for his evening lecture), it is possible to trace his facts as well as his argument to Hobson's *Evolution of Modern Capitalism*, which devoted several chapters to the subject of trusts, and was first published in 1896. Hobson was the first in England to begin the analysis of the imperialist phase of capitalism. Connolly covered all his arguments on the effect of trusts on competition, wages, employment and prices. He echoed his contention that since industry was assuming an increasingly collective character more public control was necessary. But he took one further step. The existence of trusts

> ". . . proved that industry could be carried on without competition at all. It would be futile for the working classes to think of hindering the development of the trust system, seeing that its growth was due to laws inherent in society itself. They should rather organise in order that they might make all productive property the property of the state. Their immediate aim should be to capture the political power of the state: and having secured this, they should reach out and capture all the organised powers of ministry—of those factors which today only helped to minister to the benefit of a class, but which might be made to minister to the comfort, happiness and development of the whole human race."

There was loud applause, but no questions followed. Seeing in the crowd a leading Conservative, Mr. Williamson, Connolly invited him to mount the rostrum and answer his arguments from a conservative point of view. Unfortunately the reporter did not feel bound to record these for posterity. That evening Connolly lectured again on "Socialist Teaching Made Easy".

He returned to Dublin, but was prevailed upon to spend another week in Salford immediately before sailing for America. While at home he completed his preparations. Since the *Workers' Republic* was likely to be in abeyance during his absence, and the "clear-cuts" had not yet raised sufficient funds to purchase their printing plant, he arranged that the I.S.R.P. would undertake the printing of the new paper, using material supplied by its editor, Mathieson.

Formally it was the organ of the Scottish branches of the S.D.F. but in fact it was a political challenge to *Justice*. Five numbers were printed in Dublin, the first probably under Connolly's supervision. The September number reprinted extracts from the writings of Marx on the Irish Question. In October was launched a sharp attack on "Clarionism", while the next issue contained reprints from De Leon's *Weekly People,* his translations from Kautsky, and *What Means This Strike?* Named *The Socialist,* and published in Edinburgh (it was not transferred to Glasgow till July 1912) it was in fact the British counterpart of De Leon's *People*.

The titles chosen by Connolly for his last series of lectures in Salford illustrate his keen concern with the controversies then raging in the labour movement. He spoke on "Trade Unionism—its limitations", "The Politics of Labour", "Labour and Revolution", "The Mission of the Working Class" and "Labour and Republicanism". None of these were subjects where it was easy to sit on the fence.

The Salford comrades gave him a great send-off on August 16, at the S.D.F. Club, 43, Trafford Road. T. H. Sutton was chairman, and urged them to send to the United States, through Connolly, the message "Workers of the World Unite". Connolly replied to the toast of his health by saying that one thing which he particularly wished to comment on was the practice among many branches both of the S.D.F. and I.L.P. to attach great importance and hope to the awakening of the middle class. He was inclined to think that the working class were, with all their limitations and faults, showing a disposition to work out their own emancipation and that they would eventually do so. He was always sorry to see men of the working class lacking in faith in their class for, speaking generally, they were better able to grasp broad issues than men of the middle and upper classes. The average middle-class man, though superficially well educated, was quite unable to grasp any problem outside his own narrow environment. The working class had in the main built up and still sustained and performed the work of the socialist organisations. That there were notable exceptions did not justify the leaning by some towards a hope and faith in the middle class as the ultimate lever for emancipation from present conditions.

Here was the faith of the *Socialist* given its most logical form. The toast "The International Socialist Movement" was given amid applause, and after a few days back in Dublin with his wife, Connolly sailed from Liverpool to the land of Daniel De Leon.

THE SOCIALIST LABOUR PARTY

Connolly was overwhelmed by his reception in New York. For the first time in his life he was an acclaimed personality, the honoured representative of the Irish working class. For six years he had struggled, slaved and starved. Navvy, builder's labourer, shipyard worker, publisher's proof reader, but most of all unemployed man, he had studied on an empty belly while the problem of keeping his family gnawed at the back of his mind. He had learned French and German, and written the first chapters of Ireland's first socialist classic, *Labour in Irish History*. His worth had been recognised, but his sacrifices were taken for granted. He was exactly halfway through his political career.

Born revolutionaries dedicate themselves twice, first in the flush of youth, then in the realism of maturity. No transition to outstanding leadership is possible without the second, which Connolly was now approaching. The failure of the Republican movement to seize the opportunity of the Boer war was his life's second great disappointment. The note of exasperation in his exchanges with Quelch and Glasier indicates a certain case-hardening of personality. In two fields he was up against the compromisers and the half-measure men. But in America as yet he had no rivals or enemies. The "clear-cut" ultra-leftism of De Leon seemed the doctrine he wanted, though experience was to show the impossibility of embracing it whole-heartedly. The I.S.R.P. was essentially *social-democratic*. Just before his departure the *Workers' Republic* described its position as based on the class struggle which would lead to the "working class seizing hold of political power and using this power to transfer the ownership of the means of life ... from individual to social or public ownership". De Leon on the other hand was rapidly moving towards *syndicalism*, according to which the capture of political power was merely a signal for the use of "economic power" to effect the transfer of ownership. The reason for the antithesis was that the social-democratic thesis did not specify that the workers' political power should be exercised through a working-class state, and as a consequence the question of the source of that power was left open.

Apart from their common hatred of the opportunism eating away the principles of the international labour movement, there were more immediate interests drawing De Leon and Connolly into association. The S.L.P. had split in 1899, and it was hoped that Connolly's presence would rally the Irish to De Leon's position despite its incipient syndicalism. For that reason the *Weekly People* republished material from the *Workers' Republic*, including even insignificant matter like "Home Thrusts", which were signed "Spailpin" and resembled the miscellanies of "R. Ascal". Deering's inaccurate account of Connolly's early life was given great prominence. It was dated Dublin, July 8—a day when Connolly was in Salford lecturing on trusts, and was in fact written by Murtagh Lyng who dared not use his own name for fear of victimisation. "Don't do any colouring," Connolly had warned him, but his friends could not resist a little. A special fund was raised to pay Connolly's travelling expenses and a weekly wage while he was on the road. No doubt De Leon hoped that he would return full of the S.L.P. and become its evangelist in Europe.

The I.S.R.P. was also passing through a difficult period, when financial stringency had "left its mark deep on the character and spirits" of the members. Connolly was given permission to collect subscriptions for the *Workers' Republic* while in the U.S.A., and no doubt hoped on his return to re-establish the paper on a weekly basis.

Of the inaugural meeting at the Cooper Union, New York, the *Weekly People* wrote:

"The opening of the doors . . . was like the breaking of a dam and the releasing of a torrent. At 7.30 o'clock all the approaches to the hall were jammed with the waiting crowd . . . there was little standing room left when John J. Kinneally announced Frank D. Lyon as chairman."

The meeting had a dual purpose. It was to introduce Connolly and to inaugurate the S.L.P. state campaign in the Congressional election. Connolly had a part to play in this campaign. After a month in the east he was to go west and endeavour to reach Minneapolis before polling day. Afterwards he would tour the Pacific Coast, return to the Middle West by the Santa Fé system, and then turn north for a brief tour of Canada, thence back through Detroit to New York. The tour was scheduled to end in early December.

The period was one of trade depression and the employers were making the most of national differences. Irish labour was being introduced into trades formerly exclusive to continental workers. In one workshop dispute a man named Cahill struck a Swede, Molemberg, who was a member of the S.L.P., with an iron bar. The blow proved fatal, and bitter feelings spread. Part of Connolly's duty was to preach international solidarity to his countrymen. He was particularly qualified for speaking to exiles, he said, since he had spent twenty years of his life among the exiles in Britain. His opinion was that the national exclusiveness of the Irish abroad was largely due to the propaganda of the Home Rule party. Here, in America, he found a socialist party which refused to compromise itself with such people.

The resolution of welcome put the matter succinctly enough:

"*Whereas* James Connolly is visiting this country as the representative of the Irish Socialist Republican Party, for the purpose of enlisting the interest of Irish Americans in the Socialist Movement, and

"*Whereas* James Connolly in his mission wishes to destroy the influence of the Irish Home Rulers and the bourgeoisie in Ireland, and their allies who trade on the Irish vote in this country to the economic detriment of the Irish working men in this country, therefore be it resolved:

"*That we*, the members of the Socialist Labour Party, here assembled to receive James Connolly, cordially welcome him to 'our' shores and give his mission our emphatic endorsement."

After De Leon had spoken, Connolly replied to the resolution:

"I feel under a great disadvantage," he began, "in addressing such a large and enthusiastic body of working men as are gathered here this evening. Though accustomed to addressing audiences of the working class in England, Scotland and my own country, I never stood before such a crowd before.

"I represent only the class to which I belong, and that is the working class. The Irish people, like the people of this and other capitalist countries, are divided into the master class and the working class, and I could not represent the entire Irish people on account of the antagonistic interests of these classes—no more than the wolf could represent the lamb or the fisherman the fish."

After he had finished his address there was tumultuous applause. The audience cheered at the top of their voices, rising in their seats and throwing their hats in the air. The demonstration lasted several minutes. Pressmen crowded round Connolly. What historic Irish family did he belong to? What kings was he descended from? "I have no ancestors," he told them. His people were poor like himself.

Such was the beginning of his campaign.

The remainder did not everywhere attain such a height of enthusiasm. Some of the meetings in the small towns around New York were held in the open air. At Yonkers, Tarrytown, Peekskill, Paterson, he spoke to good audiences, which increased as he worked through Connecticut to Boston, Mass. He told the Irish that a vote for the S.L.P. was a vote for Ireland, and that they should have a better use for their money than sending it over to keep well-fed politicians in the British House of Commons. When the Home Rulers fell out they told the truth about each other, so they had to make it up when the funds fell off.

Some word of these heresies no doubt preceded Connolly to the "cradle of Liberty". At the Faneuil Hall in Boston an attempt was made to stage a counter-demonstration. A number of Home Rulers stood up in the middle of the speech and tried to stampede the meeting by walking out. "The truth has hurt them," Connolly shouted after them, "and like all such they run away from it." Connolly obtained more subscriptions for the *Workers' Republic* from that than from any other meeting, his second best being at Duluth, Minnesota. At Lawrence a similar demonstration was attempted; the Town Hall floor was being repaired and the meeting was transferred to the "Classic Hall of Dance" situated above "Pat McCarthy's rum shop". About twenty-four Home Rulers made their protest.

His route now lay west. On his way he covered towns in New York State, spending several days in the vicinity of Troy, where he had cousins, and reaching Buffalo by October 16. Almost every night he slept in a fresh town; no evening was without its lecture. From St. Paul and Minneapolis he went to Salt Lake City. Here he was for the first time tempted on to controversial ground. Possibly the fact that the elections were over permitted him to relax. A "Kangaroo" complained that De Leon had "driven thousands out of the party". Social Democrats were thus nicknamed after the Kangaroo Courts of the Civil War when bogus judges, juries and clerks descended on localities, fined everybody thoroughly all round, and then "jumped" to the next hunting ground—the Social Democrats were always jumping from one reformist stunt to another, said the S.L.P. Connolly's reply used terms the "Professor"–De Leon—would hardly find complimentary. He published it in the *Weekly People,* but it may have started De Leon's dislike for Connolly. "De Leon," said the lecturer, "struck me as a somewhat chirpy old gentleman with an inordinately developed bump of family affection." To make matters worse, Connolly then engaged the entire American nation. What precise exasperation combined with the strain of the endless alternation of travelling and speaking, we are not likely to know. "Allow me to say," he wrote in the *People,* "that in one respect the S.L.P. is thoroughly American. It has its full share of the American national disease, swelled head. When I am asked what I think of America I say, 'I don't think much of it', and watch the wonderment on the face. I am not grumbling about this egotistical feeling. It is of course highly natural towards any other nationality except the Irish; to us it is only ridiculous. In course of time we will no doubt succeed in making you realise the fact."

A week later he was in California where he spent nearly a fortnight–three days in San Francisco where he had another cousin, Captain McGinn, son of that James McGinn who had married Bridget Boyle in Glasgow and later settled in Dundee. Advertising wagons had been drawn through the streets throughout Saturday and handbills were distributed. On Monday, November 18, he spoke at the Pioneer Hall, leaving next day for San Jose and then Los Angeles. Replying to a questioner at San Jose on the attitude of the Catholic Church to socialism, he said: "This institution will exercise the precaution of not placing all its eggs in one basket, for fear they may be broken."

The Colorado meetings were disappointing. Insufficient preparation had been made. The most successful was at Grand Junction where, according to the *Daily Sentinel,* Connolly spoke at the Court House, which he filled despite competition from "Captain Jinks of the Horse Marines" at the opera house, and "made many witty remarks in his economic speech". The substance of his lecture was to show that capitalism was independent of religion by comparing economic development under governments which were Catholic, Protestant and Freethinker.

After a short visit to Canada, Connolly's last engagements were at Detroit and New York. It seems likely that he spent Christmas at Troy. In his final speeches he summed up the experiences of his tour, and contributed a special article to *Detroit Today.*

"The increasing emigration from Ireland inspired my journey," he said. "The population of Ireland is only 4,000,000 and, as there is an annual emigration of 40,000, it is becoming quite a serious question as to how long the Irish nation will exist at this rate of deportation. Naturally we desire to find out whether those people who emigrate are really permanently benefited by the change; or rather whether they could not achieve as great a change for the better in their economic conditions by making a more determined stand at home. We believe—that is, the Irish Socialist Republican Party—that the conditions in America are not so rosy as they are painted by Irish middle-class politicians, and that if Irishmen were to remain at home and fight for socialism there, they would in the near future attain to better conditions of life than is possible by merely throwing themselves on the labour market of the United States.'

"Undoubtedly the standard of comfort here is much higher than at home, and to that extent the fortunate worker who gets employment is for a time improving himself. But the intensification of labour is greater here than at home, machinery is developing more rapidly, and in my opinion the worker is an old man in this country when he is still regarded as being in the prime of life at home. In other words, the emigrant sacrifices his future for his present for the sake of a few extra dollars."

He gave his cousin the same opinion.

At the Bamlet Hall he held the attention of the audience for two hours. His subject was the history of socialist ideas, "beginning with the French Aristocrats[1] and ending when the working class made socialism their own". He traced the development of capitalism and showed the origin of poverty, colonialism and war. "You have the power to prevent it," he said, "yet you go on voting for the men who rob you." He urged support for the S.L.P.

Once more in New York, he addressed his farewell meeting at the Manhattan Lyceum Annex on January 2. F. D. Lyon was in the chair again and Connolly was given another ovation. There were "tremendous cheers, ending with a rousing 'tiger'."

---

[1] [*Sic*.] Presumably Connolly said "Physiocrats".

"America is far too big a proposition to take in all at once," he confessed, "the opinion is almost general that there is nothing under the sun like the United States, but nothing surprised me more than the absolute disregard for law that is prevalent, especially among the capitalist class. Breaking law is regarded as a common occurrence and instead of meeting with disapproval it is considered smart . . . this I attribute to what may be called a lack of civic interest. This is an individualistic country and in no country is individualism so systematically pursued, both as a theory and as a policy."

He thought this individualism was brought by immigrants who came to seek their fortune regardless of the interests of the community. Individualism in Europe was restrained and not so remorselessly followed. Mutual acquaintance due to longer settlement and tradition bred civic interest. The so-called higher classes were animated by the spirit that there were other orders that must be respected and the ruling class acted as a buffer to the capitalist class. Here capitalism was unrestrained by tradition or any other limits.

He found the same spirit of individualistic lawlessness influenced trade unions. They were not curbed by old traditions and looked on betrayals by labour leaders as a piece of smartness rather than a matter calling for disapproval. Indeed, he believed on the whole that the U.S. was behind in the conception of the class struggle. His observations of Labour men had led him to believe that what was wanted was not conciliation, a broad platform that would embrace all of them, but a narrow platform, broad enough for any honest man but too narrow for any crook to put his foot on.

Though he reaffirmed his faith in the S.L.P. there was much heresy in his speech, and De Leon went out of his way to insert an important claim into his valedictory address. "The United States," he said, "is the country on which the emancipation of the workers of Europe depends." So the tour ended. Connolly had already despatched funds more than sufficient to put the *Workers' Republic* out of jeopardy for a long time to come.

Physically exhausted, but jubilant, he set sail for Ireland, warmed by his experiences, enlarged in his vision and immeasurably strengthened in self-confidence.

He reached Dublin in mid-January, in time to fight another municipal election campaign in Wood Quay ward, once again with the support of the United Labourers. His campaign was necessarily brief. There was every reason therefore to frame a programme which would present sharply the most burning immediate issues. Connolly chose to fight the election on socialism.

"Our defeat of last year," his election address ran, "brought about as it was by a campaign of slander and bribery, and a wholesale and systematic debauching of the more degraded section of the electorate, did not in the slightest degree affect the truth of the principles for which we contested. These principles still remain the only principles by which the working class can ever attain its freedom.

"When the workers come into the world we find that we are outcasts in the world. The land on which we must live is the property of a class who are the descendants of men who stole the land from our forefathers, and we who are workers are, whether in town or country, compelled to pay for permission to live on the earth; the houses, shops, factories, etc., which were built by the labour of our fathers at wages that simply kept them alive, are now owned by a class which never contributed an ounce of sweat to their erecting, but whose members will continue to draw rent and profit from them while the system lasts. As a result of this the worker in order to live must sell himself into the service of a master—he must sell to that master the liberty to coin into profit his physical and mental energies."

Connolly then developed Marx's thesis that the worker is not paid the value his services create, but such part of it as is necessary to enable him to reproduce those services. The fact that he bought his rations himself, instead of having his master buy them for him, was the sole difference between capitalism and chattel slavery. The only solution was the socialist republic, "a system of society in which the land and all houses, railways, factories, canals, workshops, and everything necessary for work shall be owned and operated as common property."

There was only one way to attain that end, he continued, and that was for

> ". . . the working class to establish a political party of its own, a political party which shall set itself to elect to all public bodies in Ireland working men resolved to use all the power of those bodies for the workers against their oppressors, whether those oppressors be English, Scots, or sham Irish patriots. Every political party is the party of a class. The Unionists represent the interests of the landlords and big capitalists generally; the United Irish League is the party of the middle class, the agriculturists, the house jobbers, slum landlords and drink-sellers."

After contrasting the universal condemnation of the taker of an evicted tenant's farm with the plaudits showered by the Home Rulers on blacklegs and strike breakers, Connolly turned to the subject of his opponents with the suggestion of "taking lesson by the municipal election of last year".

> "Let us remember how the drink-sellers of the Wood Quay ward combined with the slum owner and the house-jobber: let us remember how Alderman Davin, Councillor McCall, and all their fellow publicans issued free drinks to whoever would accept, until on the day before election, and election day, the scenes of bestiality and drunkenness around their shops were such as brought the blush of shame to every decent man and woman who saw them. Let us remember the threats and bribery, how Mr. Byrne of Wood Quay told the surrounding tenants that if 'Mr. Connolly was elected their rents would be raised'; let us remember how the spirit of religion was prostituted to the service of the drink-seller to drive the labourer back to his degradation; how the workers were told that socialism and freethinking were the same thing, although the

Freethinking Government of France was just after shooting down socialist workmen at Martinique for taking part in a strike procession; let us remember how the paid canvassers of the capitalist candidate—hired slanderers—gave a different account of Mr. Connolly to every section of the electors. How they said to the Catholics that he was an Orangeman, to the Protestants that he was a Fenian, to the Jews that he was an anti-semite, to others that he was a Jew, to the labourers that he was a journalist on the make, and to the tradesmen and professional classes that he was an ignorant labourer; that he was born in Belfast, Derry, England, Scotland and Italy, according to the person the canvasser was talking to.... If you are a worker your interests should compel you to vote for me, if you are a decent citizen, whether worker or master, you should vote for me, if you are an enemy of freedom, a tyrant, or the tool of a tyrant, you will vote against me."

This manifesto consists of a direct appeal to proletarian class interest, and contains neither an explicit appeal to republican sentiment nor a set of immediate demands. Griffith in *The United Irishman* of January 10 declared that Connolly deserved the vote of every nationalist in the ward. He was foremost among the able and honest men going forward, who (Griffith declared) could be counted on the fingers of one hand. But whether Griffith had received the manifesto when he made his pronouncements is very dubious.

Connolly made his appeal to trade unionists in reference to industrial struggles. He appealed to the workers as a whole to do away with capitalism. The ballot box was the means, but reform was thought not worthy of mention. This was essentially De Leon's position. Connolly had found in De Leon's scathing exposure of reformist opportunism a support for his own revolutionary convictions. He had not yet appreciated the extent of De Leon's dogmatism and sectish rigidity, and difference unformulated is often agreement by default. Hence, without openly proclaiming it, he put into practice De Leon's thesis that reforms were "banana peelings under the feet of the proletariat", and tacitly implied that the revolution could best be achieved by the political party of the working class concentrating on the winning of a majority of votes in elected bodies.

His vote dropped from 431 to 243. Stewart had done better than this in an election for Alderman. There was an increasingly sectish tendency in the I.S.R.P. which led members to turn inwards. From this followed personal differences which had grown serious during Connolly's absence. The members were mostly unemployed. In the summer the younger ones would walk in Phoenix Park or swim at the Bull Wall, while the older ones sat around the city. When winter came the rooms at Liffey Street served as a kind of club. It was there that Mullery taught Bradshawe to play draughts (ignoring Connolly's advice to play chess instead) while *Labour in Irish History* was being written in a corner.

Unfortunately, while Connolly was lecturing in Britain MacLoughlin, though himself a teetotaller, conceived the plan of installing a licensed bar. When Connolly left for the U.S.A. a committee was elected to look after the printing machinery, clubroom, etc. On his return he found the remittances he had sent on behalf of the *Workers' Republic* had been spent on making good the losses incurred by the bar. His attempt to depose the committee, which had kept no proper accounts, was interpreted as a slur, and ill feeling already engendered was increased.

The leadership during Connolly's absence was shared by Thomas Lyng and E. W. Stewart. Lyng was an indefatigable worker, but lacked *savoir faire*. Stewart was a great conversationalist over a pint of stout, and could find apt words to describe and satirise the weaknesses and misfortunes of others which kept the whole company paralysed with laughter. On the other hand, he was sensitive of the slightest ridicule of himself and could cherish implacable hatreds on the most slender grounds. The decline in morale was illustrated by Lyng and Stewart forming a plot to get Bradshawe drunk (he was a moderate drinker) and being drunk under the table themselves. An increase of membership was registered. When the accounts failed to tally some of these were (almost certainly wrongly) accused of financial misdemeanours, and the other members lined up for or against them.

When Connolly returned the organisation was in chaos. While the election campaign was in progress there was a temporary improvement. The January issue of the Edinburgh *Socialist* was duly printed; Jack Lyng had been initiated by Connolly and later became a printer in the U.S.A. But there was no February number, and the March number was printed in Edinburgh on a press secured by Gerald Crawford. On February 14 the *United Irishman* carried an advertisement of the *Workers' Republic* as an eight-page penny monthly whose current issue contained an instalment of *Labour in Irish History* (as did also the January *Socialist*). But on February 18 the storm broke. Connolly proposed the payment of an account in order to avoid foreclosure on the press. To his surprise the motion was rejected. He urged with increasing vehemence that the loss of the paper would be the end of the party. They were under a contractual obligation to the American subscribers who had made it possible to continue. His arguments were of no avail. Finally he tendered his resignation.

The acrimony of the proceedings had gone to the heads of some members. One of them leaped up with a motion: "I propose that we accept." Connolly returned home in a mood of deep dejection. "I resigned as a protest," he told his wife, "in hopes of proving they were pursuing a suicidal policy."

"They wouldn't accept?" said Lillie incredulously.

"Wouldn't they? They did."

The mood passed. Connolly's shots had missed their mark. He must continue the battle by other means. He had acted hastily at a meeting that was not fully representative. He must swallow his pride and prepare a statement of his case for all members to consider. About a fortnight later, after the members agreed to reverse their previous decision, he withdrew his resignation and, as his principal antagonist, Stewart the secretary, put it, was "readmitted into membership". This was the signal for Stewart to resign and a split in the party took place. Tom Lyng, Mullery, William O'Brien and others, while not embittered like Stewart, felt resentment against Connolly and temporarily dropped out of activity. His strongest supporter was Jack Lyng. The open-air meetings which had been held in January and February abruptly ceased. An attempt was made to establish a "Kangaroo" Socialist Labour Party with the object of deceiving the Americans. The finances which might have been restored were thrown into disorder once more, and the I.S.R.P. as such ceased to exist.

Connolly was confronted with the old economic problem in its acutest form. He could scarcely expect a lecture tour that would take him through the summer. England was virtually closed to him now that he was the acknowledged European apostle of De Leon. And even if this were not so, what was one summer's propaganda to a man now thirty-five? His acceptance of the invitation of the Scottish District Council of the S.D.F. to spend five months lecturing in Scotland was probably no more than tentative, though the enthusiasm which he brought to the work led them to think otherwise.

His engagement was due to begin on May 1, but he appears to have crossed to Edinburgh about a month before this and edited the last two issues of the *Workers' Republic* from Scotland. The need for securing some established trade was impressing itself on his mind, and his associates in Edinburgh say he took classes in linotype operation at the Heriot Watt Technical college, presumably under the auspices of "Typographia". As the college's own classes closed on May 8, and its day classes continued only till June 5, it seems unlikely that he can have attended the full course, unless "Typographia" continued into the vacation. It may be, however, that he had begun his training the previous year, when government-assisted linotype classes were started in Dublin and the printers were up in arms because, under the provisions of the Act, education could not be confined to existing members of the trade. It is said, furthermore, that when

Connolly qualified in Edinburgh he was unable to secure admission into the trade union. This may have contributed to his subsequent decision to leave Scotland.

The centre of gravity of Scottish socialism was shifting to Glasgow, but Edinburgh contained a core of able Marxists who were strongly under Connolly's influence. Drummond, Geddes and Robertson, together with the composer Gerald Crawford, Conlon and Walker formed a compact "impossibilist" group (as the "clear-cuts" were called) in the capital. John Leslie refused to join them, and Connolly teased him mercilessly whenever they met.

Several days of each week Connolly would spend in Glasgow, where he lodged with Thomas Clark (subsequently an Executive member of the A.E.U.) in London Road, Bridgton. In the Glasgow branches were young people like Tom Bell, William Paul and Neil MacLean, who were not only up in arms against Hyndman's "Millerandism" but resented the "snobbery and pretentiousness" which marred so many of the S.D.F. leaders. It was alleged that they took the young men drinking in order to turn them into "fakirs". Connolly was entirely free from this fault. He was a teetotaller. He sang an Irish song at their evening socials, or accompanied them on their excursions, ready to talk with everybody, and soon became their hero.

From the first publication of the *Socialist* it became clear that a split was impending in the S.D.F. Quelch, visiting Edinburgh and seeing the new press being assembled (its parts were purchased piecemeal as the money came in), expressed keen anxiety at this rival in the north. In the March number of the *Socialist*, Yates sounded the trumpet in an article on the forthcoming Easter conference at Shoreditch Town Hall. His charges against the leaders were set out in tabulated form. They had "altered revolution to reform" for the sake of the "fleshpots of office and influence". Their manifesto at the Coronation had commenced with the servile word "Sire". While abandoning revolution they had gaily opened the door to anarchism. Had not Quelch declared at

Birmingham that he would "favour any method from the ballot box to the bomb"? This quotation was a little unfair to Quelch, who had been hard pressed in debate at the time. But Yates was out for blood. Members of the Finsbury Park branch had been expelled after a "farcical trial" for daring to send to the *Weekly People* their protest against Quelch's failure to publish the I.S.R.P. manifesto. When the branch refused to sanction the expulsions it was dissolved at the behest of "escaped parsons" and "penny-a-line journalists". There was no democracy in the S.D.F.

Although the *Socialist* published pamphlets on "territorial expansion" and "the New Trusts", showing a marked awareness of the new problems of imperialism, it does not appear to have made proposals for transforming the S.D.F. This was its weakness. Constructive criticism places the onus on the responsible leaders. Negative opposition can only lead to a split. The preliminary broadside from the *Socialist* sharpened tempers to the utmost and made this inevitable. The mistake of 1884 was about to be repeated.

When the S.D.F. conference opened, Finsbury Park was discussed first. Hunter and Cotton moved reinstatement. Friedberg they argued, had only written to the *People* after being denied space in *Justice*. Quelch replied that the *People* had been for months slandering and attacking the S.D.F. The Irish manifesto had appeared while he was fighting the Dewsbury election. "The theory of these people," he went on "is that you should find out something that would injure you, and do that; you should make as many enemies as possible." Friedberg was not reinstated.

Most of Saturday was taken up with a controversy over Yates's management of the *Socialist*. The E.C. insisted that it should conform to official policy or cease publication. Yates was charged with a campaign of persistent vilification. He had refused to sell *Justice* and instead distributed the New York *People* in whose columns he had described the S.D.F. Executive Committee as liars. As a result of his "mischief" Glasgow branch had been reduced to a "handful of men" who either "could or would not pay their dues".

Yates replied that there was vilification on both sides. Since he went to Glasgow in 1900 the branch had increased its membership from 6 to 70 or 80, and they had held 400 propaganda meetings. After a lengthy discussion Yates's expulsion was upheld by 56 votes to 6. The resolution furthermore prescribed expulsion without right of appeal for anybody else who "adopted the conduct or tactics for which G.S. Yates was expelled". A resolution condemning the whole tone and conduct of the *Socialist* was then carried by 44 votes to 6. The publishers were ordered to alter it or cease publication. The six then left the conference in protest and a telegram was despatched to Glasgow, where members had gathered in the clubroom to await confirmation of the expected split. A bucket of paint had been set in readiness and on the delivery of the message the letters S.D.F. outside the premises were painted out. Those present constituted themselves the Glasgow Socialist Society. Connolly's contract was transferred to this body and Tom Bell had the duty of gathering the pence and shillings from which his weekly wage of 30s. was made up. Though frequently unpaid till Tuesday or Wednesday, he never complained.

A special meeting of the Scottish Council was called on the Wednesday after the conference, where it was agreed to report the events of the conference to all Scottish branches at a special delegate meeting on the following Tuesday, April 21. When the meeting took place, Geddes was in the chair and it was decided on the motion of Drummond to withdraw from the S.D.F. and establish a new party. Yates was reappointed editor of the *Socialist* while Mathieson was entrusted with drawing up the inaugural manifesto in consultation with Connolly.

It was in the midst of these events that Connolly wrote his "Rebel Song" which was set to music by Gerald Crawford, one of the six who had walked out of the conference. It was written during an excursion to Erskine Ferry and became the marching song of the young socialist rebels whose enthusiasm inspired it. Politically unmistakably of the S.L.P., it appeared in the May number of the *Socialist,* immediately after the split. It was followed by the "Hymn of Freedom" and "The Flag", which was written in Dublin. "Freedom's Sun" and "Freedom's Pioneers" appeared in 1904 after Connolly had settled in America. He continued to write verse but 1903 and 1904 were his most prolific years. His poetry owed much to the "proletarian lyrics", though he lacked Leslie's technical skill, and to Jim Connell. But he never attempted the lighter vein of these two authors. He most admired but could not emulate the grave and passionate dignity of Freiligrath whose poems he used to read aloud at the Glasgow gatherings. Perhaps his most remarkable performance was the translation of Max Kegel's *Sozialistenmarsch* from German into English verse. It is notable that his songs were not at first to Irish airs, but to popular tunes his young Scots comrades would know.

April and May were taken up with preparations for the launching of the new party. Connolly travelled throughout Scotland despite bad weather,[1] sometimes speaking at as many as a dozen meetings a week. His repartee became a by-word and many of his answers were long preserved. But how far they can be guaranteed original and how far they belong to the street speaker's venerable stock-in-trade is difficult to determine. Connolly added his contribution to this traditional art.

In private conversation his sharp but playful wit delighted the rebels. What did he think of De Leon, Geddes asked. "He suffers from an affectation of the throat," was the coy reply. Connolly would not explain further, but Geddes subsequently met De Leon and discovered his custom of wearing a fresh white handkerchief each day in place of a tie. These were the last days of the young Connolly. That person left for America and did not return. They were the days which gave rise to his legendary fame as a socialist leader. The sense of liberation he brought those who had suffered under the empty know-alls and erudite snobs, then edging for leadership, breathes through everything they said or

[1] 1903 was one of the worst summers on record.

wrote of him. And the word "Freedom" occurs in one title after another in his songs.

From time to time he lectured on his tour of America, making a point of contrasting the S.L.P. with the American S.D.P. The S.L.P. published a daily newspaper in English, German, Swedish and Yiddish, and a monthly in English. An affiliated organisation published a periodical in Italian. The printing works had five linotype machines, and a Hoe press capable of turning out 30,000 copies an hour. De Leon had been described in *Justice* as a "German-Venezuelan Jew", but this was typical of the anti-semitism of *Justice* which spoke of "Jewish millionaires".

The S.D.P., by contrast, had different policies in different States. In the east, where capitalism was highly developed, it paid lip service to the class struggle. In the middle west, where the petty middle class was still a force, it stood for municipalisation for the benefit of the taxpaper. In the west it argued that the basis of revolution was the farming class. Its periodicals reflected this inconsistency and sacrifice of principle. They were purely local papers like the *New York World, Seattle Socialist, Milwaukee Social Democratic Herald,* and the *Los Angeles Socialist.*

The new party in Scotland was to follow the lines of the S.L.P. and Connolly urged the adoption of the name. "It doesn't matter what you call it," he told them pithily, "it will *BE* called the S.L.P." He ascribed the "wobbling state of the movement in England" mainly to the long series of political blunders committed by Hyndman, whose character had been to "preach revolution and practise compromise, and to do neither thoroughly".

The inaugural conference opened in Edinburgh on June 7, and was attended by delegates from Kirkcaldy, Dundee, Edinburgh, Leith, Falkirk, Glasgow and Dunfermline. A message came from Cotton announcing the formation of the sole English branch in London. Connolly took the chair, and congratulated the delegates on leaving the moribund S.D.F. The manifesto was adopted with only minor changes. A move to delete the section headed "Immediate Demands" was defeated. Charles Geddes presided over the afternoon session, when Yates was confirmed as editor of the *Socialist* and Neil Maclean became national secretary. Connolly was appointed national organiser for a further period of three months. He was to spend the next full week in Kirkcaldy.

After the conference he returned to the East Meadows where he addressed a meeting with Yates, Drummond, Walker and MacLean. When it was heard that the S.D.F. proposed to stage a counter-demonstration Connolly challenged Leslie to a debate, but Leslie wisely declined. The content of Connolly's speech was typical. He showed how capitalism engendered racial strife: Belgium in the Congo, Russia in Finland, and England in South Africa. By the same token it fostered strife among the working class to further capitalist interests.

The Executive Committee of the new party met on June 13, when Connolly announced that the *Workers' Republic* had "temporarily suspended" publication. He asked that copies of *The Socialist* should be sent to its American subscribers and that a financial arrangement be sought with the I.S.R.P. which was not yet dead. Foster Place meetings had been resumed in May, when Lyng gave a detailed criticism of Wyndham's Land Purchase Bill. William O'Brien called a special meeting of all Dublin socialists in the Painters' Hall, Aungier Street, at the end of July. The I.S.R.P. meetings were resumed at 107, Talbot Street and subsequently at 46, Henry Street. The result was that the organisation felt strong enough to finance the sending of the *Socialist* to *Workers' Republic* subscribers and arrangements were made to supply the Scots paper with Irish material.

Connolly threw himself into his work as national organiser with great energy, paying visits to Edinburgh, Kirkcaldy and Dundee, but concentrating on Glasgow, where Yates's lectures on Marx's *Capital* had drawn together a band of enthusiastic young socialists full of zest for knowledge but still hazy on how to translate it into practice.

The demand for lectures and classes in the west of Scotland completely outran the supply of competent speakers.

Connolly turned to the youth. At the age of nineteen William Paul found himself conducting a large class at Clydebank. Connolly himself conducted a class for tutors in Glasgow. His method of training was original. When the students entered the room they found a large table with a chair upon it. Connolly sat in the audience with a bundle of current newspapers on his lap. The students were to apply their Marxist knowledge to some of the headlines in the papers. But in order to overcome the danger of "stage fright" they must mount the table and chair before making their speeches. Those who laughed at the mistakes of others must mount the rostrum themselves. Connolly would then pose as an opponent of socialism, throwing up awkward questions and emphasising all the time that the test of an able lecturer was the ability to explain a subject in an elementary way.

At the same time it became increasingly clear to Connolly that he could not remain a political organiser and maintain his family in Dublin. The hopes of a revival in the I.S.R.P. were aroused only to be deferred. In July he announced that at the end of his three months' engagement he intended to leave for America. He had no plans and did not know where he would settle. The decision to emigrate was precipitated when the local branch in Dundee organised a series of meetings so badly that a heavy financial loss was incurred, coming, though few saw it so plainly, directly out of Connolly's pocket. Connolly was capable of moods of deep depression, a reaction from his ceaseless urging activity.

Accordingly at the end of August he crossed once more to Dublin. Tom Bell saw him off sadly at the Broomielaw. He addressed two final open-air meetings at Foster Place, although relations between Connolly and his former comrades were still cool. The dissident element, whose sole overt plank was resistance to Connolly's "bossing", had now resigned. The I.S.R.P. proclaimed itself the Irish section of the Socialist Labour Party. It continued its work, but American De Leonism could no more provide a philosophy for the most national of movements than English I.L.P.-ism. The membership remained small. The sense of frustration continued. Individual members crossed over into Griffith's organisation, others remained inactive. But a core remained continuously at work. Leaving his family in Dublin, Connolly sailed for America on September 18. According to Mullery not one of the socialists came to see him off. Connolly spoke very bitterly of this discourtesy.

Attempts to assess the significance of the I.S.R.P. have usually taken only its Irish context. Sean MacGiollarnath, writing under the pseudonym of O'Connor, shortly after Connolly's death saw little in it but a defiance and a failure. Connolly "gained no footing among trade unionists; he neglected the Gaelic revival; he did nothing to introduce the co-operative movement into urban life. That he failed to get a grip or to hold the imagination of the workers is not a matter for wonder. He was still young; his mind had not been matured by experience which the actual solution of social problems gives; and his development had been along lines not calculated to fit him immediately for leadership of Irish workers."

This judgement does Connolly and the I.S.R.P. less than justice. Connolly's trade union activities were not so inconsiderable. He was cut off from the craft unions by their sectional exclusiveness. His efforts to influence national cultural organisations were repulsed quite early. To this day consumer co-operation has found Dublin a stony soil. The consistent struggle for socialist and republican principles which Connolly waged on every front open to him is not recognised. His failure to stir a lasting mass movement was due not to his own immaturity but to the immaturity of the objective conditions. He was ahead of his time, not behind it. The I.S.R.P. was limited by the environment in which it grew. But the key to Connolly's contribution at this period was the struggle against opportunism without which no development was possible.

X
AMERICA

The extreme magnifies the truth.
ARTHUR SCHOPENHAUER

When Connolly landed at New York in the autumn of 1903 his arrival was considered worthy of comment in the *New York Sun,* which had formed its own opinion on what he was there for, and reflected that he had a difficult task before him.

"In the United States of America all efforts to enlist Irishmen, or men of Irish ancestry, in the Socialist movements, have failed."

The *Weekly People* at once published a list of thirty-three Irish S.L.P. men, a useful list containing such names as Quinlan, Walsh and Twomey, but not M. D. Fitzgerald, first honorary member of the I.S.R.P. in the United States. Nor does it mention Barney O'Toole, the "young enthusiastic member of section New York", later credited with appearing a number of times before the National Executive Committee urging that Connolly be invited on his lecture tour. Connolly and his friends were not to think themselves the only pebbles on the Irish-American strand.

Connolly was not enthusiastically received by De Leon. "Because a situation was not given him by the party when he arrived," wrote Rudolf Katz, "Connolly began finding fault with the editor." His political differences with De Leon were not made known till the following April. On arrival it seems that he offered the *People* his services as a linotype operator and evoked a reaction which he did not expect. On his last visit he had been described as a labourer. It was now suspected, perhaps quietly propagated, that he was really a printer who had posed as an unskilled man in order to make an impression. No other shop would employ him since he lacked the A.F.L. card. After a dispiriting spell in New York

City he left for Troy, where he lived with his cousins Thomas and Helen Humes at 447, Tenth Street. There he secured work as collector to the Metropolitan Life Insurance Company. A small town, a hundred and fifty miles up the Hudson River, Troy had developed a textile industry which came increasingly to specialise in shirts, cuffs and collars which were despatched throughout the Eastern States. It attracted its share of Irish immigrants by overflow from New York and the surrounding towns, and by the time of Connolly's arrival a number of these had gravitated towards socialism. He met them in the local branch of the S.L.P., which then possessed its own meeting rooms.

Connolly's cousins were not politically inclined. But they were Americans, and nothing in the world was alien to them. Thomas Humes and his brother-in-law, Thomas Carlin, would sit up late at night tempting Connolly to expand on every conceivable topic he had knowledge of. Finally they agreed to accompany him to a meeting he was to address at Schenectady, fifteen miles to the north-west. To the surprise of all of them the meeting proved a stormy one, though no opponents of the S.L.P. were present.

Presenting what he had always understood to be the accepted Marxist theory of wages, Connolly found a strongly vocal opposition which denied the usefulness of agitating for wage-increases on the ground that these, if gained, were immediately and automatically nullified by a rise in prices. He did his best but failed to persuade them to the contrary.

No doubt his cool reception in New York had set him thinking. Unformulated differences of policy repeatedly disguise themselves as personal animosities. Possibly it was only now that he realised the dangerous strain in the S.L.P. He had overlooked this when his main efforts were concentrated on combating reformism in Britain. What he saw now was a swing to the other extreme. He picked up the *People* week by week and found there Bebel's *Woman,* first serialised then advertised in book form. Bebel's speeches were translated *in extenso* and everything was done to exalt his importance as a theorist. Partly this must have been done to stimulate the sale of the book. Though enthusiastically American, De Leon was of German education and well able to say *"bei uns"*. But Connolly here detected a political trend which he very acutely connected with another. The Belgian freethinker and Liberal, Vandervelde, was given the front page on March 19, 1904, to discuss the development of Catholic political parties in Europe. Here De Leon joined with another opponent of socialism to attack the Catholic Church. Connolly sent the *Weekly People* a letter on "Wages, Marriage and the Church". It appeared on the front page on April 9, and alongside it De Leon published his reply.

The sharpness of the controversy which ensued is usually attributed to De Leon's intolerance and dogmatism, in conflict with Connolly's stubbornness and Catholic upbringing. It was said that everybody who stood on his own two legs had trouble with De Leon. The American leader could overlook some small heresies in a missionary departing to the heathen. The same man looking for a job in New York might be a most unwelcome addition to the evangelical staff. But these factors were only contributory. De Leon was quite capable of throwing open the *People* to controversies which lasted months before he made his editorial pronunciamento. He willingly published a sharp protest against the filling of pages of the paper with his execrable blank verse translation of Lassalle's *Franz von Sickingen.* The political content not the fact of criticism aroused his ire. For Connolly raised questions fundamental to the tactics of American socialism. He challenged its traditional sectishness and separation from reality. He revealed inconsistencies in De Leon's teachings which could put in question the basis of his policy. In order to appreciate this fully it is necessary to trace some special features of American development.

The growth of the U.S.A. displayed two sharply contrasted aspects. One was the constant injection of discontented and even revolutionary elements from Europe. The other was the robbery and extermination of the aboriginal Americans, who were too independent to accept enslavement.

Hence invading capitalism expanded under conditions of chronic labour shortage. Workers were abducted from Africa for service on the plantations of the southern states. The north attracted labour from all parts of Europe by golden promises. But the availability of vast sparsely populated lands provided a line of escape by the expedient of "going West", which process spread capitalism from the Appalachians to the Pacific within eighty years, at every step expropriating the native Americans.

The social system was shot through with this contradiction. The War of Independence gave the U.S.A. the most advanced political democracy of the nineteenth century. It swept away colonial domination and undermined the vestiges of feudalism. But American democracy was a white man's democracy directed against the aborigines and excluding Negroes. These advanced from slavery to peonage thanks to the Civil War, but even Lincoln was oblivious of the interests of the races contemptuously called "Red Indians". Their inferior status was the precedent for all other forms of inequality.

Capitalism developed as nowhere else, in commerce, agriculture, consumers' products and, finally, in heavy industry. Simultaneously went the expansion of the working class. The availability of land in the west did not act as a check on trade union organisation, but it tended to restrict its aim to the economic struggle with individual employers, which was not combined with demands upon the State. The immigrants came from countries whose governments were openly despotic; in America the State was hardly noticeable. Their oppressors appeared to them as a series of separate bosses, rising in power and ruthlessness as bigger and bigger units were built up. The diffuseness of the American State, and its decentralised federal form, was a relic of the jealous rivalry between slave and non-slave states. The new territories were largely conquered, civilised and ruled by private enterprise. Finally, it was hard for any proletariat to question a State with which it was, however unwittingly, in league against the aborigines.

The rapid development of this land of opportunity produced a large and favoured "aristocracy of labour". The privileged section looked to the employers to defend its sectional interests against competition from the less favoured, and especially the immigrants. Despite its early promise, the American Federation of Labour came to represent the outlook of this section and, under the leadership of Samuel Gompers, moved over to a position of complete class collaboration, even opposing such measures as old-age pensions, health insurance and unemployed relief. It uncritically endorsed the domestic and foreign policy of successive governments on the pretext that its business was "trade unionism, pure and simple", and not politics. Its craft organisation together with sex and race prejudice, made it an object of fierce resentment among the foreign-born and unskilled workers.

It was precisely the foreign-born who were the bearers of socialist ideas to America. The American section of the First International was largely recruited from Germans, and even as late as 1889 the Socialist Labour Party which derived from it had only two Executive Committee members able to speak English. The S.L.P. conducted a struggle for the principle of a distinct independent party of the working class. It rightly criticised the craft exclusiveness and class-collaboration of the A.F.L. But, as Engels remarked in 1890, it was beset with "absurd theoretical confusion, corresponding arrogance and Lassalleanism" and it preserved political ideas which had long been exploded in Europe. These relics of Proudhon, Lassalle and Bakunin explain why the temporary conditions of American expansion were taken as proof of American "exceptionalism" and the movement was led along the wrong path.

In the next chapters it will be shown how the outmoded ideas of Lassalle and Bakunin were resurrected through the I.W.W. and thus spread through the English-speaking world, where for a time they passed for the most advanced form of socialism. For the moment, suffice it to summarise their salient points. These formed the subject of well-known polemical works by Marx and Engels, which are now generally available, but were not readily accessible between the death of Engels and the foundation of the Third International. Proudhon discouraged trade unionism on the grounds that "it is impossible for the strikes which result in an increase of wages not to lead to a general dearness". Bakunin claimed to develop Proudhon's "anarchist system" and free it of frills. He advocated abstention from political action by the working class, seeking to "impart to the workers' agitational activities an exclusively economic character" and making atheism a condition of membership of the party. He believed that the evils of capitalism arose from the existence of government as such, and thought that as a result of economic activities it was possible to bring about what he called "social liquidation", when government would cease, all land would be transferred to agricultural co-operatives, and all industries to workers' industrial co-operatives. Lassalle developed from Proudhon the "iron law of wages" according to which, no matter what wage increases the worker won, he could never improve his condition because prices would catch up with him.

Lassalle concluded that only the replacement of the payment of wages of labour by possession of the products of labour could free the working class from exploitation. It must become its own employer. Consequently the aim must be "productive associations", but instead of arising spontaneously (as Bakunin would have them) these were to be financed by the state after the return to Parliament of men "armed with the bare weapon of science". There was no universal suffrage in Germany at the time, consequently Lassalle urged a single union of all workers to bring this about.

Discredited in Europe, these ideas lingered in America, the "youngest and oldest country in the world". They existed alongside Marxism in the ideology of the S.L.P., and were even taken for Marxism. The years 1898 to 1905 saw them flower a second time and bear fruit in syndicalism.

After an unsuccessful effort to win over the Knights of Labour (a less exclusive antecedent of the A.F.L., branches of which still survived), De Leon had founded the Socialist

Trades and Labour Alliance. This failed to attract support, and a section of his party seceded and joined with the Social-Democratic Party to form the Socialist Party of America. De Leon did not then critically examine his own programme. Persisting in the false step of dual unionism, separating the vanguard from the mass, he developed the logic of his neo-Lassallean position while never ceasing to appeal to Marx. Dogmatism is characteristically raised on false opinion. Faith is only called in where reason reveals insoluble contradiction. De Leon blamed the steady decline of his party on a series of malicious conspiracies. He continued to teach that "pure and simple" trade unions were beyond redemption. Political reforms were snares, economic concessions illusory, all was false, impure and transient but "Socialism".

The S.L.P. was reduced to a propaganda machine except for elections. The party watched its vote as a seaman his barometer. De Leon did not conceal that he thought he had found a *peaceful* road to socialism. His importance was that for many years he embodied the resistance of a section of the American working class to the tide of class-collaboration.

"I find myself in complete accord with the S.L.P.," Connolly wrote, "on all questions of policy and of discipline, yet party speakers and writers give expression to conceptions of socialism with which I could not agree.

"One of our organisers in the West, in the course of a discussion with a spokesman of the Kangaroos, held that the workers could not even temporarily gain benefit from a rise in wages as 'every rise in wages was offset by a rise in prices'. When the Kangaroo quoted from Marx's *Value, Price and Profit* to prove the contrary, our S.L.P. man airily disposed of Marx by saying that Marx wrote in advance of and without anticipation of the present-day combinations of capital ... the theory that a rise in prices always destroys the value of a rise in wages sounds very revolutionary, but it is not true ... it was one of the points in dispute between my opponents at the Schenectady meeting and myself."

Connolly pointed out that there was a poor case for the Socialist Trades and Labour Alliance if the gains it won were automatically extinguished by an inexorable economic law.

He then turned to the subject of the family:

"When touring this country in 1902, I met in Indianapolis an esteemed comrade who almost lost his temper with me because I expressed my belief in monogamic marriage, and because I said I still hold that the tendency of civilisation is towards its perfection and completion, instead of its destruction. My comrade's views, especially since the publication in the *People* of Bebel's *Woman*, are held by a very large number of members, but I hold nevertheless that they are wrong, and furthermore that such works and such publications are an excrescence upon the movement. The abolition of the capitalist system will undoubtedly solve the economic side of the woman question but it will solve that alone ... men and women would still be unfaithful to their vows and questions of the intellectual equality of the sexes would still be as much in dispute as they are today ... Bebel's *Woman* is popular because of its quasi-prurient revelations of the past and present degradation of womanhood, but I question if you can find one woman who was led to socialism by it, but you can find hundreds who were repelled from studying socialism by judicious extracts from its pages."

On the third question Connolly wrote:

"The attitude of the party towards religion is another one on which I believe there is a tendency at present to stray from the correct path. Theoretically every S.L.P. man agrees that socialism is a political and economic question and has nothing to do with religion. But how many adhere to that position? The *Weekly People* of late ... and the party are becoming distinctly anti-religious. If a clergyman anywhere attacks socialism the tendency is to hit back, not at his economic absurdities, but at his theology with which we have nothing to do.

"I hold that mine is the correct S.L.P. doctrine," Connolly concluded. "Now will someone please tread on the tail of my coat?"

De Leon replied. With great show of dignity he deplored the "flippancy" of Connolly's last sentence. "We will meet him to the face," he declared. There was more than a touch of petulance in his reply. On all counts he marked Connolly down.

He granted that Marx had shown that an increase of wages did not lead to an automatically nullifying increase in prices. Marx had written: "A general rise in the rates of wages would result in a fall in the general rate of profit but broadly speaking not affect the prices of commodities."

But De Leon developed a lengthy argument which he capped with another quotation from Marx. Marx had posed an important question:

"Having shown that a general rise of wages would result in a fall in the general rate of profit, but not affect the average prices of commodities, or their values, the question ultimately arises how far, in this incessant struggle between capital and labour, the latter is likely to prove successful."

De Leon quoted what purported to be Marx's answer that "despite all the ups and downs, and do what he may, the working man will on the average only receive the value of his labour power. . . ."

If a wage increase resulted in an improved standard of living, then this Marxian principle was abrogated. The Kansas organiser was right. Connolly was wrong. Such was De Leon's triumphant conclusion.

But if De Leon had Marx's *Value, Price and Profit* in front of him when he wrote, he was guilty of a questionable subterfuge. Marx had put up this argument precisely so as to knock it down. His actual words were "I might answer . . . that despite all the ups and downs . . ." But he did not propose so to answer. He had something else to say which he prefaced with a "But". He explained that the value of labour-power differed from the value of other commodities in possessing a historical or social element. It depended on the customary level of consumption among the working people.

The value of labour-power, Marx explained, is not a constant. It is a slowly changing quantity in its own right, as a result of factors which are in the immediate sense non-economic. De Leon had vulgarised Marx. Marx had argued that the economic laws of capitalism all rested on mutable relations between people, however much they were passed off as eternal laws of nature. And the apparent abrogation of the law of value was simply an expression of that fact. De Leon had replaced this with Lassalle's "Iron Law of Wages".

On the question of woman, De Leon accused Connolly of "projecting capitalist conditions into socialism", and declared that the "monogamous family owes its origin to property". Connolly's notion that the economic aspect alone would be solved by socialism he thought unscientific. It denied the "controlling influence of material conditions upon any and all social institutions". There would therefore be no such thing as jealousy or unrequited love under socialism.

Connolly was on familiar ground in this controversy. Ten years previously in Edinburgh he had heard and criticised Edith Lanchester and other Bohemian socialists who advocated "free love" in its various forms. He had followed the controversies in *Justice* in which Eleanor Marx and Belfort Bax had taken part. He had long ago read Lewis Morgan, who argued that the monogamous family was "capable of still further improvement until the equality of the sexes is obtained", and probably he had read Unterman's translation of Engels's *Origin of the Family*, published in Chicago in 1902, in which Engels took a similar view.

Religion was the most delicate question. Here De Leon claimed that the freethinker Vandervelde was simply stating facts in saying that the Belgian Catholic Church had converted itself into a political machine. But that did not mean that the S.L.P. accepted Vandervelde's reactionary political views. As for the argument that when priests attacked socialism only the economic fallacies and not the theology should be attacked, De Leon claimed that he was working on precisely that principle. When a Cardinal had said socialism was un-American, he had replied that the Cardinal had taken an oath to the Pope who was also non-American.

It seems likely that De Leon did not understand Connolly's position on religion. Connolly had been for many years working out a *modus vivendi* between scientific socialism, without which the working class could never become the victors, and Christian beliefs, for the sake of which many Catholics would forego all earthly benefits. He was anxious to remove from Catholics' minds a deadening conflict between interests in this world and hopes of the hereafter. Connolly likened scientific socialism to such a science as mathematics. It did not require the hypothesis of a God only because it was exclusively concerned with material things. As mathematics was *numerical*, socialism was *human*, and was limited to establishing certain relations between men, irrespective of religious belief. Connolly had already written so much in the *Workers' Republic* and had polemised with the Dublin clergy along such lines.

Connolly's starting point was doubtless the Erfurt programme of 1891, which was issued during his membership of the S.S.F. in Edinburgh. This declared that "religion is a private matter". He was less likely to have known of Engels' criticism of this formulation, contained in a document suppressed by Kautsky, though it was published in German in 1901. Engels complained of the substitution of a declaration that religion was a private matter among Social-Democrats and for their party, for a political demand that governments must declare religion a private matter in relation to the State. Engels did not, however, make much of this issue. Lenin, writing in 1905, offered a strong defence of Engels' formulation on the grounds that since scientific socialism was materialist (in the philosophical sense of regarding mind as one of the properties of matter, thus deriving ideas from things and not things from ideas), a party founded upon it "must necessarily explain the actual historical and economic roots of religion". But, he added: "We must not allow the forces waging a genuinely revolutionary economic and political struggle to be broken up for the sake of opinions and dreams of third-rate importance."

Connolly's political position thus coincided with that of the Erfurt programme. There is much uncertainty as to his private opinions on the subject of religion. But the sum of the evidence seems to be that Connolly meant just what he wrote. "We cannot undertake to correct all errors because we are not the possessors of all knowledge." He therefore refused to allow the religious issue to disrupt the movement and cultivated his political garden as the needs of the day required. His capacity for keeping his thoughts to himself has deprived posterity of clearer proof than this. Not once does he express a political idea which originates in religious teaching, nor does he offer political comment on religious questions.

Needless to say, the S.L.P. would have no talk of compromise. A lively discussion followed De Leon's reply. One correspondent congratulated De Leon on delivering the knock-out blow. Patrick Twomey declared that it was absurd to think that the seller of labour-power could in the end secure more than its "market value" [*sic*]. The same man failed to see how reading Bebel would lead to the practice of plural marriages. Finally, he argued, "We certainly deny theology and should not be mealy-mouthed in so stating. We must fight organised Church fakirdom." Here spoke the ex-Catholic, more anti-Christian than the devil, the Irishman who had broken away from all past connections and swung to the opposite pole. Another writer, Jelks, declared most emphatically: "We do attack theology," and Metzler added this advice on leading Christians to socialism:

"If you meet a fellow who thinks he cannot agree with you because of his religion, show that in spite of his imagination he has no religion to hang on to because capitalism has destroyed religion as well as the family. It has made a business out of religion as well as of matrimony. Show him that his religion does not uplift him as a man, as it ought to, but degrades him to a beast of burden."

Zolot of Peekskill attacked Connolly's "new-fangled theory of surplus value" and reasserted the "principle" that "a nominal rise in wages was followed by a nominal rise in prices". The price of labour-power could *never* rise above its value. As for the future of Woman, nothing could be known about it and therefore Connolly was wasting time discussing it. The S.L.P. was not too harsh but too lenient with priests who slandered the movement. Only in one respect did he agree with Connolly, and that was to reject the bourgeois freethinkers as well, for Vandervelde had a "Kangaroo mind".

The controversy raged at this level throughout May and June. One correspondent proposed that men who took money in respect of life after death should be imprisoned for false pretences, and that "love should be free". Then came proposals to make a disciplinary matter of the conflict of opinion. Passono, secretary of Troy Branch, wrote that if Connolly was guilty of attacking the party, he should be punished. He invited De Leon to submit his suggestions to the branch. De Leon informed them that he would not send out documents "without notorial seal" but that the National Convention was being held in six weeks' time and he hoped Connolly "would manage to be present". He would have the right to reply. The Lawrence Branch were smitten with a sudden compunction. They held a discussion on the controversy on May 29 and decided to protest against the matter being debated at the Convention.

> "If these debates take place," they wrote, "they will be circulated among the wage-slaves in order to make them more prejudiced against us. Comrades, be cunning and cute as the capitalists are. Don't bother yourselves with wages, marriage and the church!"

Oblivious of the Gilbertian situation that was developing, De Leon delivered an address in the New Auditorium in Newark. There he announced that "the union's claims for political triumph are false; driven from defeat to defeat the union can gather for the next defeat only". His solution was that workers should abandon the A.F.L. and join the S.T.L.A. which aimed at abolishing the wages system. On marriage and the church he was mercifully silent.

Meanwhile it was becoming clear to Connolly that De Leon's assurance of the right of reply at the conference was unaccompanied by any right to reply in the *Weekly People*. He therefore explained his position in a lucid article in the Edinburgh *Socialist*. The same issue contained his poem "Freedom's Sun". Here he made it clear that his opposition was directed against the tendency of socialists to make any cranky or unconventional ideas free of their platforms. Bebel and Bax had sought to identify socialism with hostility to monogamic marriage. He then quoted De Leon's own past utterances for his discomfort. When a Catholic assassinated President McKinley, De Leon had resisted anti-Catholic agitation on the grounds that the assassin's religion was irrelevant. Of sex, De Leon had said: "Socialism has nothing to do with it." And on the question of wages, De Leon had said: "The theory that increased wages means increased prices, and that therefore an increase of wages is a barren victory, is frequently advanced by half-baked Marxists."

At the National Convention on July 2, at the Grand Central Palace, forty-five delegates assembled. Passono's credentials were accepted and he gave the views of Troy Branch. But his fellow-delegate Boland was seated only after a struggle. The Irish section in Troy had supported Connolly. Connolly's right of reply was only conceded on the insistence of Gilchrist, and a resolution was passed endorsing the action of the "National Editor".

After the "Connolly matter", as it was termed, was laid to rest, Patrick Twomey proceeded to fresh triumphs of dogmatism. He agreed that the "duty of the hour" was to "build the alliance plus the party" but he wondered what attitude should be taken towards those who in order to live were compelled to join "pure and simple" trade unions? In view of the danger of victimisation, would it not be best to refuse picket duty? Another correspondent, Rever, had no doubts as to the answer. S.L.P. men, he declared, must refuse all office in "pure and simple" trade unions. "Indeed," he concluded, "we must do our duty even if we were to be swept out of existence." It is only necessary to add that they did, and in time they were.

Connolly had addressed the Troy Branch on "Revolts of the Poor" in May, and continued to be active. He was now concerned to bring his family over. The price war between the White Star and Cunard companies had reduced the cost of passages to a fraction of its previous level, and Connolly seized the opportunity to send tickets to Dublin. One Saturday afternoon he travelled to New York City so as to meet them on the Sunday. Walking aimlessly through the city he was surprised to meet Jack Mullery, the tailor, who had emigrated since Connolly left Dublin. He was working in New York, but had not made contact because they were still not on speaking terms. The quarrel was forgotten in the surprise of the encounter, and Mullery found Connolly accommodation for the night.

He stayed there much longer than he expected. One boat after another he met with rising anxiety. Finally he was summoned to Ellis Island to claim his wife and children, six children as he expected. There were only five. The eldest was missing. Tearfully Lillie explained what had happened on the very day they were due to leave. Mona, then thirteen years old, had gone to look after an aunt's house, to enable the aunt to help Lillie with her packing. Lifting a pot from the fire with the aid of her apron she set her clothes ablaze and ran out of the house screaming. Neighbours assisted, but she was so badly burned that she died in hospital next day. The family had given up its house, but was taken in by the Wilsons. The doctor advised Mrs. Connolly against delaying in Dublin. Her brother changed the tickets, and a week later the family sailed from Liverpool. De Leon, on a lecture tour in Scotland, was told of the incident by Geddes and was extremely upset, perhaps not without a twinge of remorse. Certainly relations between him and Connolly appeared to improve. Sleeping dogs were let lie. During the winter of

1904–5 Connolly was invited several times to lecture in New York. He spoke on February 12 at Clark's Hall, Northwest Corner, on "Everyday Illustrations of Socialist Teaching", on March 12 on "Labour Laws and Trade Unionism", and on March 18 on "The Unfulfilled Mission of Trade Unionism".

The family had reached America in August, four girls and the baby boy: Nora now the oldest, a bright imaginative child who astonished her teachers by her forwardness, Aideen with more of her mother's placidity, little Ina, chubby, angelic and kittenish, very much her father's girl, Maire, and Ruaidhre only a toddler. The house which Connolly had secured for them at Troy was at 76, Ingalls Avenue, only a stone's throw from where the Humes family lived. It delighted them with its many rooms and garden with fruit trees. But scarcely had they settled in when Connolly's appointment with the Metropolitan came to an end.

This was in November and he was reluctant to leave Troy. But at the end of the month prospects seemed no brighter. He wrote to Mullery, somewhat tentatively, suggesting a visit to New York. "I would have more than a chance of a job at the insurance business," he thought, and asked his friend if he could "get me a bed anywhere until I get an exploiter. I will look after the grub part of it myself, but the bed item is one you cannot economise on very well. One must sleep somewhere. . . . Don't be afraid to write if you cannot do it."

Mullery contrived some accommodation in his own lodgings in Greenwich Village, where Connolly stayed for several months. The depression was slowly lifting but work was hard to get. Connolly used to grow desperate thinking over his family in Troy and how to find a few dollars to send them. For a time he secured temporary work as an insurance collector. Scarcely had he done so when Mullery became unemployed. When Mullery was re-established, Connolly was out of work; for scarcely any part of their joint *ménage* in Greenwich Village were both men employed. Jack Lyng had settled in New York. He kept open house but could never forgive Mullery for the stand he took in Dublin, though Connolly had completely ceased to think about it.

His attitude to developments in Ireland best emerges from his correspondence with Mullery:

"Mrs. Connolly informs me that the Socialists of Dublin showed great sympathy for her in her last great trouble. I am thankful to them for that proof of kindliness, and also as a token that old-time relations were not entirely blotted out."

But when six months later an account of the revival of the I.S.R.P. appeared in the *People*, he made it clear that past differences still rankled.

"Now about O'Brien's letter, of course I was glad to hear that the party in Ireland was doing well, although I did not agree with all that Bill said. I certainly thought that they might have told of their good fight to the readers of the *People* without going out of their way to tell how much better a fight they made than we had made before. . . . But all that is hardly worth while disputing about. It is enough that they are doing well. If I was as satisfied that the propaganda is as clean and true to Socialist principles as I in my 'bullying way' strove to keep it in my time, I would be happy even in my banishment in this cursed country. For after all it is to Ireland all my thoughts turn when dreaming of the future. I suppose I will never see it again, except in dreams. But if Ireland and the Socialist cause therein ever find another willing to serve them and fight and suffer for them better or more unselfishly than him they cast out, who is now writing to you, they will be fortunate indeed. As to what O'Brien said about me going back, I do not know how the idea got about. Certainly I never wrote or expressed such ideas to anybody. I have spoken more freely to you than to anybody else about the matter, and you know that I always regarded such a thing as being outside the pale of possibilities. Handicapped as I am with a large family it is not an easy thing to move about the world. And at any rate I regard Ireland, or at least the Socialist part of Ireland which is all I care for, as having thrown me out, and I do not wish to return like a dog to his vomit."

While resentful of his treatment in Dublin, Connolly did not brood over it. He set about learning Italian. There were groups of Italian socialists in Troy, and many more in New York. He thought their problems resembled those of the Irish, and he had Mullery busy with the key while he answered questions of grammar. He could seldom get home to Troy. At the weekends he would walk to the ferry with Mullery or the Lyngs. The two men frequented the cheapest restaurants where a meal could be had for ten cents. Connolly invented names for them; one was the Waldorf, another the Netherlands; a third was the "coffee without onions"—so-called from the cup of coffee which appeared with fried onions in the cup. Next time Connolly asked the waiter for "coffee without onions" and shook his sides laughing when the waiter bawled it down the hatch in so many words. Mathieson sent the Tynans and Beatties to see them. They missed a meal that day when their visitors ordered a huge dinner, intending to pay for the whole company, and did not understand why Connolly and Mullery ordered only a cup of coffee.

Early in April Connolly returned to Troy where there was an opening as agent for a Sick and Accident Benefit Society. But his previous employers (the Hancock Company of New York) placed against him a deficit on account of business which they alleged did not pay. Lacking reserves, he wrote to Mullery asking the loan of the necessary four or five dollars. Mullery immediately went to the Hancock Company's office and paid the account. But for some reason he failed to inform Connolly of this. He, in turn, knowing that Mullery had only one half-hour's lunch break, did not think the account was paid, and failed to pursue the agency. He remained unemployed till May, when the Eastern Manager of the Pacific Mutual Life Insurance Company wanted a representative in Troy.

"I am as deep in the mud as ever," Connolly wrote regarding this appointment, "although to judge by this paper on which I am writing it would seem to you that I have landed a soft place. But this job is only a commission job, and although in a year *if I can hold it so long* it will be one of the best jobs in the country, yet at present I cannot earn bread and butter. I have the right to employ agents and have a big enough margin of profit left to pay them more than they would get from most companies, but as the company is new to this district agents are hard to get. In a while, when the company gets better known, I will be on the warm side of the fence. At present I am taking side-leaps with the hunger, although to get on this job I had to represent myself as worth 3,000 dollars and get a bond for 2,000 dollars from the National Surety Company. I was playing the American capitalists at their own bunco game, and succeeded so far."

His optimism was belied by the outbreak of the local industrial struggle which cost him his new job. In the preceding August the Cluett-Peabody collar trust had introduced new starching machines which, since they were claimed to double output, were made the excuse for a series of dismissals. The machines did not come up to expectation, and the employees, whose piece rates had been halved, were subjected to severe speed-up, then sweeping American industry. Conditions of work were worsened in all other factories whose owners belonged to the Employers' Association. The threat of unemployment was used to introduce a new system of fines for spoiled work, and talking on the job was dealt with by instant dismissal. One girl was dismissed for sneezing.

Throughout the winter, organisation with the A.F.L. Starchers' Union proceeded steadily. Talks were begun with the employers just as Connolly was entering his office in the Fulton Buildings. The workers demanded the restoration of the eight-hour day, modification of the fines system and an end to petty tyranny. The talks broke down on May 11 and on May 14 the nine Association factories were closed. The strike was bitterly fought and lasted fourteen weeks. The employees were almost entirely young girls. The Churches, Catholic and Protestant, equally denounced them. The Chamber of Commerce cried woe for the trade of the town. Many families, in this year of trade depression only slowly lifting, were dependent on young wage-earners. It was the worst time to try to introduce a new insurance company. Connolly had not even the heart to press for contributions from the subscribers he had. Instead he collected money for the strike fund. But this was no use to the Pacific Insurance Company. The blank book told its own story. Connolly decided to go.

To seek another appointment in strike-paralysed Troy was hopeless. The town was small and he had become notorious as a socialist agitator. He therefore decided to try and settle in New York City and wrote on this subject to Mullery on July 31. He applied for the post of Connecticut State organiser of the S.L.P. but was turned down. The more promising prospect of becoming Pennsylvania organiser, at Gilchrist's instance, also failed. In any case these appointments were only for a matter of weeks. He found an appointment at Paterson, New Jersey, for a short spell. He tried his luck as a tiler. The American method of job-hunting was now becoming clearer to him. At Newark he represented himself as an engineer (machinist in American parlance) and "told a fairy tale about the places I had learned my trade in, and the places in this country I had worked in".

"It is a great joke to be passing myself off as an engineer," Connolly wrote, "but I am doing the trick all right. Of course I have to study at night on the theoretical part of the work, and having a fairly good knowledge of geometry it helps me in drawing the designs, and I think I will pull it off. Since then I have been offered another job in Singers Sewing Machine shop, but have declined it for the present."

Connolly's difficulty in this period of speed-up was his extreme short sight. He had to bring the blueprint close to his eyes in order to read it, and at that time in the U.S. employers did not look favourably on men who wore spectacles.

Nevertheless he held the job until after a while he yielded to the suggestion of Magnette, an S.L.P. man who was a foreman in Singers, to transfer to the Elizabeth factory.

He had made Newark his temporary abode while working in New Jersey. It was convenient to stay there. Half-way between Elizabeth and New York, it was a dormitory town with a character of its own, centre of Essex County whose history went back to 1666. At one time it had a university. It was a centre of many industries rather than great factories, cosmopolitan, and a port. It was quiet enough to make residence pleasant, but busy enough and near enough to New York to be free from the provincialism of Troy where "if a man was hard up everybody knew it". The family moved temporarily to New York to stay with the Lyngs; but by autumn he found them a house in Newark.

THE INDUSTRIAL WORKERS OF THE WORLD

Follow your path, and let people talk.

DANTE

While Connolly was job-hunting in New York and New Jersey, Chicago was the scene of one of the most historic congresses of the American labour movement. The foundation of the Industrial Workers of the World seemed to transform the situation.

It grew out of Debs's American Labour Union under the stimulus of the Colorado miners' strike. Under the leadership of W. D. Haywood, the Western Federation of Miners had struggled for nearly a year under conditions bordering on civil war. They had defended themselves gun in hand against the mineowners' private armies of Pinkerton thugs and professional hoodlums. They had come to accept revolutionism as a matter of course. Their great strength was the union of all trades in one organisation; they were defeated only when the agents of the American Federation of Labour were able to disunite them. Their experience strongly influenced the Labour Union, to which the miners were affiliated.

Debs and Haywood interested Trautman, an editor in the service of the Brewers' Union, and together they called a preliminary meeting at Chicago to discuss the establishment of a new trade union centre which would displace the A.F.L. and give the entire American working class the benefits of industrial organisation.

De Leon was kept informed. He hesitated at first to join with the "Kangaroo" Debs. While he cogitated the difficult tactical question, he permitted Bohn, national secretary of the S.L.P., to attend the meeting as he passed through Chicago from his mid-western home town. Around the turn of the year the call was issued for a National Convention to be held in Chicago on June 27, and along with the names of Haywood, Moyer, Trautmann, Haggerty, Unterman and Mother Jones, appeared that of Frank Bohn.

Having put his foot in the door, De Leon had to decide whether to enter bodily or not. He opened the columns of the *People* for a discussion on the issue. To go in would be to merge the S.T.L.A. with an organisation which might come to be dominated by the Socialist Party. By remaining outside he might permit the establishment of a rival to the S.T.L.A. which would eventually swallow it up. The first risk seemed less than the second. He could not afford to stand aloof.

Hillquit, Spargo and the right-wing of the Socialist Party made clear their opposition to the new venture. They clearly recognised De Leon's illegitimate brain-child, and noted the series of lectures during the spring of 1905 in which he expounded his theory of the transition to socialism. This was in essence that a majority must vote for the S.L.P. but that industrially organised trade unions must act as the power to enforce its will. He thought the presence of industrial unions in the background would ensure the "unconditional surrender" of the capitalist class.

> "The might of the revolutionary ballot consists in the thorough industrial organisation of the productive workers organised in such a way that when that ballot is cast the capitalist class may know that behind it is the might to enforce it."

The prominent S.L.P. man Justus Ebert welcomed the preparations for the convention at Chicago, and in a lecture on the history of American trade unionism from 1742 to 1905 expressed the view that craft unionism was the "bulwark of capitalism", while industrial unionism was the "framework of socialism".

It was possible to pass from these views to a purely Bakuninist conception of revolution, in which the workers seized the factories, land and mines and worked them co-operatively, the State being ignored altogether. But any tendency to make such a transition was hotly combated by De Leon, who was therefore in a somewhat illogical position. He regarded the State as identical with the legislative assembly. He regarded the securing of a parliamentary majority as identical with conquering State power. His reply to those who asked what the workers would do if the capitalists refused to hand over control of industry was that the workers, through their industrial unions, would take it themselves. He had then to explain why it was necessary to go through the solemn mummery of ballot and parliament. Why not simply start the industrial organisation and seize the factories as soon as they were strong enough to do so?

Confusion on the subject of the State was typical of these years. For this in part the Erfurt programme was to blame. In fear of the re-enactment of the anti-socialist laws, the German socialists had formulated their conception of political power too loosely. They had omitted the essential in the Marxian teaching on the State, namely its coercive character, as an organisation for applying sanctions. Consequently while opportunism could sleep secure in a simple faith in parliament, revolutionism was deprived of its focal point.

The delegates at the Convention were not theoretical men. They heard De Leon say the working class should take power. The provisory minutiae with which he hedged his argument did not impress them. A middle-aged professor must be allowed his foibles. And if such things were important, was it not best to leave them to those who understood them? The men from the east took him for gospel, the men from the west took him for granted. But unfortunately neither of these things can be done with impunity. It requires some theory even to boil an egg. Those who reject theory do no more than draw on the junk-pile of ideas and experiences which fill the back of every man's mind, and what is all this but bits of theory, some right, some wrong, often contradictory? The choice, then, was De Leonism or confusion.

The Convention was an unqualified success. Enthusiasm abounded. At last it seemed that the unskilled and the disfranchised were finding a way to their own. The bright promise reflected itself in the reporting of delegates. Everywhere branches of the I.W.W. were set up as the message of industrial unionism caught the imagination, stimulated to vigorous action and generated intense class-consciousness.

The S.L.P. called a meeting in New York with Connolly in the chair and De Leon as the main speaker. Though little over fifty years of age, De Leon affected a stoop and slow gait suitable to a man twenty years older. He entered at the back of the hall and moved slowly up the side aisle towards the platform. When he had traversed two thirds of the distance an admirer noticed him. "De Leon!" he shouted, and for the remainder of the great man's transit to his place in the sun the hall rocked with cheers and applause. Connolly's voice was drowned, and experienced speaker though he was, he felt nonplussed and angry. He believed that De Leon had deliberately staged the scene as a personal affront. The ill-feeling between the two men began to reawaken.

S.T.L.A. locals began to fuse and affiliate with the I.W.W. A meeting was held in Newark, also addressed by De Leon, and there he expressed the hope that the "General Executive Board of the I.W.W. will be the central administration of the nation". In the weeks that followed Connolly threw himself into the work of open-air propaganda with the help of Patrick Quinlan, a Tipperaryman of flamboyant self-confidence and the possessor of a "brass neck". He had met Connolly at the closing meeting of the 1902 tour and bestowed on him the admiration he could spare from himself. But he was a hard worker and good street orator. The two men made the I.W.W. known in Newark.

Musicians, engineers, workers of all nationalities, organised in the I.W.W. locals. A United Labour Council of Newark and vicinity was set up. Working together in the new organisation, S.L.P. and S.P.A. members began to lose their mutual hostility, and shortly after De Leon's visit the New Jersey sections of the two parties agreed to a conference to discuss amalgamation. Essex County S.L.P. chose Quinlan as delegate and the conference held a number of meetings early in 1906. The New Jersey unity conference was not alone, but attracted far more attention than those held in California and New England. Questions which agitated contemporary European socialists were not even touched upon. The State, dictatorship of the proletariat, colonialism, militarism and war were regarded as extraneous to American conditions. Dominating all the delegates was the supreme issue of trade union organisation. The S.L.P. wished to make support for industrial unionism exclusive and obligatory in accordance with its views that in this way was to be created the framework of socialism, within the shell of capitalism. The Socialist Party, on the other hand wished to leave the A.F.L. in possession of the 20 per cent of the American workers they had organised, while urging the remaining 80 per cent into the I.W.W. The agreement reached was near to the S.L.P. position, and it was not therefore surprising that a referendum of the S.P.A. rejected it.

Connolly was an enthusiastic supporter of unity. He believed that the establishment of the I.W.W., by opening the road to industrial unity, automatically wiped out the need for two separate socialist parties. He thought it likely that the I.W.W. would establish its own political party with which the others would merge. He attended the State Convention at Paterson on behalf of Essex County and strongly urged this point of view. But the failure of the unity talks temporarily halted progress in this direction.

Meanwhile an event took place in the west which rallied the supporters of unity. The leaders of the Western Federation of Miners, Haywood, Moyer and Pettibone, were arrested at Denver at the request of the Idaho State authorities. Denied an opportunity to consult their legal advisers, they were deported from Colorado in defiance of the laws of the State and lodged in Boise jail. The charge was complicity in the murder of Governor Studenberg, who had lost his life as a result of a cattle feud on December 30. A member of the W.F.M., who subsequently proved to be a Pinkerton agent, was arrested a few days afterwards and obligingly implicated the union leaders. The kidnapping took place on February 17. The local newspapers boasted that the trade unionists would never see Colorado again. Their brazen announcement of impending legal murder shook the entire working-class movement. Sherman and Trautman called for a campaign of protest which proved one of the hardest fought in history.

Haywood was not released until the end of July 1907, and Moyer was in jail till early 1908. The absence of Haywood was a serious hinderance to the I.W.W., since he was acceptable to both S.P.A. and S.L.P. factions.

A strong resolution of protest was passed at the New Jersey convention, where Connolly's gifts as publicist were recognised by his appointment to the press and literature committee. He and Quinlan were responsible for organising the Newark Haywood-Moyer defence committee, of which Quinlan became secretary. The protest movement rapidly gained ground. Kurz's coliseum was crammed when De Leon came to speak on April 3. Once again Connolly took the chair. The gathering was cosmopolitan. Over two-thirds of the Newark population were foreign-born, the largest minorities being the 50,000 Italians, the 40,000 Germans and the 30,000 Irish. Lott spoke in German, Arturo Caroti in Italian. The Brewery workers marched to the hall in a body led by their fife and drum band. As a result the Newark Workingmen's Defence Committee was established and a series of indoor and outdoor meetings was held under its auspices throughout the year.

It was at one of these meetings that Connolly first met Elizabeth Gurley Flynn, the schoolgirl of seventeen whose severely simple dress contrasted so strangely with the forceful and sparkling oratory which could spellbind audiences composed of people of three times her age. On this occasion they spoke from a wagon in Washington Park. Somebody spilled a glass of water in Connolly's hat. "I hope it won't shrink," he grimaced. "It's the only hat I have." She recalled him in her memoirs as a "short, rather stout plain man, with a big moustache and dark sad eyes, who rarely smiled".

In Newark was a branch of the Italian Socialist Federation of which Caroti was a leading member. This organisation had been represented at the Chicago convention by Tresca, and published a periodical called *Il Proletario* from its headquarters in Philadelphia. It had branches in most eastern cities, including Troy, but had recruited but a small fraction of the Italians in the U.S.A.

The reason for its failure was its incredible sectishness. Local reports in *Il Proletario* consisted not of accounts of activities but of diatribes and debating points against religion. Meetings were held on Sunday mornings so as to clash with Mass. *Il Proletario* published contemptuous articles to mark each feast of the Christian calendar and decorated its pages with such delicacies as a poetic "Hymn to Satan", and banner headlines declaiming that "God does not exist". Non-existent God received far more attention than existent capitalism. But the Italian priests seem to have treated these militant atheists with good-natured tolerance, one of them even urging in a debate at Milford, Mass. that "after all, the International itself had said that religion was a private matter".

Apart from anti-clericalism the Federation was immersed in Italian affairs. Feuds, arising from a sense of aimlessness, were perpetual. It was the I.W.W. which first began to introduce a practical note into its affairs. As early as September 1905, Caroti spoke in favour of working-class unity. A conference was then held in Newark to unite the New Jersey sections into a State organisation. The result was an influx of young Italians who followed closely the reports of the Unity Conference which appeared week by week in *Il Proletario*.

Connolly was in the midst of this activity. He believed the Italians could be won for the S.L.P. He translated important articles from *Il Proletario* and published them in the *Weekly People* with prefaces of his own.

Italians were strongly represented at the "meeting of socialists of all nationalities" held by the Newark I.W.W. in March 1906. Under Connolly's influence they began to hold more public meetings. Their increased activity began to arouse the attention of the City Police who, seeing a red flag displayed from the window of their premises on March 18 when they commemorated the Paris Commune, took it upon themselves to enter and remove it. On May 1 the police confiscated a red flag from their procession. But this time the Italians appealed to the American socialists.

Connolly drew up a memorial to the Mayor. He protested against the unconstitutional action of the police and announced an open-air indignation meeting for June 23, at the corner of 7th Avenue and Cutler Street. Miccoli took the chair, speaking in Italian. Connolly then addressed the crowd in English. Police gathered round with drawn truncheons. But something new was happening. Italian and American had united. After another Italian, Di Fronso, had spoken, another "American", Kembal, took the rostrum. The red flag flew unharmed. The result created a tremendous impression on the Italians who had hitherto regarded themselves as a powerless minority who must suffer not without protest, but without redress.

Bertelli became editor of *Il Proletario* in June. He had been strongly influenced by Connolly's arguments, and introduced into his paper a new practical note. Not that the strident anti-clericalism was at once muted. But alongside it went a realistic examination of the problems of Italians in America. At the end of July he threw down the gauntlet in an editorial entitled "Our organisation", which demanded a complete reorientation. He asked why, of the 650,000 Italians in New York, only 200 belonged to the Socialist Federation. Of 140,000 in Philadelphia there were only 100 members. Could not the reason be exclusive absorption in Italian affairs and the failure to realise they had a part to play in America? Italy was too far away for them to influence. They were allowing others to influence their countrymen in America. The Italians, he declared, could only affect the American situation by combining with other nationalities.

He drew the conclusion that the Italians in the U.S.A. must become politically speaking "as much American as Italian". They must abandon the exclusive preoccupation with Italian affairs, seek affiliation to the S.L.P., take up the defence of immigrants' immediate interests, break down the anti-clerical prejudice which cut them off from their compatriots who were not socialists, and seek to unite all Italians within the I.W.W.

Connolly believed that this change of front was largely due to his translation and preface. He wrote to the *People* urging that the new mood of the Italians should receive every encouragement. He hoped for some welcoming gesture, especially as there were "Italian Kangaroos" trying to undermine Bertelli's position. But none was forthcoming. Bertelli's proposals were discussed at the Boston Conference of the Federation, which took place in November. Though Connolly himself addressed many Italian meetings throughout the summer and autumn, more was required. The conference endorsed the I.W.W. but decided to defer the question of party affiliation for two years in the hope that in this period the two socialist parties would agree to amalgamate.

Connolly's prestige among New Jersey socialists soared. It rose even higher when he undertook the work of organising the Singer factory in Elizabeth. This huge establishment employed eight thousand workers, or "wage-slaves" as it was the fashion of socialists to call them in those days. Early in November S.L.P. organiser Bernine visited New Jersey. He was invited to speak at the gates of Singers. The first meeting was attended only sparsely. But on the second day the word had spread. Workers bolted their lunch and came out to listen. A literature stall was set up and an appeal was made for fifty men to picket the gate for trade unionism and the S.L.P.

As a result of his participation in this work, Connolly became a marked man in the factory. In the following months his foreman was under continuous pressure to dismiss him, and finally Connolly resigned rather than jeopardise his colleague's appointment.

New Jersey S.L.P. decided to send Connolly as their delegate to the twice-yearly National Executive Committee which met in New York on January 5, 1907. This meeting marked the zenith of Connolly's status in the S.L.P. Immediately afterwards De Leon resumed his vendetta with sudden fury. The occasion was a seemingly innocent resolution proposed by Connolly at this meeting.

The S.L.P. practice was to elect an E.C. on a delegate basis, and for this body to depute its functions to a sub-committee consisting of members living in or around New York City. There had been disagreements over the jurisdiction of this sub-committee. One opinion was that it should have the full powers possessed by the N.E.C. Another was that its function was purely co-ordinative, that it must not concern itself with policy.

The January 1907 meeting had before it a communication from De Leon, which was in effect a protest to the N.E.C. against action taken by the sub-committee.

A request for financial assistance had come from the Transvaal Independent Labour Party. The sub-committee had rejected it. De Leon agreed with their rejection. But his complaint was that the sub-committee's reply had been published in the *People* during his absence from New York. His assistant, Ebert, in other words, was acting as if he was responsible to the sub-committee.

Connolly proposed a resolution that the "N.E.C. and its sub-committee" had the right of unconditional access to the columns of the *People*. The wording of this resolution was unfortunate, for the right of the full committee was not being challenged. Connolly proposed his resolution with the object of making the powers of the two committees identical. Acceptance meant guaranteeing the rights of both; but rejection meant extinguishing them together. After being elected himself to the sub-committee, he returned to New Jersey and made his report to the State Committee on February 22. He explained quite calmly that his resolution had been defeated and that from now on the N.E.C. claimed no right of access to the party press. A number of delegates expressed disapproval. But the intensity of the storm that followed can only be understood in relation to other events.

On February 1 the *Daily People* carried the report of a meeting of Irishmen in New York City where it was decided to "form a socialist organisation of men and women of Irish race and extraction". Its purposes were:

1. To develop the spirit of revolutionary class-consciousness among the Irish working class of America.
2. To spread a knowledge of and help to sustain the socialist movement in Ireland.
3. To educate the members upon the history and development of the class struggle in Ireland.

Broadly speaking the conception was that put forward by Bertelli for the Italians.

During Connolly's early days in Newark a group of Irishmen had gathered together in New York under the initiative of the old Fenian, M. D. Fitzgerald, who was settled in the U.S.A. since 1873. They took part in election campaigns under the title of the "Irish Volunteers". Never numerous, they were organised simply to disprove the frequently published statements that no Irishmen were socialists. Quinlan, who was always in and out of town, became interested. After the election campaign was over the Volunteers contented themselves with social activities, and Connolly attended one of their dinners. His experience with the Italians led him to suggest the establishment of an Irish body similar to the Italian Socialist Federation, and he suggested the change of name in order to make this clear. Connolly's advice was not based on Irish national sentiment but on his estimate of the needs of a socialist movement growing in a cosmopolitan environment.

The inaugural meeting was announced for the first week in March. The acting secretary was Jack Lyng, 113, West 60th Street, and the committee included two other former members of the Dublin I.S.R.P., James Connolly and John Mullery, together with Elizabeth Gurley Flynn and Patrick Quinlan. The Committee met at the house of Elizabeth's father, Thomas Flynn, at 795, East 139th Street.

The first ball was fired by the faithful De Leonist Stromqvist from Arizona, who wrote a withering attack on race federations, though these had already been accepted within the S.L.P. The next step, said he, would be to organise all the socialists from one district or with one dialect into a federation apiece. Irish people spoke English. What reason was there for separating them from other English-speakers? What with the Hungarians and Swedes, he concluded, soon the only race without a federation would be the Red Indians. It was typical that a reference to national rights for the aborigines was regarded as a *reduction ad absurdum*. His final shaft was directed against the link with Ireland. "If we cannot educate them without splitting them up then I would sooner see them left to get their own education," said this practical man.

Connolly replied on February 19. He was opposed to dividing the *party* on racial or linguistic grounds. But he thought broader organisations would serve to link a heterogeneous population with its necessarily American leadership. A German federation was a crying need. It would eliminate much friction between German and American socialists. An Irish federation was specially necessary since Irish politics were obtruded into the U.S.A. by bourgeois organisations established for the express purpose of assisting capitalist parties in Ireland, to do which they must spread their ideas. "We propose to fight these tricksters," said Connolly. The link with the socialists in Ireland would give the federation standing with the Irish in America.

Quinlan sprang to Connolly's support. Why should the Hungarians and Swedes be allowed race federations within the S.L.P. and the Irish not? No ruling class in the English-speaking world had opposed socialism with such fury as the Irish. Why were the emigrants to be forbidden to express solidarity and support? In the course of the next few weeks the controversy raged. Few indeed were the letters published in Connolly's favour. The average level of understanding may be judged from the contribution of Kopald. All the trouble arose, he thought, from the original sin of "politics". The long intervals between elections left socialists with nothing to do but "drink tea with their compatriots". This limitation of "politics" to electioneering was characteristic of the S.L.P. and identical with the position of the opportunistic Labour parties De Leon so fervently denounced.

It was in the midst of this controversy that the N.E.C. resolution became the focus of the struggle between Connolly and De Leon. A group of New Jersey State Committee members wrote asking De Leon to confirm or deny that the N.E.C. had relinquished its right of access to the *People*. This query should have been addressed to the secretary, who had the minutes. But De Leon, who was suspected to have prompted the enquiry, told Zimmerman, Kerrschaft, Hossock and Katz that Connolly's report was entirely wrong. In four of the *People*'s gigantic columns he explained that the right of publication of the N.E.C. had never been questioned and that the resolution (which Connolly had proposed) could not possibly bear the interpretation he placed upon it. He added much to reduce the prestige of the sub-committee. He had taken alarm at its tendency to interfere in the business and mechanical departments of the *People* and he feared such interference from those without sufficient knowledge of law to avoid possible libel actions. For himself, he was prepared to vacate office at any time but only at the behest of the full N.E.C.

De Leon's position had not been even remotely called in question. Why did he threaten resignation? Connolly's supporters believed he had an agreement with the *People* by which he received a salary far beyond the capacity of the paper to pay. The monthly deficit was credited to De Leon's account. Resignation would mean cessation of publication. De Leon was accused of whipping the staff into line. "Holding the party to ransom," Connolly commented.

The members of the N.E.C. were circularised for their recollection of the meeting. Most of them believed that they had merely rejected a motion extending the right of publication to the "N.E.C. sub-committee". Connolly stoutly maintained that his resolution meant what it said. It said "N.E.C. and its sub-committee". But the majority of the members denied any recollection of the words "and its", and since Bohn was out of New York the minutes were not available.

At the sub-committee meeting of March 10 Connolly objected to the New Jersey enquiry being dealt with by the editor rather than the secretary. De Leon ought to have passed it on to Bohn. The editor had circularised the members of the N.E.C. rather than await the return of the secretary; and alone of all the replies received, Connolly's had not been published. He had made it clear that his intention was to delegate to the sub-committee the full rights of the N.E.C. A committee of three was elected to investigate the matter.

Meanwhile, with the help of his daughter Nora, he transcribed thirty copies of his own statement and posted them to the N.E.C. members. His letter (which was now printed in the *People*) stated that he had the original of his motion before him and that the words "and its" were there as large as life. This was now confirmed by Bohn, who disclosed a copy identically worded and in the handwriting of Olpp. De Leon brushed all this aside. Minutes were not minutes until they were passed. What determined the content of the minutes was the recollection of the majority.

The following week the *People* contained a violent attack on Connolly written by Eck, who accused him of opposing De Leon in the same spirit as had prompted his criticisms of Bebel's *Woman*. To make matters worse, he had called De Leon "a Pope". Quinlan, whose interventions did not always improve matters, wrote that at the New Jersey meeting Connolly had used no such expression, but that he had called De Leon a dictator, and added that the action of the N.E.C. reminded him of the passing of the Act of Union. This reference to the most corrupt event in Irish history may have been lost on some, but its general import was plain enough. Bohn, who had been present, testified that Connolly's manner had been moderate and unprovocative and that the complainant Eck had not been present. Other heresies reared their heads. Quinlan returned to criticise the anti-political trend of the S.L.P. and suggested that it should cease interfering with the I.W.W. and concentrate on its own task of socialist propaganda.

On March 29, somewhat later than was intended, the unintimidated Irish founded the Irish Socialist Federation at a meeting at 79, MacDougal Street. Jack Lyng was confirmed as secretary. The Federation was to preach "revolutionary socialism" and publish literature dealing with the class struggle in Ireland. But it was not to affiliate to any political party for the time being. The I.S.F. held both indoor and outdoor meetings throughout the summer. Connolly's pamphlets were reprinted. For the time being the controversy on race and language federations languished.

The committee of three reported on April 14, its decision being that Connolly's complaint should be dismissed. But Connolly was able to secure a postponement of the sub-committee's vote by intimating that a further complaint relevant to the matter was in the post. He alleged that De Leon had exerted private influence on the committee members. Next month the committee of three, unable to confute Connolly, but unwilling to challenge De Leon, recommended referring the dispute to the "Sections Grievances Committee". Connolly opposed this measure and the result was a tied vote of six either way.

A letter from Pennsylvania suggested the sensible course that the N.E.C. deal with the issue of substance, namely the rights of the sub-committee. The membership in that State was in favour of Connolly's conception of full delegation known today as "democratic centralism". Olive Johnson on the other hand, a fanatical admirer of De Leon, wrote from California demanding the removal of the sub-committee for "insubordination and incapacity". Connolly moved that the committee of three draft an answer to Mrs. Johnson and this was done.

Although he had won to his side half the sub-committee, and was selected as one of the principal speakers at the May Day demonstration against "patriotism, anti-immigration, Russian Czarism, American Moyer-Haywood outrages and craft unionism", Connolly realised that his position on the N.E.C. was extremely unsafe. His own State E.C. had in effect repudiated him. He must seek the suffrages of the general membership. He therefore sent in his resignation, which was discussed at the end of May. Instead of merely accepting it and announcing a fresh election, the committee, possibly with a view to the election, decided to humiliate Connolly by calling on the sections to vote on his recall. Meanwhile members of the N.E.C. were being canvassed to declare unconstitutional the vote already taken to accept the Hungarian and Swedish race federations into the S.L.P. A motion came from Ohio demanding Connolly's removal from the sub-committee. But he had decided to continue his attendance until he was forced out.

New Jersey voted. Only the four Plainfield votes were against the acceptance of the resignation. There were 7 votes for accepting it and 24 for recall, of which Passaic contributed 13 and Hoboken 9. But an odd feature of the referendum was that no returns were received from Essex, Elizabeth and North Hudson, that is to say from Connolly's own districts. A new election was announced and Essex nominated Connolly. He agreed to stand. South Hoboken nominated Eck. The half-yearly N.E.C. met in July and expunged the offending "and its" from the minutes. It had now to endorse Connolly's recall, which was quickly done, and await the result of the by-election. The only strong opposition came from Gilchrist of Pennsylvania.

In the election Connolly received 22 votes, Eck 59. But Connolly's vote included no less than 13 out of the 16 cast by Essex and all six from Plainfield. The sub-committee, somewhat inconsistently, chose to regard him as a member until a further resolution was passed. His removal was proposed and carried, the reasons advanced in its favour being his "double-dealing", his "persecution" of members of the New Jersey N.E.C. and subsequent "persecution" of the editor of the *People*. A brief protest against the "falsification" of the minutes, by Duffy of Pennsylvania, was answered in several columns by De Leon. When the regular election to the N.E.C. took place in October, Connolly did not stand. He had decided to resign from the S.L.P.

When Singer's had grown too hot to hold him, he had accepted an appointment as organiser of the Building Section of the New York I.W.W. For a time he travelled daily between Newark and the City, when necessary spending the night with the Lyngs. He was reluctant to uproot his family once more, or to deprive Lillie of the quietness and cleanness of the suburbs and the little garden of which she was so fond. But the accumulation of evening meetings made it impracticable to continue. By the end of the year the family had moved to Elton Avenue, Bronx, where they occupied one of the notorious "fire-trap" tenements a few hundred yards from the Flynns. During 1907 the youngest daughter, Fiona, was born, the only child born in America.

The move to New York brought him to much closer quarters with De Leon, and was the signal for renewed hostilities. For while Connolly had been defending his position in New Jersey a section of the New York membership had expressed strong criticism of De Leon. These included Frank Bohn and Justus Ebert. When Connolly resigned scores of members left with him, and De Leon feared Connolly's arrival might be the signal for a further exodus. The arena was now transferred to the I.W.W.

Nothing was further from Connolly's intentions than to try conclusions with De Leon. He wanted no career in America, where he was lonely and dissatisfied. He was the last man to push himself into the limelight. He signed articles with pseudonyms. On one occasion, when Cody was introducing him from that famous I.S.F. rostrum whose gaspipe legs were used as means of defence in emergencies, he was thoroughly embarrassed by the chairman's succession of sugary compliments. He seized Cody by the shoulders, bodily removed him from the platform, and started to speak himself.

A full knowledge of De Leon's motives must await a definitive biography of the American leader. His critics usually ascribe to him jealousy and the inability to stand the sight of a man of superior abilities in his entourage. These estimates merely reverse the claims of his admirers, who see him as the apostolic successor to Marx, challenged by such pygmies as Connolly, Bohn and Ebert, who aspired to his editorial chair and were thrown into combination by their common frustration.

But the basis of the conflict was certainly political. "We differed on policy," Connolly told his daughter. The eccentricities of De Leon merely distorted the form of the struggle, which originated in the stage through which the American movement was passing. De Leon regarded himself as Marx's successor in America, but had in fact revised Marxism. He had adopted the position of dual unionism. Although he did not fully appreciate it, Connolly's position on wages and prices implicitly challenged this. Second, De Leon was against any accommodation with the Socialist Party. Connolly was openly and increasingly in favour of this. Third, Connolly's conception of a broad national approach to the huge polyglot population of the New York area, aiming at unity in diversity, diversity in unity, an American Party acting as the gathering point, cut across De Leon's conception of a tribeless, nationless socialist *élite*. The issue of religion and morals was of less fundamental importance, but bore directly on the possibility of creating a socialist movement of a genuinely mass character.

De Leon appeared as an opponent of reformism in its European form, but offered only a form of Lassalleanism against American reformism. All sections were reactionary but the proletariat. All tendencies were untouchable but his own. His influence on the I.W.W. had its positive aspects in the early stage. He resisted the efforts made by Sherman to disrupt the organisation. When Sherman and McCabe tried to starve out the visiting delegates by a filibuster, he supported the vote of one-dollar-fifty a day expenses. R. M. Fox is mistaken in identifying him with Sherman's shady manœuvre. When the defeated filibusters seized the union offices and tried to set up a breakaway, his support for Trautman and St. John helped to hold the organisation together. But after Moyer was "got at" in jail, and the western miners decided to disaffiliate, the I.W.W. became an alliance between the S.T.L.A. element around New York and the full-blown syndicalists of the west who, Jourdain-like, were talking Bakunin without knowing it. At the 1907 convention De Leon's polemical skill won the day. Those who wished to exclude all politics were defeated. "Direct action" to "have and hold" all industrial plants made its appeal, neither convincing nor being convinced. The Lassallean formula of distributing to the workers the full product of their labour was adopted instead. At the head of the *Industrial Union Bulletin* ran the streamer "Labour is entitled to all it produces". But De Leon's growing arrogance made many enemies who were still unable to answer him. He may have feared that these would make use of Connolly to oust him.

Connolly threw himself enthusiastically into his work as an I.W.W. organiser, revealing aptitudes which surprised even his friends. For the first time—and he was nearly forty—he could devote his main energies to work he believed in. He was secretary of the "Building and Constructional Workers Industrial Union". But the I.W.W. was flexible in matters of demarcation. Soon he was also organising tramwaymen, moulders, garment workers, milkmen and dockers. He made great use of outdoor propaganda, especially on the waterfront among the Irish of Brooklyn and the Germans of Hoboken. As New York Correspondent of the *Industrial Union Bulletin*, he became nationally known.

Such spare time as was left to him he spent with the Irish. In Mott Haven he was less isolated than in Newark. As well as the Flynns, who kept open house, there were the two families of Glasgow socialists who had arrived. Though Mullery had returned to Dublin, John Lyng remained and Quinlan was always turning up. This group in the Bronx formed the core of the Irish Socialist Federation, whose green banner bearing the words *Faugh a Ballach* was carried at all working-class demonstrations. When there was neither union nor I.S.F., Connolly would sometimes take a soft drink in a little Irish saloon where men talked and sang the songs of home. He was desperately poor. His eighteen dollars a week was paid irregularly. But he had little occasion to go far from home, and enjoyed a rare spell of settled family life. During this period he completed *Labour in Irish History*.

Working for the union was arduous. A fresh slump set in during the autumn of 1907. In three months over seventy banks and financial houses closed their doors. Connolly could remark that the typical "American institution" was the bread-line. Employers grew contemptuous of the workers. Crafts became doubly jealous of their privileges.

"Not a day passes," Connolly wrote in the *Bulletin*, "without some of its (I.W.W.) members being fired off jobs as a result of the action of walking delegates of the pure and simple unions."

At Brownsville, near Brooklyn, where Connolly had organised plasterers and turners, the A.F.L. delegates were accompanied by a gang of hoodlums who ejected the I.W.W. men from the site. It was a commonplace to be informed by an employer that the A.F.L. men had refused to work with the "Wobblies".

Generally speaking the rank and file of the craft unions had better instincts than their leaders, and showed what could have been done if dual unionism had been abandoned. The I.W.W. organised steel-erectors, bronze workers and carpenters into Local 95. For a time they used A.F.L. halls for their meetings. But the leaders tried to prevent them. A number of A.F.L. members protested against the refusal of the House-smiths Union to permit such a letting, and as a result Connolly was invited to address the General Council of that union on the aims of the I.W.W. His case received a hearing but his members got no accommodation.

Connolly made a bid for the leadership of the Yonkers tramway strike. He thought its course illustrated the "correct instincts" of the working class when "unhampered" by "pure-and-simpledom". The workers had organised of their own initiative and appointed a negotiating committee which declared that, failing immediate satisfaction of their demands, no trolley-cars would be running next day. The manager asked a resumption of work while negotiations proceeded. "You mean while you get scabs," they replied. The strike took place and was solid. But electricians and engineers continued working. "They took a firm grip on their union cards," said Connolly, "and scabbed it on the men on strike."

On the first day, Jacobsen, an I.W.W. man in Yonkers, sent for Connolly. The teamsters union also sent their organiser. Connolly arrived first and was given the floor. He advised the men to concentrate on bringing out the electricians and engineers by besieging them in their own homes. If these were to strike their demands were as good as won. Jennings of the teamsters then spoke. He made scant reference to the strike. His speech was composed of "invective against the I.W.W." to which Connolly gave measure for measure. But the men had already decided to affiliate with the A.F.L. All Connolly could do was to warn them as he departed that they had entrusted their future to Judas Iscariot. Next day the newspapers flaunted the headline "Victory for Strikers". They had gone back to work. The teamsters union was "recognised" and issues disputed referred to arbitration.

Even within the I.W.W. itself old craft traditions could linger. For example, Connolly discovered that a branch affiliated to Local 95 was exacting an "examination fee" from all new members. It was three dollars a man and mostly went to the publican. They had divided the workers into three grades with different rates of pay. When Connolly ordered an investigation the committeemen destroyed the books.

In addition to recruiting, competing, and investigating, there was the defence of victimised members to arrange. A particularly notorious case was the charge of murder levelled against Preston for shooting a hoodlum who drew a gun on him while he was picketing. Connolly called a conference of all working-class organisations at his office at 60, Cooper Square, and established a defence organisation. This meeting took place on November 30 and the green banner of the I.S.F. played its part in the ensuing campaign.

Constant activity, tireless initiative, earned Connolly great respect in New York. When he first crossed swords with De Leon he was taken to task for presumption. Now things had

209

changed. The wages and prices controversy was reopened in July 1907 by the Californian I.W.W. man Frank Reed, who restated the "iron law of wages" in its current form. James P. Thompson, New Jersey organiser, sharply contradicted him. If Reed was right, Marx was wrong. Ashplant and others, mingling Marxian phrases with a hotchpotch of bourgeois economics, offered the counter that the "capitalist system always works like clockwork for the capitalist".

The controversy was in progress four months before Connolly entered. Now he made a contribution so conclusive that not one correspondent replied.

The story of how De Leon failed to publish an answer throws a curious light on his mental processes. He was urged to reply, but was afraid to lower himself. He therefore induced Katz to write to Edwards, editor of the I.W.W. *Bulletin*, suggesting that the issue of wages and prices be referred to him for an answer. The Chicago office received this request with some impatience. Trautman's secretary, Justh, had been complaining of attacks on the I.W.W. in the *People*. De Leon replied that only the contributor was responsible. He wrote to Trautman complaining of Justh, and relations between the two centres became strained. Edwards did not accept Katz's suggestion, and De Leon then complained that "Justh had joined the Connolly crew". Once more, instead of a political difference De Leon detected a conspiracy. He grew embittered against Trautman.

Almost immediately after this interchange took place, Connolly opened up negotiations with the Waterside Workers of New York, for a mass entry of twelve thousand dockers into the I.W.W. These men had been members of the Knights of Labour, and regarded the A.F.L. as a blackleg organisation. They constituted about a quarter of the longshore labour force in New York, Brooklyn and Hoboken. Connolly considered the Germans the most advanced, but Italians and Irish too were "free from the graft and corruption of Gompersism".

Here was a splendid opportunity for the I.W.W. to consolidate itself in America's largest city. But De Leon professed to see in the merger only a plot by Connolly to swamp the I.W.W. with Irish and Italian Catholics and submerge the influence of the S.T.L.A. He decided on a frontal attack and demanded that the General Executive Board, which sat in Chicago, should hold a special meeting in New York so as to investigate his complaints. Trautman was at first inclined to refuse. A visit to New York would be expensive. There was a tradition of rivalry between the big cities and prestige was felt to be involved. Finally he agreed, and the meeting was opened two days before Christmas.

De Leon had lost his case before he arrived. On the first day Connolly was empowered to discuss the waiving of certain I.W.W. rules if he could secure the longshoremen's affiliation. He was given leave of absence from the General Executive Board to attend the Waterside E.C. Just before he left, Katz accused him of "pouring cold water" on a strike in Lancaster, Pennsylvania, and saying that Katz "had no right to bring the men out". The allegations being denied, it was agreed to defer the matter till witnesses could be brought.

De Leon did not arrive until Connolly had left. But he had no hesitation in opening a tirade in his absence. First he charged Connolly with teaching "false economics" on wages and prices. Worse, he had tried to sabotage the *People* by demanding it employ I.W.W. labour. The only men who could set English were A.F.L. members. De Leon did not mention that Connolly himself could set English, and there were possibly others. He accused Connolly of "deliberate disruption" on behalf of the Catholic Church. He had sought to "inject the religious question" so as to divide the workers. When this proved a failure, he had tried to "inject" the national question. His whole career in Ireland proved him a wrecker[1] and destroyer. The I.S.R.P. was defunct. Its paper was finished. His attack on the Lawrence strike showed his attitude to trade unionism. That he was "an agent of the Jesuits" De Leon attempted to prove by a "chain of evidence"

[1] A reference in one of Connolly's letters to the "party I wrecked" is a sarcastic comment on this favourite charge of De Leon's.

which is lost to posterity since the *Bulletin* rejected it as libellous. In the midst of the denunciation Cole left the room, and returned blazing with anger at the "Star-chamber proceedings" against Connolly. He insisted that the meeting should adjourn until Connolly could be present. The chairman agreed and Connolly was notified to attend next morning, when De Leon repeated his charges. The committee had had all night to reflect upon them.

The meeting resumed in a calmer atmosphere, favourable to Connolly, although he had so far failed to clinch the agreement with the Waterside Workers. De Leon's allegations of "Ultramontanism" could carry little weight against Connolly's known record. This "Jesuit agent" had, indeed, through the I.S.F. carried a campaign of protest to the very church doors of Monsignor Brann, who had denounced a Moyer-Haywood release demonstration from the altar. Dr. Brann had been compelled to apologise and admit he had been misinformed about the I.W.W. The Executive Board was unconvinced by the "chain of evidence". The members were irritated by De Leon's arrogance and lack of moderation. They would have preferred to be at home for Christmas and wanted the matter despatched quickly. Connolly's refusal to be drawn into a slanging match enabled them to bring matters to a quick conclusion.

Williams, as chairman, ruled all matters relating to the S.L.P. and I.S.R.P. "political" and irrelevant to the position of an I.W.W. organiser. As for indisputably I.W.W. matters, Yates suggested that the G.E.B. could not constitutionally act until they had gone through the full administrative procedure. Only Katz objected when Williams upheld Yates, and De Leon was reduced to asking what this procedure was. He was told to complain to Connolly's own local, and appeal against their decision if necessary.

Katz did his best. He moved that Connolly be disqualified from acting as an I.W.W. organiser by reason of his attitude to the Lancaster strike. But Connolly's witness, Campbell, corroborated his denial of disparaging statements. Williams declined to allow action on Katz's hearsay.

When the minutes were published Katz objected to the non-inclusion of the "chain of evidence". But the minutes were allowed to stand. In only one respect did Katz and De Leon have their way. The storm of controversy they had raised round Connolly's head made it inadvisable to continue his "Notes from New York" in the I.W.W. *Bulletin*. But the decisive battle had gone against De Leon.

XII

THE HARP

It is extremely difficult to search for truth on any other road than the one we have been accustomed to follow.

ANTOINE LAVOISIER

A few days after the New York Executive meeting appeared the first number of Connolly's monthly, *The Harp*. Official organ of the I.S.F., it was to be Connolly's main means of appealing to the Irish in America to support socialism. The way had been prepared by monthly meetings at Cooper Square, open-air propaganda, and reprints of poems and pamphlets. With twelve quarto pages it was in many ways the most personal of Connolly's papers, showing him in a stage of mental travail, struggling for a certainty he could never attain in the American environment.

He had supported the S.L.P. thanks to De Leon's insistence on class struggle as opposed to class collaboration. He opposed him on wages, marriage, the church, and the National Associations, in the belief that S.L.P. narrowness was repelling workers from the party of class struggle and driving them into the camp of the collaborators. But Connolly had not the equipment for a thoroughgoing critique of De Leon's theoretical position, which arose from a misunderstanding of the State. Connolly never became completely clear on this subject, and for the moment turned the professor's conclusions against him, without abandoning his false premises. He became a De Leonist against De Leon.

In his first editorial he made it plain that he blamed the socialists themselves for their failure to recruit the Irish in America. One objective factor he may have missed, namely, the ease with which opposition to British imperialism could be transmuted into support for its American rival. He laid stress on features of American socialism which Irish workers were bound to find repugnant, among them heresy-hunting dogmatism. Making a shrewd thrust at De Leon he chose his sub-title not from Desmoulins, but from the Jesuits: "In things essential, unity; in things doubtful, diversity; in all things charity." *The Harp* carried this quotation for eighteen months.

Referring to the existence of two socialist parties whose warfare caused nothing but confusion, he wrote:

"In their mutual recriminations many wrong things have been said ... we are convinced that if American socialists had been more solicitous in finding points they had in common, and less eager to stretch the importance of the points on which they differed, a great party ... might ere this have been built in America."

With a sly reference to the "Internationale" he complained of the surfeit of "saviours" whose reputations had been built on disunion and who would "prefer a party of ten sycophants to a million who could think for themselves".

Here he all but paraphrased Marx's letter to Schweitzer on the subject of Lassalle:

"The sect sees the justification for its existence and its 'point of honour' not in what it has in common with the class movement but in the *particular shibboleth* which *distinguishes* it from it."

So far Connolly's insight carried him quickly. But because he did not trace De Leon's dogmatism to its theoretical foundation (as Marx did with Proudhon and Lassalle) he proposed, instead of theoretical clarification, the submergence of theoretical differences.

He so strongly recoiled from dogmatic pseudo-science as to waive the claims of science. This is the significance of his judgement upon the Hervé-Vollmar controversy at the Stuttgart International Socialist Congress of 1907. The *Weekly People* and the I.W.W. *Bulletin* were all for Hervé's demand that soldiers should be urged to desert or mutiny on the outbreak of war.

"Heroic folly," Lenin called it, while he described Vollmar's "national defencism" as opportunist cowardice. Connolly sought to reduce the issue of substance to a difference of presentation. French people were by tradition "hot-headed" while Germans were "cautious", and each made a contribution. At this time he speculated much on the meaning of national differences, especially as they concerned the Irish. The Irish, he thought, proceeded too rapidly from thought to action but reached their real objective nearly as quickly as the more systematic Germans. He connected this in part with the dogmatic character of Catholicism; the Irish Catholic was inclined to require a completely committed position, and on moving from one standpoint to another scorned all inter-mediate stations. This he saw among the Irish in America, divided between socialist and anti-socialist dogmatism. Some of these speculations found place in *Labour in Irish History*, but Connolly had clarified his own mind before its publica-tion in book form, and these questionable generalisations were then omitted.

He was in the dilemma of many an American socialist who could sit neither on the needle of the S.L.P. nor in the bog of the S.P.A. Finding neither party satisfactory, he clung to the I.W.W. while slowly accustoming himself to the idea of membership of the less "revolutionary" party.

"The I.W.W.," he wrote, "has it in its power to solve the problem of socialist unity."

In one sense he was right: that is to say, insofar as the I.W.W. embodied the principle of mass action. But the rea-son he gave was the De Leonist reason that the I.W.W. pre-pared and organised the administrative framework of future society while simultaneously fighting the encroachments of the master class. It was the old American illusion in a new form. American socialist papers were full of new titles for this "future society" ranging from Gronland's "Co-operative Commonwealth" through "Industrial Republic" and "Indus-trial Democracy" to "Social Democracy" and Connolly's own "Workers' Republic". The I.W.W. understood much the same by all these titles, namely "industrially organised" society considered without relation to state power.

Connolly himself described a society in which all workers elected their foremen, these in turn their managers, and where supreme administrative responsibility rested in a committee elected from constituencies representing various industries. Following De Leon in attributing the *policy* of trade unions exclusively to their *structure*, he placed working-class power in the sphere of organisation. Hence his belief that the I.W.W. would solve the problem of socialist unity, which was De Leon's thesis also.

De Leon claimed the authority of Marx. He dealt with the relation of political to economic struggles in his pamphlet *As to Politics*, a reprint of a discussion conducted in the *Weekly People* from November 1906 to February 1907. In this he tried to rally the faithful to the conceptions he presented to the I.W.W. convention. He quoted Marx as follows:

> "Only the trade union is capable of setting on foot a true political party of labour and thus raising a bulwark against the power of capital."

Connolly paraphrased this statement in the full belief that it came from Marx. De Leon had been challenged at Stuttgart by the Austrian socialist Bäer, whom he told contemptuously: "Not from Marx? Read the whole of Marx, sir." But the extract is, of course, not from Marx at all, but from an interview Marx was alleged to have given Haman, who recorded it in language most unlike Marx's. Marxist scholars have been unanimous in rejecting the interview as spurious. Not till late in 1908, however, did the I.W.W. *Bulletin* admit that the quotation was dubious and substitute extracts from the *Geneva Manifesto*. It was from this bogus source that De Leon derived five major points of his platform, namely:

1. That a true political party of labour is bound to carry into the political arena principles of the revolutionary economic organisation which it reflects.
2. That the revolutionary act of achieving the overthrow of capitalism and the establishment of socialism is the function reserved to the economic organisation.
3. That the "physical force" called for by the revolutionary act *lies inherent* in the economic organisations.

4. That the element of force consists not only in a military or other organisation implying violence, but in the structure of the economic organisation.
5. That the economic organisation is not transitory but is the present "embryo of the future Government of the Republic of Labour".

But what was the "revolutionary act" but Bakunin's "social liquidation", when economic organisations of the workers replace the old state which magically disappears in a social *dies illa*? The ghost of the old anarchist must have chuckled to see the followers of Marx accepting in his name a compote of Bakuninism and Lassalleanism. Throughout 1908 the *Industrial Union Bulletin* slipped closer to the anarchist position.

Early in 1908 Connolly founded the I.W.W. propaganda leagues. The purpose was to aid recruiting by an explanation of the general purposes of industrial unionism. De Leon protested to the New York Industrial Council and demanded the immediate dissolution of the leagues and the dismissal of Connolly from his post, adding an insult which Connolly could not ignore. He described him as a "police spy". Consequently, as De Leon entered his complaint at Connolly's local, so Connolly lodged a complaint at De Leon's and demanded his expulsion from the I.W.W. for slandering one of its officials. In each case the local refused to move and both Connolly and De Leon appealed to the convention, where a battle royal was promised. If Connolly had realised the need and the possibility of demolishing De Leon theoretically, American socialism might have saved many lost years and the labours of W. Z. Foster, who took up the task in a later epoch, would have been rendered far easier.

In his speech at the McMahon Hall, when the Leagues were first established, Connolly developed another aspect of theory, supporting a conclusion he had already reached. His speech was published in the *Bulletin* and is at present available in the pamphlet *The Axe to the Root*. He was trying to draw syndicalist conclusions from the *Communist Manifesto*, and postulated three stages in the mental development of each subject class in world history "corresponding to the inception, development and decay of the oppressing powers". In the first the oppressed sought to re-establish the conditions of the past; in the second they fought for amelioration within a present framework they accepted; in the third they tried to "conquer the future". The second period ended, in Connolly's estimation, for the English bourgeoisie with the great civil war, "because the growth of the industrial system had made the capitalist class realise that they could at any moment stop the flow of its life-blood so to speak, and from so realising it was but a short mental evolution to frame a theory of political action which proclaimed that the capitalist class was the nation."

Connolly then described three periods of working-class evolution, beginning with Luddism, passing through reformist or craft trade unionism, and culminating with the I.W.W., of which he concluded:

"The fact that it had its inception among men actually engaged in the work of trade union organisation ... and not in the theories of any political party ... is the most hopeful augury of the future."

These ideas permeate the declaration of principles of the I.S.F. and are in turn linked to another theory, namely, that the victory of the working class is only possible after a prolonged accumulation of "economic power". What this meant concretely was best explained in the April issue of *The Harp*:

"The first act of the workers will be through their economic organisations seizing the organised industries; the last act the conquest of the political power."

Connolly continued:

"In this the working class will, as they must, follow the lines traversed by the capitalist revolution of Cromwellian England ... the capitalist class had developed their economic power before they raised the banner of political revolt."

That one to whom the *Communist Manifesto* was so familiar could thus stand Marxism on its head testified to the ut-
ter confusion reigning in the American movement. Marx and
Engels, it is true, distinguished stages in the development of
working-class consciousness. But while "all preceding classes
that got the upper hand sought to fortify their already
acquired status . . . the proletarians cannot become masters of
the productive forces of society except by abolishing their
own previous mode of appropriation."

Hence the triumphant conclusion:

"The first step in the revolution of the working class, is to
raise the proletariat to the position of ruling class." It will
then "use its political supremacy to wrest by degrees all
capital from the bourgeoisie."

Or as Marx put it elsewhere:

"The economic emancipation of the working class is therefore the *great end* to which every political movement ought
to be subordinate as a *means*."[1]

But to Connolly, at this stage of his evolution,

"The struggle for the conquest of the political state of the
capitalist is not the battle, it is only the echo of the battle.
The real battle is being fought out, and will be fought out,
in the industrial field."

When in April 1908 the Socialist Party Convention took
place, Stirton of Hancock, Michigan, expressed a related idea
which Connolly took up in *The Harp*:

"Political institutions are not adapted to the administration of industry . . . only the industrial form of organisation offers us even a theoretical constructive Socialist programme. There is no constructive Socialism except in the
industrial field."

[1] My italics. C. D. G.

Connolly took this conception further, to the point of saying:

"Under socialism, states, territories or provinces will exist only as geographical expressions and have no existence as sources of governmental power, though they may be seats of administrative bodies.

". . . the administrative force of the Socialist Republic of the future will function through unions industrially organised."

In the first years of the century many socialists failed to distinguish between fully developed socialism (communism) and the transitional stage which ushers it in. In the final stage, government by coercion disappears because no antagonistic class interests remain. This is what Connolly had in mind. But this period must be preceded by that interval known as the "dictatorship of the proletariat",[1] when there is governmental power exercised by the working class.

Nowhere was confusion on this subject more pronounced than in America. The ideas then prevailing have been described in memoirs by Elizabeth Gurley Flynn and W. Z. Foster. The origin of Stirton's statement is also easily traced. It comes almost verbatim from the *Economic Determinism* of the Texas anarchist Ward Mills, which was serialised in the I.W.W. *Bulletin*. It coincided with the last of De Leon's five points, but Ward Mills had assimilated it entirely to Bakunin's ideas. In his book he gave a lengthy exposition of Morgan's theory of the genesis of the State. He then skipped lightly through feudal and capitalist epochs, as if the existence of one or other form of state was the only thing that need be known about them. He then declared that "the downfall of the political State sounds the knell of private property" and that after the "death of the political State" there would be established "industrially organised society".

This being the theoretical fare fed to thousands of organ-

---

[1] Lest this phrase gives rise to misunderstanding, let it be noted that Marx identified the "dictatorship of the proletariat" with "democracy"–government by the people. It does not, of course, imply an era of repression.

ised workers, it was not surprising that a German socialist should write critically to the *Bulletin* asking: "Why don't the I.W.W. grow faster?" He answered his own question by blaming the use of the *Bulletin* for "Marxian political wrangles". Thus was theory further discredited. And the ironic upshot was that the two rival revisionisms of De Leon and Ward Mills (roughly speaking Lassalle and Bakunin *redivivi*) presented themselves as the "right" and the "left" at the fourth I.W.W. convention. All that was absent was Marxism. The door remained closed to both through lack of the conception of the dictatorship of the proletariat, and consequently of the role of the working-class party.

Events in April and May 1908 slowly convinced Connolly that instead of a new I.W.W. party, which might attract or even absorb the S.L.P. and S.P.A., there was needed a concentration of all socialist forces within the S.P.A. He was persuaded of this partly by the favourable reception given *The Harp* at the S.P.A. Chicago convention, when a special literature stand was made available for its display. He was also impressed by the party's visible signs of growth. At the end of May the S.P.A. launched the *New York Evening Call,* a socialist daily as lively and popular as the *People* was dead and airless. It was an immediate success. On the other hand every day brought fresh defections from the S.L.P. These included Bohn and Ebert, and many other followers of Connolly. When the S.P.A. hired a railway train and sent the "Red special" across America to boost Debs for president, it became clear which party had the lease on the future.

Still Connolly hesitated. The right-wing of the S.P.A. were reformists of a stamp he knew too well in Europe. He did not take kindly to membership of a non-Marxian party. The issue of the presidential election finally decided him. The I.S.F. could not stand aside from this struggle. Its "Manifesto to Irish wage-slaves" was published in full in *The Call,* whose manager, Mailley, became a member of the I.S.F. Connolly advised socialists to join the party which tolerated the greater freedom of opinion. The S.L.P. believed that the "social revolution could only be accomplished by men and women with a clear understanding of the economics of capitalism, and that therefore a clear and definite programme is a first essential, and in the interest of maintaining that programme it is imperative to expel . . .all who are not in the strictest harmony with its 'clear-cut' principle." The S.P.A. on the other hand held that social revolution "depends in the last analysis upon the growth of class-consciousness . . . and therefore the chief task of the socialist political party is to educate . . . by clearing the minds of the members, not by a process of weeding out."

There was much new wisdom here. Liebknecht gave De Leon similar advice just a year later, when he told him: "Join the larger party." But Connolly was prepared to tolerate diversity, in part, because he was feeling disillusioned with parties. Elections, he said, were but the "dress parade" of the industrial struggle, though they were important in making the working class conscious of its identity and transcending craft and industrial differences. He had no conception of a political party as the general staff of a class. While he rightly said "a political party must be catholic enough to tolerate differences of opinion among its adherents, provided they unite to face the common enemy," he reiterated the syndicalist position when he added by way of explanation that "since the political body does not accomplish the revolution, but only leads the attack on the political citadel of capitalism, there no longer exists danger in the unclearness of its membership." Social revolution was to proceed from economic organisations, so the Augean stable of political confusion need not be cleansed.

It was some time before Connolly once more began to modify his views, and for a number of years he described himself as a syndicalist. His able presentation of the syndicalist case made an instant appeal. This was because he directed his attack against actual evils, and not abstractions. His hearers immediately realised that he was setting his mind to the solution of their problems. He counselled less theorising and more fighting because the S.L.P. had degraded theory from its proud position as a guide to action. He demanded that instead of abstruse economic and casuistical treaties, socialists should explain simply how poverty, violence, tyranny and degradation arose from capitalism. He wanted people to rally and put an end to it. His message of action against present evils was his great strength, and this drew him to the I.W.W.

If Connolly's contribution to the American movement was to urge toleration in place of dogmatism, he had something more intimate to give the Irish. Here the warring of socialist sects was less noticeable in face of the over-riding need for an independent republic, "the only purely political change in Ireland worth crossing the street for", as Connolly put it. The nearer he was to Ireland the clearer sighted and happier; only twice did he obtrude syndicalist theory into purely Irish affairs, once in comparing the I.W.W. with the Land League, and again in seeking a parallel between "building the framework within the shell" and Sinn Fein.[1]

In an editorial already referred to, he gave his opinion that Irishmen in America "as soon as they became socialists" adopted a line of conduct fatal to the best interests of the socialist cause amongst them.

"The first result of the winning to socialism of a worker of the Irish race should be that he should become ... a channel for conveying the socialist message to others of his race.

"But this he could only do as long as his socialism did not cause him to raise barriers betwixt himself and his fellow-countrymen and women, to renounce his connection with, or to abjure all ties of kinship or tradition that throughout the world makes the heart of one Celt go out to another, no matter how unknown. Yet this is precisely what their adoption of socialism has caused in the great majority of cases among Irishmen.

[1] Sinn Fein, founded by Arthur Griffith, believed in boycotting the Westminster Parliament, but winning local authorities which at a certain point could combine to administer the country independently.

"Led away by a foolishly sentimental misinterpretation of the socialist doctrine of universal brotherhood, or internationalism, they generally began by dropping out of all the Irish societies they were affiliated with, no matter how righteous their objects were, and ended by ceasing to mix in Irish gatherings or to maintain Irish connections. The results upon the minds of their fellow-countrymen were as might be expected. . . .

"We propose to show all the workers of our fighting race that socialism will make them better fighters for freedom without being less Irish."

Now for the first time he claimed revolutionary significance for the Gaelic revival.

He saw the industrial struggle bestriding national boundaries, but as a liberating, not a restrictive force. His socialism was national in form, international in substance. And that his view of it was not confined to Ireland he showed by two well-documented articles acclaiming the advent of the Indian national movement and headed *The Coming Revolt in India.*

During the early months of its publication De Leon was ever inveighing against *The Harp* as an organ of the Jesuits. The religious question, therefore, involved polemics on two fronts. In his reply to De Leon, Connolly showed how Yankee sectarianism (typified in the anti-Catholic "Know-nothing" movement of the last century) had thrown the Irish into the arms of the Democratic Party.

On the other front Connolly sustained a campaign against every clerical interference in political affairs, insisting on the right of a Catholic to be a socialist while remaining a Catholic. He gave, it is true, evidence of familiarity with the materialist explanation of religion as an "inverted world-consciousness" but he applied this only to the development of its successive forms, and that only in passing. In his day "historical materialism" was usually presented mechanically as "historical determinism" or as the not even necessarily materialist "economic determinism". The philosophical aspect seems to have repelled him, and he did not develop it.

Cardinal Logue visited New York in May 1908 and promised support for the Irish National Party "in demanding for Ireland autonomy consistent with the unity of the British Empire".

In the midst of the rejoicing and mutual congratulations there was one discordant note, from the little group who sold *The Harp*. Connolly prefaced his welcome to the Cardinal with the words: "With him as an ecclesiastic we have nothing to do." Having directed each cobbler to his last he went on: "He stepped out of place to interfere in secular matters." Then followed an account of the suppression of Patrick Kenny's *Irish Peasant*, which had been published in Navan and was now transferred to Dublin and taken over by W. P. Ryan.

As a logical consequence of the denial of the right of the clergy to claim religious justification for attacks on socialism, Connolly refused to countenance attempts to quote religion in its defence. A pamphlet by Patrick Cooney was praised for defending the right of Catholics to independent political opinion, but criticised for coquetting with "Christian Socialism", with its implication that socialist doctrines came within the province of the Church.

Connolly and his small band of helpers would station themselves outside East Side meeting halls to sell their papers. A voluntary staff would post them to the growing number of subscribers throughout the U.S.A. Soon the issues were being completely sold out. The *Gaelic American* quoted them and Catholic periodicals offered exchange arrangements.

The welcome extension of *The Harp* outside New York led Connolly to arrange a lecture tour on its behalf. This was the more necessary since J.E.C. Donnelly, the Donegal man who printed it, was incurring a loss which could only be met by an increased circulation. A few dates were secured in response to an advertisement. Connolly left New York in July 1908, so as to take part simultaneously in the "Debs for President" campaign. Though De Leon had added to his slate of grievances Connolly's refusal to accept him as an

I.W.W. speaker on the May Day platform, he had not succeeded in securing his dismissal. But withdrawal of S.L.P. support meant the gradual decline of the work. Unemployment had reached three times the highest figure of 1904; the I.W.W. was the organisation of the oppressed and the victimised. Eighteen dollars a week was just not there. Connolly shut his office and went on the road. The I.S.F. transferred its meetings to the Murray Hill Social Club.

He first toured New England, was in Bridgeport from July 25 to 27, then in Boston, Leominster, Lowell, Malden and Springfield. His headquarters in Massachusetts was Malden, a suburb of Boston, where he stayed with Mr. John D. Williams whose wife was away on holiday. Williams recalled him as a quiet, knowledgeable man whose mission met with too little success. The S.L.P. were resentful, the S.P.A. suspicious of him. Only in Boston itself was he well received. He pushed on into New Hampshire, Vermont and Maine before cutting back across New York to Philadelphia. He worked the State of Pennsylvania from a headquarters at Pottsville, leaving on September 3, and holding meetings in Buffalo, Gloversville, Auburn and Detroit on the way to his goal—Chicago, where he was to try final conclusions with De Leon.

No minutes were taken at the fourth I.W.W. convention. The slump had all but beggared the organisation. There was no means of paying a stenographer. The official report was expanded from Trautman's notes. Delegates had to meet their own travelling and catering expenses. But the indomitable spirit of the Wobblies was equal to the occasion. Theoretical confusion there might be, but from the Lakes to the Pacific coast had gone forth the warning that De Leon was descending with a hundred devils to swing "politics" on the convention. The famous "overall brigade" rode into Chicago on the rods of railway carriages. From New York came Elizabeth Gurley Flynn and her husband. When the convention gathered, no term of abuse was so low as "intellectual", and the strains of "Hallelujah, I'm a bum" floated round the hall as often as De Leon put in an appear-

15*

ance. "The bummery," he contemptuously called them. "I'd like to get in a bang at the Pope," said one of them.

On this occasion De Leon met his Waterloo. His credentials were challenged. But he was allowed the floor, where he showed he had lost all capacity for political accommodation. He may have been theoretically less wrong than his unthinking opponents, but the delegates would have none of him. Politics had become identified with either dogma or treachery. He was isolated and refused a seat. His attack on Connolly was of no avail.

Connolly's credentials were accepted. His report on the work of the propaganda leagues was approved and he was congratulated. His appeal against the refusal of Local 58 to expel De Leon was upheld by the committee, but it was finally decided to refer the matter back to the local.

This was superfluous. De Leon would be Caesar or nothing. He had irrevocably lost control of the I.W.W. His first step was to demand that the *Industrial Union Bulletin* repay the capital loaned it by the S.T.L.A. A few more issues were brought out, but the paper could not survive. He then led a breakaway of the Eastern Branches which in effect amounted to the withdrawal of a much diminished S.T.L.A.

The I.W.W. adopted a new preamble, which Connolly applauded in *The Harp* because of its vigorous stand on the principle of the class struggle. He was asked if he approved of its repudiating the principle of political action. He laughed, "It will be impossible to prevent the workers taking it."

XIII
PREPARING FOR RETURN

Connolly remained long enough in Chicago to establish a branch of the I.S.F. Its secretary, Bernard MacMahon, held a responsible post in the City Hall and was competent enough to defy attempts to dismiss him. He and the writer Miss Reilly, of the left wing of the S.P.A., introduced Connolly to the Kerrs and Unterman of the *International Socialist Review*. It was pointless to hurry back to New York. The moment De Leon left for his hotel, breathing vengeance on the "bummery", the fate of 60, Cooper Square was finally sealed.

The Kerrs offered to republish Connolly's articles on industrial unionism so as to encourage the idea that political unity would result from the replacement of craft by industrial unionism. "Political scabbery is born of industrial scabbery," said Connolly. In the American edition of *Socialism Made Easy* four expository articles were prefaced by extracts from the "Talking Points" of the *Workers' Republic*. These "Workshop Talks" were models of simple argument for the man at the bench, carrying Connolly's special passionateness into the realm of everyday things. Two distinct phases of his political thought were thus combined in the pamphlet which appeared just before Christmas.

This was the first pamphlet from which Connolly earned money. Its impact was immediate and spread far afield. The following May, Tom Mann, then in Australia, greeted it enthusiastically and even discarded one of his own in its favour. The expository section was in 1911 incorporated into the Year Book of the Australian "One Big Union" movement under the title of *The Axe to the Root*. Distributed in Britain it helped to infuse the idea of class struggle into both trade unions and I.L.P., and was still being reprinted in Ireland in the thirties. Echoes of its arguments could still be heard in the debates of the Republican Congress movement. On the other hand it helped to popularise the unscientific ideas of syndicalism.

On his return to New York, Connolly found the I.S.F. without a secretary. Jack Lyng had succumbed to malaria, from which he had suffered intermittently for several years. This was at the very time when a national as well as a New York secretary was essential. Brady, whose pamphlet *The Historical Basis of Socialism in Ireland* had been published by the S.L.P. wing of the old I.S.R.P., recently arrived in New York, now took on the national secretaryship temporarily. For New York secretary Connolly put forward Kathleen Flynn, Elizabeth's younger sister, then only fifteen years old. His own daughter Nora also began to help. Socialist Party branches in Irish districts were circularised with the offer of assistance and the Federation's open-air lecturers were heavily engaged. Every Saturday Quinlan, Walsh, O'Shaughnessy, Brady and Shanahan took their stances together with Connolly himself.

In December Connolly returned to Boston. The I.S.F. branch, which had been meeting each Sunday at 724, Washington Street, booked the Faneuil Hall for a mass meeting. The title of Connolly's lecture was "The Labour Movement in Ireland and America". He repeated the speech in New York a week later, at the Brevoort Hall in East 54th Street, William Mailley, manager of *The Call*, taking the chair. Brady relinquished the secretaryship at Christmas 1908, after which the headquarters were transferred to Chicago. Connolly revisited the city and persuaded Bernard MacMahon to take over. He spoke at Gloversville, Auburn and Detroit on the way. Generally speaking, the I.S.F. found more favour in the Middle-West; anti-Irish prejudice was less developed and the S.P.A. more revolutionary, just as the S.L.P. was less dogmatic.

But already Connolly's thoughts were gravitating back to their old centre. In mid-1908 he had told Mother Jones that he was tired of America and was awaiting an opportunity to return to Ireland. As *The Harp* extended its influence, his correspondence with Ireland and the Irish in the U.S.A., Australia and Argentina, continually increased. The balance of the paper's contents so far shifted that some American readers protested at its preoccupation with Irish affairs.

These were commanding attention. The arrival of Larkin to lead the transport strike in Belfast had shown that Catholic and Protestant could unite for their immediate demands. Connolly reprinted the great solidarity speech of the Independent Orangeman, Lindsay Crawford. In his struggle in Ireland, Larkin seemed to be putting into practice just what Connolly found best in the I.W.W. of America—the united struggle of all trades, using all tactics from guerilla action to the sympathetic strike. Larkin himself had imbibed syndicalist ideas in Liverpool and was no sooner in Dublin than his fellow socialists told him legendary tales of the great Irish Marxian across the Atlantic. When in January 1908 Larkin founded the Irish Transport Union, Connolly hailed it with delight. Industrial unionism had come to Ireland.

The winter of Dublin Socialism which descended in 1902 proved briefer than seemed likely at its onset. It had seemed as if its republican allies had gone over to Griffith while its own forces were hopelessly divided. But when Griffith established Sinn Fein and tried to supplement his consistent opposition with a positive programme, the issues Connolly had raised in the nineties came up again.

The break-up of the I.S.R.P. scattered socialist emissaries in all directions. Some joined Sinn Fein and influenced the Gaelic revivalists, among whom W. P. Ryan, Standish O'Grady and Douglas Hyde were paying increasing attention to property questions. Others made contact with younger republicans like Ceannt and Sean MacDermott. *Inghinidhe na h'Eireann* revived.

When Maud Gonne wrote to Connolly telling him of her separation from John MacBride, he replied: "I hope you will now be Maud Gonne again." She herself never again played quite the same part, but doughty lieutenants followed her, among them Helena Molony and Constance Gore-Booth, by marriage Countess Markiewicz. Some of the trade unions were now showing signs of transferring their allegiance from the Nationalist Party to Sinn Fein. In this process a leading part was played by P. T. Daly, Sinn Fein member of the Dublin Trades Council.

There were now several socialist groups shifting and changing their names as in the eighties; but broadly speaking two tendencies existed. First was the I.S.R.P. group led by William O'Brien and Tom Lyng, which maintained contact with Connolly and the Edinburgh socialists. This section was first split into the S.L.P. and the Socialist Party of Ireland, then amalgamated as the Irish Socialist Party. The organisation was continuous, but the membership remained small. Distinct from them was the section derived from the second Dublin I.L.P. founded in 1907, which now attracted a section of the Fabian supporters.

From Griffith on the right to O'Brien on the left, these groupings comprised the forces which Connolly had gathered against the Jubilee and the Boer War. His first concern was with Sinn Fein. In January 1909 he argued that while socialists must reject its social teaching, which Griffith had taken from the German economist List, the principle of national self-reliance was common ground. But could Irish socialists be united on this point? The I.S.R.P. group believed in the precedence of the national question. But in Dublin there was also the I.L.P., highly impressed by the way the most vocal nationalists were "merciless grinders of the faces of the poor", and hence mistakenly rejecting the conception of national independence as a distraction from socialist tasks. In Belfast were those who, having learned socialism in the struggle against the shipyard owners and linen magnates, felt that a green flag was no substitute for higher wages and could not see the connection between national independence and socialism. Connolly suggested that all socialist sections should meet in conference and seek a common platform. A united socialist movement could then decide its attitude to Sinn Fein. Connolly's advice was published in W. P. Ryan's *Nation* and made a great impression.

Connolly did little more for the I.W.W. except to speak at the 1909 May Day meeting when Trautman came from

Chicago. The New York S.P.A. still regarded him as a dangerous "red" and gave no place to the I.S.F. in the afternoon parade. The Irish, smarting under the affront, noted with irony the cloudburst that broke over the city at exactly 3 p.m.

The centre of gravity of the S.P.A. was Chicago. In New York socialist politics had been bedevilled by De Leonism. On the initiative of Unterman, Louis Berger persuaded the National Executive to put Connolly on the road as a national organiser. He took up his appointment in June 1909 and was assigned to the Middle-West. He did not return to New York for nearly eleven months. His wage was three dollars a day, but this time it was paid. The S.P.A. was meticulous over its accounts—every cent was not only accounted for to auditors, but published in its bulletin down to the minutest detail. Connolly's last year in the U.S.A. was relatively prosperous.

His departure created difficulties for *The Harp*. In May Donnelly decided his pocket could stand the loss no longer. It was not issued in June. The July issue, in eight pages of larger format, was published late. It contained an appeal for financial support, which seems to have been sufficiently forthcoming to tide the paper over the next year. In the midst of these difficulties, Connolly had to leave. The remaining issues were dominated by the serial *Labour in Irish History* and a minimum of technical work was required. "Spailpin" sent home editorials written on long rail journeys during which he is said to have "devoured libraries".

National organisers, of whom the S.P.A. employed six, were travelling lecturers who addressed meetings and gave advice to branches. The Socialist Party bulletin shows how extensive and effective an organisation had been built up on this basis. After travelling all day, Connolly would have to address a meeting in the evening and possibly sit up half the following night discussing politics with his hosts and a few visitors. But he succeeded in controlling the general policy of *The Harp* and conducting a varied correspondence.

His suggestions for socialist unity were taken up in Dublin

and, on the initiative of William O'Brien, a conference was called at the Trades Hall, Capel Street, on June 13. Over one hundred and fifty were present, "including several ladies". O'Brien from the chair urged the two socialist societies in Dublin to "sink their differences", and a unity committee was established. This included William and Daniel O'Brien, Peadar Maicin, Seamus Pike, Michael Mallin, Francis Skeffington, Tom Lyng, Walter Carpenter, Fred Ryan and O'Brien-Hishon, the last representing the group Larkin was gathering around him. Amalgamation was announced on August 28, the common platform being independent-labour representation on electoral bodies, support for the national language (strongly revolutionary in the very month when Dr. Hickey was dismissed from Maynooth for advocating it), the ultimate aim of socialism and democratic discussion of the means of achieving it in Ireland, and its lecturers included Larkin, Maicin, Dudley Edwards (of the League of Progressive Thought), R. H. Mortished and Mrs. Despard. For the first time for many years socialist meetings drew attendances of up to four hundred.

Relations with Sinn Fein did not fall out satisfactorily. Griffith was strongly opposed to any association with Labour. The group around *The Nation* hesitated to provoke a split by making their paper avowedly socialist. It was then that discussions began over the transfer of *The Harp* to Ireland, which was agreed upon in the autumn. The December issue was missed, but in January 1910 *The Harp* reappeared in Dublin. Connolly was still titular editor, but Larkin was Dublin editor. Nora Connolly was New York business agent. The technical supervision was W. P. Ryan's, and the paper was published from the office of *The Nation*.

Meanwhile differences within Sinn Fein were sharpening. At a stormy meeting of the Executive in December, Griffith shocked his colleagues by proposing the merging of the organisation with William O'Brien's "All for Ireland Movement" which had been established by the Home Rule M.P. as a breakaway from the U.I.L., now dominated by the sectarian "Ancient Order of Hibernians (Board of Erin)". Griffith was backed up by Brady and O'Brien, and opposed by P. T. Daly and the Countess Markievicz. The consequence was that, though Sinn Fein did not dissolve, many of those who fought Griffith on this issue became disillusioned and slowly drifted into the S.P.I. Sinn Fein fell into eclipse as socialism advanced. Its decline became more rapid after the Liberal government decided to sponsor a third Home Rule Bill.

The new Socialist Party of Ireland recruited members in Cork, Waterford, Dundalk, Castlebar, Cahirciveen, Carrickmacross, Derry and Belfast. For the most part they were readers of *The Nation* or subscribers to *The Harp*.

While on his travels, Connolly contributed two articles to the *International Socialist Review*, one an answer to Berger's enquiry about the tactics to be adopted in the event of a capitalist administration refusing to accept the verdict of the polls. Use the strength of industrial unionism, said Connolly. In the other he rejected the policy of working within the A.F.L. whose craft organisation was "the most dispersive and isolating force at work in the Labour movement today". Similar considerations lay behind his editorial in the first Dublin *Harp*. Here he urged that a "Workers' Union of Ireland" should enforce the principle of "Sinn Fein" by refusing to handle imports of articles which could be made equally well in Ireland. This article contains a sentence which has been taken from its historical context in order to justify opportunism on more than one occasion:

"But we have come to the opinion that in the struggle for freedom the theoretical clearness of a few socialists is not as important as the aroused class instincts and consciousness of the mass of the workers."

Abstractly speaking, it was of course quite unscientific to counterpose the clarity of the few and the instincts of the many. But Connolly was writing at a particular time and in a particular place. Theoretical clarity is useless if it is isolated from the class movement. This is what Connolly was getting at. He was at war with the narrow sectishness which had so seriously weakened the American movement.

He explained that he wanted the socialists to put into practice the teachings of the *Communist Manifesto*, that the vanguard of the working class had no interests apart from those of the class and at all times represented the interests of the whole. He was fighting not theory but dogmatism.

During the winter the Dublin socialists returned to the plan of bringing Connolly back to Ireland for a lecture tour, with the possibility that he would remain permanently. Both William O'Brien and Larkin, through his accountant Hishon, approached him. In March an appeal for funds was issued and invitations were sent to Wheatley in Glasgow, his brother John Connolly in Edinburgh, now active with the Trades Council, and to friends in Leeds, London, Liverpool, Manchester and Merthyr. This seems to have been Larkin's initiative. But then came the trumped up malversation case against Larkin, and O'Brien took over the preparations for Connolly's visit.

When the prospects of an alliance with Sinn Fein faded, Connolly elaborated proposals for an Irish Labour Party, based on the broadest measure of agreement and including the trade unions. He thought the Dublin Trades Council might take the lead in calling a conference which would then stimulate the same in other cities. All hope of the Sinn Fein alliance was not abandoned, but the attitude of Labour to other parties would have to depend on the attitude of the others towards them. This awaited the outcome of a struggle that was still proceeding. Connolly was, in sum, aiming at a broad labour-republican alliance under socialist leadership.

The rapid growth of socialism in Ireland in 1909–10 alarmed sections of the clergy. The masses were being rendered receptive by industrial upheavals led by Larkin. A Jesuit, Father Kane, decided to devote his Lenten lectures to its denunciation. "If Connolly were here there would be a reply at once," said the socialist Loughran, and on his motion it was proposed to publish a symposium from Connolly, Wheatley and Father Haggerty. But Connolly, who suspected "Christian Socialism" at this period, offered to write a special pamphlet. He had accumulated ample material and probably drafted the main outline during the last days of his tour, as he moved eastwards from Fort Wayne to Chicago and so on to meet his family in New York, shabby, tired but happy with achievement.

It remains uncertain whether the reply to Father Kane was not first envisaged on a somewhat grander scale than the pamphlet published under the title of _Labour, Nationality and Religion._ Posthumously published notes indicate that Connolly was contemplating a general exposition of the socialist attitude to religion. He extracted copiously from the writings of Kautsky on the Reformation. But it is not certain that these notes relate to this work, or even this period, though it is likely. He finally decided to confine himself to refuting Father Kane.

Father Kane had launched his main attack, not on socialist ideology, but on the practicability of socialism as a system of society. He defined it as "state ownership of all wealth-producing power". He was therefore speaking not upon faith or morals but upon politics. Connolly was quite happy to meet him on this ground, and opened his pamphlet with a preface in which he listed no less than sixteen examples, known to most Irishmen, of the Irish Hierarchy taking a stand on politics which was subsequently generally admitted to be mistaken.

After disposing quickly of Father Kane's criticism of the labour theory of value, and surplus value, Connolly showed that the Irish land system denied every principle of property ownership which Father Kane upheld. To the allegation that socialism was based on covetousness, he quoted St. Chrysostom's aphorism: "The rich man is a thief." To such infantilities as allegations of "compulsory equality", "state ownership of children", "free love", "destruction of incentive", "inability of socialists to agree", "impossibility of planning" and "obligatory atheism", he made replies which were not only scientifically and historically acceptable within the limits of Catholic teaching, but threw a piercing light on the realities of Irish history in general and the class struggle in particular.

Larkin suggested St. Patrick's day for Connolly's homecoming. Although a postponement became necessary, Connolly did not renew his engagement with the S.P.A. On April 28, 1910, he addressed the I.S.F. on "Recent Developments in the Labour Movement in Ireland". Then Larkin proposed a further postponement until September, when he hoped to arrange a lecture tour in Britain. Connolly therefore accepted Ebert's invitation to assist in the Free Speech campaign in New Castle, Pennsylvania. This was his last struggle in the United States.

The tinplate workers had been on strike since July 1909. The I.W.W. was strong and supported by two local papers, the *New Castle Free Press* and *Solidarity*.

The authorities filed an action against the editors for seditious libel. On March 2 they were arrested on the charge of failing to comply with imprint technicalities, and lodged in the county jail. The Federation of Labour called a State convention to decide on appropriate action.

The socialists fought back. They proved that the leading local capitalist paper had for years violated the same imprint technicality they were arrested for ignoring. The police were compelled to arrest the *Herald* editor as well but, to show their impartiality, balanced the account by entering and wrecking the S.P.A. rooms. The *Herald* editor had committed six hundred violations and was liable to a fine of 120,000 dollars. He was found "not guilty". But the *Free Press* was fined 600 dollars for only two violations. The staff of *Solidarity* were also fined, but refused to pay, waived their appeal and went to jail. The *Free Press* editors appealed, but were refused bail. Defence funds were thereupon launched in New York and Chicago. Big Bill Haywood hastened to the scene. Ebert was constantly to and fro between New Castle and New York. When Connolly arrived in New York he was met with the urgent request to go at once to New Castle and edit the *Free Press* till editor McKeever was released.

Connolly immediately realised that the purpose of the technical charge was to secure evidence to be used in the prosecution for seditious libel, and to hamper the preparation of the defence. He issued a statement to that effect, and threw doubt on whether the offence "seditious libel" existed in American law. The employers were anxious to use this case as a precedent. In order to prevent the prisoners consulting their attorneys, the Governor alleged a diphtheria epidemic and declared the county jail a quarantine area. The *Free Press* had maintained itself through its jobbing printing business. Now its customers were threatened with subpoenas in the seditious libel prosecution. They were told their attendances would not be required if they did no more business with the *Free Press*. Connolly frankly admitted that the struggle had reached a point beyond anything in his experience.

He met the situation by rallying the support of the socialists, and he and Ebert raised funds in New York and New Jersey. The trial began on June 17, and lasted three days. The jury disagreed and a new trial was announced for September. But on June 29 the judge suddenly announced that he would settle for a fine of 100 dollars. McKeever and his colleagues accepted, and Connolly relinquished the editorship of the paper and returned to New York. There he received a telegram from Dublin. O'Brien had made arrangements for his lecture tour to begin at the end of July. On July 14 the I.S.F. announced a farewell banquet, which was held at Cavanagh's restaurant. Bohn and Ebert were among the speakers, together with Quinlan, Cassidy and Patrick O'Donohue. Connolly sailed on the sixteenth.

The June issue of *The Harp* was the last. Larkin has been blamed for its discontinuance. Six libel actions are said to have been threatened as a result of his first editorial (in February). But it was not, however, until the June issue that *prima facie* defamatory matter appeared. Larkin went to the Dundalk T.U.C. meeting at Whitsun where he exploded a bombshell by proving that its chairman, E. W. Stewart, was not a member of any trade union at all. His reporting of the conference showed that success easily went to his head, and there may have been grounds for libel actions in that issue.

But it is doubtful if these were more than a minor contributory factor in the paper's discontinuance. The June issue contained the final instalment of *Labour in Irish History*. The subscriptions collected the previous year then ran out, and about the same time Larkin was sent to jail.

Labour, Nationality and Religion was revised and brought out soon after Connolly's arrival in Dublin. *Labour in Irish History* appeared in book form the following November. A few changes were made. *The Harp* had in the first few chapters followed exactly the text in *The Socialist*. Now a preface based on Connolly's review of Alice Stopford Green's *Making of Ireland and its Undoing* was added. The chapters were renumbered, the quotations redistributed, a few passages cut and one brief addition made. According to Quinlan, footnotes were supplied to an American edition, but Quinlan is mistaken as to the contents of the Irish edition. The work had reached its final form through twelve years of varied and strenuous activity. It was noteworthy that so little revision proved necessary. It was of striking unity both in style and outlook. Its language was simple and popular and glowed with feeling.

It began where Leslie left off. Starting from the conception of the class struggle in Ireland, Connolly rewrote history from the standpoint of the working people. For the first time the heroes took a back seat. The "masses" held the stage. Leslie's conceptions of upper-class treachery, the derivation of national from social exploitation, and the missionary objectives of the Catholic Church, were fitted neatly into the proper compartments of a synthesis on a larger scale.

"Whenever the social question cropped up in modern Irish history, whenever the question of labour and its wrongs figures in the writings or speeches of our modern Irish politicians, it was simply that they might be used as weapons in the warfare against a political adversary, and not at all

240

because the person so using them was personally convinced that the subjection of labour was in itself a wrong."

Hence Connolly's title. Labour was to have its rightful place in Irish history. The indifference of the politicians was to be exposed. The influence of economic conditions on Irish history was to be demonstrated. The Irish question was a social question. That was the kernel of Connolly's explanation, and in the second chapter he acknowledged that he owed his central proposition to Karl Marx, "the greatest of modern thinkers".

Connolly has been accused of romanticism because he made his starting point the fact that Anglo-Norman feudalism found and destroyed in Ireland the last surviving primitive communist society in western Europe. Yet this is precisely what the arch-materialists Marx and Engels discovered. He was correctly placing the "property question" in the forefront of his subject. In Ireland, foreign rule *meant* a foreign property system. The struggle for the land was for centuries the mainspring of Irish affairs, and it would be absurd to discuss this without reference to the land system (with its accompanying legal and cultural superstructure) which had disappeared. It is certainly true of property relations that violent deaths produce ghosts which may haunt for centuries. In Ireland private property was enforced on a people economically and mentally unprepared for it. Connolly was therefore right in seeing it as in Ireland at most an interlude of a few centuries, whereas in Egypt it survived over as many millennia.

Connolly fully understood there is no return. Social development is a vector and irreversible. Like Engels (in his footnote to the fourth edition of *The Origin of the Family)* he saw clan vestiges around him, in the capacity for tacit solidarity of the Irish as a people, in their ability to co-operate and combine which did not exclude local jealousies and persistent feuds. Connolly regarded the Gaelic revival, not as a means of restoring an ancient social order, but as a means of strengthening democratic consciousness. The old order was not to be re-established but consummated in socialism. In this sense he described his book as "part of the literature of the Gaelic revival".

The treachery of the "gintlemen" in Ireland, illustrated by example upon example, Connolly explained by their bad title deeds. The propertied classes looked before and after and clove hard to what was. Neither from the next wave of planters nor from the aborigines was there toleration or comfort. Through course of time, they learned methods for dealing with their precarious situation and envolved a technique of opportunism haloed round with mystification, whence the demagogue parliamentarian and the gombeen man with "Holy Ireland" on his lips. These tendencies had reached their apex in the Redmondite party. Only betrayal could be expected of them. Taking this to be a general rule, Connolly concluded that the result would be that the working class would apply the methods of the Land League to all major means of production and "progress towards the mastery of those factories, workshops and farms upon which a people's bread and liberties depend".

In identifying this process precisely with national liberation, Connolly oversimplified under De Leon's influence. It was the speciality of the Lassalleans to deny any progressive significance to the capitalist class. But he had reasons. The Irish capitalists had a "thousand economic strings in the shape of investments binding them to English capitalism". That is to say, political independence is not identical with economic independence. "Only the Irish working class remain as the incorruptible inheritors of the fight for freedom in Ireland," Connolly argued.

For some time Connolly seems to have been undecided on whether Sinn Fein (or I.W.W.) tactics would bring both political and economic independence so to speak at one blow, or whether the winning of political independence was an intermediate objective to be tackled on its own. Ultimately he decided on the second, most people agree correctly. Hence the road to Easter Week.

Through the chapters of *Labour in Irish History* the social struggles of the Irish people were unfolded. It is eloquent testimony to this work of genius that so few have dared to assail its main tenets. Apart from O'Faolain's accusation of romanticism, already noted, criticism has been confined to details. The positions of the main classes at the great climacterical points of Irish history was undoubtedly correctly described. Professor George O'Brien, in his studies of Irish economic development, criticised only one chapter, that on Grattan's parliament, and correctly identified Connolly's weak point.

Connolly was inclined to discount the value of "legislative independence". He ascribed the relative prosperity of Grattan's epoch in Ireland to the influence of the industrial revolution in England (not in Ireland, as Professor O'Brien seemed to think), which created an exceptional demand for certain Irish products. The result was to strengthen the hands of the Irish capitalists and lead them to demand greater independence. When economic conditions became less favourable, came the Union. "Industrial decline having set in, the Irish capitalist class was not able to combat the influence of the corruption fund of the English Government." But contemporary sources do indicate a sharp increase in tillage and the production of certain home industries, which, it should be noted, started at an extremely low level. Merchant capital was finding its way into industry, and it would be wrong to deny the effect of the protectionist measures adopted by Grattan's parliament.

While Connolly was quite correct to trace the economic motivation of the Irish capitalists, he was on less certain ground in denying progressive significance to their political demands. Political power is the demiurge of economic revolution, while it is itself always the product of economic development. Connolly overstressed one side of this picture and Professor O'Brien restored the balance by stressing the other.

Connolly's contempt for Grattan was only exceeded by his contempt for O'Connell, whom he accused of obscuring the true reasons for the decay of Irish industry. O'Connell attributed it to the removal of the Parliament and its hangers-on from Dublin to London, Connolly to the invention of machinery and the use of steam-power in Britain.

In place of O'Connell, Connolly exalted the great democrats of Irish history, Tone, Emmet and the Fenians, who saw a change in class relations as essential to the salvation of Ireland.

Connolly was the first to insist on the continuity of Irish socialist tradition from the time of William Thompson to his own day. Thompson he regarded as the first Irish socialist, bearing the same relation to Marx as the pre-Darwinian evolutionists to Darwin.

That there was no special repugnancy to socialism in the Irish temperament he showed by the illustration of Ralahine, an agricultural colony after the style of New Lanark. The ease with which the ancient traditions of co-operation were revived was demonstrated in practice. More important for the history of the socialist *movement* was the identification of the Dublin trades with Chartism, which O'Connell resisted with all his powers. The fusion of scientific socialist thought with the working-class and national movements began when working-class Fenians began to join the First International.

Connolly's reference to Devin Reilly perhaps requires some explanation. "We are not Communists," wrote Reilly, "we abhor Communism for the same reason as we abhor poor law systems, and systems founded on the absolute sovereignty of wealth." Connolly commented: "Students of socialism today will recognise that many who are earnest workers for socialism today would, like Devin Reilly, have 'abhorred' the crude Communism of 1848." Connolly is here referring to the preface to the 1888 English translation of the *Communist Manifesto*, where Engels explains why the word Communist was preferred to Socialist. In those days socialism was a middle-class movement, communism a working-class movement. "It was a crude rough-hewn purely instinctive sort of communism," said Engels. This crudity consisted in lack of scientific development, not in an inclination to political excess. But since 1874 there had been an increasing tendency for the followers of Bakunin to adopt the title "Communist", and in the first years of the twentieth century the anarchists regularly advertised meetings as "Communist". The connotation of the two terms had changed, as it has changed again. Connolly possibly thought Engels's "crude" communism betokened something akin to the anarchism which was still being fought in his early years in the socialist movement. He was certainly not referring to the communism of the *Manifesto,* which he repeatedly quoted.

The final chapter of *Labour in Irish History* summarizes the effect of the land reform. The Land Acts acting in conjunction with the development of transatlantic traffic were converting Ireland from a feudal into a capitalist country. "Today the competition of trust-owned farms of the United States and the Argentine Republic is a more deadly enemy than the lingering remnants of landlordism or the bureaucratic officialism of the British Empire. Capitalism is now the enemy. . . . The merely *political* heresy under which middle-class doctrinaires have for nearly 250 years cloaked the Irish fight for freedom has thus run its course . . . the Irish toilers from henceforward will base their fight for freedom not upon the winning or losing of the right to talk to an Irish Parliament, but upon their progress towards the mastery of those factories, workshops and farms upon which a people's bread and liberties depend."

Labour in Irish History established Connolly's reputation as a socialist thinker. It received favourable reviews and a wide distribution. While it contains many formulations which smack of syndicalism, it remains the best exposition of the role of the property question in the history of Irish politics and is being periodically reprinted up to the present day.

THE SOCIALIST PARTY OF IRELAND

Connolly returned to a Europe in which the revolutionary tide was flowing once more. In Britain the Conservative party had suffered the rout of its history. Twenty-nine Labour M.P.s alongside a huge Liberal majority announced that henceforth the working class was in politics. The Liberals won two further elections in January and December 1910, and the conflicts of the ensuing period struck ever nearer to the roots of social discontent.

After a trade recession somewhat milder than America's came a period of relative prosperity when, despite fluctuations in employment, rents and prices steadily advanced and each month brought a turn of the screw. The Liberal government was committed to an arms race which, though modest by mid-century standards, placed a dead-weight on the economy. Its efforts to head off discontent by introducing social services alarmed the Conservatives while winning little gratitude from the workers. As the Tory party fell back on its inner defences of Lords, Crown and Army, the Liberals were compelled to rally popular enthusiasm in one constitutional crisis after another. With brave words and lead in their hearts they set the masses in motion. From 1911 onwards Britain suffered the "great unrest", a crisis in some ways as severe as that of the eighties, and arising on the new basis of fully developed imperialism.

The sharpest wage-offensive of the twentieth century became inextricably interwoven with democratic demands, the most important of which were women's suffrage and the supremacy of the Commons. The middle class acquired a vicarious backbone from the example of workers. The eunuch Home Rule became a whole man again. In Belfast and Dublin especially were focused struggles of world-wide import, how inevitably may be judged from a simple review of living standards.

Dublin (and for most purposes Belfast too) differed from

London in two important respects, first in a lower average wage, and second in a greater differential between skilled and unskilled workers. Between 1905 and 1912 the cost of living rose by 8 per cent in London but by 12 per cent in Dublin. The principal item of working-class expenditure was then, far more than today, food. The 12 per cent general increase in Dublin derived from a 15 per cent increase in food prices, rents rising by only 1 per cent. While it was true that in Dublin meat remained 20 per cent cheaper than in London, other foodstuffs which formed the staple diet of the unskilled workers were 7 per cent dearer. As for wages, printers enjoyed 90 per cent of the London rate, skilled building workers 72 per cent, while labourers were separated by a further great gulf: they received only 54 per cent. All circumstances thus combined to bear disastrously on the worst placed sections of the Irish working class.

The cause of the continual turmoil in Dublin was thus not Larkin but what Larkin found awaiting him. Here was no aristocracy of labour confronted by the masses of non-privileged, but a class of untouchables set far below the by no means sumptuous standards of average subsistence. The death rate in Dublin exceeded that of Moscow and was the highest in western Europe. Even so, twopence-halfpenny could still look down on twopence. The skilled trades had for years conducted their struggles without reference to the interests of the labourers. Now Larkin was leading these, to use their ubiquity and weight of numbers with equivalent disregard for the convenience of the "proud artisans".

In Britain the theoretical confusion of socialist thought remained the dark aspect of a promising outlook. The S.D.F. (re-named the S.D.P.) preserved the tradition of scientific socialism, but after the breakaway of the S.L.P. in 1903, and the S.P.G.B. in 1904, Hyndman's supporters faced no major challenge for a number of years. Few followed his outright advocacy of a strong navy to fight Germany, but many went half way with him. Alongside Hyndman's opportunist acceptance of the main purpose of imperialism, the defence of the Empire against German encroachment, went much sectish face-saving. *Justice* condemned the suffrage movement as an affair of "bourgeois women". Home Rule was a matter of small consequence, to be supported but not sacrificed for. The political leadership of the workers struggling for wage-increases was thus handed to Lansbury and his associates, the militancy of whose *Daily Herald* was dismissed contemptuously as its "rebelly tone". The importance of uniting the democratic movement was not understood. Its agitations proceeded "side by side", only gradually harmonising. Many of the most active workers were attracted to the practicalist outlook of syndicalism, whose characteristically British form became an odd emotional amalgam of revolution and reform, very appealing to the old militants of the I.L.P.

Attempts were made, as twenty years previously, to transplant British exotics into Ireland. Now they made less impression. Purely British politics were confined to Belfast where there was an S.D.P. branch led by Rennie, an S.L.P. group with anarchist leanings led by the brothers Orr, and about four branches of the I.L.P. Local elections were still conducted by trade union endorsement of approved individuals, but a demand was growing for more consistent and co-ordinated policy and organisation. The only centre round which Irish socialist societies could group was the Socialist Party of Ireland. This much the I.S.R.P. had established, that Dublin socialism was comparatively uncomplicated by cross-channel influences. Though not clear or united on programme or tactics, its aims were presented in a form whose merit was their simplicity—an Irish state with a socialist government. The S.P.I. was the pivot on which Connolly proposed to balance and unite north and south.

He landed at Derry on Tuesday July 26, 1910, and was met at Amiens Street, Dublin, by old friends and supporters. His first action was to pay a visit to Larkin in Mountjoy Prison. On the Thursday a reception was held in his honour at the Antient Concert Rooms in Pearse Street (then Gt. Brunswick Street). While he busied himself with finalising the text of *Labour, Nationality and Religion* during the day, he returned each evening to the old propaganda places. His old associates noticed his increased self-assurance and maturity, mingled with greater restraint and a dourness which some mistook for arrogance.

At the end of a fortnight he went to Belfast. An indoor meeting had been called by the brothers Orr, which was attended by Danny McDevitt, D. R. Campbell (president of the Irish T.U.C.), James Mitchell, Tom Johnson and others. It was decided to establish a branch of the S.P.I. in Belfast. This was on Sunday morning, August 7. In the afternoon the socialists went to the Custom House steps where Connolly spoke again. During the next few days he addressed two branches of the I.L.P., and from those he convinced of the need for a united Irish Socialist Party he drew together his Belfast Branch. Among the earliest recruits were Sean McEntee, who became literature secretary, Sean Crawford, Sean Murphy and William McMullen, then an apprentice in the shipyard.

Next week he was back in Dublin, speaking at Dun Laoghaire green and at St. James's fountain, under Transport Union auspices. The High Street branch was busy in the campaign Hishon had organised for the release of Larkin. The Trades Council had endorsed it on June 14, and Larkin Release Committees were collecting signatures to a petition. Connolly found Larkin's activities had already changed the outlook of the people. There were no cabbage-stalks this time.

Though he had spoken every night for three weeks, Connolly then went to Cork, where a group of socialists already existed. The most outstanding was John Dowling of Cobh, but the central figure, corresponding to Danny McDevitt in Belfast, was William O'Shea. He had been president of the Young Ireland Society which gave support to Con O'Lyhane in the gasworkers' strike of 1901. A publican with a house in Buckingham Street, on the quays, he provided a rendezvous for both local and visiting socialists, many of them seamen. The first public meeting on Saturday August 20 drew six hundred people. The second drew "two thousand earnest, eager working men and women". There was not a hostile note. George Parker, a tailor, was chairman. The meetings proceeded each night and afterwards members and those interested repaired to O'Shea's bar, where Connolly sipped lemonade and answered further questions. At the Foresters' Hall there was founded a branch of twenty-four members, among them Hearsey (an Englishman employed by Clyde Shipping), Michael O'Callaghan, Gerald O'Riordan, a carter, and Daniel Coveney of Carrigtuohill. A chirpy young Dublinman, William Travers, had constantly interrupted Connolly, twitted him on his "Napoleonic pose" and made himself a regular pest. Connolly met him accidentally on Parliament Bridge. "Any more questions?" he asked. The heckler replied that he had. Accepting an invitation to O'Shea's, Travers was convinced by Connolly's arguments and joined the S.P.I. It was typical of Connolly that he quickly made him chairman of an open-air meeting and he developed into a capable speaker. At one of the meetings, held in Daunt Square, two thousand people gathered, and two hundred copies of *Labour, Nationality and Religion* were sold. Cork could stomach this, but that a similar intrusion of socialism into Cobh took this particular form had its consequences later.

The backbone of the S.P.I. consisting of railwaymen, the Railway Servants Hall in Marlborough Street became the branch headquarters. Charles Hearsey was the first secretary.

After a final meeting in Cork on August 27 Connolly returned to Dublin in time for a meeting at Phoenix Park, but immediately on its conclusion continued to Belfast, where he spent another week. By mid-September it was possible to hold a delegate conference in Dublin at which Francis Sheehy-Skeffington presided and a national executive committee was elected. P. S. O'Hegarty indignantly denied a report that members of the Cork branch of Sinn Fein had deserted to socialism. But scarcely a week after his protest, P. T. Daly in Dublin joined the S.P.I. just after Connolly crossed to Glasgow to lecture to the Clarion Scouts and made contact with Thomas Johnston, editor of *Forward,* and John Wheatley of the Catholic Socialist movement. From October 1 Connolly contributed regularly to *Forward.* Things promised so well that he borrowed and scraped the money to bring his family back from America, "the millionaire's family" they called them on the boat. "They mean the madman's family," laughed Connolly. But he told his wife, "You are not returning to the misery you left." The S.P.I. had decided to retain his services permanently at £2 a week and about the same time issued its official statement of aims and objects, which was probably adopted at the delegate conference, or by the Executive Committee set up by it.

The manifesto runs:

"The Socialist Party of Ireland seeks to organise the workers of this country, irrespective of creed or race, into one great Party of Labour. It believes that the dependence of the working class upon the owners of capitalist property, and the desire of these capitalists and landowners to keep the vast mass of the people so subject and dependent, is the great and abiding cause of all our modern social and political evils—of nearly all modern crime, mental degradation, religious strife and political tyranny. Recognising this, it counsels the Irish working class to follow the example of the workers of every civilised country in the world, whether subject or free, and organise itself industrially and politically with the end in view of gaining control and mastery of the entire resources of the country.

"Such is our aim; such is Socialism. Our method is: Political organisation at the Ballot Box to secure the election of representatives of Socialist Principles to all the elective governing Public Bodies of this country, and thus to gradually transfer the political power of the State into the hands of those who will use it to further and extend the principle of common or public ownership. We mean to make the people of Ireland the sole and sovereign owners of Ireland, but leave ourselves free to adapt our methods to suit the development of the times. The Socialist Party of Ireland may, as the occasion seems to warrant, either enter the political field with candidates of our own, or assist in furthering every honest attempt on the part of organised Labour to obtain representation through independent working-class candidates pledged to a progressive policy of social reform. We know that every victory won for progress today is a victory for Socialism, even when the victors most anxiously repudiate our cause.

"We live in times of political change, and even of political revolution. More and more civic and national responsibility is destined to be thrust upon, or won by, the people of Ireland. Old political organisations will die out and new ones must arise to take their place; old party rallying cries and watchwords are destined to become obsolete and meaningless, and the fire of old feuds and hatreds will pale and expire before newer conceptions born of a consciousness of our common destiny. In this great awakening of Erin, Labour if guided by the lamp of Socialist teaching may set its feet firmly and triumphantly upon the path that leads to its full emancipation. But if Labour does not rise to the occasion, and allows itself to be swallowed up in and identified with new political alignments, scattering and dissipating its forces instead of concentrating them upon Socialist lines, then indeed will our last state be worse than our first.

"We therefore appeal to all workers, and to all honest friends of progress in any rank of life to throw in their lot with the Socialist Party of Ireland, and assist it in giving force, clearness and effectiveness to the gathering Working-Class Movement of this country. And on its part that Party, conscious of its high mission, pledges itself to pursue, unfalteringly and undeviatingly, its great object—common ownership of the means of producing and distributing all wealth. In other words, common ownership of our common country, the material basis of the higher intellectual and moral development of the future."

This statement is remarkable for its restitution of social-democratic in place of syndicalist conceptions. The opening paragraph owed inspiration to the Statutes of the First International, which Connolly paraphrased so often. But then followed the classical presentation of state power as a means to "extend the principle of common ownership". Considerable flexibility of tactics was permitted and the socialists were to support every democratic movement, every partial reform, while seeking to guide the entire people with socialist theory. The appeal, though primarily to the working class, included all friends of progress. On the other hand, the question of state power was still not clearly formulated. The S.P.I. hoped by securing control of one local government authority after another, "to gradually transfer the political power of the state" into the hands of socialists. But the issue of an independent central government for Ireland is not even mentioned.

How is the contrast between this and the frankly syndicalist manifesto of the I.S.F. to be explained? Not by Connolly's conversion. The next manifesto shows that. Most probably, and Connolly indicated this later, the 1910 manifesto was substantially the unity manifesto of 1908 and it was considered unwise to alter its basis when the party had just made a great expansion.

Immediately after his return from Scotland, Connolly approached the Women's Franchise League and *Inghinidhe na h'Eireann* with a suggestion for a joint campaign to extend to Ireland the Act providing for the school-feeding of necessitous children. The Trades Council was invited to receive a deputation, and consented. On November 10, just as his family were sailing, Connolly accompanied Maud Gonne to the Executive Committee where it was decided to hold a special meeting of the Council the following week. Connolly, Maud Gonne and Miss Magee urged the case, and Larkin backed them up strongly with sharp criticism of the failure of the Parliamentarians. The Trades Council agreed to approach the Lord Mayor for the calling of a conference. At first he did not respond. So on December 6 the socialists and feminists waited upon him and compelled him to call a meeting at the Mansion House on December 12.

Meanwhile Connolly had met his family at Derry and brought them to Dublin. A social evening was organised at the Antient Concert Rooms; the younger children recognised only Jack Mullery. The personnel had changed since the old days. Tom Lyng, William and Daniel O'Brien, MacLoughlin and a few more remained. Carolan remained in sympathy but was now inactive. Murtagh Lyng had died suddenly. Tom O'Brien was teaching languages in France; Bradshawe and Arnell were in London. The family found accommodation in the Ballsbridge area.

Despite tentative moves, there were no Labour candidates in the general election which took place in December. In Belfast, rather than enter politics the Trades Council drove a bargain with Joe Devlin, who had appealed to them not to split the vote. They lost the affiliation of the cabinet-makers in consequence. While unable to finance candidates, the S.P.I. issued a manifesto on the election signed by Fred Ryan (national secretary) and Connolly as national organiser, together with W. O'Brien and T. J. Lyng for Dublin, George Coulter and Thomas Johnson for Belfast, and J. Dowling and O'Leary for Cork. Connolly also discussed the election in *Forward*, taking up arms once more against his old enemy the U.I.L. which advised Irish workers in Britain to vote Liberal. Connolly's advice was to vote Labour.

After the elections Connolly resumed his campaign for school-feeding. Arrangements were made for a deputation to the Home Secretary in London. To mobilise public opinion Connolly decided on a campaign in the south, where Cork Corporation granted him the use of the City Hall. His open-air meetings, except at the National Monument, began to meet with strong organised opposition, and on March 7, 1911, there took place at Cobh, which Connolly described as "that nest of parasites feeding upon parasites", a fracas which might have ended like O'Briens "Battle of Bantry" the preceding autumn.

The Cobh (then Queenstown) Urban District Council had granted the use of the City Hall, but withdrew it at the last minute. Connolly therefore decided on an open-air meeting.

Healy, a small master painter with an interest in a local laundry where girls earned 2s. 6d. a week, appeared on the scene with his "voting tackle". It was this councillor who had secured the cancellation of the Town Hall letting. Connolly's address was listened to in silence. Then Healy asked him: "Did you write in a book that the Jesuits killed Popes?" To the sound of resentful murmurs Connolly declared: "This is an appeal to prejudice, but I will not be intimidated. My answer is that Father Kane the Jesuit denounced us in his Lenten lectures and I wrote a reply showing that the mud he had thrown at us could be more fitly thrown at him and his Order. The Jesuits and Dominicans had been expelled from many countries for political intrigue."

"What about free love?" squealed a woman's voice. "Up de Mollies!" came the answering shout from the crowd, "Three cheers for Donellan! Rush'em! D'Mollies!" The mob charged, smashing the soap box Connolly had been standing on. He and Jack Dowling fought them off as best they could till the police arrived and told them to "get back to Cork as fast as they could". They escorted them to the bar of the Rob Roy Hotel where they took refuge till merciful rain dispersed the mob. Under police protection they were escorted to the station.

Connolly's last words from the platform had been: "We'll be here again on Thursday." The police were very anxious to dissuade him. The following day every member of the S.P.I. was visited by detectives unknown to the others and advised not to go to Cobh. Not one took the advice given.

Travers took the chair on Thursday and appealed for a fair hearing, mentioning that the Young Irelanders had been chased out of Limerick. Dowling was there again, and Hartland, a worker in the naval dockyard at Haulbowline, showed rare courage in attending. On the other side there were now three local councillors, soon to be joined by their chairman, Mr. Hennessy. Beside the contestants stood District Inspector Topping's posse of fifty R.I.C. men. This time the mob was armed with chairlegs, ashplants, stakes and pokers. There was no offer of a hearing. Through the constant banging of tins and upturned buckets by crowds of small children came cries of "atheists" and "soupers". Dowling gave up after a while. Hartland did his best. Connolly was speaking when the chairman of the Council intervened. The policemen clicked heels and saluted.

"Are you against religion?" asked Hennessy.

"We are not," Connolly replied.

The crowd grew quiet with menace as Hennessy stepped forward. "Keep back boys," he called several times, interrupting himself *sotto voce* over his shoulder with "Be at 'em! Be at 'em!" He waddled over to Connolly and told him: "Look here, my good man, the decent people of this town want neither ye nor yer doctrine, and let ye take yerselves and yer followers out or I'll not answer for what may happen ye!"

Connolly grew angry and declined to move. He remarked audibly on the resemblance the chief citizen bore to a codfish standing on its tail with its mouth open. A policeman plucked him by the sleeve: "Now, Mister Connolly, will yeh please go along with Mr. Hennessy." Connolly roughly shook off the policeman's hand: "I'd die a thousand deaths before I'd go anywhere with a scoundrel like that." Hennessy elbowed his way through the crowd and Healy returned to the attack. A few more words were exchanged before the crowd charged. The socialists left their box where it was and beat a hasty retreat through a shower of stones, sticks and other missiles.

"This way," shouted Connolly as he led them through an archway to where a solitary sidecar stood. He leaped up beside the driver and with a gruff "You'll be paid," seized the reins. The others clambered aboard as the car gathered speed, and they galloped away with the Hibernians screaming behind them. They did not stop till they reached Rushbrooke station, four miles away.

No more meetings were attempted in Cobh. By a coincidence a week later Cardinal Logue denounced the A.O.H. (Board of Erin) as "a pest, a cruel tyranny, and a system of organised blackguardism". Father Lawrence O'Neill described it as a "grand old Catholic society". For once the capitalist press followed the priest and ignored the cardinal.

Throughout March the Mollie Maguires[1] continued their hooliganism against O'Brien's supporters. This accounts for the fact that the *Cork Free Press* alone gave Connolly's campaign a mention. A curious polarisation was taking place in Ireland, under the stress of the simultaneous intensification of national and social struggles. The same social strata were affected to differing degrees in the different districts, and played correspondingly different parts. Each section developed its forward and its retrogressive wing. Thus the socialists of the I.L.P. differed from those of the S.P.I. in Belfast. There were "political" and "non-political" trade unionists. Griffith appeared to the right of the Gaelic republicans, Pearse, Ceannt and MacDermott. But the more right-wing "All for Ireland Movement" which he had sought to merge with, was resisting the Molly Maguires in the south. Even the Liberal party was producing Liberal Unionists alongside the Liberal Home Rulers who had held the field so long.

Of the A.O.H. (Board of Erin) Connolly said they were the "foulest brood that ever spawned in Ireland", and Pearse commented that their "narrowing down of Nationalism to the members of one creed is the most fateful thing that has happened in Ireland since the days of the Pope's Brass Band".[2] Their function was to divert the national movement down sectarian channels, while Redmond discussed forms of devolution even less far-reaching than Home Rule. Sectarianism was easier started than stopped. It contributed enormously to the confirmation of Orange bigotry in the north, and thus helped to divide the working-class movement.

On returning to Dublin Connolly found fresh disappointments. Party funds were proving insufficient to maintain him. There was a tendency among some of the members to capitulate to the A.O.H. attacks. Indeed after his removal to Belfast the Dublin Branch approached the A.O.H. with a

---

[1] So-named after an Enniskillen woman of the sectarian land war whose craziness expressed itself as exaggerated Catholicity.

[2] The derisive name given to the Parliamentary party of Sadleir and Keogh who made a parade of their Catholicity in order to sidetrack support for the Tenants' Right League in the eighteen- fifties.

17 Greaves; Connolly

most humbly worded appeal not to interfere with their meetings. The Spring-Rice family had been contributing to the party, but now withdrew their support for private reasons. Connolly had the problem of employment for his older daughters, and maintaining the younger children. He crossed to Scotland, visited Edinburgh and told John Leslie that he was contemplating settling in England. The set-backs in Cork, and the slow growth of the movement must be measured against the urgency of his economic situation. "My first mistake was to go to America," he said, "my second was to leave it." Leslie encouraged him to return to Ireland. "You'll find a niche in the temple of fame," he told him. He went back, but it was to Belfast, whither he brought first his daughter Nora, and then the rest of the family. He took up temporary residence with Danny McDevitt at 5, Rosemary Street, "the bounder's college", where every conceivable rebel group met at some time or other.

In Belfast he joined the Irish Transport Workers' Union. When its Dublin members had left the National Union of Dock Labourers, Belfast had refused to follow them. P. T. Daly, who had joined Larkin's staff, made excursions to the north without success. The I.T.W.U. was regarded as a "Fenian" breakaway and there was some resentment against Larkin, such as often persists after an industrial defeat. Only seven members attended Connolly's first branch meeting, which elected McKeown as delegate to the I.T.U.C. meeting in Galway. Connolly was disappointed at not winning the nomination himself. He wanted to support a resolution calling for the establishment of an Irish Labour Party. Some ill-considered remarks passed by Larkin led him to suspect he was being "frozen out". Larkin was not a member of the S.P.I. but had claimed membership during a tour of Scotland. Yet not once had Larkin invited Connolly to speak while he was living in Dublin. Like many a man of the heart, identifying himself with the cause, Larkin quite unthinkingly identified the cause with himself, and trod on other peoples' toes mercilessly. His ebullience and unpredictability always riled Connolly, who squirmed when he heard him support quite sound courses of action with the most appallingly wrong arguments. He tolerated him for his ability to come down on the side of the angels, while venturing to doubt that this was due to a private telephone connection with God.

There were stormy scenes at the I.T.U.C. The proposal for an Irish Labour Party "to fight the capitalist parties of Ireland on their own soil" was countered by William Walker's amendment pledging support for the British Labour Party. Walker won by 32 votes to 29. As Connolly put it, "The unborn Labour Party of Ireland was strangled in the womb by the hands of the I.L.P.-ers." Agreed on all economic questions, the I.T.U.C. had been rendered politically nugatory because of a fundamental divergence of socialist opinion. Socialist unity must be achieved as quickly as possible, and Connolly addressed himself to this question in an article in *Forward*, which was published on May 27, 1911.

> "The I.L.P. in Belfast," he wrote, "believes that the Socialist movement in Ireland must perforce remain a dues-paying organic part of the British Socialist movement ... whereas the S.P.I. maintain that the relations between Socialism in Ireland and in Great Britain should be fraternal and not organic, and should operate by exchange of literature and speakers rather than by attempts to treat as one, two peoples of whom one has for 700 years nurtured an unending martyrdom rather than admit the unity or surrender its national identity. The Socialist Party of Ireland considers itself the only International Party in Ireland, since its conception of Internationalism is that of a free federation of free peoples, whereas that of the Belfast branches of the I.L.P. seems scarcely distinguishable from imperialism, the merging of subjugated peoples in the political system of their conquerors."

To Connolly an absolute condition of socialist unity in Ireland was the acceptance of the minimum programme of the national movement. William Walker, on the other hand, had pledged himself to oppose Home Rule and support the

Protestant succession (and thus incidentally a "socialist" monarchy!). Connolly dealt uncompromisingly with his pledges.

"Why sacrifice all Ireland for a part of Belfast?" he concluded, and proposed a convention at which the I.L.P. and the S.P.I. would discuss unity from the standpoint of an Irish-based socialist movement asserting Ireland's right to self-government.

Walker was game enough to reply. But he proved an unworthy opponent. His conception of socialism was completely reformist. He pointed with pride to the progress of "municipal socialism" in Belfast. Did they not "collectively own and control" gasworks, waterworks, harbour works, markets, tramways, electricity, museums and art galleries? They had even organised a police band. Walker saw no more in socialism than an extension of these things. If of such were the world's greatest goods, why should Irish people not concentrate on securing more of them throughout Ireland? To the "sweatshops under the Orange flag" he made no reference, nor to the conditions of dockers and carters in the municipal paradise. Himself representing the extremity of Belfast's peculiar parochialism, he accused Connolly of lack of true internationalism and a "conservative temperament".

But he was acute enough to quote Fintan Lalor's remark that "the land question contains and the legislative question does not contain the materials from which victory is to be manufactured". Walker quoted Lalor, but he forgot to quote himself. He had ascribed the increasing conservatism of the larger farmers to the reformist Land Acts. The extension of the parallel did not occur to him and he concluded that it was a "peculiar brand of socialism that aims at legislative independence before socialism". Then, with the typical inconsequentiality of Carlisle Circus, he grew lyrical over the "wonderful organisation" of the United Irishmen and boasted of the number of Protestants who were rebels for Ireland.

Connolly, in his reply, quoted Marx's famous letter to Kugelman, which had been published in *Neue Zeit* in 1902.

In it Marx had argued that the British workers should take the initiative in dissolving the Union in their own interests. Failing that, said Marx, the English people, in league with their rulers against the Irish, would be forever dependent on them. The Irish question was not merely an economic question, it was also a democratic question, a question of national independence. Connolly did not omit to remind Walker that the Protestant United Irishmen he cited with such pride would all have argued against him. And to all this Walker, in his next rejoinder, could do no more than describe as "frothy talk" the claim that internationalism did not exclude nationalism. Words overmastered him, things were beyond him.

There was no common ground. Whether he knew it or not, Walker was the forerunner of that type of imperialist organiser who goes to a colonial country to teach that a tenth of a loaf is better than no bread, and to promote "advancement within the framework of the Commonwealth". Needless to say when the war broke out with imperial Germany, internationalism was engulfed in nationalism, and the British lion was quite another thing. The controversy was closed by Tom Johnston when Walker, all else failing, descended to an abusive personal attack on Connolly. Thinking as he did, it was quite logical that (very soon afterwards) he should quit the Labour movement for an official position under the new Insurance Act. Several others followed him, of those approached only Sam Haslett declining. Connolly thought bitterly over what is now called "right-wing Labourism". "You train them, and we buy them," a Duchess remarked to Hyndman.

The polemic drew to its close during the wave of chauvinism which surrounded the coronation of King George V. Once again black flags flew in Limerick and Kilkenny. John Daly declared that he was "still a Fenian" and while Connolly was speaking to the same effect in Beresford Place, police made a charge on Countess Markiewicz's meeting outside the Sinn Fein office in Harcourt Street. Rival crowds sang "God save Ireland" and "God save the King". The coronation enthusiasm was confined to the middle class and the most depressed sections of the "lumpen-proletariat". Three days before the coronation the international seamen's strike began. Coronation night was marked by wild scenes in Liverpool, bricks and bottles flying freely. On June 26, three hundred and fifty Dublin dockers struck for a wage increase. The new monarch nonetheless decided to make the personal acquaintance of his loyal subjects in Dublin.

In connection with the royal visit Connolly drafted the famous manifesto, for distributing which Walter Carpenter received three months imprisonment.

It read:

"Fellow workers,

As you are aware from reading the daily and weekly newspapers, we are about to be blessed with a visit from King George V.

Knowing from previous experience of Royal visits as well as from the Coronation orgies of the past few weeks, that the occasion will be utilised to make propaganda on behalf of royalty and aristocracy against the oncoming forces of democracy and National freedom, we desire to place before you some reasons why you should unanimously refuse to countenance this visit, or to recognise it by your presence at its attendant processions and demonstrations. ...

The future of the working class requires that all political and social positions should be open to all men and women; that all privileges of birth or wealth be abolished, and that every man or woman born into this land should have an equal opportunity to attain to the proudest position in the land. ...

Fellow workers, stand by the dignity of your class. All these parading royalties, all this insolent aristocracy, all these grovelling, dirt-eating capitalist traitors, all these are but signs of disease in any social state ... public ownership must take the place of capitalist ownership, social democracy replace political and social inequality, the sovereignty of labour must supersede and destroy the sovereignty of birth and the monarchy of capitalism.

Ours be the task to enlighten the ignorant among our class, to dissipate and destroy the political and social superstitions of the enslaved masses and to hasten the coming day when, in the words of Joseph Brennan, the fearless patriot of '48, all the world will maintain–

> The Right Divine of Labour
> To be the first of earthly things:
> That the Thinker and the Worker
> Are Manhood's only Kings."

Such was the creed Connolly instilled into his comrades of the Socialist Party of Ireland.

BELFAST ORGANISER

While Connolly's polemic with Walker revealed the gulf between the revolutionary and the reformist, the great unrest was invading Belfast as it were to try the case by practice.

Scarcely had the seamen gained their demands, when the dockers, who had come out in sympathy, preferred their own. The seamen were prepared to help those who had helped them, and by the end of June paralysis was creeping round all coasts. The cross channel dockers in Belfast were most intimately involved. These enjoyed regular employment and were for the most part Protestants. The more casual work provided by deep-sea vessels was left to the Catholics. Connolly grasped the idea that by bringing out the deep-sea dockers in sympathy with the cross-channel seamen, he could accomplish three aims at once. He could rebuild the Transport Union organisation which had languished since 1907, secure a complete victory over the employers, and unite the port workers irrespective of religious affiliations. It was the shrewd calculation of a man of practical imagination. Few would have risked trying to put it into effect.

William O'Brien, of the Dublin Trades Council, knew well the difficult struggle Connolly and his family faced in Belfast. The withdrawal of the contributions of middle-class supporters had coincided with the controversy with Walker. The S.P.I. could not support an organiser in Belfast on funds raised in Dublin, and Connolly's indignation knew no bounds when some well-meaning member pointed to the advantage of having daughters of employable age. O'Brien and his colleagues had for some time been urging on Larkin the desirability of appointing Connolly Belfast organiser of the Union. Larkin demurred, but the spread of the dock strike made the advantage of such a step so obvious that it was now taken. Connolly received a telegram enclosing two weeks' pay. He visited Dublin on July 16, addressed a meeting of strikers in Beresford Place, and returned to open his office in Corporation Street and look around for members. He speedily allied himself with Bennett of the Seamen's and Firemen's Union. For a time, the local newspapers imagined him to be an additional organiser for that union. They soon learned better.

Organisation began not in the office but on the job. He went to the lower docks, and introduced himself during the lunchtime break. A docker called Clarke found him a conveniently placed barrel from which he addressed the men. The Head Line was then holding out against the seamen's settlement. On July 19 he brought out three hundred dockers in sympathy and marched with them to meetings at Garmoyle Street and the Custom House steps. There, arrangements were made for picketing the cross-channel boats. At the same time the dockers stated their own claim for increased pay, cessation of speed-up and shorter working hours.

The Transport Union was without funds. The S.F.U. could pay only its own members, and was moreover but poorly connected in Belfast, even lacking affiliation to the Trades Council. Quick to realise the difficulties of the new union, and remembering 1907, the employers plastered the quays with notices demanding an unconditional return to work on Monday, on pain of a general lock-out. To their surprise the men stood firm. For this Connolly's tireless ingenuity was responsible. Enthusiasm was never allowed to subside. He secured players from both Catholic and Orange bands, and combined them into what became subsequently the "Non-Sectarian Labour Band". Using I.W.W. technique he paraded through Belfast taking up street collections for the strike fund. The Trades Council held a special meeting on the 30th at which D. R. Campbell warmly pledged full support, and invited the S.F.U. to affiliate. Thanks to help from Dublin, Connolly made two strike benefit payments of 4s. 6d. one week and 5s. the next.

As a result of the Trades Council meeting, attention was focused upon the conditions of the dockers for the first time since 1907. Public sympathy veered strongly in their direction. Men were being paid one penny for shovelling a ton of iron ore, the rate for corresponding work in Britain being fourpence. Grain workers had to lift one hundred tons a day for 5s. If they lifted one hundred and twenty, each member of the gang earned a bonus of 6d. Hours of labour were unlimited. If a winch broke down for fifteen minutes, a quarter of a day's pay was forfeited. So accelerated was the pace of work that men could not stand it for more than three days a week. Hence by labour which "strained every muscle to the breaking point" and "feverish recklessness menacing life and limb", they could contrive to earn 15s. a week.

The Burns Laird Line was the first to offer a settlement with their seamen, but the S.F.U. refused to return without the dockers. Their resolve was strengthened when, following reports from Liverpool, the cross-channel dockers ceased work. Things began to look serious in Belfast and the employers elected an "executive" to act on behalf of all companies using the port. Wild scenes took place when coal, grain and flax carts were upset and their contents scattered over the cobbles. But sectarianism was absent.

As the enemy grouped their forces, Connolly grew a little dubious of victory. His first supporter, Clarke, caught him standing, head in his hands, elbows on the bannisters of the union premises, hesitant over his meeting at the Custom House steps. What was he to do next? Clarke gave him the evening paper which reported that the employers had decided to offer a compromise settlement which included recognition of the union and a shilling a day extra for one hundred tons. Connolly's face lit up and he seized the paper eagerly. "We'll accept," he declared. "Better take what we can and avoid a prolonged struggle." The meeting was transformed into a victory meeting. Next day he issued a press statement, drawing attention to the employers' concessions and calling on the public to see that they kept their promises. Belfast remained the lowest paying port in the United Kingdom, but the wage increase averaged 3s. a week and there was some lightening of labour.

In the temporary calm following the shipping strike Connolly was able to find a house at Glenalina Terrace at the head of the Falls Road, and bring his family from Dublin. Nora had already secured work in the ware-room or making-up department of a linen mill. In her memoir she recalled her surprise at learning she was a "papish" and at the absurd system of craft snobbery which divided the linen workers.

It was a strange, fascinating, yet not incomprehensible city which was his home for the next few years. A seething Brummagem planted on one of the finest sites in Europe, it owed its existence to two industries, linen and shipbuilding. Through the Lagan valley it tapped a hinterland stretching to Cavan, Sligo and Donegal, and became a considerable port and commercial centre, in Connolly's day the most populous city in Ireland.

The social composition of Belfast was peculiar and cannot be understood apart from its history. Unlike Dublin it was a product of the industrial revolution. In 1757 its population stood at only 8,500. By 1831 it had reached 50,000 and thereafter doubled in twenty years. It continued to grow rapidly throughout the latter half of the century. By tracing the causes of this rapid growth, and the origin of the new population, it is possible to understand many of the peculiar features of the labour movement which grew up in it, and which Connolly had to contend with.

For many years the linen trade rested on a cottage industry dispersed throughout north-east Ireland. Throughout Ulster the small farmers grew their own flax, which they spun, wove and bleached by the aid of their own families. In this respect Ulster differed from the other three provinces, where cottage woollens were slowly eliminated and replaced by nothing else. If the Ulster peasant could now no more clothe himself than his counterpart in Leinster, he was producing a commodity whose market price would clothe him and to spare. As British imports ousted the southerner's cottage product he was offered no avenue of capitalist development. To him land became everything. Get land or get out was the dilemma which produced one agrarian revolt after another. In Ulster the dual character of the tenant's function, as peasant on the soil and the producer of an industrial product essential to the trading class, was reflected in the system of land tenure known as the "Ulster custom". Under this arrangement not only had the landlord a right to his rent. The tenant possessed a goodwill which must be paid to him by his successor. Landlords frequently deplored this arrangement, but their connections with mortgagors and merchants were close enough to afford them corresponding compensation.

As capitalism developed, first one and then another subdivision of linen manufacture separated itself from the land. The first was bleaching, the final stage in the process. By ceasing to spread their webs in the fields to bleach in the sun, and instead taking brown linen to market, the farmers saved valuable land. This became possible only after the invention of chlorine bleaching. The brown linen trade concentrated in the markets of the larger towns. The bleaching companies then began to enter weaving, in turn centralising this branch of the industry. The process led inevitably to the introduction of steam-powered machinery, the dependence of which on imported coal drew everything towards the port of Belfast like an economic magnet.

The ultimate application of power to spinning deprived the cottager of his last base. From the eighteen-twenties onwards, countless small producers were ruined. Farmers disposed of their tenant right and drifted into Belfast. The hard-pressed cottager had for years employed his whole family, frequently eighteen hours a day, in the vain endeavour to keep his independence and his plot of land. Habits of drudgery were deeply ingrained. Accordingly, it was easy for employers to save factory space by introducing "outwork" in the finishing processes which did not lend themselves so easily to existing forms of mechanisation. Girls and boys were recruited to the mills. When it became obligatory for them to attend school they worked in the mills as "part-timers". From the period of the fifties, when the great shipyard expansion began, the income of a working-class family was the sum of a number of sweated wages. The availability of cheap labour, seeing salvation in hard work rather than in combination, attracted enterprises from Scotland and England, which further contributed to the rapid rise of Belfast.

Workers being thus assembled together, organisation was inevitable. But certain factors tended to retard it. The most important was sectarianism. This had been inculcated with disastrous results before 1798 as a means of dividing the tenant farmers. It was still strong in the country, while dormant in Belfast till the fifties. Employers made full use of the fact that Catholic and Protestant ex-farmers presented themselves in Belfast as competitors. They carefully balanced the numbers of each religion in their workshops. The Protestant majority could thus be led to believe that their best protection would be an all-Protestant shop. In the event of a Catholic majority (a less usual state of affairs), the Catholics would feel similar anxiety to be free of the competition of the Protestants. The growth of working-class sectarianism was thus a perverted form of the tendency of the working class to eliminate competition in its own ranks. It was the correctness of the instinct which gave it its terrible power, the narrowness of its application turning it into its opposite. Into sectarian feeling was also translated some of the resentment of the older weavers against the mill-workers who were now undercutting them. But it was left to the Protestant clergy, at a time when sectarian feeling was being whipped up in Britain also, to create a philosophy in which the love of God was identified with the hatred of fellow men.

The Belfast workers contained a high proportion of new arrivals. They were naturally lacking in the dogged if parochial solidarity of the Dublinmen, which had taken centuries to breed. When the Presbyterian Reverend Hanna warned his flock that their "blood-bought cherished rights were imperilled by the audacious and savage outrages of a Romish mob", they really believed themselves in danger.

In the riots which ensued, Catholics established in predominantly Protestant areas (that is, along the roads leading to Protestant districts of the countryside whence their inhabitants had originally come) were forcibly ejected and the ghetto-like character of the Falls Road area began to develop. At the same time it should be noticed that following the down-fall of Chartism sectarian riots occurred in Britain also.

Sectarianism was the employer's safeguard. Through it he was enabled to maintain a system of low wages, long hours and exploitation of entire families. It was not surprising therefore that organisation, when it developed, entirely lacked the strongly indigenous quality noticeable in Dublin. Members of skilled trades, after immigration from Scotland or England, demanded conditions customary for craftsmen across the channel. Shipbuilding and linen were large-scale industries absent from Dublin. The link with Britain, which might beggar his employer and put a Dublinman out of work, was on the contrary seen in Belfast as the worker's only safeguard. By the same token the industrialists were strong Home Rulers, willing to sacrifice the landlords in order to become the exclusive exploiters of the people. All this silently wrote itself into the consciousness of the Protestant worker. His consciousness was the reflection of his material conditions, not some mysterious perversity incapable of rational explanation. The Catholic, on the other hand, required the protection of his co-religionists outside the Belfast area, voted for national candidates, and having less to lose was more prepared to take his chance in any political reshuffle.

The centre of working-class organisation was the Belfast Trades Council. Founded in 1881, it had not the long pre-history of its sister in Dublin. It gathered its forces slowly, through affiliation of branches of the large amalgamated unions. Lacking breadth of tradition it was less the prey to illusions. It passed few resolutions exalting the patriotism of the employers, and was protesting against the Liberal-Labour alliance with the U.I.L. long before Connolly took up the cudgels. Quite early in its history its leadership fell to men who were socialists according to their lights, and its record of solidarity was second to none.

In some respects Belfast was ahead of Dublin. Granted that the socialist sects meant little taken separately, there was a strong total sentiment for independent working-class political action. Parliamentary candidates were offered long before such a thing was thinkable elsewhere in Ireland. But though they were certainly unconscious of it, these tended to uphold the interests of the skilled workers only. From the unskilled they were separated by a wall of sectarianism. Without winning the suffrages of a section of the Catholics they could never be victorious. And to do this it was necessary to transcend the limitations of I.L.P. socialism and take up the national struggle against imperialism strongly enough to win away sufficient Catholics from their adhesion to Joseph Devlin. Neither endorsing Devlin nor ignoring him could succeed in doing this. As long as Labour was bounded by such limitations it was open at any crisis to blows which could hurl it back close to its starting point.

Belfast was thus a supreme challenge to Connolly, a city bursting with revolutionary potentialities, but bedevilled by a special imp of disunity arising from its historical development. It was a hard nut which he failed to crack. At another time he might have succeeded. But for three years after the time of his arrival, the entire resources of Tory reaction were concentrated on this one city. With all his skill and experience Connolly had not time to rally forces of comparable magnitude. The outcome of the struggle, which became an issue for the entire British Empire, was the polarisation and ultimately the enforced partition of Ireland. Connolly's efforts to prevent this provide a classic illustration of socialist resourcefulness and adherence to principle.

An unexpected opportunity came his way on October 4, 1911, when a number of mill-girls, striking spontaneously against a speed-up introduced by the masters to evade an agreement to restrict output, approached Connolly for advice. Among them were the wives and daughters, indeed the mothers, of the dockers he had just organised. It was Troy over again. Throughout the shops notices were posted an-

nouncing a system of fines for, among other things, singing,
laughing, talking, or even "adjusting the hair during working
hours". The introduction of sweets or knitting needles into
the mill spelled instant dismissal.

The mill-girls were mostly unorganised. The Trades
Council was indeed aware of a widespread discontent, now
erupting, and had sponsored the formation of a linen-work-
ers' union under the leadership of Miss Mary Galway. Characteristically, she had concentrated on the better-paid Protestant workers in the making-up section. She declined to
assist the mill-girls in their "unofficial" struggle against the
new rules, and when some of her own members joined the
strikers and went to listen to Connolly's meeting, she held
a counter-demonstration to denounce the strike. Connolly
held several open-air meetings and finally booked the St.
Mary's Hall, which was crammed with 1,500 women.

With great astuteness Connolly had preferred a wage-claim
as well as demanding the rescission of the rules. The band was
brought out again and the collecting boxes gathered enough
to give each striker 2s. a week. Some Catholic priests denounced the strike, and one sermon was a diatribe against
syndicalism, socialism, Connolly and all his works and
pomps. He attended this Mass and sat impassive through the
invective. When it became clear that the masters would not
negotiate, he showed how well he understood that a disciplined army can retreat to victory. The strike had given the
women a unity of will which they had previously lacked. He
advised them to go back, but to disregard the rules. If one
girl was checked for singing, let all sing. If one was dismissed
let all walk out. Production would be reduced to chaos.
The masters gave in. The rules became a dead letter, and
meanwhile Connolly set about organising the textile workers'
section of the Irish Transport Workers Union.

The new organisation was founded at the end of November, Mrs. Tom Johnson being the first secretary. Its establishment was not allowed to pass unchallenged. At a meeting of
the Trades Council, upon which Connolly now represented
the Transport Union, Miss Galway complained of "inter-

ference" and requested Connolly to "confine himself to the class of workers he was sent to represent". There was a sharp debate, in which Walker's followers were vociferous in support of Miss Galway. Walker had been working hard to prevent a Home Ruler representing the Council at the British Labour Party conference. The unholy alliance of Connolly, Campbell and Johnson filled him with alarm. Widely divergent as their views were, to Walker all three were "Fenians". He was anxious to keep Connolly's influence down and to prevent a second Transport Union delegate reaching the Council.

Connolly repudiated the allegation of poaching. There were 18,000 textile workers unorganised. When he was approached by the strikers he had asked were they members of Miss Galway's union, and was told they were not. Unparliamentary language had been used to emphasise this point. They now had rooms and offices in York Street and they were going to stop there. He was not going to allow eighteen thousand women to remain unorganised just because the Trades Council had organised the Textile Operatives Society. To those who had criticised his activities on the docks he answered that before the end of the year—he was speaking a week before Christmas—there would not be a worker on Donegall Quay who was not in the Transport Union.

Connolly was able to back up his word. In November he had attempted to secure the 6s. rate for an eight hour day, but had agreed to a compromise of 6s. for an eighty ton day. It was difficult for Miss Galway to place much against the fact, and she therefore agreed to "seek an amicable settlement".

Meanwhile the Belfast bakers had been on strike, and a prolonged struggle for union recognition had taken place in Dundalk. There is a tradition that Connolly spoke in Dundalk during this struggle. Certainly both Belfast and Dublin representatives of the Union spoke there, and Connolly may have spoken at one of the numerous open-air meetings which were held. Wexford, however, he certainly visited in Jan-

273

uary 1912, in order to take part in one of the most hard-fought struggles of Irish labour history.

After the settlement of a strike on Wexford Quays, the workers of the three foundries had followed the dockers into the I.T.W.U., but the ironmasters did not wait for their demands. They closed down their works and informed the men that they were dismissed. This was towards the end of August 1911. P. T. Daly was sent from Dublin, held a protest meeting in the Bull Ring, and shortly found himself confronted with a general lock-out. The quay labourers made a fresh wage demand and resumed their strike. Three hundred extra police were drafted into the town and one of their baton charges resulted in the death of a worker, Michael Leary. As a consequence, Daly enrolled the "Workers' Police", the first proletarian defence force recorded in Ireland.

The strike afforded Arthur Griffith an opportunity to express sympathy with his countrymen fighting tyranny, and *Sinn Fein*[1] published a blistering attack on Larkin. The result was a strong and dignified protest from Eamonn Ceannt, who from that time disengaged himself from Sinn Fein and moved towards Pearse and MacDermott who were working on the Republican paper, *Irish Freedom*.

"You have no condemnation of the Employers' Federation," Ceannt told Griffith, "or is there one law for them and another for their servants?" He urged that Sinn Fein should encourage Irish trade unionism, and not insult it at every opportunity.

The strike dragged on through the autumn. The employers haughtily declined offers of mediation by the Corporation. The men received support from the ever-willing Dublin Trades Council, and Connolly organised a meeting in Belfast at which the Wexford men put their case and took back a collection. P. T. Daly toured the countryside asking for support, thus spreading the influence of the rebel union to New Ross, Enniscorthy and even to quite small villages. Oulart Irish Trade and Labour League (a survival of Davitt's old

[1] Journal of the Sinn Fein party replacing the *United Irishman*.

organisation) voted funds. Shopkeepers provided credit. The Gaelic Athletic Association organised games in support of the strikers and the police broke their heads for them when they paraded with black flags. Daly and local secretary Peter O'Connor recruited sturdy lieutenants in Corish and Furlong, but not a dint could be made in the employers' determination to resist to the end. The Wexford strike was the first great labour struggle in which important sections of the small middle class went over to the side of the workers.

In mid-October the employers announced their intention to re-open with scab labour. This came in driblets, escorted by police. The locked-out men were kindly permitted to apply for reinstatement on condition they abjured the union. Not one did so. They held out over Christmas, and the employers were then faced with the necessity of conducting their business entirely with imported labour. This created an accommodation problem. Brushing aside the protests of the clergy, anxious to avoid such an injection of infidels into their flocks, they attempted to provide hostel accommodation on the one hand, and on the other urged landlords to evict Wexford men for non-payment of rent. They declared their willingness, however, to employ trade unionists provided they were not members of the Transport Union. It was at this point that Connolly was sent to Wexford.

He arrived on January 30, only to find Daly had been arrested and lodged in Waterford jail. Charged with "persistent following" of a blackleg, he refused to give bail to desist from this nefarious practice, on the grounds that it was not unlawful. A case was then stated for a higher court. Shortly afterwards a meeting took place where police were so thick that the public could scarcely enter the Bull Ring. Preparations for Daly's arrest had been made with great secrecy. He was allowed to return to his office. The building was then sealed off. When Daly emerged he was seized and taken to an emergency court in the police barracks, tried in camera and, a true bill being found, was taken by train out of Wexford. When the workers learned of it there was a huge protest demonstration at which further arrests were made.

Connolly's first difficulty was to discover exactly what had happened. He took a room in the hotel where P. T. Daly had stayed, and asked for the organiser's papers. "Not even his wife would get them without his personal instructions," said the proprietress, and all of Connolly's best persuasions were in vain. He must proceed by horse-sense and guesswork.

His approach was, as ever, political. He consolidated the support of the shopkeepers by pointing out that the iron industry might leave Wexford for ever. He was there to try and prevent that, by means of a just settlement. He did not wish to ruin the foundries. He proposed taking the employers at their word. They would accept any union but the Transport Union. He would therefore establish a new union, which would affiliate nationally to the Transport Union in Dublin. There remained the issue of the imported workers. Most of these did not wish to stay; he would therefore advise a return to work on the understanding that the imported workers would be sent away as soon as possible.

These proposals proved acceptable, and the final terms were negotiated through the good offices of Cruise O'Brien, editor of the *Wexford Free Press*, who acted as intermediary between Connolly and the employers.

"A drawn battle," Connolly commented, as he organised a victory demonstration. The Bull Ring rang with "Freedom's Pioneers" to the tune of the "Boys of Wexford". But returning from a visit to P. T. Daly in Waterford jail, he found a fresh dispute threatening. Doyle's foundry had refused to dismiss the scabs till the Wexford men were actually at work. The men refused to start till the scabs were gone. The settlement of February 8 was back in the melting pot. Connolly called a meeting in the Bandroom and insisted that the men carry out strictly the terms of the agreement. During the next few days the imported workers left the town.

But now Connolly must conduct a campaign for the release of Daly. This kept him in the south until early March. The organiser was charged with "incitement to riot", a misdemeanour only known among men of the left. Connolly declared that Daly's detention was illegal and demanded a public enquiry. He took the matter up with Mr. Field, M.P., who asked a question in Parliament. A compromise was reached on this issue also. Daly had to find sureties to be of good behaviour in Wexford, and was thereupon permitted to return to Dublin.

Connolly availed himself of the waiting period to set the organisation of the Foundrymen's Union on a firm footing, and to spread the Transport Union through Co. Wexford. The branch at New Ross had suffered a decline and he decided to try to revive it. On arrival in the town he and Peter O'Connor were met by the local police chief who confidentially passed on a terrible warning that had reached him in his professional capacity. Connolly's open-air meeting was to be the object of a planned attack by local hoodlums. For his own safety he urged him to abandon the notion of speaking in New Ross. "I'm not accustomed to being bluffed," Connolly replied, and proceeded to hold an attentive meeting in the presence of thirty-six policemen, after which the recruits to the union marched to 96, Mary Street to fill in their application forms.

Once more in Belfast, with only a month before the Home Rule Bill was to be introduced, Connolly must hastily gather up the threads of interrupted political work. The seeming imminence of Home Rule raised urgent questions. Like Pearse and Griffith he welcomed Home Rule as an instalment, though a modest one, of national independence. He regarded it as a natural political consequence of the Land Acts and the removal of the landlord garrison. It was the legislative acceptance of an economic *fait accompli,* the establishment of a capitalist garrison. He does not appear to have distinguished between different sections of Irish capitalists. He regarded the Unionism of the Belfast industrial magnates as a purely political reaction, solidarity with their blood-brothers of English Conservatism rather than arising from the unwillingness of monopoly capitalists to come under the heel of shopkeepers and farmers. Once the landlords had gone there was no single possessing class capable of ruling all Ireland. Only the democracy could do that.

While necessarily unaware of the terrible force with which this truth would assert itself, Connolly followed it as his lodestar. Throughout the autumn and winter he had sought opportunities to address the I.L.P. branches. He invited their members to joint discussions at Rosemary Street. It was essential, he argued, that the Irish legislature should have a Labour opposition. He pointed to the record of the Parliamentary party on social questions, their opposition to the extension of the school meals service to Ireland, and the medical benefits of the Insurance Act. Now he made final preparations for a conference which took place at Easter in Dublin. Of the five Belfast branches of the I.L.P., only one (William Walker's) let the S.P.I. invitation "lie on the table". The Belfast branch of the British Socialist Party (a fusion of the Social-Democratic Party, formerly Federation, with left-wing I.L.P. elements grouped round Victor Grayson) was also represented. The S.P.I. had delegates from Belfast, Dublin and Cork.

The conference was held in the Antient Concert Rooms. The B.S.P. delegates left early. The occasion was a skittish prank played by one of the Dubliners. A Union Jack was spread on the floor in place of a doormat. Trampling on the symbol of the forcible fusion of nations was more than the representatives of the revolutionary proletariat could stomach. The I.L.P. laughed off this regrettable contretemps and out of the conference arose the new "Independent Labour Party of Ireland".

Connolly's approach to the all-important question of the working-class party was tentative and experimental. Throughout his life he groped for the correct formula. Recoiling from Hyndman's opportunism, he embraced the dogmatic ultra-leftism of De Leon. Recoiling from De Leon's dogmatism he urged on the S.P.I. a constitution capable of attracting diverse trends of thought. As if repenting of this vagueness, but unwilling to insist on ideological purity, he produced the

I.L.P.(I.) programme which is remarkable in containing both social democratic and syndicalist formulations side by side. Connolly may have been influenced by an article by Jaurès which appeared in *L'Humanité* about this time, when it was argued that the two conceptions were not really at variance. The aim of the new party was presented as an "Industrial Commonwealth" based on the common ownership of the land and instruments of production, distribution and exchange, with complete political and social equality between the sexes. The means were:

1. *Political*: Organisation of the forces of labour in Ireland to take political action on independent lines for securing the control of all public elective bodies, and for the mastery of all the public powers of the State, in order that such bodies and such powers should be used for the attainment of the above object.

2. *Industrial*: Furtherance of the Industrial Organisation of the wage-earners, with a view to securing unity of action in the industrial field as a means to the conquest of industrial power, the necessary preliminary to industrial freedom.

Having placed the political and industrial means in this curious apposition, the manifesto then declared that "the I.L.P. of Ireland has been formed as the political weapon of the Irish working class, and is open to all men and women, irrespective of their past political affiliations, who desire to see the working class of their country organised upon the political field".

The statement contains no reference to the struggle for national independence. It was "no longer a question of Celt against Saxon or Catholic against Protestant, but of *all the workers against all the exploiters*".

Why the omission of the demand Connolly was so insistent upon? On April 11 the Home Rule Bill was introduced at Westminster. The Dublin gathering met in the firm expectation that Ireland would soon have her own government. This might be restricted in power, and be but an instalment of true independence. But the remainder was to be secured through the "reconquest of Ireland". This conception Connolly explained in a series of open-air lectures at Library Street during the spring. After publication in the *Irish Worker,* they were later expanded into the well-known pamphlet of the same title.

The programme of the I.L.P. (I.) was preserved when the party reverted to its old title of "Socialist Party of Ireland", and this circumstance caused endless political confusion. The programme was applicable only to the period *after* Ireland had legislative independence and as soon as the Unionist counter attack delayed the achievement of independence it became out of date. What exercised Irish socialists in 1912 was not *whether* a Home Rule Act, but *what* Home Rule Act.

The Home Rule Bill, once published, confirmed the worst prognostications of the Socialists. John Redmond explained that it was based on the ill-fated bill of 1893 with minor alterations. Unlike the Parliament of 1782 which was co-ordinated with the British, the Home Rule Parliament was to be subordinate. Autonomy was to be confined to "purely Irish" affairs. The subordinate Parliament was to have no power whatsoever relating to the Crown, peace and war, army and navy, treaties and foreign relations, colonial relations, dignities, treason, naturalisation, aliens, light-houses, coinage, legal tender, weights and measures, trade marks copyright and patents, trade with any place outside Ireland, quarantine, navigation except in Irish inland waters. "Provisionally" excluded from its control were land purchase, old age pensions, national insurance, labour exchanges, collection of taxes, the Royal Irish Constabulary, Post Office Savings Bank, and all public loans made before the passing of the Act. Finally, there was a specific provision forbidding the favouring or penalising of any religion.

Who would imagine that autonomy so hedged with limitations would fail to be granted? On March 31 Pearse had spoken from the same platform as Redmond, supporting Home Rule, but warning him that this was the mountain's last parturition. Now *Irish Freedom* was scathingly contemptuous of the ridiculous mouse. Connolly seized sharply on the class aspect of the bill, which Redmond, busily listing its restrictions and safeguards to show his baby was "only a little one", had refrained from mentioning.

A schedule attached to the bill showed that apart from two University constituencies, 168 seats were provided for the Dublin Parliament on the basis of between 5,000 and 6,000 electors each. Thus Waterford would qualify for a member, but Kilkenny and Newry would do so no longer. The urban voters, comprising one third of the population, were restricted to 34 out of 170 seats, or about a fifth. To the Westminster Parliament, 34 county and 8 Borough members were to be returned, the balance thus weighing even more heavily against the urban population.

Connolly accused the Redmondites of conniving at a gerrymander. The Belfast branch of the I.L.P.(I.) organised a meeting in the St. Mary's Hall which was filled to its capacity of one thousand five hundred. Tom Johnson took the chair and Connolly, who was uproariously applauded by the mill-girls, urged the acceptance of a resolution demanding proportional representation, the excision of the proposal for a senate, payment of members and election expenses, and suffrage for women. Except for a solitary "No" to the last point, which was urged by Sheehy-Skeffington from Dublin, the resolution was accepted unanimously.

It was Connolly's strength that he suspected every action of a class enemy. The proposal to pay members of the Irish legislature had met with the indignant expostulations of the Redmondites. What an intolerable restriction on the indefeasible sovereign rights of a nation! Connolly stripped the cloak of self-righteousness from these skilled demagogues, showing the vulgar mercenary aim of placing financial obstacles in the way of Labour representation.

It was Britain's duty, insofar as she withdrew from Ireland, to leave democracy behind her.

Arthur Griffith roundly condemned the stand of the I.L.P.(I.) *Irish Freedom,* on the other hand, gave cautious approbation. But Connolly had not done. At Whitsun the

Irish T.U.C. was held in Clonmel. Larkin proposed a resolution demanding adequate representation for urban areas, adult suffrage, payment of members and election expenses, which Connolly and O'Brien supported. Then Connolly proposed the resolution of the Belfast Branch of the I.T.W.U. that an Irish Labour Party be established.

The proposition was that "the independent representation of Labour upon all public boards be, and is hereby, included amongst the objects of this Congress". One day at least should be devoted to this subject at future annual meetings. Affiliated bodies should pay a political levy of 1s. per annum per member, to defray the expense of political activity. Connolly argued that the loss of the medical benefits of the Insurance Act was directly traceable to the absence of a Labour Party in Ireland. Now that the old parties were going to be disrupted by Home Rule, independent working-class organisation was more essential than ever before.

Another Belfast delegate seconded, and Larkin, John Dowling of Cobh and Tom Johnson supported. Objections from the craft unions of Dublin and Belfast were answered by D. R. Campbell and William O'Brien. In an astutely worded reply Connolly, who was becoming no mean diplomat, complimented his opponents on the form of their speeches and his supporters on their substance. The influence of the Home Rule Bill was decisive. The resolution to establish the Labour Party was passed by 49 votes to 18. Once more there was illustrated the principle that the working class of a subject nation turns to independent political action to the degree that the struggle for national independence makes this possible. The Clonmel resolution was one of the greatest triumphs of Connolly's life. It represented the consummation of sixteen years of labour.

At the same time it must be noted that, like the I.L.P.(I.), the Irish Labour Party based its programme and tactics on the assumption of Home Rule. In Home Rule Ireland there were to be two working-class parties, corresponding roughly to the Labour Party and the I.L.P. in England. The first unified all forces under the auspices of the trade unions and was non-socialist. The second was primarily a propagandist organisation and its purpose was to spread the knowledge of socialism. It seemed to the founders that after the establishment of an independent legislature in Ireland, the two countries would politically draw apart to the extent that the labour movement accomplished the "reconquest of Ireland". The weight of the imperialist counter-offensive could not even be guessed at the time. The conditions envisaged in the two Labour programmes never came into existence.

COUNTER-REVOLUTION

Conservative apologists were maintaining even in 1957 that the Liberals had "no mandate" for the Home Rule Bill. Let those talk of mandates who respect them. But facts are facts. It was generally recognised that Home Rule was an essential part of Liberal policy since 1886. Hence the repeated demands that the Liberals should "drop" Home Rule from their programme. The "mandate" issue was raised in 1912 to justify the Tory campaign against the Bill, and has been repeated by Tory apologists ever since, although clearly answered at the time. The Bill was announced in the autumn of 1911, introduced in April 1912 and the constitutional crisis it gave rise to had not ended when world war broke out in August 1914.

Redmond stated categorically that: "In January 1910 and in December 1910, Home Rule was specifically placed before the electors by the Prime Minister and his colleagues, coupled with the declaration that, amongst the first uses to which the Parliament Bill would be put, would be the passage of a Home Rule Bill through the House of Commons ... on every Unionist platform in both these elections Home Rule was put in the very forefront by Lord Lansdowne, Mr. Balfour, Mr. Chamberlain and all the lesser lights."

July 1911 passed without untoward incidents. Despite the protests of the Conservatives there was no reason to expect anything more violent than what normally stirred the parliamentary tea-pot. Connolly and his colleagues were quite justified in basing their calculations on the expectation of Home Rule. Ulster's instantaneous revulsion to the dreadful news is a figment of Unionist imagination. Ulster as a province of nine counties was in favour of Home Rule. Belfast was divided, but the demonstration *in favour* of Home Rule on October 30 at the Ulster Hall showed how many influential Protestants welcomed it. The meeting was under Liberal auspices and had the support of Lord Pirrie, Ulster's leading industrialist. Mr. Hemmerde, Recorder of Liverpool, was the main speaker. He earned great applause in Belfast. Twenty-five years later he was still being snubbed by the Liverpool Tories for what earned him compliments at the time. The organist was Teasdale Griffith, of Belfast Cathedral. Things changed for him too, and he migrated to Birkenhead. Sam Porter, once of the I.S.R.P., was on the platform, together with eighteen Justices of the Peace, five leading lawyers, and a galaxy of aldermen, doctors and business people. There were capitalists in Belfast who could still play their normal role as a "national bourgeoisie".

But a month previously there had been held a more sinister gathering at Craigavon. Representatives of the Orange lodges of all Ulster had heard Edward Carson announce that "if necessary, tomorrow, Ulster would march from Belfast to Cork, and take the consequences, even if not one of them returned". Like the fascist wild talk of a later generation his speech was dismissed as hot air, and to this day there is a tendency to emphasise the element of bluff in Unionist pronouncements.

Comparatively little notice was taken of an announcement made on September 25 that the Ulster Unionist Council was preparing to set up a "Provisional Government" to keep Dublin's writ out of the nine counties of Ulster, which it would hold "in trust" for Westminster. The will of the people had been tested at an election. The Lords seemed powerless to do more than delay. Here were the Ulster Unionists proposing armed counter-revolution with the aid of the Crown and high military personnel. "It couldn't happen here," thought the public.

The Unionists' first necessity was to silence all contrary voices among the bourgeoisie. After the Ulster Hall meeting a violent press campaign was instituted against Hemmerde. Liberals who protested found their Orange associates reluctant to do business with them. The storm-troopers of Unionist reaction were recruited from the brazen hoodlums of the Belfast slums. The leaders who directed them were mostly the brainless pups of aristocratic families. They appeared anachronistically from their parks and demesnes to join with their most abject victims in putting the clock back. Orange elements hitherto too respectable for ruffianism learned the example from their betters, and a pressure of intimidation · was started which increased day by day.

The Ulster Hall had been made available to Hemmerde in October. In January 1912 its doors were barred to Winston Churchill himself. He must remove his profane gathering to a football field. Little was omitted that could exacerbate sectarian feeling. The First Lord of the Admiralty, although protected by seven thousand troops, was glad to get out alive. A week later Lord and Lady Pirrie were waylaid at Larne by a mob of "roughs led by well-dressed blackguards" and pelted with bad eggs, flour and ordure. Thereafter Liberalism, more interested in its money than its life, bowed to the inevitable. An artery was opened through which the lifeblood of Britain's greatest political party drained away in ten years.

There were radical Protestants, among them the Rev. J. B. Armour and the landlord Gold-Verschoyle, who were still resisting as late as April 1912. They remained a breach in the Unionist front, and a testimony that Home Rule was not Rome Rule. They were therefore ignored in public and intrigued against in private.

While Lord Cecil, F. E. Smith and Bonar Law followed Carson's inflammatory speeches with even better ones of their own, and actually began to procure arms, Connolly concentrated on drawing together the labour forces. He continued his speeches in Library Street, the content of which can be studied in the files of the *Irish Worker* and the pamphlet *The Reconquest of Ireland*. The first two lectures developed Connolly's old thesis that the conquest was twofold, "the imposition upon Ireland of an alien rule in political matters, and of a social system equally alien and even more abhorrent". The ruthless land-robbery of the Cromwellian settlement provided the general text, Lord Lansdowne and Carson's entourage the local illustrations. Connolly's encyclopaedic knowledge of Irish history won a hearing even among workers of Unionist persuasion. To these he explained the social basis of sectarianism in Lalor's phrase: "The conquest of our liberties and the conquest of our lands." He rattled their faith in the Battle of the Boyne by showing it was no battle at all. And as for William of glorious memory, his victory was celebrated with Te Deums in Rome and Madrid. He reminded them that until comparatively recent times, Presbyterians had been persecuted equally with Catholics. "The thin clothing and pale faces of honest Protestant workers are still in evidence in Belfast," he declared. "Let us hope that they will ere long be marching again to storm the capitalist system." This was the reconquest of Ireland, returning to the people collectively what was stolen from their ancestors severally.

Three further lectures were published in the *Irish Worker,* two on Dublin and one on Belfast. Their purpose was to provide an immediate programme for the newly-established Labour Party. "A people are not to be judged by the performances of their great men," Connolly wrote. "A truer standard by which the spiritual and mental measurement of a people can be taken . . . is by that picture drawn of itself . . . at the ballot box." He noted with surprise that little use had been made by the Irish workers of the powers conferred by the Local Government Act of 1898, and gave a picture of social conditions in Dublin only less appalling than the indifference of its leading citizens. The rich lived as long as the rich anywhere, but the poor were decimated by overcrowding and sweated labour. He demanded that the Corporation use their powers to "revolutionise the tenement house system". It should acquire land for cemeteries and end the "scandalous robbery of the poor practised by the Catholic Cemeteries Committee at Glasnevin". But its existing powers were inadequate and fresh powers should be demanded.

By contrast Connolly showed that Belfast had been granted every kind of legislative sanction for its municipal activities, which Dublin had been denied. Its central areas had been built on land let on long leases at moderate rents, and its boundaries had been extended as the built-up areas grew.

There were no districts like Rathmines and Rathgar, enjoying the advantages of city life and paying country rates. Yet an examination of the reports of the Medical Officer of Health showed an exceptionally high incidence of premature births, tuberculosis and industrial injuries. The aspect of Belfast most astonishing to a visitor would be the part-time system or "little children working". The demands which Connolly urged the labour movement to make were:

1. The abolition of the early morning start.
2. The abolition of all task or piece work.
3. Reduction of the working day to a maximum of eight hours.
4. Workmen's compensation equal to full wages.
5. Pensions for widows of men killed in industrial accidents, to be a charge on the employer, collected and disbursed by the State.

Throughout it was assumed that Home Rule would become effective, and the fact that *The Reconquest of Ireland* did not appear as a pamphlet until 1915 must not obscure this. Whether in Dublin or Belfast, Connolly's means were one, namely, the building of a "party of Labour" to reform and then to revolutionise the mode of production. But by the end of June 1912 it was becoming clear to him that the Clonmel resolution was not being given effect. The T.U.C. had broken up without giving the secretary concrete instructions. It was necessary to circularise all trade unions and trades councils, urging them to hold meetings for the furtherance of labour representation. Connolly suspected that Larkin was lukewarm towards the new party. After Clonmel he had suggested the publication of *The Reconquest of Ireland* as a Labour Party pamphlet, but since then he had grown unaccountably reticent. It later transpired that Larkin was having differences with his colleagues on the N.E.C. as a result of which he resigned from the chairmanship. At this meeting the N.E.C. decided to initiate the campaign Connolly desired with a meeting at the Antient Concert Rooms. Larkin refused to speak. When O'Brien invited Connolly to take his place, he declined. He explained, in a letter dated September 13, that to speak without Larkin's approval would be to invite the criticism that he had neglected his members in the north to go to Dublin against Larkin's wishes. He advised cancelling the meeting pending Larkin's co-operation. "This seems tame and slavishness," he wrote, "but it is the only way to get him on the move again. He must rule or he will not work, and in the present stage of the Labour movement he has us at his mercy." In Larkin's extenuation be it said that he was not the first nor the last great mass leader to blemish his repute by intractability in collective enterprises. "I am sick of all this playing to one man," Connolly concluded. "But as things are I am prepared to advise it for the sake of the movement." As things in fact fell out, the delay proved of little consequence.

Even had the Labour Party campaign been expedited, it seems likely that it would have been overtaken by events in Belfast. Orange sectarianism had grown through the spring of 1912 and was being met, to Connolly's disgust, by Catholic sectarianism. The taint of Unionism was beginning to touch even the working-class movement. Just as German and Italian Social-Democracy prepared the way for Hitler and Mussolini, so Walker's social-chauvinism left the intensely parochial movement of Belfast ideologically disarmed before Carson. Stewart and Campbell were forced to resign from the Juvenile Labour Advisory Committee on the grounds that the city was being divided up according to religion. Only Protestants must pay visits to Protestant areas, or the Orangemen would disapprove. Societies like the St. Vincent de Paul then chose to see a menace of proselytising by a continuance of Protestant visiting in Catholic areas. Every child born alive had to be one or the other, and remain it. The Trades Council deplored sectarianism but urged its delegates to resume their duties.

The rising excitement on the Home Rule issue tended to distract from trade union organisation, but the Trades Council continued its work and Connolly attended regularly, on one occasion moving a resolution urging the dismissal of

Mr. Justice Craig on grounds of partiality in workmen's compensation cases. The Textile Workers' Union kept functioning with more difficulty despite its predominantly Catholic membership. In May, Connolly instituted open-air meetings under its auspices in the Falls Road area. The collection, which was scrupulously handed in to Mrs. Johnson each day, was 7s. 5d. at the first meeting and rose steadily week by week till in the autumn it reached a maximum of 12s. 6d. This was a substantial collection for those days. He also tried to introduce social activity with an Irish dancing class which began in early June. Here Connolly was forced to retreat. The girls were not very interested in Irish dancing, and it became necessary to include ballroom dancing. In the summer fresh difficulties arose from the sickness of the secretary; Mrs. Johnson was replaced by Winifred Carney on September 1.

July 1912 brought license for every sectarian lunacy and speeches more inflammatory than ever. Despite the continuous incitement, the mounting fever had not yet unbalanced the main body of the working class. But the Castledawson provocation gave just the pretext the Unionists required. On June 29 a Protestant school outing at Castledawson was attacked by members of the A.O.H. (Board of Erin), who thus once more played directly into the hands of Unionist reaction. That the Hibernians were constantly subject to provocation, were quickly outnumbered by local Orangemen and forced to retreat, was not weighed in the press reports. Hatred was wanted and the bellows were applied to its flames.

Disturbances began in Workman-Clarke's shipyard. Its Director, Mr. George Clarke, was a member of the Unionist Council. Orange workers taunted Catholics over Castledawson. Taunts led to blows. Antagonism grew so sharp that a number of Catholics left work and went home; three were taken to hospital. During the next few days assaults continued. One man was deprived of every stitch of clothing and kicked in the face till he was unrecognisable. Maddened Orangemen held heated rivets at the mouths of their fellow-workers, refusing to let them go till they had cursed the Pope.

The management felt no indignation over this misuse of time they were paying for.

The disturbances spread to Harland and Wolff's later in the week. Here it did not please the (Liberal) management. But the example of the other yard, combined with the incendiary speeches of the Carsonites, proved more than could be withstood. Two thousand Catholics were disemployed in the first ten days of July, and with them were four hundred Englishmen and Scotsmen whose sole crime was to refuse to assist the Orange bravos. Secret Unionist clubs had been set up in the shipyards in preparation for the July days. And while men were being kicked insensible not a policeman was to be seen.

These events shocked English progressive opinion. But they also confused it. On the one hand those taking action were unmistakably workers. On the other hand, every socialist or radical was a "Fenian get" who must retire before triumphant reaction. The Orange chorus grew louder. The ropeworkers employees were the next victims. Here Catholics were less numerous and they went home voluntarily. This did not satisfy the Unionists. Every girl, however devout a Protestant or non-political herself, who had a relative known to be connected with the labour and trade union movement was also told to take her leave.

The management of Workman-Clarke had thus performed great services for the Empire and now felt justified in claiming its reward. It was announced that labourers would be engaged to replace those who had been driven out. But it was clearly stipulated that Socialists or Home Rulers would be unacceptable, even if as irreproachably Protestant as King William himself. New wage-rates were applied. Labourers were given 16s. a week, little more than the former boys' rate. Harland and Wolff's, on the other hand, issued a statement to the effect that continued disturbances were endangering production and threatened a general lock-out. But they and other employers availed themselves of the opportunity to tear up the "closed shop" agreements, and to employ non-unionists, together with labourers on tradesmen's work. Apprenticeship agreements likewise went by the board. The sole contribution to the cause of law and order on the part of the authorities was to arrest a Tipperaryman for using a revolver while retreating under a hail of rivets. The expelled men were still without work in September. The government in London, which could have ended all this in a week, made no effort to intervene.

The superb courage with which Connolly infused all who worked with him was shown before the month of July was out. While the barbarian madness was still at its height, he organised a "Labour Demonstration", under the auspices of the I.T.G.W.U.,[1] "the only union that allows no bigotry in its ranks". Headed by the "Non-Sectarian Labour Band", the procession of dockers and mill-girls left 122, Corporation Street at 7.45 p.m. and passed by way of Victoria Street, Edward Street and Cromac Street to Cromac Square, where Miss Savage, Flanagan and Connolly addressed a meeting. From then on, not a Sunday evening at Library Street was missed. If Connolly was in Dublin, MacMullen took his place. "Civil and religious Liberty" was the most frequent subject, but women's suffrage was never forgotten. Connolly contrasted the freedom for riot and sedition enjoyed by the Unionists, with the brutalities of the Liberal Government against the suffragettes to whose meetings in London and elsewhere he sent many a message of support.

One of these ran: "When trimmers and compromisers disavow you, I, a poor slum-bred politician, raise my hat in thanksgiving that I have lived to see this resurgence of women." Winifred Carney, like Mrs. Johnson, was enrolled from the ranks of the suffrage movement. It is noticeable, however, even at this time, that while Connolly ever uncompromisingly held out for Home Rule, some of the Belfast members of the I.L.P.(I.) were inclined to avoid discussing it, and confined themselves to the economic issues of the day.

[1] In the early literature this union is referred to as both I.T.W.U. and I.T.G.W.U.

Having split the working class more thoroughly than at any time since 1886, the Unionists could now proceed with the organising of counter-revolution. "There are things stronger than Parliamentary majorities," said Mr. Bonar Law. "I can imagine no length of resistance to which Ulster will not go." On September 28, 1912, a "Solemn League and Covenant" to "use all means which may be found necessary to defeat the present conspiracy to set up a Home Rule Parliament . . . and . . . to refuse to recognise its authority" was signed in the blood of its sponsors and offered to the public for endorsement. Over two hundred and nineteen thousand signed. The feelings of those who did so were mixed. A lesson in the temper of the extremists had been given in July. Employers collected the signatures of their workpeople. Landlords passed the "list" to their tenants. Customers offered it to tradesmen. In the shipyards those who declined their hand joined the unemployed "Fenians" and socialists outside the gates. In December every signatory was invited to enrol either for political or military service against Home Rule. The Ulster Volunteers were established, and the Tipperaryman who did time for unauthorised self-defence could note how correctly Carson applied to the magistrates for authorisation to arm his men, and how correctly the magistrates granted it.

Connolly had no means of resistance but propaganda. He was tied to Belfast by his trade union duties. Moreover quite possibly he believed that the Unionists were bluffing and that the Liberal Government, with its strong majority and support from all parts of Ireland, would call their bluff, which they so obviously could do. Had he believed otherwise he had little freedom of action. He busied himself with organising and lecturing.

On November 23 he issued his famous manifesto *To the Linen Slaves of Belfast*. From 1911 onwards there had been many exposures of sweated conditions in the linen mills. The Sweated Industries Act laid down a minimum wage of 3*d*. an hour for women workers. But the Belfast mill-owners were not paying it. Connolly urged the women to organise to secure the application of the law in Belfast, and the abolition of all fines. Realising that the spinning room held the key to the whole industry, he made a special appeal to reelers and spinners who received a wage "less than some of our pious mill-owners spend weekly on a dog". He urged that preparations should be made for a general stoppage in the industry.

About the same time he was involved in polemics in the *Catholic Times* of London, which had commented on a *Daily Herald* review of a reprint of *Labour, Nationality and Religion.* Catholic theoreticians were much exercised with Labour policy. At the Annual Conference of the Catholic Truth Society, Father Fullerton's declaration that most labour leaders "could not point to an honest day's work done in their lives" was strongly criticised by Father Lawrence. Father Fullerton was urging "co-partnership" as the "grand remedy by which to allay social disturbance". Cardinal Logue remarked on Fullerton's report that "notwithstanding Father Lawrence's rather severe criticism, the paper was considered a beautiful one". *Catholic Democrat* discussed the same questions, and it was against this background of Catholic "social policy" that Father MacEarlean, S.J., took Connolly to task in an article entitled *Rome and Irish Catholics.* The controversy revolved round the question of whether the Catholic Church had been mistaken in political matters, and after a number of clerical and lay contributors, including Connolly, had made their points, Father MacEarlean (while maintaining all his truculence) reluctantly half-admitted that this had indeed been so. The controversy and Connolly's handling of it greatly enlarged his reputation among the Catholic circles who surrounded the *Daily Herald,* and brought him to London to debate with Hilaire Belloc at the Irish Club in Charing Cross Road. On this occasion the audience was astonished at the ease with which Connolly trounced one of the leading intellectuals of Britain.

Despite the darkening skies in the northern city, Connolly decided to contest Dock ward in the municipal elections. This was a "mixed" ward containing the homes of many I.T.W.U. men. Adopted by these at a meeting in the ward, Connolly also secured the official support of the Trades Council. In his election address he argued that since the National Health Insurance Act delegated certain duties to the City Council, there was a need for a Labour councillor to see they were properly performed. The City Council would be urged to pay more attention to school feeding than to "the perpetuation of religious discords which make Belfast a by-word among civilised nations". His programme included direct labour on city contacts, a closed shop for Corporation employees, a minimum wage of 6d. an hour, the provision of special covered cars for workers in the mornings and evenings, and the promotion of a Bill to democratise the Harbour Board.

Such were the immediate demands Connolly placed in the forefront. But the remaining third of his manifesto declared his political position without concealment. He advocated socialism. This was to be achieved as a result of the "continuous increase in the power of the working class", that is to say, essentially by social-democratic means. He declared himself openly as a lifelong advocate of national independence for Ireland and a supporter of Home Rule. He stood for equal rights for women, and asked the electors' votes as "a member of the working class".

The Dock Ward Campaign was the most curious of his career. Hesitantly members of William Walker's branch of the I.L.P. came forward to help the Labour candidate. They were not all opposed to Home Rule, but held a view which Connolly fought strongly among his own adherents, namely that a socialist could be for it or against it with equal justice. This type of opportunism was readily generated in Belfast, where parochial oppositions are met by ostrich compromises. After tempering the wind to the electoral lamb, they were disconcerted when the candidate rounded on them and insisted on his policy. "He thinks nobody knew anything till he came," grumbled Sam Geddis, whose speech was "corrected" publicly from the platform immediately he had made it. They thought Connolly inflexible, even doctrinaire. Were there not too few socialists already, without all this fuss about policy? They could not understand that some issues are determinants of a man's class position, because they did not understand the class struggle. Even Connolly's most active workers, D. R. Campbell and the Johnsons, whose integrity and intelligence were alike unassailable, had doubts upon where this insistence was leading. Catholics like Jim Grimley, Ellen Gordon and Winifred Carney were of course willy-nilly nationalists. But could not the Protestants enjoy the luxury of their own sectarian tent also? It was only among the youth that Catholics like Connolly's children, and young Protestants like Jack Carney, drew around them a group which increasingly referred to themselves not as young socialists but as young republicans.

If support was two-sided, so was opposition. A.O.H. hooligans stoned the socialists out of Barrack Street. The police on the other hand tried to prevent their meeting in Protestant areas. Once a cordon was drawn up across the road between one Catholic district and another. "March on, boys," said Connolly, and band and procession broke straight through. In the result Connolly won the nationalist vote and polled 905 to his Unionist opponent's 1,523.

After the election, the socialists of the I.L.P.(I.) began to exchange speakers with the I.L.P. Connolly was highly suspicious of his new allies, and at first would hardly speak to some of Walker's former stalwarts. Even after the establishment of a joint committee he advised against joint open-air meetings. In this he was overruled by his committee, but devoted many a speech to correcting the errors of his unwanted colleagues. The events of July 1912 had affected a permanent change. It became impossible to hold meetings in Protestant areas. Library Street was permissible from being in the main business centre. The socialists found another refuge at Clonard Street, off the Falls Road, where Connolly and Campbell urged the establishment of a Labour Party, and showed how politics were used for depressing wages.

The Home Rule Bill passed its third reading in January 1913 and was promptly rejected by the Lords. It must then be reintroduced in two separate sessions before the veto could be overridden. The first hint of partition had been given in what was at the time thought merely a "wrecking amendment" the previous year. Now Carson demanded that Ulster be excluded from the Bill, notwithstanding the fact that of the thirty-three members returned by the province only sixteen were Unionists. In other words, he demanded that a minority of a minority defeat the will of the two majorities. Simultaneously the importation of arms was accelerated, and a scheme for setting up a Provisional Government with its own judiciary and administration was adopted by the Ulster Unionist Council. With the help of Sir Henry Wilson, Chief of the Imperial General Staff, retired army officers were provided to train and command the military force of able-bodied Covenanters. Instead of arresting the counter-revolutionaries, the Liberal Government played into their hands by offering compromises. It was still jailing and torturing suffragettes. It was still encouraging the employers to resist wage demands. But as Lenin put it, "The Liberals of England, the lackeys of the money-bags, are capable only of cringing before the Carsons."

The first months of 1913 were a time of gloom for Connolly. The I.T.W.U. had registered as an approved society under the Insurance Act, and he was involved in much detailed administration, engaging clerks and organising the new department, while reaction gathered around him. The insurance staff was paid from Dublin. The five shillings a week the Textile Workers' organiser received he paid from his own pocket. Sometimes at a quarter to six he would tire of the office chair, and hustle Winifred Carney and Ellen Gordon on to the Falls Road tram, his spirits steadily reviving, while they secretly prayed for a traffic jam. As they passed a sandwichman he would laugh, "There now—two shillings a day and his board." When they told him of the man who had come in to ask for an "eternity form" he laughed, "You should have sent him to the Salvation Army."

The Textile Union grew very slowly. Only the dances, now making no educational pretences, held it together. The girls had no religious scruples about Connolly. He might not raise his hat when he passed a church (once when it was pointed out to him that it might be policy for him to do so, he lifted it, looked at Danny McDevitt quizzically, scratched his head, and replaced it). He might even have written that dreadful book, unsold copies of which lay round the premises. He could tell Grimley that he had "long ceased to practise religion". They also sensed the other thing he told Grimley: "I would die for the Irish Papist." They felt his sympathy and understood his complete partisanship. He made no intellectual demands on them as he did on his socialist colleagues, who because they could not understand him regarded him as aloof. The mill-girls were light-hearted and lively spirited. When the Countess Markiewicz came to speak at the gates they threw snowballs at her in the best of good humour. Such was the material Connolly had to work with. It was at its best on the job, and the employers learned to respect it. The manifesto "to the Linen Slaves" was followed in March by an ultimatum "to the Linen Lords". Its gravamen was "pay now, or fight", and they paid like lambs.

The Textile Union had its difficulties with the flax roughers who tried to break up one of its meetings. But in mid-April these workers were compelled to strike for their own demands and Connolly immediately gave them unconditional support. An effort was made to strengthen unity by holding a May Day demonstration. On May 1, the Textile and Transport Workers' Unions paraded the Falls Road and passed through Royal Avenue to the Custom House steps, a point it was now possible to touch upon only with overwhelming strength. Flanagan, Shields, Ellen Gordon and Connolly were here joined by Malcolm of the railwaymen in a call for working-class international solidarity. On May 2, once more in the Falls Road—whither independent Labour activity was being steadily driven back—Connolly and Ellen Gordon spoke by invitation at a meeting of the flax roughers and all speakers called for one big union for the linen trade.

April and May were months of illusory sanity in Belfast. Carsonite provocation had slackened while the Lords veto held, namely, till June. It was therefore possible for Connolly to make a slight advance in the docks. The N.U.D.L. had declined to oppose the I.T.W.U. with a Protestant union for the cross-channel men, and when Connolly won a 3s. increase for his own members, these benefited also, thanks to the good offices of the S.F.U. Some of the cross-channel men now joined the Transport Union and even began to take an interest in "socialism", though there were subsequently some backsliders following an "ungodly" speech Connolly made in Dublin.

From May 12 to 14 the T.U.C. met in Cork City, and once more Connolly represented the Belfast Transport Workers. William O'Brien delivered a presidential address full of confidence in the new-found powers of Labour. While the Belfast movement had been fighting its rear-guard action against counter-revolution, Labour elsewhere had made advances. Indeed, the contrast was occasioning some misunderstanding between Connolly and Larkin, who was impatient and inclined to blame his lieutenant because Belfast was not Dublin and 1913 was not 1907. There were many mutual irritations, suppressed for the sake of the movement. Larkin would cheerfully break the Bank of Ireland. He unblushingly raided the insurance funds to pay strike benefit, and Connolly had to go to Dublin and thump the table for his clerks' pay. The opposite of Larkin in temperament, accurate in recording, exact with money, precise in expression, but lacking positive imagination, was William O'Brien. If Connolly and Larkin irritated each other, Larkin and O'Brien were at daggers drawn. Larkin could be right in substance but impossibly, even ludicrously, wrong in his mode of presentation. O'Brien was inclined to demand things in the correct form before he was prepared to look at the substance. Lacking the soaring inspiration of Larkin, he saw the ground, and the pitfalls, when the other chose to ignore them. He was thus a very necessary man for the Irish movement. He laboured steadily, doing much more than was seen, looking after machinery that would have ground to a standstill but for his timely oiling. His reward was not in the climate of those days. The agitator not the administrator was history's darling, and O'Brien could only come into his own subsequently, when Labour had lost the vision the agitators shadowed forth.

The debates of Cork continued those of Clonmel. Connolly was this time determined to make the Labour Party more than a pious belief. He dwelt on the gerrymander implicit in the Home Rule Bill, still not doubting it would become law. The T.U.C. had sent a deputation to the British Labour Party to ask them to insist on proportional representation. "Was sending a deputation to London an innovation?" asked the West British McCarron with heavy irony. "Everything we do is an innovation," answered Connolly. It was better to appeal to their own class across the water than to their enemies in Ireland. A Special Committee consisting of Connolly, Richard O'Carroll (of Dublin) and Lynch (Cork) drew up a resolution which proposed a Parliamentary Committee of ten persons (Larkin's amendment made it twelve) which must draft a constitution and:

1. Endeavour to give effect to political decisions of the T.U.C.
2. Watch all legislative measures affecting Labour in Ireland.
3. Indicate legal action as required.
4. Secure independent Labour representation on all public boards.
5. Support the British T.U.C. in all matters affecting the United Kingdom as a whole.

There was to be a sub-committee, or standing committee, to meet every month, and the full committee would meet each quarter.

The Cork decisions marked a substantial advance. Indeed, it was at Cork rather than at Clonmel that the Labour Party was launched. William O'Brien proposed the resolution demanding proportional representation, Connolly seconding. Connolly then moved a resolution expressing detestation of the Liberal Government's use of coercion against the suffragettes. The Government "ran away from Carson, and prosecuted women". Indeed at that very time it was prosecuting his schoolgirl supporter Anna Munro for "obstruction" at Marble Arch. He also spoke in favour of extending the medical benefits of the Insurance Acts to Ireland. If these were not made available, he would advise people not to pay their contributions.

The T.U.C. had aroused some alarm among Cork Nationalists. The U.I.L. *Examiner* had conducted a campaign under such slogans as "Keep Larkin out" and "Refuse hospitality". But 1913 was not 1908 in the south either. The employers' conspiracy, which had broken the Cork Branch and left its handful of members to pay their dues in secret, was powerless now that Dublin had become a Labour stronghold and the centre of a united T.U.C. The I.L.P.(I.) held a meeting in Daunt Square at which Dowling presided and Tom Johnson and Lynch (of Cobh) spoke. Now it was Cork which rang with "Freedom's pioneers". Alex Turner, Connolly and finally Larkin took the rostrum. On the following Tuesday an I.T.W.U. meeting was held with the same speakers. Next morning Ellen Gordon and Connolly addressed the millworkers at Blackpool and organised a new branch of the Textile Workers' Union. In the evening they went to Cobh, where the meeting held under I.L.P.(I.) auspices was addressed by Connolly, Larkin, O'Brien, Dowling and Ellen Gordon. The police had taken elaborate precautions. But no trouble came. The crowd was friendly, at times even enthusiastic, and made ample amends for their behaviour two years previously.

Connolly returned to Belfast to find that there also a stiffening of working-class resistance was taking place. On June 9 there was a demonstration to demand the application of the Trade Boards Act to the whole linen industry. Connolly attributed this advance to his "consistent propaganda at mill doors". He had resumed his contributions to *Forward* at the beginning of May, but complained that a "spate of strikes" left him no time for writing. He was called to Larne the very week his brother John paid a visit from Edinburgh. The visitor had to be left in charge of Danny McDevitt.

The Larne aluminium plant workers were showing dissatisfaction with an 84-hour seven-day-week, and three hundred of them joined the I.T.W.U. They were followed by a number of dockers and a strike followed on June 9. The men had been accustomed to work a seven-day week. Some had never been to church for seventeen years. The strike left them free on the Sunday, and the local clergymen took advantage of their availability to invite them to the services on June 15. While Connolly was in Belfast raising the strike pay, every Protestant church in Larne rang with sermons against the wickedness of the strike which had brought them their congregation. They declared that the strike was a "Fenian" and "Papist" plot. It was a Christian duty to go back to work and trust to the generosity of the management. This they did, to Connolly's great chagrin, and gained thereby precisely nothing but a speed-up. Connolly commented ruefully that the confraternities of Wexford could not break a strike, but the Protestant parsons could. North-east Ulster, not the south, was the priest-ridden part of Ireland.

The return of July naturally halted the recovery of the forces of democracy. The strength of the workers was "dissipated by Carsonism" once more. Not that July 1913 saw scenes as violent as July 1912. Once was enough. The purpose was achieved. Moreover, those liable to attack made themselves scarce during the week of bacchanalia. Guns were pouring into Ulster and military manœuvres were the day's order. The young republicans asked Connolly's advice on how to pull the devil by the tail. He wrote them a manifesto commenting upon the way in which the Orangemen, in celebrating the Battle of the Boyne, were commemorating a papist festival, and told about the Te Deums in Rome when King William won. The manifesto was printed on adhesive paper and plastered the route of the procession on the twelfth.

August 1913 proved stormier than July. Belfast Orangemen travelled by special train to Derry, keeping up a fusillade of shots from the windows. Once more it was Orange confetti, and Magdeburg quarter.

The same weekend the I.T.W.U. and Textile Workers Union held their annual outing to Portrush. From early morning till late night the Midland Railway terminus was besieged by Orangemen from the shipyard. A force of police was required to get the party on to the platform. From 7 p.m. the crowd was enlarged by a steady stream of hoodlums, who began to sing "Dolly's Brae" and fire revolver shots. By the time the excursion returned there was a crowd of ten thousand. Police and railway officials in collusion had cut off the van containing the drums and banners at Ballymena. The band thus returned without instruments, and the members had to run the gauntlet of stones and sticks as they left the station under "police protection".

The Carsonites had created conditions in which they could arm and drill with impunity. There was a terror directed equally against the nationalists and the labour movement. The I.T.W.U. was an oasis of working-class strength in the general confusion. Had there been a leadership in the nationalist party which had the vision to join with the forces of Labour, the counter-revolution could still have been halted, even in face of the government's inactivity. Devlin would have to stand for wage-increases, women's suffrage, extension of medical benefits to Ireland, school feeding, ending of sweating in the linen industry, and proportional representation. But it was precisely the aim of the Home Rulers to make Home Rule cheap rule. This insistence confirmed the repulsion of the Orange element, and divided the nationalist workers. Instead of Carson's army being split along class lines, it was the working class who were split along religious lines. This Connolly represented at Library Street in his lectures on "Politics and Wages", which continued throughout the month of August.

As the *Northern Whig* became more repulsively bigoted on the one side, the *Irish News* heaped fuel on the flames from the other, and Connolly bitterly reproached the British Labour Party for its uncritical support of the Nationalists. Irish capitalism now entered a period of betrayal. Unable to rise above parochial divisions, the working class was powerless to rescue the country from the path which led to the death of Connolly, the partition of Ireland, and the victory of opportunism within the most revolutionary labour movement of Western Europe. At the very moment when Carson was driving the Liberal Government back on its pledges, the bourgeoisie declared war, not on Carson, but on Irish Labour in its citadel of Dublin. Sectarianism was the alibi for national abdication.

XVII
THE GREAT LOCK-OUT

On Friday August 29 Connolly received a telegram. Industrial war had broken out in Dublin. Larkin had been arrested and charged with seditious libel and conspiracy, together with O'Brien, Lawlor and P. T. Daly. Connolly left at once for Dublin where he found the defendants out on bail and holding a protest meeting in Beresford Place. One of the greatest labour struggles in West European history had begun. For Ireland, indeed, it was a climacteric as fateful as 1916.

In inception it resembled one of those chess openings when pawns fling themselves into the centre of the board only to freeze into minatory deadlock, behind which the real forces manœuvre for position. The employers had political reasons for trying conclusions with Larkin. Not only had he stirred up those who carried the whole of Dublin society on their backs. His organisation had infused a new spirit into both Trades Council and T.U.C., and the political outcome was a Labour Party. They were expecting Home Rule, and whether it was to be "Rome rule" or not, they intended to be the beneficiaries. He had disturbed their dream of an Ireland safely insulated from the "profane class struggle of the sinful world". Self-government was being conferred only to be snatched away on the one hand by Carson, on the other by the resurgent mob. The dream became a nightmare. How could they defend Home Rule with Larkin on their flank? How could they, on the other hand, defend it without him?

The Dublin employers had founded an Association in 1911 in hopes of "meeting combination with combination". Little headway was made with it, for Larkin held the initiative. His organising activity seemed tireless and endless. Each week he produced ninety thousand copies of the *Irish Worker*. Raucous, sensational, even hysterical at times, it was a stentorian voice of the people. The smaller employers shivered in the blast, fearing while they hated, until big capital was ready to do battle.

From April to August 1913 Dublin was talking conciliation. The Chamber of Commerce met representatives of the Trades Council under the chairmanship of the Lord Mayor. Both Larkin and Connolly afterwards accused the employers of talking peace the better to prepare war. But O'Brien and the Trades Council took them seriously. So did *The Irish Times*. According to his apologist, Wright, it was in April that William Martin Murphy decided to slay the blatant beast. His heart bled for Jacobs and the shipping companies who were struggling in the "tentacles" of Liberty Hall. He had ample resources and knew how to bide his time. Conciliation was a useful smokescreen, but there was always the danger that it might be successful.

Tramway boss, newspaper proprietor, owner and investor from Ramsgate to Buenos Aires, he decided to provoke a struggle before the conciliation scheme came to be accepted as a practical possibility. That the A.O.H. helped to shape his course cannot be doubted. Throughout the summer there was talk of a compromise between Redmond and Carson, involving partition, devolution, or "Home Rule within Home Rule". The bourgeoisie looked apprehensively around and wondered what would happen if the working class took up the national flag when they dropped it. "The A.O.H. felt itself endangered by Larkinism," wrote Hilaire Belloc's *New Witness*, adding after the arrests: "Larkin was prosecuted at the instance of a Nationalist politician," namely, Devlin. The political motivation of the lock-out which followed has received little attention, but helps to explain the extraordinary implacability of the employers. After Home Rule, whose rule? The future of their class was at stake.

Martin Murphy has been described as a "good employer". His tramwaymen did not think so. Nor did the public; he charged twice the fares for a service inferior to that of Belfast. The description "good employer" dates from the Trades Council's sycophantic days, when any large employer was good. It is surprising that writers with Labour sympathies should have used Wright's *Disturbed Dublin* as a serious source book. In August 1913, said Larkin, "dog or devil, thief or saint" was being invited to work for the Tramway Company. Hostilities commenced on Friday August 15, when Murphy called together the employees in the despatch department of the *Independent* and offered them the choice of the union or the job. The following Monday, as they were leaving work, forty of them were paid off. The city newsboys thereupon refused to sell the *Independent* and *Evening Herald*. Motorcars and vans were pressed into service and were followed down Middle Abbey Street by hostile crowds. A young clerk, Martin Nolan, clinging to the reins in the face of lashes from the driver's whip, was overpowered by four policemen and arrested for "obstruction and intimidation". The men of Suttons, the carriers, then stopped work.

On Tuesday the dispute spread to Eason, wholesale and retail newsagent. Their men refused to handle the *Independent*. Murphy's next act of provocation was on Thursday, when he announced that he "expected demands" on the Tramway Company. His directors decided to suspend the parcels service, and the men were paid off. The political aspect of the struggle emerged more strongly next day. Special Constables were sworn in. But Larkin was a tactician. There were no flamboyant threats. Union officials were seen making contact with the tramwaymen without giving a clue as to what was afoot. Once more Murphy struck. He issued a circular which was sent to every employee by post. It demanded a pledge to continue to work in the event of the union calling a strike. The tramwaymen then held a meeting in the small hours of Sunday morning. Larkin was empowered to call a lightning strike at his discretion.

This was Horse Show week, the height of the Dublin "Season". *The Irish Times* regarded a strike at such a period as unthinkable. But Murphy declared grimly that he had four men for every potential striker and could moreover supply other employers with all the scabs they wanted. He was determined on a trial of strength. The union had no option.

Work stopped on Tuesday at 10 a.m. Tramwaymen informed their passengers that they were going no further. Leaving their trams standing, drivers and conductors got off and walked home. On that day Murphy visited Dublin Castle. He was assured that the state forces were at his disposal. A marquee was erected at Dun Laoghaire to receive police from Co. Cork. Meanwhile there were clashes between strikers and the few employees still working on the trams. On Wednesday August 27 it was announced that the "skeleton service" would be discontinued at dark.

Each night Larkin held a giant meeting by the Custom House. On Wednesday he announced a demonstration in O'Connell Street for the following Sunday. The police provoked some disorder and next day the press demanded the proclamation of Sunday's meeting. Larkin replied defiantly he would hold his meeting proclamation or no proclamation. If the police insisted on fighting, the workers would arm themselves. It was for this speech that Larkin was arrested.

"Now arrest Carson," retorted the *Daily Herald*. The London Trades Council and British Socialist Party sent indignant protests to Chief Secretary Birrell. The Dublin Trades Council demanded the immediate release of Larkin, and issued an appeal for funds. He was allowed £200 bail, and it was then that Connolly joined him at the meeting in Beresford Place.

The expected proclamation had by then been issued. Larkin held the document aloft before the crowd, and at the conclusion of a fiery speech struck a match and burned it before the crowd. He declared he would hold the demonstration "dead or alive", and then made himself scarce.

Connolly continued in the same vein. He noted the banned meeting was one to be held in "Sackville Street",[1] but he thought people might take a stroll through O'Connell Street if only to see if a meeting was being held there or not. He denied the right of His Majesty the King of England to prevent Irish people from gathering in their principal thoroughfare.

Friday's meeting was also broken up by police, but Connolly and Partridge were not arrested till early on Saturday afternoon. Mr. Justice Swifte sat specially to hear the case.

[1] The "Ascendancy" name of O'Connell Street.

It is not true, though it has been stated, that Connolly refused to recognise the court. He utilised the legal machinery that was available, while explaining what he thought of it.

"One point in the indictment," he said, "is that I do not recognise the Proclamation. I do not, because I do not recognise English Government in Ireland at all. I do not even recognise the King except when I am compelled to do so." Regarding the O'Connell Street meeting, he had advised people not to "hold a meeting" but to "be there". At the same time he claimed that "the only manner in which progress can be made is by guaranteeing the right of the people to assemble and voice their grievances". He refused to give bail to be of good behaviour and was sentenced to three months' imprisonment.

Once the leaders were out of the way, police violence began in earnest. A football crowd at Ringsend showed its resentment against scabs playing in one of the teams. Police quelled their protest with batons. Later in the evening there were clashes between strikers and "loyal" tramwaymen in Pearse Street (then Gt. Brunswick Street). Wild baton charges followed both there and around Liberty Hall, until after nightfall when a "bright and promising" young worker, James Nolan, was clubbed to death. Another, James Byrne, received serious injuries from the police who were copiously supplied with drink. Employers and authorities had the scent of victory in their nostrils.

As the terror mounted, William O'Brien did what he considered the sensible thing. Larkin was missing. Connolly was in jail. He transferred Sunday's demonstration to the I.T.W.U. recreation ground at Croydon Park, "in the interests of peace". This action was speedily repudiated by Larkin, who had made his own plans. It is the explanation of the fact that so few strikers were in O'Connell Street when Larkin drove up to the door of the Imperial Hotel wearing a false beard and Count Markiewicz's frock coat. He was bowed into the foyer and made his way, still bent almost double, to the balcony, where straightening himself, he announced that he had kept his promise. He was soon arrested and led away. But the effect was electrical. This spectacular defiance of authority seemed symbolic of the workers' invincibility. The cry went up "It's Larkin", and then followed the historic baton charge which gripped the imagination of Europe and completely identified the political and industrial aspects of the conflict. The police laid into the crowd with savage and indiscriminate violence, sparing neither age nor sex. Many of those present were simply passers-by or worshippers returning from Mass in Marlborough Street. That night, and on many nights that followed, the police ran berserk, breaking into workers' homes, shattering delph and furniture, arresting without provocation, clubbing without mercy or compunction. That Sunday there were over four hundred civilians injured against thirty constables. James Byrne died in hospital during the morning.

But "law and order" had overreached itself. So great was the revulsion of feeling that even the Cork A.O.H. protested against the police terror. At the British T.U.C., then meeting in Manchester, Larkin's arch-enemy, Sexton, moved a resolution demanding freedom of assembly in Dublin.

On Monday morning, September 1, Larkin was charged once again. This time bail was refused. Now that the workers' leaders seemed likely to remain locked up for some time, the smaller employers took heart. Jacobs and the coal merchants locked out their men that same morning. Two days later four hundred and four employers, including some who had not previously been members of the Association, bound themselves by "solemn vows and still more binding financial pledges" (as Connolly put it) not to employ any worker who refused to sign an undertaking not to become a member of or assist the I.T.W.U. in any way. It was an undertaking so sweeping as to be unique in Labour history, and caused consternation on both sides of the channel.

Larkin was remanded till the following Monday, and events moved with vertiginous speed. Keir Hardie landed in Dublin, visited Connolly in jail and went on to Belfast where he secured the support of the Trades Council. It was on that day that Connolly's cross-channel dockers resigned in protest against his "ungodly speech". A British T.U.C. delegation arrived in Dublin and conferred with the employers in the Shelbourne Hotel, while strikes spread on the North Wall and the master builders gave notice of a lock-out in accordance with the employers' agreement. Twenty thousand people marched in the funeral procession of Nolan, and the police dared not intervene. Nor were they in evidence at Byrne's funeral or the mass meeting in O'Connell Street called by the British labour leaders, whose main preoccupation was to settle the strike before it spread to England. The Dublin employers were unaffected by their sweet reasonableness. The issue was engaged; the deadlock was plain to be seen. One side must give way. The issue of action in England dominated the struggle until December.

Connolly's first action after being sentenced was to send for Danny McDevitt from Belfast. He must collect a small bag from Moran's hotel, pay his bill and take the bag back to Belfast. The bag was unlocked. McDevitt was surprised at this request. Was there nobody in Dublin to be entrusted with such a small thing? Connolly offered no explanation, but McDevitt gathered that he was not anxious that the financial condition of the union in Belfast should be too well known in Dublin, and felt the open bag would prove too much of a temptation to the curious. His other request was for grammars of the Irish language. These were sent in, but by the time they arrived Connolly had decided that too much was going on outside. Study must wait. On Sunday September 7 he went on hunger strike.

His detention was of doubtful legality. Great indignation was aroused when it leaked out that Mr. Swifte, the magistrate, was a substantial shareholder in the Tramway Company. The authorities tried to keep the hunger strike dark, and no forcible feeding was attempted. But as protests mounted they became alarmed. This mood of the people was completely new. They had rebelled, and heaven had not fallen in on them. A new air of confidence that they had power and could use it affected the entire working class.

Lillie and Ina visited Connolly on the seventh day and found him weak and feverish. A deputation composed of William O'Brien, Sheehy-Skeffington, P.T. Daly and Eamon Martin of the Fianna waited on the Lord Lieutenant. Mrs. Connolly was staying at the Martins' home. In the afternoon the vice-regal car appeared at the door, bearing orders to the Governor of Mountjoy that Connolly should be released. Mrs. Connolly and Ina thereupon returned to Mountjoy with Martin, and took Connolly by taxi to the house of Countess Markiewicz. The preceding Thursday Larkin was allowed bail, though a true bill had been found against him. The higher authorities were beginning to wonder whither events might lead. The weapon of thuggery had to be replaced by another, the weapon of starvation.

Connolly rested at Surrey House, Rathmines, for a few days. Meanwhile the efforts of the British T.U.C. leaders to effect a compromise were bogging down and a sympathetic strike movement began in England. Liverpool dockers came out, and were quickly followed by railwaymen in Birmingham, Yorkshire and South Wales. The *Daily Herald*, utilising the services of Sheehy-Skeffington and W.P. Ryan, constantly urged support for Dublin. Even there, not all forces were yet engaged. The master builders declared their lockout, and with the completion of the harvest the farmers of Co. Dublin followed suit. The struggle engulfed one section after another. Even the children were drawn in. Pupils of Rutland Street school refused to work with textbooks distributed by Easons, and were evicted from the premises by the police.

Connolly completed his recuperation in Belfast. Before returning he wired Nelly Gordon. He was determined to use his reappearance in order to stimulate solidarity in the north. She brought out the Non-Sectarian Labour Band and a demonstration of dockers and mill-girls awaited him at the G.N.R. station. At the same time Orangemen gathered in Shaftesbury Square singing "Dolly's Brae". From the one came drumrolls and cheers, from the other catcalls and volleys of stones. Despite brickbats and some revolver shots, a meeting was held. Flanagan made a strong attack on religious sectarianism and Nelly Gordon welcomed Connolly back to Belfast. The procession returned to the union office. It was ironical that on that same day when the Orangemen discharged their shots, a section of the clergy in Dublin condemned "socialism" and demanded the formation of a breakaway union. One or two "yellow" sheets were started with employers' money. But the A.O.H. move was unheeded by the strikers.

While Connolly spent his few days in Belfast, the promising sympathetic strike movement across the channel came to an end. J. H. Thomas, instead of standing by the railwaymen who were victimised for supporting Dublin, helped the employers to dismiss them, and there were one or two cases of severe hardship. The T.U.C. leaders made statements that they were in Dublin in a purely "judicial" capacity. The older leaders hated Larkin, and hated militancy even more. The *Daily Citizen* openly sneered at him. *Justice* damned by faint praise, and only Lapworth's *Daily Herald* remained stoutly pro-Dublin. As the leaders of the British workers cajoled and bludgeoned them into treachery, representatives of the employers crossed to London seeking sustenance from their own class abroad. They obtained it without difficulty. They represented themselves as the defenders of business morality against the syndicalist Larkin who had torn up agreements and justified the sympathetic strike with the terse words "to hell with contracts". So ended the first phase of the struggle.

From condemning sympathetic strikes the British leaders turned to obstructing the "blacking" of goods in transit to Dublin. Here less sacrifice was involved and they had to face a rank-and-file vociferously demanding action. Unfortunately, they knew the weaknesses of their own people. For years it had been Britain's tradition to let others fight her battles while she supplied the weapons. Now the splendid solidarity movement was sidetracked into a campaign to send foodships to Dublin. As an adjunct to a sympathetic strike movement or boycott this would have been admirable. It was to be a substitute. In vain Larkin could reason or storm. The price of strike action was stated clearly on the ticket. It was London control of the I.T.W.U. Otherwise union funds were not to be risked on the Dublin intransigents. The right wing were endeavouring to confine British support to food and fuel, practical rather than political help, while making Larkin, who wanted the latter, seem ungrateful. Instead of the struggles of the two peoples being treated as one, the British were encouraged to think they were magnanimously sustaining the Irish in an essentially domestic affair, which to some extent they had involved themselves in foolishly. The leaders grudged. But the rank-and-file did not grudge. There was no mistaking the intense class feeling which brought pennies and sixpences from remote villages in Yorkshire and South Wales into the Dublin relief fund. But Larkin was right in his belief that sympathetic strike action alone could defeat the employers.

If it had been taken, the history of Western Europe might have been different. An issue of policy within the British labour movement thus contained the Dublin struggle like the banks of a stream and this explains Larkin's periodical outbursts against the right-wing leaders, as well as the tactics they adopted in Dublin. To Larkin they were guilty of industrial treachery. To Connolly there was also an explanation which lay deeper. It was to be found in the old Liberal-Labour alliance with the Home Rulers, which he had fought for twenty years. It was an aspect of the parliamentary opportunism of British Labour.

On his return to Dublin Connolly found a grimmer mood among the locked-out workers. When the Liverpool men returned to work the hopes of sympathetic action in Britain were finally dashed. A threatened split in the employers' camp had been healed by timely subventions from Britain. Connolly's return freed Larkin for lightning visits to Britain, where at packed meetings he urged without avail the resumption of the sympathetic strike. The leadership of the strike from now on slowly passed to Connolly. Starvation was on the way. Dublin suffragettes opened a soup-kitchen at Liberty

Hall, where Countess Markiewicz supplied free dinners to the most needy. This service was augmented when the first foodship, the s.s. *Hare,* paid for by the British T.U.C. and loaded with £5,000 worth of C.W.S. food, arrived at the North Wall from Manchester on September 27. It was a fine gesture of solidarity and seemed to herald more active assistance to come. Enthusiasm was intense and Connolly was not the man to damp it. Yet he struck a reflective note within his speech of welcome. He compared the arrival of the ship to the breaking of the boom in Derry, the Unionist anniversary being now "put in the halfpenny place". But he went on:

> "The chapter of Irish history dealing with the relief of Dublin by the labouring men of England will be a long and bright one. In order to obtain relief the trade union has surrendered nothing, not one particle of our independence. We have not been asked to surrender anything. We on our part are willing to accept the proposals of the Lord Mayor as a basis of negotiations. There may be some things in it that we may want to get out, but as a basis of negotiation it is an eminently reasonable proposal."

The essential condition insisted on by the union—withdrawal of the stipulation against union membership—had been accepted by the Mayor.

The employers on the other hand were dreaming of total victory through the use of blacklegs and were negotiating for a ship in which to quarter them in the safety of the Liffey.

"Moderate as I am," said Connolly, "I know what it means. If this ship is brought to Dublin by the Shipping Federation and they begin to discharge their cargo—I mention no names, as I want to give them a chance of withdrawing—I know, you know, and God knows, that the streets of Dublin will run red with the blood of the working classes."

Seddon attended a meeting of the Trades Council Executive under whose stamp the food was to be issued—1s. 8d. worth a head for sixty thousand persons. Supplies also came in from Aberdeen and Dumfries Co-operative Societies. The same day the employers rebuffed the Lord Mayor, and a

Board of Trade Enquiry, presided over by Sir George Askwith, the "licensed strike-breaker", was announced. Connolly thought it would "investigate what everybody knew", but when Gosling invited the Trades Council to nominate witnesses, he accepted delegation along with Larkin, O'Brien, Johnson, O'Carroll, D. R. Campbell, MacPartlin and Rimmer. Robert Williams, the enthusiastic but unstable militant, attended for the Transport Federation, and despite the vituperative eloquence of T. M. Healy (the "most foul-mouthed man in Ireland") who enjoyed his brief for the employers, Murphy and his colleagues were publicly exposed as aggressors and protractors of the struggle. On October 7, George Russell (A. E.) wrote a celebrated letter to *The Irish Times* which described them as "blind Samsons pulling down the pillars of the Social Order", and told them: "You are sounding the death-knell of autocracy in industry ... so surely will democratic power wrest from you the control of industry."

The statement of the workers' case was drawn up by Connolly.

"With due respect to this Court," he began, "it is neither first nor last in our thoughts today ... the ultimate tribunal to which we appeal is not this Court, but rather the verdict of the class to which we belong.... The learned Counsel for the employers says that for the past five years there have been more strikes than there have been since Dublin was a capital. Practically every responsible man in Dublin today admits that the social conditions of Dublin are a disgrace to civilisation. Have these two sets of facts no relation?"

He accused the employers of "enforcing their rights with a rod of iron and renouncing their duties with a front of brass".

"They tell us that they recognise Trade Unions.... They complain that the Irish Transport and General Workers' Union cannot be trusted to keep its agreements. The majority of shipping firms in Dublin today are at present working, refusing to join in this mad enterprise ... with perfect confidence in the faith of the I.T.G.W.U. They complain of the sympathetic strike, but the members of the United Builders Labourers Union ... have been subjected to a sympathetic lock-out."

The verdict was quite favourable. Askwith proposed a new basis for negotiations, involving reinstatement, withdrawal of the employer's pledge, and an arbitration agreement relinquishing the sympathetic strike for two years except when an employer rejected conciliation. "The strikers must not be victimised," declared Gosling. "On this point the masters will not yield," replied Healy. "Then," said Gosling, "we will fight."

A group of prominent citizens, anxious to succeed where officialdom had failed, seized upon these proposals to establish a "peace committee". Its delegates attended the Trades Council Executive. O'Brien pointed out that the workers had not rejected overtures. Connolly suggested an attempt to find an acceptable intermediary, the object being to bring the two sides together. But by early October both Protestant and Catholic Archbishops had declined that honour. The peace committee speedily learned that only the workers' side maintained a vestige of social responsibility.

The employers now clinched matters by declaring that no settlement was possible without the removal of Larkin and the appointment of new officials approved by the British joint Trade Board. Its experiences resulted in a complete change in the character of the peace committee.

Foodships were arriving at weekly intervals. The third arrived on October 13. The employers' demand for Larkin's removal (a subtle attempt to suborn Connolly) arrived when Larkin was beginning a tour which took him from Glasgow to Hull, Birmingham and London. He was taken ill at Nottingham and compelled to abandon his meeting in Aberdeen. Newspapers were not slow to point to the "responsible" alternative, but Connolly dashed their hopes by declaring "the position is unchanged" and organising a procession through the streets of Dublin on October 15. Four thousand marched with bands and banners.

At the meeting which concluded this demonstration, he announced that evictions had begun. "Pay no rent," Larkin had said. The advice was of course unnecessary. Families could not do so if they wished. One worker whose book was clear previous to the strike was served with an eviction order. He refused to move. R.I.C. men were sent to eject him, but being countrymen they declined. This was not the work they were called to Dublin to do. "There was a limit to the brutality of the R.I.C.," said Connolly. But the Dublin police were not so squeamish. They broke in the door and smashed the remaining furniture, beating up both man and wife. The four children marched out defiantly singing "God save Larkin, said the Heroes". Such was the spirit of the working class.

The solidarity movement grew steadily and irresistibly. Both British and Irish suffrage movements rallied to the aid of the women and children. Committees were set up everywhere, encouraged by the *Daily Herald* and the *Glasgow Forward,* where Connolly wrote each week. The London Gaelic League forgot its pretended "non-political" character so far as to establish a special committee to raise funds for Dublin. The Trades Council was the general clearing house for raising and distributing funds, co-ordinating, and ironing out disputes and difficulties. Even in Belfast belated sympathy began to rise. The men who had left the union in August, on account of the "ungodly speech" of their leader, applied to rejoin now. The employers at once gave them an unsolicited 2s. 6d. a week to keep them out. On the other hand workers of six or seven mills applied for membership of the union that was waging this titanic battle. Cathal O'Shannon, Nora and Ina Connolly took collecting boxes round church doors. The Gaelic League of Belfast came in. Finally Thomas Johnson was able to issue an appeal to the shipyard workers to forget sectarian differences and support their own class, and many of them responded. Such was the second phase—total deadlock.

In mid-October the cause suffered a set-back. Up to then the obvious reasonableness of the workers contrasted with the employers' intransigence had carried all before it. In October secondary effects of the strike began to appear. Small businessmen closed down through lack of materials. Established Corporation employees, laid off for the same reason, were told that they had lost their seniority. Shopkeepers and small landlords began to feel the pinch. These classes read Arthur Griffith's *Sinn Fein*, the only paper (apart from the yellow sheets of the A.O.H.) which saw no harm in the employers. Griffith saw in the foodships, not solidarity taking the only course left open to it, but a nefarious plot to advance British exports over the ruins of Irish trade. He thundered against "Marx's iron law of wages" and the "neofeudalism of Marx, Proudhon and Lassalle". An ignoramus in all theoretical and scientific matters, he was unaware that his own suspicion of Trade Unionism was shared by Proudhon whom Marx had immortalised by destroying his reputation. When the pent forces of solidarity broke through at a fresh point, the backward strata were quick to misinterpret and condemn. The precondition for what took place was, however, the refusal of the British trade union leaders to take sympathetic action.

A group of suffragettes connected with the Daily Herald League in London proposed a plan for bringing the children of the strikers to be cared for in the homes of British workers. A similar scheme had been adopted in the New England Textile strike and it is surprising that Mrs. Montefiore, who was widely travelled, did not fear a repetition of the sectarian repercussions which wrecked it in America. The Parliamentary Committee of the British T.U.C. gave no countenance and insisted that its own funds must be devoted to supporting children in their own homes. But the T.U.C. was suspect owing to its obstruction of sympathetic action, and was unfortunately in this instance not heeded. An announcement brought many applications from parents anxious to spare their children the miseries of Dublin. Foster-parents were found in London, Edinburgh, Plymouth and above all in Liverpool. Later the scheme was extended to the outskirts of Dublin and to Belfast, as it caught the imagination of sympathisers.

Larkin seems to have given tacit approval. Connolly was extremely dubious but, presented with a *fait accompli,* left Dublin to fulfil engagements in Edinburgh and Dundee. He spoke at Leith, where students tried to break up the meeting, and from the bandstand in the centre of the Meadows, his old stamping ground. At Dundee his brother John had the temerity to appear at the platform in the uniform of the Edinburgh City Artillery, and was denounced in fine style. He went on to Glasgow and Kilmarnock, to reach Dublin once more on October 28. He found Larkin in jail, under a seven months' sentence, and outside a seething pot of Hibernian provocation. The suffragettes had gone quietly about their business while Larkin was occupied with his defence. A true bill was found on the twenty-first, and Larkin was convicted on the twenty-seventh as fifteen thousand men, women and children cheered encouragement from outside the court. The jury was composed of his opponents the employers, and one, with more compunction than the rest, who declared his interest, was refused exemption. "A packed jury," Larkin commented. He was within an ace of victory in his English campaign. So deftly had he laid about him that Labour leaders had asked the strike committee to "restrain him". "Larkin must go" became the right-wing cry, because "he stands in the way of a settlement". But after his speech at the Picton Hall, the Liverpool dockers declared themselves ready to strike once more. The employers and Hibernians had therefore good reason to try to discredit him during his trial and prepare the way for the importation of scabs. They found their opportunity in the campaign against the "deportation" of the children.

Four days after the first children left on the seventeenth, the Archbishop of Dublin broke his judicial silence. He denounced the "deportation" as a danger to the children's faith. The Hibernian rags then published a membership certificate of the Orange Order in the not uncommon name of James

Larkin, and accused the strike leader of proselytising. Some children reached Mrs. Criddle and Fred Bower in Liverpool, others the Pethwick-Lawrence family in Surrey. Then the riots began. With fanatical young priests at their head, howling mobs surrounded the quays and stations. Both parents and children were injured in their attacks. Despite the declared fact that the only Protestant accommodation in Belfast was that offered by D. R. Campbell, Amiens Street was the scene of wild hysteria. Mrs. Montefiore and her colleagues were arrested. Palpable evidence that religious facilities were fully available was ignored or brushed aside. Under this smokescreen "free labour" was brought over from Manchester. When Connolly found himself acting general secretary of the union it seemed only one more tribulation was necessary. Seddon and Gosling announced their intention of paying another visit with a view to "settling" the strike.

Connolly's handling of this complex and unfavourable situation was masterly. His strength was the tremendous momentum the mass movement had by now attained. Within three weeks he had turned the tables on all his adversaries, and got Larkin out of jail. The first step was to inform the press that in view of the opposition the transmigration scheme had been abandoned. Instead, he demanded that the children be supported in Dublin. He then suspended all free dinners at Liberty Hall. "Go to the Archbishop and the priests," he told his supporters. "They are loud in their professions. Put them to the test." They failed to pass. Catholic relief and charitable organisations were so overwhelmed with demands that Archbishop Walsh was compelled to adopt a conciliatory tone. Now at last he issued an appeal for the settlement of the dispute.

Dinners were resumed after a week. To workers who had been carried away by the hysteria, Connolly was indulgent and helpful. His old neighbour, Mrs. Farrell, had been arrested during a riot in which Sheehy-Skeffington was injured. He visited her in jail, bailed her out and offered to arrange defence counsel. By this means he drew back into the struggle workers who had strayed.

He rallied the locked-out men in Beresford Place. To his question "Will we give in?" husky voices cried, "No surrender!" The imprisonment of Larkin had an effect opposite to that which was intended. It was hoped that Connolly would seize the opportunity to oust Larkin and become leader himself. He was in his own testimony "subjected to influences that none could imagine", particularly from across the channel. But instead, his skill and firmness saved the situation. "Messrs. Seddon and Gosling are coming over again to negotiate," he told the *Daily Herald*, "and we heartily accept the co-operation of our comrades across the water *as our allies*. The moment they are anything less than that we are ready to dispense with their co-operation. If we are to judge by the capitalist press, some of our English comrades are susceptible to the blarney of soft-spoken Dublin employers, but we are giving them the credit of not being easily wheedled out of their allegiance to the working class."

To the Dublinmen he was even more outspoken. "If the trade union leaders from across the water are prepared to accept peace at any price, and threaten to withdraw their foodships and support . . . then I would say 'Take back your foodships, for the workers of Dublin will not surrender their position for all the ships on the sea'." Seddon and Gosling arrived. The Trades Council Executive rejected their proposal for a settlement without the I.T.G.W.U. Connolly's refusal to disavow Larkin left no room for manœuvre.

Securing Larkin's release was the next problem. His imprisonment was widely held to be illegal. He was acquitted on all counts save that of sedition. But among his seditious utterances the worst that could be listed were such dynamite-laden statements as that he denied the divine right of kings, opposed the Empire and that "the employing class lived on rent and profit". The sentence, said Connolly, showed the class character of the administration of the law. At a protest meeting he announced his plan to defeat the Liberal candidate in each of three by-elections which were pending.

"It doesn't matter," Connolly declared, "whether it is a Labour man or a Tory that is against the Liberal. The immediate thing is to hit the government that keeps Larkin in jail." If these measures were without effect, bolder ones would be taken.

A manifesto was wired to Keighley, Reading and Linlithgow. "Locked-out Nationalist workers of Dublin appeal to British workers to vote against Liberal jailers of Larkin and murderers of Byrne and Nolan." Belfast Branch of the I.L.P.(I.) followed with a telegram to Keighley, where Devlin was busy helping the Liberal. On the exposure of the strike-breaking activities of his A.O.H. (Board of Erin), that gentleman hastily cancelled his meetings and slunk out of the town.

Partridge was despatched to Reading where he joined Lansbury in support of the Labour candidate. At the funeral of James Byrne, secretary of the Dun Laoghaire Trades Council, who had died on hunger strike, Connolly declared: "The government must go if Larkin stays in." The occasion became a great anti-government demonstration which filled the Home Rulers with a deep uneasiness. Every shop in the town closed while the procession passed.

"My heart swelled with pride," said Connolly, "that the workers are at last learning to honour their fighters and martyrs. Byrne as truly died a martyr as any man who ever died for Ireland." He remarked that the employers had at last been forced into a semblance of negotiation. They would now try to protract discussions while they brought in fresh scabs.

The news of the government defeats in Linlithgow and Reading caused great jubilation in Dublin. Sky-rockets were fired from the roof of Liberty Hall. "We are doubtless to be told we are attacking Home Rule," said Connolly. "Dublin working men are as firm as ever for national self-government. But they are not going to allow the government to bludgeon them and jail their leaders and comrades and place all the machinery of the law, police, and military at the disposal of the employers without hitting back. Reading is the first blow. Follow it at Keighley, and at every election till Larkin is free."

On November 12 the Liberals were defeated at Keighley also. The prestige of the Home Rulers fell disastrously. The Dublin working class now understood the meaning of Home Rule under the Hibernians. Two months of struggle taught them the truth of Connolly's twenty years' propaganda.

Lost by-elections did not suffice to move the government. Nor did the rapidly mounting release campaign in Britain, which was now joined by the Liberal newspapers, the *News* and *Chronicle*. Scabs poured in, fifty from Manchester on the 29th, and one hundred from Liverpool on November 5. The *Daily Herald* called for a general strike, Robert Williams for a special conference of the T.U.C. Connolly did not wait. Throughout Dublin he posted his own manifesto. Everywhere groups of men were to be seen reading and discussing it. It was headed "Importation or Deportation?" and flayed the hypocrisy of those who "prostituted the name of religion" by pouring "insults and calumny upon the Labour men and women who offered the children shelter and comfort ... but allow English blacklegs to enter Dublin without a protest."

The manifesto then announced that "individual picketing" was abolished. Mass picketing was to be the rule, and those who shirked were to be refused food tickets. It concluded:

> "Fellow workers, the employers are determined to starve you into submission, and if you resist to club you, jail you, and kill you. We defy them. If they think they can carry on their industries without you, we will, in the words of the Ulster Orangemen, take steps to prevent it. Be men now, or be for ever slaves.–James Connolly."

The authorities replied by arming the scabs. One of them, driving a load of cement, drew a revolver and shot a boy in the knee. He was not arrested, but his load of cement was soon strewn about the road.

It was the struggle of the workers against the police-protected armed scabs which gave rise to the Citizen Army. Its origin has been disputed but seems clearly ascertained. When the first rumours of the introduction of scabs were noted, the *Daily Herald* issued the slogan "Arm the Workers". But it was not giving voice to any new conception, certainly not in syndicalist propaganda. Larkin attributed the notion of a citizen army to Fearon of Cork in 1908. But in the U.S.A. it would have been unthinkable *not* to arm pickets where this was possible. The Workers' Police of Wexford has already been referred to.

On October 31 a correspondent in the *Daily Herald* had urged the T.U.C. to create a "Civil Guard" to protect civil rights. At Dun Laoghaire Connolly also had referred to the need to arm the workers. Talk of workers' defence was in the air; it arose from the inescapable needs of the situation, and required but a catalyst to set it in action.

On November 11 the Industrial Peace Committee dissolved. A majority decided to abandon the position of impartiality and give full support to the workers' side. The events which precipitated this decision were the use of three companies of Surrey infantry to protect Jacobs' scabs and the government decision to increase the pay of the police who were trying to disperse the massed pickets. A new committee was formed, under the chairmanship of Captain Jack White who had resigned his commission on account of his anti-imperialist views. The inaugural meeting of the "Civic Committee", as the majority called itself, was held on the twelfth at 40, Trinity College, and one of the proposals made by the Captain was a "drilling scheme" as a means of bringing "discipline into the distracted ranks of Labour". It is of course hard to believe that Captain White did not envisage the possible consequences of such a course. He approached Connolly, who had just played his trump card for the defeat of the scabs and the release of Larkin.

This was the *Manifesto to the British Working Class,* calling on them to stop all traffic from Messrs. Guinness, Jacobs and other scab firms. Connolly had thus resumed the struggle for sympathetic action, and appealed over the heads of the right-wing leaders.

"We are denied every right guaranteed by law," he declared, "we are subjected to cold-blooded systematic arrests and ferocious prison sentences. Girls and women are jailed every day. 'Free' labourers are imported by hundreds.

"We propose to carry the war into every section of the enemy's camp. Will you second us? We are about to take action the news of which will probably have reached you before this is in your hands."

That news aroused even the "respectable" classes to grudging enthusiasm, and on the mass of the workers its effect was electrical. Connolly had closed the port of Dublin "as tight as a drum". All over England "vigilance committees" were elected. Meetings of railwaymen decided not to handle tainted goods in Liverpool, Birmingham, Holyhead, Swansea, Bristol, Heysham, Manchester, London, Nottingham, Crewe, Derby, Sheffield, Leeds and Newcastle. This action opened the fourth phase of the struggle.

In vain the Dublin shipping companies pleaded their agreements. This was no ordinary dispute, Connolly told them. The result was almost magical. Larkin was released at 7.30 a.m. on the thirteenth. The two men then drafted a further appeal to the British workers calling for a general strike to stop the transit of scabs. That Thursday night there was a great victory meeting and procession, the biggest yet held. Until after midnight boys and girls lit bonfires in the streets. Larkin did not speak, however. He was suffering from a nervous reaction. Frothing and fuming in his cell he had not been able to orient himself to Connolly's strategy. Men of feeling tend to think mechanically. Why had Connolly accused Murphy of refusing agreements and then torn them up himself? Larkin's frustration could only be purged in action. He left for Liverpool on the Friday, thence to carry his "fiery cross" throughout England. It was Connolly who startled the victory meeting with these words:

"I am going to talk sedition. The next time we are out for a march I want to be accompanied by four battalions of trained men with their corporals and sergeants. Why should we not drill and train men as they are doing in Ulster?"

He asked every man willing to join the "Labour Army" to give in his name when he drew his strike pay at the end of the week. He had competent officers ready to instruct and lead them, and could get arms any time they wanted them. The announcement was greeted with deafening cheers.

Connolly remained acting general secretary and editor of the *Irish Worker*, but left McKeown in temporary charge while he joined Larkin in Manchester where four thousand assembled in the Free Trade Hall with another twenty thousand outside. "The working class of Dublin is being slowly murdered," Connolly told them.

In this fourth stage of the struggle, practically the entire working class of Dublin was engaged. The bulk of the intelligentsia had joined them. Republicans like Pearse and Clarke looked on with admiration at such a stupendous resistance, and slowly a new comprehension dawned. Both sides were receiving thousands of pounds a week from Britain. But it was a condition of working-class victory that the employers should be prevented from producing or distributing. The steady trickle of scabs enabled the more fortunate businesses to tick over, and though not a ship left Dublin, Derry and Belfast were still open. For this reason the fight against scab labour in Dublin was little more than a holding operation until there was sympathetic action above all in Liverpool and Glasgow.

Connolly accompanied Larkin to London where they met the Parliamentary Committee of the T.U.C. on the Tuesday, urging either a general strike or a total boycott of Dublin. There was no response. Nor was there immediate consent to Williams' proposal for a special meeting of the T.U.C. Next day the two colleagues spoke at the famous Albert Hall meeting, when students risked burning the place down in an attempt to plunge the auditorium into darkness. Fortunately they were too ignorant of electricity to achieve either. Instead they swarmed over the balconies, interrupting the quieter speakers, creating pandemonium until they were ejected by a group of burly stewards led by Con O'Lyhane. Once more Connolly and Larkin stressed the need for sympathetic action and demanded a special T.U.C. meeting. They were joined by George Lansbury, Will Dyson, Robert Williams, George Russell, George Bernard Shaw and Sylvia Pankhurst.

Connolly made a flying visit to Belfast, where he addressed a meeting at the low docks. The local men had been called out because the Head Line had transported scabs to Dublin. There was to be no return till the Dublin men won. The example of Dublin was increasingly impressing the Protestant workers, and it is noteworthy that when a meeting at King Street a thousand strong celebrated Larkin's release, "Dolly's Brae" was silent, and a mob of Hibernians tried to break it up. Noteworthy also was the fact that the police arrested not the Hibernians but the trade unionists.

Reaching Dublin the same night Connolly attended the first public meeting of the "Civic League". Captain White had advised Trinity College students to absent themselves from lectures as a protest against police protection of the scabs. The authorities replied by announcing that any student who attended "Captain White's Home Rule meeting" would be deprived of his rooms. The Mansion House being refused to them, the Civic League hired the Antient Concert Rooms and Connolly was delighted to see over a hundred college boys arrive in a procession. They were allotted seats on the platform. Among the speakers were Rev. R.M. Gwynn and Professor Collingwood of the National University, Countess Markiewicz, Sheehy-Skeffington and Darrell Figgis. A telegram from Roger Casement supported the "drilling scheme" as a step towards the foundation of a corps of national volunteers. Connolly had referred to the proposed force in his Albert Hall speech as "a citizen army of locked-out men" and the name "Citizen Army" seems to have been adopted immediately after Captain White's meeting. It was first used officially on Sunday November 23, when after a further recruiting meeting two companies were formed. It was thus at first essentially a labour defence force, though Connolly's speeches and Casement's telegram show that there were inklings of its ultimate destiny. Captain Monteith was on his way to join when he met Tom Clarke, who dissuaded him on the grounds that his help was required in the purely nationalist "Volunteer" movement then being prepared.

The Citizen Army drilled with hurley-sticks and wooden shafts at Croydon Park. For practical purposes the shafts were sometimes "shoed" with a cylinder of metal. A favourable reaction was immediately noticeable among the police. Scabs still came in. Devlin still screamed for the establishment of a "Catholic Labour Union". But he merely isolated himself. The working class had already won its moral victory. When the annual Manchester Martyrs procession took place, the I.T.G.W.U. dominated it with the largest contingent of all. The A.O.H. deemed it prudent not to appear. The working class had dislodged them from the body of the nationalist movement. In the same week the British T.U.C. conceded Larkin's request and announced a special meeting on December 9.

The two weeks preceding this conference were crucial. Larkin travelled from city to city arousing intense excitement. At Birmingham and Liverpool, Connolly joined him. No day was without at least one meeting. Cardiff, Swansea, East Ham, Hull, Leicester, Edinburgh, Newcastle, Leeds, Preston, Glasgow, and Stockport were covered before the conference, and Larkin made one brief appearance in Dublin. The right-wing leaders also mobilised their forces. Fearing the opinions of their members, they called not a delegate conference but a conference of paid officials. J. H. Thomas gave orders that on the first occasion the Transport Union unloaded a ship, all his men must return forthwith. Havelock Wilson denounced sympathetic strikes and encouraged his members to work the Head Line ships. The *Daily Citizen* attacked Larkin bitterly and incessantly. Larkin, unfortunately, saw these attacks not as signs of a political trend but as acts of personal apostasy. He replied in kind and with interest. Liverpool carters and motormen struck work. When two

Llanelly railwaymen were dismissed for refusing to handle goods for Dublin, the resultant strike spread throughout South Wales. Funds were now arriving from Australia and America, and news arrived that the French workers were preparing to close the ports against all goods originating in Dublin.

Protected by the staves of the Citizen Army, Connolly now led processions past Mountjoy to sing rebel songs for Frank Moss, who was on hunger strike. He skilfully outwitted the police so as to pass singing by the Convent where Mary Murphy was imprisoned. As many as twelve thousand gathered in Beresford Place. The remaining support for the employers ebbed steadily. When the Irish Volunteers were founded on November 25 at the Rotunda, Lawrence Kettle, whose family employed scabs on Co. Dublin farms, was hooted off the platform amidst pandemonium. Pembroke Urban Council decided to apply penalty clauses against builders who had ceased work on its housing scheme. Archbishop Walsh appealed once more for peace and, most significant of all, the *Freeman's Journal* crossed over to the position of *The Irish Times,* urged the employers to give up their ban on the Transport Union, and left the *Independent* alone on the employers' side. Sharp divisions appeared in the Dublin Chamber of Commerce, where Murphy's dictatorial behaviour was becoming more and more resented.

England was decisive. Boycott Dublin goods for two weeks, and the employers would have to cave in. Larkin saw the Parliamentary Committee once more. Instead of blacking Dublin goods, they elected one more delegation, the "strongest yet", which visited Dublin determined to effect a settlement at all costs, if need be over the heads of the local committees. The employers could scarcely decline to talk. The *Daily Mail* was clamouring that "Larkin and Murphy must *both* go" and Murphy knew his position was now none too strong. Connolly and Foran represented the union, O'Brien and MacPartlin the trades council. Arthur Henderson tried desperately to jockey the Irishmen into an unacceptable settlement. The employers sat in one room, the workers' representatives in another, and the British passed back and forth between them. Only for fifteen minutes did both sides sit together. Experienced diplomats they might be, but the Englishmen could find no half-way house between Gabriel and Beelzebub. The conference broke down after an allnight sitting, on the question of reinstatement—two days before the special T.U.C. in the Memorial Hall, Farringdon Road.

Before leaving for London, Connolly posted up another manifesto in which he laid the blame for the breakdown squarely on the employers. The conference was on December 9, and ostensibly there were two alternative policies presented to it for a choice. The right-wing proposed a 1d. levy to send Dublin £12,500 instead of the present £5,000. The left-wing demand was for a boycott of Dublin goods and, if necessary, a national strike to prevent victimisation.

On the eve of the conference J. H. Thomas settled the South Wales strike on terms of "abject betrayal". The attacks on Larkin intensified. Larkin himself grew more openly contemptuous of the "milk and water" cross-channel leaders. His emotional outbursts probably did far less harm than his occasional mechanical attempts to think his way out of a difficulty. He was billed to speak at Grimsby, but declined on the ground that the proposed chairman, Ernest Marklew, had divorced his wife. Most probably his motive was to avoid any other possible clash with the Catholic Church on a moral question. But the refusal created a very bad impression in Britain while it was scarcely noticed in Ireland. Blatchford's *Clarion* published a blistering "Open Letter" to him. Sick with a sense of defeat and betrayal he laid about him even more determinedly. *Clarion* described him as a "devoted Catholic". While the B.S.P. was the backbone of the solidarity movement, *Justice* had remained serenely detached. It now suggested that Larkinism was a Catholic plot to discredit the trade union leaders, with the complicity of the *Daily Herald*. Yet at the Sun Hall, Liverpool, Larkin had described Father Hopkins as "masquerading in a cassock and gold cross" adding: "We want none of these sky-pilots; we can pilot ourselves."

Six hundred delegates attended the conference, representing three hundred and fifty unions. But a glance convinced Larkin that he was on trial, and before a jury of his enemies. Robert Williams and he both complained the delegates had been neither elected nor mandated. Williams himself was excluded, on the grounds that as secretary of the Transport Federation he was paid by nineteen unions and was therefore not eligible.

At the outset it became clear that far from being called to assist Dublin, the conference was assembled to betray it. The first item on the agenda was the resolution accepting the report of the deputation to Dublin. It was moved by Henderson, who dropped his bait in the form of veiled insults directed at Larkin. Gosling, on the other hand, gave a fair account which laid the blame for the position on William Martin Murphy. Connolly smoothed things over by assuring Henderson that he need fear no opposition from Dublin should the T.U.C. feel disposed to open up fresh negotiations at any time.

Ben Tillet then moved a resolution condemning "unfair attacks" on trade union leaders. J. H. Thomas accused Larkin of sowing dissensions in the ranks of British railwaymen. Havelock Wilson said there was "Murphyism" in the trade union movement as well as among employers. Larkin, overworked and exhausted, taunted and exasperated beyond endurance, gave himself the pleasure of speaking his mind clearly for fifteen minutes.

"Mr. Chairman, and human beings," he began, and in a speech which was continuously interrupted he spoke of the "foul, lying attacks" made against him. "Not a man in this hall has been elected," he thundered, and demanded the blacking of Dublin goods. The resolution was carried on a card vote with a big majority.

Then came the resolutions to call conferences, continue consultations, use every legitimate means, and so on. Generosity was not unending, it was hinted. The situation should be an object lesson to those who tried to create dissension. The gas-workers' delegate, Jack Jones, had the clarity of vision to suggest fighting capitalism not Larkinism, and proposed the boycott. Davis of the Vehicle Builders seconded. Railwayman Williams described the proposition as "silly". Robert Smillie objected that the rank-and-file had given no mandate for a national stoppage. Delegates supporting Larkin were constantly heckled, and the Jones amendment was lost by two million to two hundred thousand. One of the meaningless resolutions was then carried.

Larkin was speechless with indignation. Lacking theoretical understanding of the mainspring of the treachery before him, he was stupefied like many an honest man who sees duplicity his own mind cannot encompass. He had been hopelessly outmanœuvred on a stage which had been cunningly set. It was Connolly who found words, and he spoke moderately.

"I and my colleagues from Dublin," he said, "are here under a deep sense of humiliation. It would have been better for the conference to have first endeavoured to try and settle the Dublin dispute and afterwards wash their dirty linen. The reverse has however been the case." He thanked them for the help they had given but warned them: "We in Dublin will not necessarily accept all the resolutions passed at this conference."

Larkin left for Glasgow. Connolly returned to Dublin. On the way he leant out of the carriage window at Crewe and bought a newspaper. To his surprise it announced the resumption of work at the North Wall. Thomas had already ordered his men back to work before the conference met. If they did not return they would get no strike pay.

In Dublin there was no weakening, and Connolly confined himself to a simple statement of what had passed. But the final stage of the struggle had now opened. The foolish obduracy of Murphy precluded a settlement. But neither side was in any position to fight on. There could only be a disengagement. The remarkable fact is that this disengagement took as many months as were required to reach the crucial deadlock. Peace talks were begun again, and dragged out with intermissions. No settlement was ever come to between the main contestants, but step by step their allies resumed the *status quo,* or something near it. The London conference, which wrecked all hope of a workers' victory, released the smaller employers from their dependence on Murphy. *The Irish Times* demanded the unconditional reinstatement of all locked-out men–a category which included all but those tramwaymen who had struck in protest against the dismissal of the parcels men.

In mid-December this outcome could not be clearly foreseen. Connolly resumed his meetings, devoting much attention to the municipal elections, which he hoped to make a dazzling demonstration against the employers and government. The armed scabs grew more arrogant as their numbers increased. An old woman was shot, without any arrest being made. But when the same treatment was offered the Vice-Chairman of the Docks Board it was a different matter. The scab without respect for the gentry, when arrested, was bailed out by his employer. The Citizen Army continued to drill and defend the pickets, but shortage of arms drove many to transfer to the Volunteers.

When it was clear that Devlin's attempts to start a sectarian breakaway were doomed to failure, A.O.H. hoodlums broke into the *Irish Worker* printing office, smashed the formes and scattered the type. Police arrived. They prevented further damage but refused to make any arrests. A few days previously Hibernians had broken up a meeting of the Irish Volunteers in Cork city.

Less than a week after the London conference, British leaders dealt fresh blows at Dublin. The Seamen's and Firemen's Union ordered its members to man the boats of the Head Line though they were being discharged by Shipping Federation scabs. In both Dublin and Belfast the members refused. They were then informed that union men would be brought from England to fill their places. A consignment of Guinness refused in Dublin was despatched to Sligo. Connolly wired his local branch. Blacked in Sligo, it was taken by rail to Derry, where N.U.D.L. dockers loaded it, N.S.F.U. men took it to Liverpool and Sexton's dockers discharged it.

Connolly called a meeting of his Executive Committee. There was obviously now no point in keeping up the port-workers' strike. Foodships had ceased and contributions were rapidly falling. The T.U.C. had done nothing but promise another mediation team. It was decided to permit dockers to return to work "without prejudice to negotiations or a subsequent settlement". The smaller firms accepted them willingly, and they went back "with the Red Hand up".

On the day of the E.C., Larkin returned. He held an impromptu meeting at Dun Laoghaire and reached Dublin just in time to be evicted from his house. He had paid no rent since August 18. But he was full of fight. "The struggle is not half over," he declared. His spiritual stature was shown in those days of destitution and betrayal. He knew the E.C. decision was inevitable, but may have discharged his nervous tension through some words upon it. Newspapers reported a quarrel between Larkin and Connolly, to which they attributed Connolly's return to Belfast before Christmas.

This was the Christmas of hunger and heroism. "Dublin lies in the grip of the power of the purse," Connolly wrote. Every effort at mitigation was made by the union's faithful auxiliary workers. A huge marquee was erected at Croydon Park, and twenty thousand children were given a square meal. The O'Mahony provided Wicklow venison for one thousand men. Most of the prisoners in Mountjoy were released for Christmas, but not from good will. The warders threatened to strike themselves if their duties were not lightened over the holiday.

Connolly spent Christmas expanding *The Reconquest of Ireland* for pamphlet publication. On his return, Larkin and he issued a joint manifesto; it was made clear that Larkin had made a rough sketch, Connolly had drafted it, and both had signed it. So much was required to silence the tongue-wagging of those who were aiming for a split. The manifesto affirmed their intention of continuing the struggle and called for increased aid from both Ireland and Britain.

On January 4, 1914, they spoke together at the funeral of Alice Brady, a sixteen year old girl who died after being shot by a scab. Her assailant, then on bail, was taken in a second time and charged with murder. He was acquitted on the Judge's direction. Connolly seems to have caught a chill at the funeral. He returned to Belfast to lecture to the I.L.P.(I.) branch on the tenth and remained there a fortnight while his wife nursed him through his only recorded illness. He was not well enough to attend the Belfast office until January 20 and could not accompany Larkin to London to seek clarification of the position of the T.U.C. Larkin and O'Brien came back with the news that all aid to Dublin had now ceased. The fund was formally wound up on February 10, the thousands who had been on strike for nearly six months being handed over callously to their starvation. It is significant that two days later Asquith announced his first scheme for the partition of Ireland.

Taking Connolly's place in *Forward* during his sickness, Larkin explained that despite a number of settlements there were still nine thousand strikers. The election results showed the mood of the people. There were 12,026 pro-Larkin votes against 14,978 for the nationalists. Labour was within an ace of a majority, and the Archbishop congratulated the Mayor on his narrow escape. But Dublin was isolated and Dublin was starving. Visitors described the terrible plight of the people, women dressed in shawls and skirts, in mid-February devoid of a stitch of underclothing, children ten years old dressed entirely in sacking. Reactionaries took heart. Father Kane resumed his attacks on socialism. The A.O.H. started to develop a new tactic of infiltrating into trade unions and secured a complete capitulation by the United Labourers, which destroyed the union. Martin Murphy demanded that the government deport Larkin to England. At Liberty Hall, meetings were held at which lists of firms who still operated the employers' pledge were drawn up. The workers of all others were advised to return. By this means the burden on the union was gradually diminished.

As soon as Connolly was fit, the two leaders went to Glasgow, where they appealed to the "advanced section in Britain" not to desert Dublin. For the remaining two months of the struggle the B.S.P. carried the main burden of organising relief. British Labour indeed paid its own price for December 9. The middle-class backers of the *Daily Herald* forced Lansbury to dismiss Lapworth. "Too much Dublin" was the complaint. At the end of December London master-builders locked out their own workers. The *Herald,* under its new management, was reduced to eight pages. The great unrest quieted; once more British democracy suffered defeat because it failed to extend its full solidarity to the people of an oppressed nation. Only one union, the A.S.E.,[1] voted a $3d$. levy in response to Larkin's new appeal. In the months that followed the British people were being led by their leaders ever nearer the slaughter of the first world war.

Connolly now returned to Belfast, while Larkin continued to raise funds in Britain to cover the retreat of his army. Aid now took on another form. The socialists organised meetings and concerts for Dublin. Delia Larkin took a troupe of players through Lancashire. The Lord Mayor of Liverpool was prevailed on to patronise a distress fund in that City. Connolly's weekly articles in *Forward* returned to the subject of Dublin again and again. No experience had moved him so much in his life. He must dwell on it all the time. His old friends of the S.L.P. in Glasgow, from whom he had been estranged since the final breach with De Leon, began to rally round him again. But the socialist advance-guard, however welcome, was a poor substitute for the main army of labour.

A thousand I.T.G.W.U. men in Belfast were still locked out, and no arguments would persuade the Head Line to employ them. Connolly visited Glasgow and London in an effort to get the Stevedores Union to boycott the company. By mid-March, however, it was clear that the employers refused to distinguish between the I.T.G.W.U. and the S.F.U. men. Negotiations were opened between the two unions with a view to joint action. Adversity had forced them to compact. The same week, Jacobs' girls returned to work.

Lenten pastorals denouncing socialism and syndicalism had

---

[1] Parent body of the Amalgamated Engineering Union.

no influence on the starving workers. Connolly challenged the Hierarchy to name one point the union had refused to concede which the Archbishop himself, placed in the same position, would have conceded. Men now signed the Murphy pledge, but many remained members of the union. They continued to pay their subscriptions at Liberty Hall. There were no sackings. The pledge for which the capitalists had starved, murdered and tortured men for eight months was now reduced to a scrap of paper whose provisions they could not enforce. They could humiliate their returning employees, scoff at their emaciation and raggedness. Yet the battle was drawn. The employers had gained nothing they set out to gain. Their weaker members were bankrupt, and they dare not repeat the challenge to labour. It was too strong. But the Irish national struggle had been dealt a deadly blow.

In his weekly articles Connolly showed deep insight into the dynamics of the struggle, its importance for the British working class, and its connection with the Home Rule question. In *Old Wine in New Bottles* he tried to answer theoretically the question why the British unions had failed to respond to the call of class solidarity. He naturally avoided the vulgar nationalist pitfall of blaming them because they were British, though it is doubtful if he ever again felt any sense of confidence in the British labour movement. He did not, like Lenin, link up opportunism in the labour movement with the growth of imperialism. This was not yet clear. Rather he looked back to the early I.W.W., "the first Labour organisation to organise with the definite ideal of taking over and holding the economic machinery of society". He explained the syndicalist ideal of industrial unions linked into "one great union" where one membership card covered the "whole working-class organisation".

Then he raised questions which led beyond the syndicalist horizon. He had observed the process of amalgamation and affiliation which had produced, for example, the Transport Workers' Federation. The enlargement of organisation had been accompanied by "a freezing up of the fraternal spirit". The sudden strike, which had "won more for Labour than all the great labour conflicts in history", was replaced by the war of massed battalions "on a field every inch of which had been explored and mapped out beforehand". The amalgamations and federations had been, without exception "used in the old spirit of the worst type of sectionalism".

"Fighting spirit is of more importance than the creation of the theoretically perfect organisation," Connolly concluded. But how was it to be maintained? "The only solution of that problem is the choice of officers, local and national, from the standpoint of their responsiveness to the call for solidarity." Here he stopped short. Who was to look after the keepers? The De Leonist duology had become a trilogy: trade unions for "direct action", a Labour party for organising votes, and a socialist party for propaganda. But the socialist party was relegated to third place. Connolly needed and was feeling for the missing link, the socialist party of a new type which would provide the working-class movement with its incorruptible cadre. Without it he could only advise in general: "Choose the right man." The tragedy of his untimely death two years later is that his political advance was cut short. Nobody in Ireland developed these questions further, and underestimation of the role of the party has dogged the Irish labour movement for forty and more years.

XVIII
PARTITION

The British Constitution does not exist.
MONTESQUIEU

The last second reading of the Home Rule Bill under the Parliament Act was moved on March 9, 1914, while Connolly was negotiating with the waterfront unions. If the Commons passed it now, the Lords were powerless to reject it. Not that that promised to be the end of the matter. The Unionists were sabre-rattling all winter and intensifying their intrigues among courtiers and brass-hats as the point neared where the Liberals would either give in or compel them to make good their threats of civil war.

Throughout the period when the employers had levied total war on the workers, on the national front the air was thick with rumours of compromise. As suddenly and finally as his great predecessor was "converted" to Home Rule, Asquith embraced the doctrine of two Irelands, and proposed that any county wishing to be excluded from the operation of the Act might do so on a simple majority vote of the electors. This first proposition was hedged round with safeguards. But the principle of partition was there. A hole was stabbed in Home Rule, and the Unionists seized every tool to enlarge it. This was made easy enough for them when Devlin and Redmond hastened to accept Asquith's amendment, and from then on Home Rule and Partition were identical.

Carson affected dismay at the poorness of his bargain and demanded the permanent exclusion of four counties. To add portentousness to his claim he allowed it to be known that the Ulster Volunteers intended raiding arms dumps around Belfast. Only eleven days after the second reading, Sir Arthur Paget was ordering troops north from the Curragh. And at the direct instigation of the Chief of the Imperial General Staff, fifty-seven officers resigned their commissions. Far from being court-martialled or stuck in irons like a ship's cook, the mutinous gentlemen were assured that the army would never be used against the Unionists. The troops remained where they were. A deal was made within two days, and War Secretary Seely handed in his insignia of office as handsel. So passed the crisis which revealed in a flash the realities of the British "Constitution" so aptly summarised by Montesquieu.

Connolly was preoccupied with the strike and its aftermath when the storm broke. He reported to the I.T.U.C. in Dublin on his negotiations, and joined Captain White in addressing a proclaimed meeting in O'Connell Street. After more vicious baton charges White was carried away covered in blood. The Citizen Army had dwindled, though White did great execution with his blackthorn.

At the first intimation of partition, Connolly had sent his estimation to the *Irish Worker*. In the issue of March 14 he wrote:

"The recent proposals of Messrs. Asquith, Devlin and Redmond ... reveal in a most striking and unmistakable manner the depths of betrayal to which so-called nationalist politicians are willing to sink. ...

"Such a scheme as that agreed to by Devlin and Redmond, the betrayal of the national democracy of industrial Ulster, would mean a carnival of reaction both North and South, would set back the wheels of progress, would destroy the oncoming unity of the Irish labour movement, and paralyse all advanced movements while it endured.

"To it, Labour should give its bitterest opposition, against it Labour in Ulster should fight even to the death if necessary, as our fathers fought before us."

In his brief statement in *Forward,* on March 21, he declared his belief that "such a scheme would destroy the labour movement by disrupting it. It would make division more intense and confusion of ideas and parties more confounded."

At his instance the I.T.U.C. Executive passed a resolution condemning partition, which was followed by one from the Trades Council. The Citizen Army was reorganised and, on

Sean O'Casey's suggestion, a written constitution was adopted. Connolly was anxious to enlist Larkin's dynamism in rebuilding it, and also to help him orient himself towards new tasks. He proposed a public meeting where Larkin could take the chair and this took place on the twenty-second. Thereafter Larkin grew increasingly interested. He appealed to every union affiliated to the T.U.C. to establish a company and during the spring and summer held recruiting meetings throughout Co. Dublin. On the twenty-second also took place the first Sinn Fein function to which representatives of organised labour were invited. It was a conference called to discuss action against partition.

From Dublin Connolly went on to Cardiff. The Head Line had offered to take back the Dublin men, but they refused to go back until the Belfast men were reinstated. The Head Line then secured the services of five hundred scab stevedores, and the Dublin S.F.U. men refused to work "black" ships. On the Company then introducing the Shipping Federation ticket, a joint conference of all unions affected was held in Cardiff, on the twenty-third. No agreement was reached and the conference arranged to resume on April 14. Returning to Belfast, Connolly booked the St. Mary's Hall for a protest meeting. The press refused his advertisements, but he was able to fill the hall in three days. William MacMullen presided. Captain White came from Dublin with his head swathed in bandages, and received an ovation.

A manifesto was prepared and distributed at chapel doors. It ran:

"In this great crisis of Ireland, I desire to appeal to the working class ... to take action to prevent the betrayal of their interests by those who have planned the exclusion of part of Ulster from the Home Rule Bill. ... Meetings are being rushed through in other parts of Ireland, and at these meetings wire pullers of the United Irish League and the Ancient Order of Hibernians (Board of Erin) are passing resolutions approving of the exclusion whilst you who will suffer by this dastardly proposal are never even consulted."

Connolly pointed out that the claim made by the U.I.L. that exclusion was "only temporary" was belied by the prospect of two general elections during its proposed duration of six years. "It would require only the passage of a small Act of not more than three or four lines to make the exclusion perpetual."

"As the officers of the Curragh have stood by their class, so let the working class democracy stand by its class," the Manifesto concluded. "Let it be heard and understood that Labour stands for the unity of Ireland—and Ireland united in the name of progress, and who shall separate us?"

Such was Connolly's policy. But at no time was Irish Labour worse placed to carry it out. In these closing weeks of the great lock-out there came to the fore a delayed sensation of defeat, which Larkin bravely but not always effectively sought to dispel. If Dublin was dispirited, Belfast was hopelessly divided. The only possibility was that the British labour movement might strive to wreck the bill rather than tolerate partition. Both Connolly and the Irish T.U.C. urged this course upon them.

It must not be forgotten what while Home Rule was to the Redmondites the final settlement, to Republicans it was an instalment only acceptable in so far as it did not close the door to further development. Pearse, and even Griffith, had supported it on this express condition. From the standpoint of Westminster, on the other hand, it was a British administrative measure pure and simple. It provided for the better exploitation of Ireland, and had written into it guarantees limiting its use for any other purpose. Connolly fully appreciated the reactionary element within the Home Rule proposals, and indeed this aspect was the rational element in the mass opposition of Belfast Protestant workers, which would otherwise appear totally nonsensical. The progressive aspect was that the moment Home Rule was granted the Irish people could take an independent course and destroy the limitations which were imposed. Having failed to destroy the organisation of the working class, the Home Rulers must now acquiesce in its division. Political betrayal necessarily followed industrial stalemate. The question now was whether British Labour, guilty of betrayal on the industrial field, would behave any better on the political.

The negative answer came quickly. Mr. George Barnes, replying to a letter of protest by Tom Johnson, justified the right-wing position simply:

> "I have taken my line along with all my colleagues from the Irish Nationalists. . . . The Nationalists of Ireland have sent men to Parliament and the Labour men have not."

The Liberal Government, which had used batons on the Liverpool transport workers and shot down the miners of South Wales, declared that "Ulster" must not be "coerced". Those who dissented from the majority of the Irish people on a matter of national sovereignty were to be given a sovereignty of their own. And the Labour leaders became apologetic accessories in the name of self-determination and peace.

"Nobody defends it on its merits," pleaded Barnes when finally driven into a corner. "It is put forward as the price of peace. If peace is not brought by it, then it goes by the board. And so I leave it."

Connolly commented with much bitterness. He spoke of "that tired feeling" which came across Irish socialists when they witnessed "the love embraces which take place between the Parliamentary Labour Party and our deadliest enemies—the Home Rule Party. . . . It will not help on a better understanding between the militant proletariat of the two islands."

The conclusion that he drew was that the Irish movement must expect to paddle its own canoe. This year he declined the annual invitation to address May Day meetings in Glasgow. He gave as his reason that he was too busy in Ireland. But he had willingly given the Clarion Scouts a lecture in February. His disillusionment with the British movement was expressed at its sharpest in his May Day article in *Forward*, which he headed "Fraternity or betrayal".

> "I cannot this May Day felicitate you or the working class

of the world in general upon the spread of working class solidarity," he wrote. "Instead of it I see much mouthing of phrases, much sordid betrayal of our holiest hopes."

He summarised the position of the Irish *vis-à-vis* the British movement in the reproachful quatrain:

> "Aye, bitter hate, or cold neglect
> Or lukewarm love at best
> Is all we have or can expect,
> We aliens of the west."

The "betrayed Transport Union" hovered over their festivities "like Banquo's ghost".

At the same time he tried once more to assess the new situation. In his article "Changes" he contrasted the early socialists' insistence on the "legislative" eight-hour day and their preoccupation with "the ballot box", with the syndicalist tendency to belittle political action. The latter he attributed to disappointment with the record of the Labour M.P.s elected in 1906. Now he thought he detected a new tendency to belittle industrial action, decry strikes and counterpose these to "politics".

> "The development of the power of the modern state should teach us that the mere right to vote will not protect the workers unless they have a strong economic organisation behind them, that the nationalisation or municipalisation of industries but changes the form of the workers' servitude whilst leaving the essence unimpaired; and that in the long run the forces of reaction will be able to dominate and direct its political powers."

Connolly never fully understood the State, and here again, in the midst of much practical good sense, he exactly reverses the actual position by adding: "Within the social order of capitalism I can see no possibility of building up a new economic organisation fit for the work of superseding the old on socialist lines, except that new order be built upon the lines of industries that capitalism itself has perfected." The transition to socialism was still seen as economic pressure compelling political changes, rather than State power compelling economic changes. The coming of the working class to power was the end of the process rather than the beginning. Thus between "economic power" and "the ballot box" the relation remained as mysterious as the "revolutionary act" which was to bring them into conformity.

Recognition of some unformulated lacuna in his train of thought must have prompted his last sentence, which ran: "I realise that human nature is a wonderful thing, that the soul of man gives expression to strange and complex phenomena and that no man knows what powers or possibilities for good or evil lie in humanity.... I try to preserve my receptivity to new ideas, my tolerance towards all manifestations of social activity." He could scarcely have intended this literally. It was a means of rounding off a subject on which he had come to doubt his own clarity. From that time on, indeed, his writings showed him searching for the explanation, and the way out, of the impasse which the world proletariat seemed to be marching into. Something had happened to the leadership. That he recognised clearly. But the reason, the imperialist bribery of the labour aristocracy, and the remedy, the new type of socialist party, eluded him. He could consult nobody. He continued to cultivate his garden, above all determined to end the dependence of uncorrupted Ireland upon corrupted England. This necessity, which was correctly understood, occupied and dominated his mind throughout the two remaining years he was to live. What would have been the result if he had established a scientific socialist party within the Labour Party, and permitted the Citizen Army to fuse with the Volunteers, is a matter for speculation. Such a course was not obvious enough to suggest itself to him; historical conditions thereby rejected it, and what occurred was therefore historically necessary.

The Irish T.U.C. met in Dublin on June 1 and became the Irish T.U.C. and Labour Party from that date. On the eve of the opening a procession three-quarters of a mile long wound its way to Phoenix Park, where at the sound of a trumpet speeches from two platforms were to commence simultaneously. "Jim was never in better form," wrote Connolly in *Forward*. But at the meeting itself he had been so angry when Larkin, too impatient to await the agreed time, had the trumpet blown prematurely and started to speak on his own, that he refused to say one word himself, though men had come from Cork to listen to him. Larkin, to give him his due, sensing something was amiss, loudly praised his colleague and asked rhetorically who in Ulster could face Jim Connolly. Mutual loyalty drew together these contrasting men, Larkin domineering and unpredictable, Connolly disciplined but a trifle inflexible.

Larkin was in the chair at the T.U.C. sessions. The eccentricities of his chairmanship caused much amusement and goaded William O'Brien into unconcealed fury. His enemies contented themselves with describing Larkin as "a remarkable man". The masses were firmly with him. He was head and shoulders above the petty negotiators who would fix anything over a pint, and the people recognised his incorruptibility. Connolly played the leading part in the deliberations of Congress, and was now elected to the N.E.C. But not once did he permit himself to cross swords with Larkin. He recognised the power of the mass movement to "impose unity".

The Parliamentary Committee reported the long negotiations with the British Labour Party and the attempt to induce them to oppose partition and the gerrymandering of Irish constituencies and demand the extension of medical benefits and school feeding to Ireland. Both Ramsay MacDonald and Henderson had declined to move. Deputations waited on them without result. A protest meeting was held in O'Connell Street and correspondence was exchanged galore. The response was entirely negative. Connolly proposed and Daly seconded the motion condemning partition. Labour was the only section in Ireland to fight a consistent campaign against it. British Labour, said Connolly, had flouted every opinion of Labour in Ireland. There were only three dissentients.

Connolly opposed the introduction of the card vote, declaring that the smaller unions were more democratic than the larger ones. He also opposed the transformation of the Irish T.U.C. forthwith into a Labour party—he wanted an "Irish T.U.C. *and* Labour Party". He seconded a motion calling for women's suffrage, and proposed another condemning the Sirocco works for introducing a "no union" pledge and simultaneously drilling Ulster Volunteers on their premises.

Three weeks after the T.U.C. he was summoned to Dublin again. Crisis was shaking the Transport Union. The newspapers reported Larkin's resignation and his decision to leave Dublin for good. A special committee meeting on June 19 had failed to dissuade him, and a general meeting of members was announced for Croydon Park on Sunday June 21. Larkin did not attend. He was at Bodenstown with the Citizen Army—on the first occasion that Volunteers and Citizen Army men collaborated. Partridge and Daly spoke of Larkin's physical and mental exhaustion, Daly making bitter references to the old enemies who had returned to the attack in the disorganisation following the lock-out. Connolly sounded a similar note. Efforts had been made to set him and Larkin at loggerheads. Larkin had raised the Dublin workers out of slavery. But now he needed a complete rest—perhaps in the U.S.A., where he could collect funds for the union. It was decided to ask him to withdraw his resignation.

Three bands were engaged to meet Larkin on his return from Sallins, where he had been delighted by his reception. A huge procession escorted him to Croydon Park. There he delivered an hour's speech, complaining of "interference" by other officials of the union. These indeed had secretly withheld £7,500 from the strike fund so as to complete the purchase of Liberty Hall. But Larkin was no accountant and as yet merely suspected it, indeed, in so far as he guessed, probably approved. At the end of the speech the members declared that they would camp all night in the grounds unless he agreed to attend a general meeting in the Antient Concert Rooms.

He acceded. Next day the meeting was held. Those who wished for a clash between Connolly and Larkin were again disappointed. Larkin declared that he had been invited to repudiate Connolly's actions (fighting the Liberals and closing the port) during his imprisonment. "I tell you here and now," he said, "that I endorsed all Connolly did." Connolly then moved a resolution assuring Larkin of the continued fidelity of the members to his leadership. His speech was punctuated by "Hear hears" from Larkin.

"Jim knows I am no follower of Larkin," said Connolly. "I stand for Jim because I believe he is the best man our class has turned out in Ireland. I am with him as a comrade, and I believe he accepts me as such." He then recalled the decisions he took while Larkin was in jail, explaining that the closing of the port would have won the strike if the British unions had not been restrained by fear for their treasuries. He professed ignorance of what had been happening in Dublin, but believed that Larkin would yet thank God that he had produced men capable of criticising him. He believed Larkin was overstrung in the last few weeks, and the committee was trying, perhaps in a blundering way, to save him from doing too much. He advised him to do less routine work. Whatever trivialities had given Larkin's opponents their opportunity, Connolly was not going to avail himself of them. Daly seconded and Foran asked: "What will I do with Jim's resignation?" "Burn it", was the reply; and Foran set a match to it amid expressions of "indescribable enthusiasm".

On July 3 Connolly brought Larkin to Belfast to present brooches to two Dublin girls, active in the lock-out, who were now working in Belfast. Two days later he himself went to Limerick where a Labour demonstration was held in support of thirty-seven members of the United Carmen's and Storemen's Society who were on strike. Limerick was notorious, then as now, for the narrow-mindedness and obscurantism of its bourgeoisie. The newsagents were afraid to stock the *Irish Worker,* and attempts had been made to drive out *Reynolds's News.* Booksellers who had displayed *Labour in Irish*

History had been intimidated, and even *The Sketch* was on the local index. Every agency had been used to poison the public mind against the demonstration. But Dublin had lit a flame outside its boundaries. There was a huge and enthusiastic demonstration which both surprised and delighted Connolly.

The stresses which followed the lock-out slowly eased. Larkin sought medical advice for his nervous exhaustion, and took no notice of his instructions. He and Connolly spoke together at the Sports and Gala Day at Croydon Park, when the South African deportees (among whom was the old Edinburgh S.S.F. man, Tuke) visited Dublin. Croydon Park had been beautified with flowers and shrubs obtained from the Liverpool nurseryman W. S. Bulley. The circumstance is worth noting that Bulley's firm (Messrs. Bees) advertised regularly in the *Irish Worker* and *Daily Herald*, and that there is no record or recollection of Larkin having to pay for his plants. Larkin's enemies acted unworthily, therefore, in stigmatising him in later years for going outside Ireland for his requirements. Bulley possessed huge private gardens which he refused to lock on account of his socialist principles, and at a time when nobody would dream of offering credit to Larkin could easily supply him from his own stock.

The summer matured and Larkin recovered his strength. Connolly wrestled with his financial difficulties in Belfast. After the gun-running at Larne, when Carson's friends landed thirty-six thousand rifles for the Ulstermen, the British authorities forbade the importation of arms into Ireland. But Erskine Childers and Bulmer Hobson conducted a spectacular gun-running at Howth. That evening British troops opened fire on a defenceless crowd in Bachelor's Walk and the regiment was hastily removed from the city immediately after dark. But the old days came to an end on August 4, when Britain declared war on Germany. The Home Rule Bill became law, with the exclusion of Ulster. So did a suspending Act preventing it from coming into operation. The summer of British imperialism ended in a whimper of lies.

IMPERIALIST WAR

According to Cathal O'Shannon, Connolly was sitting in his Belfast office when news of the European mobilisations came through. "This means war," he declared, and sat a long time silent, head in hands. Finally he announced emphatically that a blow for Irish independence must now be struck. He asked to be put in touch with the Irish Republican Brotherhood. O'Shannon told him there was to be a meeting that night, and from it discussions were arranged.

Redmond declared support for the war in a memorable scene in Parliament. He invited Asquith to withdraw all British troops from Ireland. Volunteers and covenanters would combine to defend it. "For Britain," he might have added. Redmond now controlled the Volunteers. In June he had demanded that twenty-five of his nominees should be co-opted on to the Executive. Though this gave him a majority, the Irish Republican Brotherhood (an executive within an executive) acquiesced. It was hoped to get money and guns. In their rapid growth the Volunteers had recruited many Redmondites. The I.R.B. leaders were anxious to avoid a split. Connolly had stormed from the Sidewalk but was powerless to intervene. Now the idea that sparrow and cuckoo could defend one nest began to spread through the Volunteers, even affecting members of the I.R.B.

Connolly's discussions may not have disappointed him. He learned the probable policy of *Irish Freedom* in time to publish a reply on the day it appeared. But much more had passed through his mind than "England's difficulty is Ireland's opportunity". He was a man in touch with socialist thought on an international scale. His article in the *Irish Worker* showed how widely his mind had ranged over the problems raised by the war, and that his guiding principle was adherence to the decisions of the International.

"What should be the attitude of the working-class democracy of Ireland in the face of the present crisis?" he asked.

"I wish to emphasize the fact that the question is addressed to 'the working-class democracy' because I believe that it would be worse than foolish to take counsel in this matter from any other source."

His approach was that of an international socialist concerned that first of all the working class should take up a correct position.

"I know of no foreign enemy in this country except the British Government," Connolly wrote. "Should a German army land in Ireland tomorrow, we should be perfectly justified in joining it, if by so doing we could rid this country once and for all from its connection with the Brigand Empire that drags us unwillingly to war."

Then he made his appeal:

"Should the working class of Europe, rather than slaughter each other for the benefit of kings and financiers, proceed tomorrow to erect barricades all over Europe, to break up bridges and destroy the transport service that war might be abolished, we should be perfectly justified in following such a glorious example, and contributing our aid to the final dethronement of the vulture classes that rule and rob the world."

His immediate proposal was that the labour movement should prevent profiteering by stopping the export of food-stuffs from Ireland, if necessary through "armed battling in the streets". Connolly was groping for the first step along the pathway to revolution. He concluded:

"Starting thus, Ireland may yet set the torch to a European conflagration that will not burn out until the last throne and the last capitalist bond and debenture will be shrivelled on the funeral pyre of the last war lord."

Connolly's hope was that his policy would lead to a socialist Europe. No wonder therefore that Lenin defended the Easter Rising. For the Russians and Serbs, alone among

European Socialist parties, took the same stand as the Irish. This was the stand all had committed themselves to at international congresses in Stuttgart, Copenhagen and Basle.

The Stuttgart resolution was discussed by Connolly in *The Harp*. It ran: "In case war should break out it is their duty (i.e. of the socialist parties) to intervene in favour of its speedy termination and with all their powers to utilise the economic and political crisis created by the war to rouse the masses and thereby hasten the downfall of capitalist class rule."

But Connolly had an important theoretical problem to solve alone. Was the correct course now to identify the Irish and British labour movements and endeavour to concert the overthrow of capitalism in both countries simultaneously? Or was the Irish movement for national independence *in its own right* a factor making for the overthrow of European capitalism? Connolly's answer was the logical extension of all his previous thought. But its brilliance was such that he anticipated the opinion of the world movement by a whole year. Not until the Zimmerwald Conference of September 21, 1915, was it declared that:

"Now you must stand up for your own cause, for the sacred aims of socialism, *for the emancipation of the oppressed nations* as well as of the enslaved classes, by means of irreconcilable proletarian class struggle."

That Connolly's thought ran parallel with Lenin's can be shown almost phrase by phrase. Thus, Lenin spoke of "civil war" on October 14 when Connolly was advising his hearers to arm and fight for Ireland rather than Britain. The famous slogan "turn the imperialist war into a civil war" was first employed by Lenin on November 1. Connolly's article in the *International Socialist Review* of March 1915, contains the words: "The signal of war ought also to have been the signal for rebellion ... when the bugles sounded the first note for actual war, their notes should have been taken for the tocsin for social revolution. ... Such a civil war would not ... have

353

resulted in such a loss for socialist life as this international war has entailed."

Connolly embodied these views in two manifestoes. The first was issued under the name of the Irish Citizen Army, Belfast Division, that is to say under largely nominal auspices. The Belfast Branch of the I.L.P.(I.) was at loggerheads on the tactical wisdom of publicly opposing the war in loyalist Belfast, the majority believing that that city was not the place for anti-imperialist propaganda. Connolly was compelled to tell a large hostile crowd at Library Street that in opposing the war he was speaking for himself alone, and not for the I.L.P.(I.). After that it was decided to discontinue meetings. On this account the Belfast Division was invented. Young socialists, suffragettes and republicans (the "don't care a damn brigade") posted the manifesto round the town:

"You are asked to stop and consider what this war will mean to the working class of this city and country," it read. "War will mean more unemployment and less wages. Already the mills of Belfast are put on short time.... Remember, all you workers, that this war is utterly unjustifiable and unnecessary.... We have no foreign enemy except the treacherous government of England—a government that even whilst it is calling on us to die for it, refuses to give a straight answer to our own demand for Home Rule.... We want Ireland, not for peers or the nominees of peers, but Ireland for the Irish."

Of his more timorous colleagues Connolly remarked: "They seem to have a curious idea of what constitutes a working-class propaganda. They don't seem to think that I ought to express an opinion on the greatest crisis that has faced the working class in our generation."

Their failure to follow Connolly's advice was a political disaster. It contributed to the immobilising of Irish Labour for a generation. It prevented the establishment of a revolutionary socialist party covering all Ireland. Moreover, it contributed to the centrist (neither for nor against) resolution of the I.T.U.C. at Sligo in 1916, when the Rising came up for discussion. Failing a European revolution, it made partition a certainty.

Dublin redeemed the shame of Belfast, as if to proclaim the inseparability of all democratic struggles. There the I.L.P.(I.) declared that:

"All the workers of the world are like ourselves, beasts of burden to a propertied class, their lives ordered and ruled for them by the interests of that class, their countries stolen from them by the armed might of the hirelings of that class ... to take up arms in anger to kill any of the poor driven workers of another nation at the order of our rulers is as clearly an act of murder as any crime of violence ever committed.

"Now, if we forget for a moment the vital distinction between a people and its rulers, and imagine that each of the countries outside Ireland is solid and with but one interest to conserve.... Has Germany ever harmed Ireland? No. Has England harmed Ireland? Yes....

"The Empire is founded upon the misery of the toiling masses.... Its humiliation ... will allow other peoples to take their rightful place among the nations of the world."

This line of policy was carried to the Irish T.U.C. which alone in Western Europe declared on August 10 that "a European war for the aggrandisement of the capitalistic class has been declared," and demanded the retention of foodstuffs in Ireland.

In Ireland the majority forces of Labour were thus aligned against imperialism, while a minority held aloof from the struggle. But in Britain the balance was the other way. The *Daily Citizen* disgraced itself from the start, becoming an unashamed recruiting sheet. Blatchford's *Clarion* condemned the "reactionary autocracy of Prussia" and delightedly exhibited Cunningham-Grahame's abject political recantation. The "rebelly" *Daily Herald* fell from grace nearly as precipitately. For a while it toyed with "switching the war" against the Tsar. But by September it had become a weekly, sobbing for "poor little Belgium", advertising the "Daily Mail

Rose", and concluding with "why not try Christianity?" The B.S.P. was sharply divided. The leadership, after some hesitations, declared for the Entente and participated in recruiting. But branches immediately protested. There was life in the old S.D.F. yet. Some branches even quoted Connolly against their executive committee and sent their congratulations to Dublin. Thereafter internal struggles paralysed the party in England for close on two years. The *Labour Leader* and the I.L.P. were less affected by chauvinism, taking a pacifist position, that is to say in advance of the leadership of the B.S.P. but to the rear of its rank-and-file. Only in Glasgow was there a united protest against the war. Here revolutionary feeling was strongest. The "clear-cut" tradition possessed the virtues of its faults and showed them now. *The Socialist* condemned the war, but said little about how to deal with it except "when it is over the people will see how they have been fooled". Time went by and a more practical and militant note was sounded. Unity was forged between men like Bell and MacManus of the S.L.P. and MacLean and Gallacher of the B.S.P. On the whole, *Forward* acquitted itself best, and published Connolly's fiery articles until the censorship rendered this impossible.

During the first week of the war five thousand people gathered on Glasgow Green to demand the cessation of hostilities. The speakers included Connolly's friends Wheatley and Bell, together with representatives of the B.S.P. and I.L.P.

The development of the movement against the war was thus utterly different in the two countries. It was bound to be more rapid in Ireland. But the decisive battalions were in England. This circumstance confronted Connolly with a tactical choice. Should he delay while the movement in England matured? Or would he thereby miss his opportunity in Ireland? In the event he decided to write the British movement off for *practical* purposes, and concentrate on the more rapidly developing forces in Ireland. Ireland was to kindle the blaze. This choice led to accusations of "retirement" into purely Irish affairs, but they were belied by his continuous contact with those British socialists who were actively opposed to the war.

The enterprise he had undertaken demanded the gathering together of the anti-imperialist forces under one direction and leadership. Where was this leadership to come from and how was this concentration to be achieved? This question naturally took Connolly outside the bounds of syndicalist thought, though from time to time he still expressed himself with the aid of the old slogans.

De Leonists regarded all non-proletarian classes as "one reactionary mass". The working class must not taint its purity with alliances of any kind. Hence it could offer no leadership beyond its own ranks. Connolly's task was to rally all anti-imperialists. He counter-posed on the one hand British imperialism, on the other the Irish people. Pearse reached a similar definition of the progressive camp in Ireland in *The Sovereign People*. Where Connolly differed from Pearse was in resolving the "people" into its component parts, and seeing the leading role of the working class within the class alliance. He was distinct both from those who wished to concentrate exclusively on the workers' own special aims, and those who wished to submerge the proletariat entirely and deal only with the struggles of the progressive camp as a whole. He told Louie Bennett that socialism could not be thought of in Ireland before there was national independence.

The question of organisation was more difficult. Since his I.S.R.P. days Connolly had (first under De Leon's influence, and then in revolt against it) progressively whittled off the manifold functions of a socialist party. The I.L.P.(I.) was no more than a propagandist auxiliary to the Irish T.U.C. and Labour Party. It is doubtful if Connolly gave it a thought as a general staff in the coming struggle. The conception of a *scientific* party, leading daily struggles and organised in such a way as to facilitate revolutionary action, was foreign to Western Europe in those days. Connolly must solve his problems with what he had. But the loose, scarcely congealed

T.U.C. and Labour Party was obviously no better for his purpose.

He had taught that the basis of working-class "force" was "economic". Perhaps then the trade unions were the organisers of the national struggle? That they had a role was clear, especially the Transport Union. But equally clear was it that this must be subsidiary. Thus, almost by default, the leadership fell to the military organisation, the Citizen Army. Any class alliance would then express itself as a military alliance between the Citizen Army and the Volunteers. At the call of these the Transport Union would paralyse communications, and thus the law that the State is the organ of political power avenged itself on syndicalist theory.

Connolly hurried to Dublin at the first opportunity. Larkin was confused by the war crisis, and made contradictory speeches in which recurred the theme of Irish support to Britain in return for a guarantee of dominion status. Yet for two and a half months before his departure for America, he published Connolly's article weekly, and gradually swung round to his colleague's position. A special meeting of the Executive Committee of the T.U.C. was held on August 30. Connolly recounted his experience with the I.R.B. in Belfast to O'Brien, who told him that those he had been in touch with were of no influence, and that nothing could be done without Tom Clarke and Sean MacDermott.

In Beresford Place, at a meeting held to commemorate Byrne and Nolan, he launched a bitter attack on the Redmondites who had not merely "sold" the people of Ireland.

"No, by God," he exclaimed, "they have given you away.... As an Irish worker I owe a duty to our class, counting no allegiance to the Empire. I'd be glad to see it back in the bottomless pit.... If you are itching for a rifle, itching to fight, have a country of your own; better to fight for your own country than for the robber empire. You have been told you are not strong, that you have no rifles. Revolutions do not start with rifles; start first and get your rifles after. Our curse is our belief in our weakness. We are not weak, we are strong. Make up your mind to strike before your opportunity goes."

An open-air speaker does not always weigh every word. The authorities were long accustomed to parliamentarians who clothed the tamest propositions in the most bellicose language. To some extent this may explain their curious blindness to developments between 1914 and 1916. But it is as well to note that the operative words in Connolly's speech were *revolutions* and *start*. He was not proposing that the Dublin workers should commence an *uprising* without rifles; he was proposing that they should start a *revolution . . .* which did not start with rifles, but might well end with them. His mental picture was that of a democratic revolution to put an end to the imperialist war, in Irish conditions taking a national form.

He made a flying visit to Sligo in order to discuss arrangements for the 1915 T.U.C. with the reception committee set up in that town. While he was away he wrote to William O'Brien, indicating that he had found others who shared his views on the war. Through his brother Daniel, now a member of the Volunteers, O'Brien made contact with Eamonn Ceannt, an Executive member prominent in the I.R.B. The I.R.B. leadership had met soon after the outbreak of war and decided in principle that an insurrection should be prepared now that Britain was engaged with Germany. An advisory committee had been set up on to which prominent Volunteer officers were drawn. The unusual course (for the I.R.B.) of entrusting military discussions to a broad committee was based on the political situation which existed before Redmond urged the Volunteers to join the British army. It was afterwards reversed.

In the early days of the war the lines of policy advocated by Connolly and the I.R.B. leadership ran parallel. When the I.R.B. ceased overt preparations for insurrection it was natural enough for Connolly to interpret the policy-change as an abandonment of the struggle. During the short period when policies overlapped a meeting was called in the Library of the Gaelic League at 25, Parnell Square on September 9[1] and attended by the leaders of the I.R.B., Tom Clarke, and Sean MacDermott, together with Patrick Pearse, Sean T. O'Kelly, Major John MacBride, Thomas MacDonagh, Eamonn Ceannt, James Connolly and Arthur Griffith.

According to William O'Brien, Connolly advocated making definite preparations for organising an insurrection, and making contact with Germany with a view to military support. Both of these proposals were an integral part of I.R.B. policy. But the lines of work envisaged must depend on an estimate of the political character of the coming revolution. A discussion took place on the desirability of conducting agitation through an open organisation. It was agreed to appoint two sub-committees, one to endeavour to make contact with Germany, and the other to establish an open organisation to be used for propaganda purposes.

When some time before Christmas Connolly despatched his daughter Nora on a secret errand to the U.S.A., he told her (she records in her book) that discovery would mean treason charges against Clarke, MacDermott, Connolly . . . and Countess Markiewicz. A guess may therefore be hazarded that these four constituted the sub-committee. If they were prepared to trust each other in so hazardous an undertaking at so early a date, the mutual distrust of twelve months later is in need of explanation. All the inner history of the period cannot have come to light. It should be remembered, however, that while Connolly would be aware of the existence and importance of the I.R.B. he would not be in a position to assess political developments within it, more especially since its main public expression was through the organisation of the Volunteers.

Connolly became president of the open propagandist or-

---

[1] Dorothy Macardle considers this the *first* meeting, despite Sean T. O'Kelly's statement that the first he attended took place "three weeks after the outbreak of war". William O'Brien published a list of those present on September 9. It differs so much from O'Kelly's that it is best to assume that the two men described different meetings of a series.

ganisation, which was called the "Irish Neutrality League". Sean T. O'Kelly was secretary and Thomas Farren, of the Trades Council, treasurer. The remaining Committee members were Countess Markiewicz, Arthur Griffith, Sean Milroy, J. J. Scollan of the A.O.H. (American Alliance), Francis Sheehy-Skeffington and William O'Brien. It is to be noted that the I.R.B. leaders did not participate. Nor did Larkin, who confessed nine years later that he was somewhat dubious of the new organisation. Possibly Griffith was the stumbling block. Connolly offered Larkin a "hint" of what was afoot, but he replied that he was leaving for America.

Before returning to Belfast Connolly spoke at a demonstration called by the I.L.P.(I.) to demand once more the extension of the School-feeding Act to Ireland, and, seemingly under stress of war, the Government at last considered it expedient to comply. The Belfast authorities did not want their new responsibilities and worked hard to exclude trade unionists from participation in the administration. Connolly held a number of open-air meetings on the subject under I.T.G.W.U. auspices. But now he must confine himself to the Falls and New Lodge Road districts. Library Street was unthinkable. Even in the Catholic areas people were succumbing to Devlin's propaganda. "If they will not support the war because it is just," commented a shrewd Unionist, "they should not support it because they have got Home Rule. They have not got it." But Devlin insisted that they had. "Ruling by fooling" Connolly called this, as he placed Unionist and Nationalist claims side by side and showed that each amounted to—partition. Week by week he struggled against the tide of pro-British chauvinism, and slowly the more intelligent workers began to recover their balance, especially when employers decided to encourage enlistment by dismissing men and replacing them by women and boys at lower wage-rates.

On September 20 Redmond made his notorious speech at Woodenbridge offering the Irish Volunteers to the British Government for service on the Western front. Connolly was in Belfast at the time and quickly connected the Nationalist leader's offer with the recruiting meeting Asquith was to address in the Mansion House on the twenty-fifth. A meeting of the broad committee was held, and proposals were made to seize the Mansion House on the night of September 24 and hold it long enough to make the recruiting meeting impossible. Only eighty Volunteers and forty Citizen Army men could be made available in the short time, and it is said that when it was learned that the military were already installed in the hall the attempt was abandoned. By this time Connolly was in Dublin. Although he had written: "I am afraid that our friends of the conference have not got sufficient dash and desperation to deal with the matter," he appears to have accepted the abandonment without demur.

It must be more than a coincidence that on that same night when the Mansion House was to have been raided, a raid *did* occur. Under the leadership of Clarke and MacDermott, the Volunteer premises were seized by I.R.B. Volunteers, and M. Judge read out a manifesto repudiating Redmond and announcing a convention at which a new E.C. would be elected. The Citizen Army, held in readiness for the Mansion House raid, was quietly dismissed by Connolly. But the *Irish Worker* of September 26 published the manifesto in full—a circumstance which seems to indicate that both Connolly and Larkin were well aware of what was proposed.

The Asquith recruiting meeting was hindered by other means. The whole area around the Mansion House was cordoned off by police. A brake carrying Larkin, Connolly, P. T. Daly, and Countess Markiewicz led a procession of Citizen Army men from Liberty Hall to Stephens Green. A hundred Citizen Army men carried rifles (without ammunition but with fixed bayonets). The cheers of ten thousand Dublin citizens momentarily drowned the voice of the war leader, who secured only six recruits. The sight of the Citizen Army measuring arms with the hated enemies of the people made the greatest impression since the days of the lock-out.

To Connolly it seemed that bold defiance was winning mass support. He applauded the "Napoleon-like stroke" of the Provisional Committee, although the Volunteer organisation split at once. Of the 150,000 members 140,000 went with Redmond, and only 10,000 remained with the Provisional Committee. Since, however, the National Volunteers founded by Redmond had no political basis apart from support for the British Army, within a year they were a negligible force. The Irish Volunteers, on the other hand, slowly recovered their influence.

The circulars announcing the inaugural public meeting of the Irish Neutrality League were despatched on October 5. That day Larkin was in Belfast, where he told Connolly once more that he was leaving for America. The differences which had come to a head in June still rankled. Delia Larkin had had further brushes with the committee of the union, and Larkin wrote to Quinlan that he was "not in love with the work" in Dublin. McDevitt recalls a visit to Dublin when he found Larkin pacing the corridor outside a room where a meeting was in progress. "They're deciding whether to let me go to America," he told him. Afterwards Connolly came out and told McDevitt that the point at issue was whether Larkin should represent the T.U.C. while in the U.S.A. Connolly had opposed the suggestion; he believed that the T.U.C. would be embarrassed as a result of Larkin's speeches. Perhaps reacting to this, Larkin had written somewhat petulantly in the *Irish Worker* of September 26 that personally he was "willing to nominate Connolly" in his place. But now, in Belfast, he told Connolly that he was nominating Daly; Connolly was to be in charge of the paper and the insurance. Connolly was so upset that he wired William O'Brien at once, following up with a letter urging him to induce Foran and the committee to make it clear that this arrangement would not be acceptable. It would be impossible to maintain "their understanding with the nationalists" if Daly became General Secretary of the union. The danger was that Larkin would announce his decision publicly before the committee met.

O'Brien was successful. Larkin changed his mind and within a few days Connolly was in Dublin. He presided at the Dublin meeting of the Neutrality League, where he introduced the suggestion of wearing the republican colours: green, white and orange. The main decision of the meeting was to start a campaign against recruiting. It has been stated that this was the only meeting the League held. But there were several others. The organisation seems to have fallen apart during the period of repression which began in December. It had no future once the I.R.B. revised its "broad" policy, allowed the advisory bodies to lapse and concentrated its affairs in the hands of its own committees.

After a last brief interlude in Belfast, Connolly was installed as acting general secretary and editor of the *Irish Worker*. The paper immediately underwent a striking change. The space-wasting rodomontade was eliminated. The Liverpool docker who wrote in favour of an Irish rebellion "after Germany is defeated" contributed no more. The journal became tight, disciplined and effective, a model of revolutionary journalism.

Immediately after Larkin departed on October 24, bearing with him the good wishes of the cheering crowd at Croydon Park, and an illuminated address, Connolly marked the change of management by a new defiance of British imperialism. Across the front of Liberty Hall he stretched a banner with the legend "We serve neither King nor Kaiser but Ireland". Connolly raised the flag under which he was to tackle a giant task with dogged pertinacity. The affairs of the union were in chaos. The insurance fund was insolvent and the Ministry was threatening to withdraw its approval. Debts of every kind remained as a legacy of the lock-out. Connolly reorganised the offices in Liberty Hall and streamlined the administration, let superfluous rooms to friendly organisations, and gave the building a coat of paint. He visited the branches and urged unity in face of the growing reaction. Dublin Corporation refused Trades Council representation on its committee to administer the school meals scheme. Connolly addressed a conference which demanded the democratisation of the service. Week by week the *Irish Worker* taught that "the working class alone is the anchor and foundation of any real nationalism that this country can show". It was impossible to strengthen the nation by weakening the working class.

October was the month of preparation for the crucial Volunteer Convention. The Redmondites had gone. But two trends still existed. Would the new E.C. be composed of thoroughgoing physical force men? asked Clann na Gael, the Fenian organisation in New York. They awaited each mail with mounting anxiety. Connolly had already formed the opinion that the moderates would win the day, and in an article entitled "A forward policy for the Volunteers" advocated a minimum programme to hold the waverers and win back the allegiance of those who had joined Redmond. There is no doubt that the sequence of events as they actually fell out led him to believe that the Irish Republican Brotherhood itself had joined the moderates.

The convention took place on October 25, at the Abbey Theatre. To Connolly's delight the *Freeman's Journal* reporter was refused admission. With Sean Milroy he attended in a deputation from the Citizen Army, proposing affiliation to the Volunteer organisation and two representatives on the Committee. The reason for the rejection of this proposal was that the acceptance of affiliations would make it difficult for the I.R.B. to secure the election of consistent "physical force" men to positions of trust. They were intent on a rising but proposed to use the moderates as a cover behind which to prepare it. At the crucial time I.R.B. men in key positions were to swing the rank and file, if necessary against the advice of the moderate figureheads. Connolly of course knew nothing of this. The rejection of the Citizen Army seemed evidence of a weakening of revolutionary will. Pearse, it is true, tried to make clear that he held nothing against the labour men. While the Convention was sitting, about nine hundred Volunteers held a parade in Abbey Street, after which the Citizen Army, coming round the corner from Liberty Hall, marched to Stephens Green. Connolly presided at a meeting, together with Countess Markiewicz and P. T. Daly. Eoin MacNeill and Pearse had been advertised. Mac-

Neill did not put in an appearance, but Pearse did so, this occasion being the first on which he shared a platform with Connolly.

At the Convention the moderates, epitomised in the academic figure of Eoin MacNeill, had the day as expected. But its results none the less thoroughly alarmed the authorities. In mid-November Captain Monteith, the Volunteers' most skilled military instructor, was suddenly dismissed from his Government post and simultaneously ordered to leave Dublin. He came into Liberty Hall to tell Connolly. The *Irish Worker* was being run off at the time. Connolly lifted the telephone and ordered the expostulating printer to stop the press, while he sent over fresh copy.

"If I had the handling of this matter," said Connolly, "I would put you in position in Dublin, turn out every Volunteer in the city, and say to the Government 'Now come and take him'. Tell Hobson this and if necessary I'll turn out the Citizen Army. That would stop all these deportation orders."

Diarmuid Lynch, a leading figure in the I.R.B. of this time, criticised Connolly's stand in this matter, pointing out that the British authorities were being given an opportunity to try conclusions with the Volunteers, who would certainly have been defeated. No doubt Lynch was right in thinking such a result *militarily* possible. But was it *politically* possible? Lynch, who returned from the U.S.A. about this time, was partly responsible for the abandonment by the I.R.B. of their "broad" policy. His criticism of Connolly, who grasped the significance of *victimisation plus deportation* as a mass rallying cry, shows the gap between the thinking of the best representatives of military and political republicanism. To Connolly the military struggle arose out of the intensification of the political struggle; to his critic the military struggle existed in isolation and the preservation of the leadership was the task of the leadership alone.

The City and County Board of the Volunteers decided that Monteith should obey the order and carry out organising work in the south. Connolly was disappointed. If Monteith was to leave Dublin he would prefer him to work for the Transport Union. He showed the Captain a poster advertising a protest meeting at Stephens Green. Monteith then left for Limerick. The two men did not meet again,[1] but in his old age Monteith would repeat over and over again his opinion that the *one man* of 1916 who must never be forgotten was James Connolly. The protest meeting was well attended despite heavy rain. William O'Brien presided and The O'Rahilly of the Volunteers spoke alongside P. T. Daly, Countess Markiewicz and Sean Milroy. Connolly proposed a resolution pledging those present as "fighters for Ireland" never to rest until they were privileged to see Ireland a free and independent Republic among the Nations.

The beginnings of repression, combined with the advice from America, led the I.R.B. to adopt a more cautious attitude to its allies. The "broad" policy was quietly dropped and the committees which had been formed were allowed to lapse. Connolly regarded this development as a further victory for the moderates and began to express the impatience which culminated in January 1916. He resolved to build up the Citizen Army as an independent force.

The authorities, however, considered what was going on dangerous enough. Early in December they suppressed *Sinn Fein, Irish Freedom* and the *Irish Worker.* The last issue of Connolly's paper appeared on December 5 with a blank space instead of the leading article; the censor had intimidated the printer. But the banned article was issued as a leaflet, and a further issue is said to have been published on the nineteenth "while the censor wasn't looking" under the title of *Irish Work.*

"Yes, my Lords and gentlemen," Connolly's banned editorial concluded, "our cards are on the table! If you leave

---

[1] Monteith was in Dublin again from August 24–27, 1915, on his way to America, but it seems probable that he did not see Connolly then. In the intervening period he supplied Connolly with a small hand press which was used for handbills, programmes, etc. After the Rising it was given into the charge of Kathleen Lynn, but Captain Monteith's daughter's statement that it was with Dr. Lynn until her death is not verified. It is said to have been taken to Countess Markiewicz. It was not, of course, the press on which was printed the Proclamation.

us at liberty we will kill your recruiting, save our poor boys from your slaughterhouse, and blast your hopes of Empire. If you strike at, imprison or kill us, out of our prisons or graves we will still evoke a spirit that will thwart you and, mayhap, raise a force that will destroy you. We defy you! Do your worst!"

Such a passage further illustrates how Connolly's tactics differed from those of the I.R.B. The difference arose from distinction of class. As the class aims, so the tactics. Connolly's plan was to rally the people openly for democratic revolution. At this time he was staying at Surrey House, Rathmines, the residence of Countess Markiewicz, one of those "open houses" to which Republicans of all kinds resorted, and especially the Fianna. There he met Liam Mellows with whom he discussed politics far into the night. Mellows learned much from Connolly during those days, but it would be incorrect to pretend that Connolly made him a socialist. Mellows was a man of loyalties. Connolly added one more loyalty, which Mellows never lost. So strong was the romantic appeal of conspiratorial Fenianism that not until the disastrous days of 1922 did the younger man realise the truth that revolution is political or it is nothing. On the other hand, Connolly was highly impressed by Mellows, considering him the finest of all the young Republicans. He was prevailed upon to contribute an article to the Fianna newspaper. "Irish blackguards" was its title, and it advised the Fianna not to be afraid to praise the lawbreakers of Irish history who had been proclaimed "blackguards" by the British authorities. A certain constraint entered Connolly's style when writing for the youth, and the reason is not far to seek. He had never had any "youth" himself. He wrote rather as for children.

After a few days in Belfast at Christmas, Connolly crossed to Glasgow to see his old friends Bell and MacManus of the S.L.P. It was agreed that they should print the *Irish Worker* on the S.L.P. press, and MacManus worked hard at the setting, composing and printing, finally taking the first copies over to Dublin labelled "Glass". MacManus also managed the clandestine correspondence which continued until the police traced the origin of the newspapers being distributed in Dublin. The entire issue of February 20 was seized as it was being brought off the steamer. Connolly was thrown back on his own resources.

He had already considered acquiring a press of his own, and setting it in the basement of Liberty Hall under Citizen Army guard. Crossing to Liverpool he approached Fred Bower, author of the "Don't Shoot" leaflet which had led to Tom Mann's imprisonment, and a prominent member of the I.L.P. The two men scoured the city in search of a suitable machine, but drew a complete blank. At that time the Citizen Army was bringing guns from Liverpool packed between slabs of marble. Bower introduced Connolly to some Liverpool socialists and they fell to discussing the coming revolution in Ireland. "But is the time ripe?" asked Bower. "You never know if the time is ripe till you try," Connolly replied. "If you succeed the time is ripe, if not, then it was not ripe." He made the same reply to Tom Bell, who was not satisfied at his easy dismissal of the possibility of an objective estimate of revolutionary prospects.

Early in February a dilapidated Furnival machine was found at Millers, in Abbey Street. It had to be propped up on bricks, but was motor-driven and capable of turning out one thousand six hundred copies an hour. The accumulation of type and other equipment necessarily took time. It was, however, not allowed into Liberty Hall without presenting its credentials. On February 10 P. Murray appeared before the committee to protest against the introduction of a machine which might be used "for any illegal printing that would be the means of bringing notice of the authorities on the place and having the hall closed". Connolly is said to have explained that the machine was "only a little one" and secured the agreement of the committee. Then followed discussions with the Trades Council which was interested in the project of a new "Labour paper". During March Connolly had to pay some attention to Belfast, where on March 1 the

I.T.G.W.U. dockers applied for a further wage increase of 1s. a day. Labour and trade union affairs thus occupied him for several months. The union's finances remained acutely embarrassed. He struggled to pay the debts, and this meant a struggle to institute better discipline in the branches.

A conference on Labour representation was held in Dublin on May 4. Though the T.U.C. annual meeting was postponed (it was not held until August 1916), there were preparations for Labour Day, the T.U.C. Executive meeting on May 22, and a visit to the I.T.G.W.U. branch in Cork. According to Tadhg Barry, when Connolly visited Cork he booked the Sinn Fein hall for an I.L.P. (I.) meeting but on arrival found it locked and nobody to be seen. Barry apologised profusely on his colleagues' behalf, but Connolly answered quietly, "I'm used to that." In his speech to the I.T.G.W.U. Connolly summarised the results of the wages campaign. During the winter and spring of 1915 all classes of labour catered for by the I.T.G.W.U. had applied for increases. The Stevedores had won 1d. a ton, the deep sea dockers 1s. a day, the casual cross-channel dockers 1s. a day, the constant men 8d. a day; the Dublin and General Company granted 4s. a week; the dockyard labourers secured 3s. a week; Ross and Walpole gave 2s. a week, and general carriers 2s. a week simply on the basis of a letter from the union. So much for the leadership of a man who has been accused of becoming a "pure nationalist"! On the contrary, Connolly was practising his conviction that a strong working class was essential to the struggle for national independence. The struggle for wages did not contradict the struggle for democracy. The new "Labour paper" thus appeared on May 29, the day before the trade unions and Citizen Army celebrated Labour day in Phoenix Park. Its title was The *Workers' Republic* and once more on the title page appeared in English and Irish the challenging aphorism of Camille Desmoulins.

XX
MATURING REVOLUTION

Great crises mature so gradually and deviously that advance can come clothed in the appearance of retreat. Most misunderstandings of Connolly's great last year, which opened with the publication of the second *Workers' Republic*, are based on over-simplification. O'Casey declared: "Labour lost a leader." But he should have asked: "What is required of a Labour leader?" The courageous pacifist Skeffington, who was appalled by war's carnage, urged Connolly to "return to the ways of peace". Trade unionists of the old school confined themselves to "sensible" wage demands, despising national "sunburstery" along with the nationalist party of the employers. Both fought the consequences of the war, and a good fight it was. But Connolly had glimpsed the depth of the abyss. Here was a crisis so radical as to require, and therefore to make possible, a democratic revolution. Connolly placed this objective before him and followed it like a star.

The year 1915 saw the beginning of resistance in Britain. Rents rose and prices rose. The employers tried their best to undermine trade union standards. But just as the slower-moving British began to gather way, the more advanced Irish movement seemed to slacken speed. The benefit of higher food prices was felt by the larger farmers and cattle-traders. Manufacturers were enabled to maintain their income on a smaller turnover. Profitable war-contracts distended the eyes of entrepreneurs as deputations led by Redmond and Devlin waited on the British munitions chiefs with proposals to establish arms factories in Ireland. Even recruitment brought its compensations. Separation allowances were making their way into houses that had never known a regular wage.

On the other hand, the increasing dearness of food hit the workers as consumers; that of hard goods hit the subsistence farmers. In the new conditions wage increases could now be got provided there was a moderate determination to get

371

them. Trade unionism rapidly extended throughout the country. Subordination of all else to the need for recruits placed civil rights under continuous attack and the democratic forces drew together against the threat of conscription. Amid the complexities of this fluid situation Connolly held to one principle, better expressed practically than in formal writings. The struggle for democracy, national and civil, was conducted in *conjunction* with that for the workers' economic demands. It was the abdication of this great classical principle by a later generation that brought ruin on the Irish labour movement.

Connolly held firmly to his long-established belief that the interests of labour demanded a national revolution. Hence at Phoenix Park when the Labour day gathering hailed the appearance of the *Workers' Republic* and a resolution was passed that "this meeting extends fraternal greetings to the workers of every country who are striving for the emancipation of their class", his own witty speech by-passed the economic demands on which the other speakers were concentrating, attacked the war, and advised men to join the army–the Citizen Army.

On June 1 the Trades Council considered Devlin's attempt to bespeak support for the Nationalist candidate in the College Green by-election. Connolly urged that Labour should contest the seat, and argued forcefully both at the Trades Council and the N.E.C. of the T.U.C. Four days before the election a special meeting of the Trades Council endorsed the candidature of its president, T. Farren, who was defeated by a large margin in a very low poll. The *Workers' Republic* reflected the process of knitting together a national labour movement.

The musical and athletic carnival at Croydon Park on June 12 and 13 drew from Gaelic enthusiast Edward Dalton the comment that this was the sanest attempt yet made to identify the "working population" (to the advanced nationalist the workers were still not quite "people") with the Irish-Ireland movement. At Liberty Hall Connolly discouraged the music hall songs of the Larkin period, and insisted on an

"Irish rebel" atmosphere. But despite ample pressure from interested quarters he sprang to Larkin's defence every time he was attacked. The Dublin press was full of allegations of a hiatus between Larkin and Clan na Gael. Connolly published particulars of Larkin's work in the U.S.A., quoting from *The Gaelic American*, Devoy's paper. The working class was being made the backbone of the national movement, not merely an adjunct to it. At Bodenstown on June 20 the Guard of Honour consisted of equal numbers of Citizen Army men and Volunteers, the I.C.A. thus receiving a position in very favourable disproportion to its numbers.

When Sean MacDermott and Sheehy-Skeffington were arrested under the Defence of the Realm Act for anti-recruiting speeches, Connolly addressed a protest meeting at Beresford Place together with William O'Brien and Mrs. Sheehy-Skeffington. There were similar protests against the control of employment provision in the Defence of the Realm Act, which had the effect of restricting trade union recruitment.

The day after the Bodenstown commemoration, the strike of the labourers in the railway goods yards began. An application for a wage increase had been lodged in February. But up to June 21 no answer had been received from the employers, who were endeavouring to ignore the union. The strike began under a good omen. On June 22, Connolly negotiated one penny an hour for the workers of Messrs. Judd's after a very brief strike. The goods men were paid a week's benefit, but then supervened the factor on which the employers were reckoning, the financial straits of the I.T.G.W.U.

Connolly secured a temporary respite by circularising country branches with a request to forward half their funds to head office. Meanwhile a committee meeting decided reluctantly to relinquish the lease of Croydon Park, and six months notice was given. The struggle continued until July 21, when Connolly told the committee frankly that he could not raise another week's strike pay. Realistically he advised a return to work. This was happily averted by a loan from another union, and on August 14 the employers granted an increase of 2s. a week.

During this period the *Workers' Republic* had been reporting the progress of the struggle in Wales. Connolly's first comment throws some light on his general prognosis of the war crisis, and hence on his policy in 1916. He complimented the British workers on "waking up" but added: "We fear that they are crying out too late; the master class are now in possession of such impressive powers as they have not possessed for three-quarters of a century." He painted a grim picture of the post-war impotence of trade unionism, weakened by dilution of labour and deprived of its customary means of defence.

The reason why Connolly saw in these struggles a last touch of autumn rather than a presage of spring will perhaps not readily occur to the twentieth-century mind, accustomed as it is to a steady crescendo of revolution. The last century was marked by the slow advance of democratic reforms within the general framework of capitalist class power. The suffrage movement carried the process into the new century, where the old national-democratic movements met and merged with the new colonial movements which were a popular reaction against imperialism. On the outbreak of war there seemed to be a full stop followed by a reverse process. Monopoly capitalism was asserting its true nature cataclysmically. But that it would call forth new democratic forces in proportion to the check it administered, and that these would be of incomparably greater magnitude than their predecessors it had halted, was not obvious even to those who were most actively stimulating them. The effect of the war on the labour movement seemed to Connolly wholly destructive, since it was precisely its destructive aspect which was uppermost during the year 1914–15. Therefore, he thought, something must be done *before* the sands ran out and democracy was lost for a generation. This is the origin of his deep sense of frustration which led such observers as Louie Bennett to describe him as "embittered". He was a living illustration of the historical fact that many a revolution is begun under "defensive" slogans.

Connolly protested against the proclamation of the mining area of South Wales with a touch of "I told you so". But when the pit-owners and the government were forced to climb down, he was loud in his congratulations. He made the miners' victory the subject of his leading article on July 24, pointing out that the "measure of liberty enjoyed in Great Britain has a direct bearing upon the measure of liberty permitted in Ireland", and added: "It shows again that the only rebellious spirit left in the modern world is in the possession of those who have been accustomed to drop tools at a moment's notice in defence of a victimised or unjustly punished comrade."

At the Trades Council meeting he made a speech of unusual eloquence for such a gathering. The result of the South Wales miners strike was "another signal proof of the strength and invincibility of Labour when united. Here we had the greatest and strongest government that these countries had ever seen in modern times, a government vested with powers that a few years ago no one present would have dreamt would be vested in a modern British government." A body of workers had declared they would stop the process of production and "it was found they were more powerful than all the mighty civil and military forces arrayed against them". He concluded regretfully: "If the working-class soldiers had but the moral courage to say to the diplomats that they would not march against their brothers across the frontiers . . . there would have been no war, and millions of homes that are now desolated would be happy."

Action, before it was too late, became a recurrent theme in Connolly's speeches. On July 18 he held a huge anti-conscription meeting outside Liberty Hall. He warned that there would be attempts to introduce conscription piecemeal beginning with the Unionist districts. That in fact conscription could not be and was not imposed on Ireland was largely due to the campaign waged by Connolly and the republicans. The threat was present throughout 1915 and afterwards.

The funeral of Jeremiah O'Donovan Rossa, the Fenian

exile, was made the occasion of a great republican demonstration in Dublin. A broad committee was established on which Connolly represented the Transport Union. His work on this committee was conducted during the most difficult days of the rail yards strike. In the procession to Glasnevin on August 1 once more the Volunteers and Citizen Army joined forces. On this occasion Patrick Pearse made his famous oration which concluded with the words: "Ireland unfree shall never be at peace."

Connolly published Bulmer Hobson's letter announcing the arrangements. But when Sean McGarry, who was to edit the souvenir programme, asked him for an article he at first refused. "When are you fellows going to stop blethering about *dead* Fenians?" he asked. "Why don't you get a few *live* ones for a change?" According to Ryan, McGarry reported his failure to Tom Clarke, who then used his persuasive powers with success, for Connolly wrote:

"... for generations ... the soul of Ireland preached revolution, declared that no blood-letting could be as disastrous as a cowardly acceptance of the rule of the conqueror, nay, the rule of the conqueror would necessarily entail more blood-letting than revolt against the rule."

Then he turned his attack against the moderate wing of the Volunteers, as he had struck at the parliamentarians in 1898.

"That involved the question whether those who accept that which Rossa rejected have any right to take part in honour paid to a man whose only title to honour lies in his continued rejection of that which they have accepted."

He wrote to his daughter Nora that the time was gone when MacNeill was a suitable figurehead for the Volunteers. He should be removed. At the back of his mind was doubtless the conviction that the moderates had had a hand in an attempt which had been made in June to exclude the Citizen Army from a drilling competition in Tullow, which they participated in and won. During the following month he slowly formed the opinion that the retention of MacNeill meant that none of the volunteer leaders meant business. This conviction grew, despite his increasing regard for Pearse, whose *From a Hermitage* very favourably impressed him, except for the title.

He began to dream of a plan of action in which the Citizen Army would begin the uprising and rely on the patriotism of the Volunteers to bring them out. There is a standing parallel between this plan and that then actually being prepared by the I.R.B. Each relied (the I.R.B. perhaps with more justice) on the event creating the forces to complete it. Each week since its inception the *Workers' Republic* devoted its back page to the analysis of an insurrection. Those articles with the more political cast were his own work, the more plainly military that of Michael Mallin, the silk-weaver whom Connolly considered a "great soldier". A miniature rifle range was installed at Liberty Hall and a reserve was formed from men of the Citizen Army who could not attend regular parades. A number of rifles belonging to the Redmondite Volunteers were known to be stored in the railway sheds. The strike finished on August 14. On August 15, masked men seized them and removed them. The raiders seemed to have considerable familiarity with the sheds and yards. A search was also begun for supplies of explosives, and at the end of August, the day before the Byrne and Nolan memorial meeting, there was a "military tattoo" at Croydon Park.

As always, these activities ran parallel with those of trade union organisation. Difficulties arose in the Women Workers' Union as a result of which Delia Larkin resigned and returned to Liverpool. She was a brilliant woman and had sacrificed a career in order to help her brother in the lock-out struggle, but perhaps shared with her brother an inaptitude for appreciating other people's point of view. On the other side there was some jealousy and resentment of the "outsider" which its history has made so typical a feature of Dublin. Edward Dalton had in the previous February hit on the extraordinary notion of taking a public opinion poll on the subject of who was the most popular woman in the national movement. That Delia Larkin won by a large margin did not increase the circle of immediate friends.[1] But Connolly does not seem to have regretted her departure. He was a guest of Countess Markiewicz who possessed all the temperament that was needed. After an unsuccessful attempt to engage Louie Bennett, who disapproved of political, and especially national, affiliations in trade unions, he installed some of the rank-and-file girls in the front rooms of Liberty Hall, advertised a reorganisation meeting for August 10, and addressed it together with Partridge. The union survived and was able to prevent employers dismissing women workers with a view to substituting child labour.

On August 13 he was in Belfast speaking at the Co-operative Hall on "The Labour movement in the present crisis in Ireland". Flanagan took the chair. Connolly reaffirmed his opposition to the war, denounced the D.O.R.A., the jailings and the attempted deportation of Volunteer leaders as impermissible restrictions of political liberty. Loyal Belfast with its glum opportunists had to take its medicine, after which he left for Sligo, where the Trades Council called a special meeting for him. At this time the *Workers' Republic* issued an appeal for trade union amalgamations. It was suggested that all small unions catering for general labour should meet in conference with a view to establishing "one big union", with "one card, one badge, one E.C. and one front to the common enemy, the capitalist".

Connolly fought on all fronts. It is doubtful if Western Europe ever saw such consistent application of revolutionary tactics. The war as a whole, and all its consequences, political and economic, came under his continuous fire. The announcement of the special budget was answered by a public meeting on September 26 at which Connolly issued that slogan which became world-famous under the Popular Front in France: "Let the rich men pay." "Before they were asked to pay the bloodtax of the war, it was surely right," said Connolly, "that the Irish race should have been asked to consent to waging

---

[1] The men's poll was won by Arthur Griffith.

war at all." The way to answer the budget was to demand more wages.

The wage demands went in at once. On the twenty-fourth the boatmen demanded 2d. a ton–and settled for 1d. on the twenty-seventh. The Coal Association conceded higher wage rates without ado. The shipping companies agreed to meet the union in conference on October 1 and on that day the casual shipping companies offered a rate of 7s. a day, but adjourned the discussion on overtime. The Burns-Laird line offered an increase of 2s. a day. Terms were to be discussed on the tenth. But before that date the Scottish company informed the union that, since its offer had not been accepted at once, it was now withdrawn. The matter would be placed in the hands of the Board of Trade. One may hazard the guess that the government was behind the withdrawal. Connolly's policy would nullify the effect of the budget. Almost by the same post came the withdrawal of the offer made by the Casuals. "To hell with contracts!" was Connolly's ironical comment. At the meeting on the tenth it was therefore decided to withdraw labour. An immediate appeal for funds was made to the E.C. of the Trades Council, which once more lived up to its proud record. Public meetings were held and after about three weeks a settlement was reached. Only the City of Dublin Company refused to pay, and its workers continued on strike until a few days before the Easter Rising. Wage increases were also won in Sligo and Belfast. Connolly visited Kerry at the invitation of the Tralee Trades Council, and recruited one hundred and sixty men into the union. Following the meeting the vice-president of the Trades Council was dismissed from his employment, and the campaign for his reinstatement spread Labour ideas throughout the county. In the succeeding months union branches were established at Killarney, Listowel and even at Fenit.

There is little reason to doubt that Connolly had the conception of an insurrection far more advanced in its political character than that which he ultimately agreed to. That the trade unions were to play a special part is indicated by the singling out of Co. Kerry for intensive organisation. According to T.A. Jackson, who received a letter from his friend Con O'Lyhane, there were plans afoot to land arms from America in German vessels to be seized in New York Harbour and brought across the Atlantic. Connolly was aware of the history of the 1905 revolution in Russia and must have had the conception of sporadic strikes leading to a general political strike and so to armed insurrection. In *What is our programme?* published on January 22, 1916, he informed Griffith and his colleagues (the "advanced nationalists" as distinct from the "republicans") that but for their anti-trade union prejudice the conditions for insurrection would already be to hand.

"We have succeeded in creating an organisation that will willingly do more for Ireland than any other trade union movement in the world has attempted to do for its national government. Had we not been attacked and betrayed by many of our fervent advanced patriots, had they not been so anxious to destroy us, so willing to applaud even the British Government when it attacked us, had they stood by us and pushed our organisation all over Ireland, it would now be in our power at a word to crumple up and demoralise every offensive move of the enemy against the champions of Irish freedom. Had we been able to carry out all our plans, as such an Irish organisation of Labour alone could carry them out, we could at a word have created all the conditions necessary to the striking of a successful blow whenever the military arm of Ireland wished to move."

In the literature of the Irish revolution, this passage is little quoted; when Irish Labour capitulated first to Sinn Fein, and then to the Free State, the myth of Connolly's friendship with Griffith was extremely useful, and it was overlooked. All that could then be seen in Connolly's differences with the I.R.B. men was an issue regarding the date of the Rising—Connolly was impatient, which indeed he was. The I.R.B. was all-seeing, all-provident and had "chosen the right time". In reality there were not two dates but two conceptions of the national uprising. Connolly had in mind a popular insurrection led by the working class, with the trade union movement (though not the working-class political party) as the backbone of popular organisation. Therefore the presence of enemies of trade unionism in high places of the Volunteer leadership filled him with apprehension. A popular insurrection demanded the propaganda of revolution, and the formulation of a minimum social programme for which the people were to be invited to fight. Repeatedly he urged the Volunteer leaders to state political aims, and their failure to do so led him to suspect their integrity. When Patrick Pearse spoke at the Mitchel Commemoration under the chairmanship of Griffith, and the Sinn Fein press rang with pleas for moderation, he adopted the tactic of appealing to the rank and file Volunteers over the heads of the leadership. This political struggle came to a head in January 1916.

At the beginning of October efforts were made to tighten the discipline and extend the organisation of the Citizen Army. A peremptory notice in the *Workers' Republic* instructed those who were not prepared to attend Sunday parades to hand in their guns. Others were waiting for them. During the dock strikes the reserves were expanded and Connolly slily twitted the employers on the good work they were doing for the I.C.A. As well as the regular route marches, two midnight exercises were undertaken. One of these was based on the assumption that the Castle was in the hands of insurgent forces, and the aim was to prevent its relief by the British.

Connolly's sense of urgency was deepened by the intensification of recruiting and the growing threat of conscription for which a Bill was being prepared. The Redmondites denounced those who opposed recruiting on the pretence that by so doing they rendered conscription in Ireland inevitable. This was as good as saying that if the workers did not volunteer the middle class would be conscripted along with them. The *Evening Herald* was loud in its support of recruiting and, among sundry accounts of "heroic Irish priests" killed in the Dardanelles, published pictures whose captions drew attention to the "contented faces of the dying and the dead".

On November 15 the Trades Council appointed two delegates to discuss joint action against conscription with the Volunteers. As a result a joint protest meeting was held, though not for a month. Hobson, Griffith and MacNeill were there, together with Pearse and MacDonagh. Connolly and Farren represented the Trades Council. The Mansion House was crammed and an overflow meeting of five hundred held up all traffic in Dawson Street.

But meanwhile, developments in the dock strike linked curiously with the conscription issue. William Martin Murphy urged the Association of Master Carriers to lock out all members of the Transport Union. After an anxious debate the meeting decided that the time was inopportune. But Murphy's underlying motive was revealed when four hundred and four employers were called together and heard an appeal written by the Lord Lieutenant demanding more recruits and urging them to "facilitate enlistment" as much as possible. Dismissals thereupon increased in frequency. After the initial success of "economic conscription" in Dublin, the Lord Lieutenant toured the country urging provincial employers to follow suit. The result was a wave of indignation, which now affected the best of the younger clergy, who began to separate themselves from the parliamentary war party.

Week by week Connolly made his appeal to the rank-and-file. He appealed to patriotism with Mangan's "Youth of Ireland, stand prepared". Every article breathed warnings on the danger of delay. He tried to sting into action and begged the Volunteer leaders to "break through their refined distrust of the mob". He likened them to those who "having all their lives sung the glories of the revolution, when it rose up before them they ran away appalled". Pearse's lecture on John Mitchel, he described as "brilliant", because it showed the "nature of the forces which destroyed Mitchel". In 1848 the people had been held back by talk of "premature insurrection" and "the desire of the Government to provoke us to act before we are ready". Of the Manchester Martyrs, commemorated annually in November, he wrote: "The Fenians of Manchester rose superior to all the whines about prudence, caution and restraint, and saw only two of their countrymen struck at for loyalty to freedom." "Should the day ever come," he wrote in another article, "when revolutionary leaders are prepared to sacrifice the lives of those under them as recklessly as the ruling class do in every war, there will not be a throne or a despotic government left in the world." But instead the people were being invited to struggle against conscription much as they would organise a cattle-drive, or make a still of poteen.

In "Trust your leaders", published on December 4, Connolly's invective sharpened. "In Ireland we have ever seized upon mediocrities and made them our leaders." Was conscription to be fought with phrases, or "do you prefer the method of that Catholic priest who recently advised his people to send a deputation of their ten best shots to meet the conscriptors?" His polemics were taken up in other republican papers, where he forced a discussion of tactics. Yet throughout all this urging and prodding he made it clear that he based his advocacy of early revolution on objective factors. He answered in advance critics like Bower, who quoted his previous strictures on the "physical force" insurrectionism which believes it can "make" a revolution out of factors only present in the mind. He wrote:

"We believe in constitutional action in normal times; we believe in revolutionary action in exceptional times. These are exceptional times."

Connolly realised that there was a crisis affecting all classes of society which demanded and made possible a revolution. And he never ceased to make clear the working-class aims which would be realised through a democratic republic.

"We want and must have economic conscription in Ireland, for Ireland. Not the conscription of men by hunger to compel them to fight for the power that denies them the right to govern their own country, but the conscription by an Irish nation of all the resources of the nation, its land, its railways, its canals, its workshops, its docks, its mines, its mountains, its rivers and streams, its factories and machinery, its horses, its cattle *and* its men and women, all co-operating together under one common direction that Ireland may live and bear on her fruitful bosom the greatest number of the freest people she has ever known."

This remarkable passage shows Connolly's thought at its maturest and most profound. The coming revolution in Ireland was to be a "people's revolution" leading, not to the formal democratic republic of the bourgeoisie, but to a "popular republic" as it might be called today. Moreover, all trace of syndicalism was now sloughed off in the heat of mental and practical struggle. The cohesive force was to be the direction of a democratic state. In the *Workers' Republic* of January 15, 1916, he made matters clearer still:

"As the propertied classes have so shamelessly sold themselves to the enemy, the economic conscription of their property will cause few qualms to whomsoever shall administer the Irish Government in the first stage of freedom.

"All the material of distribution–the railways, the canals, and all the land stolen from the Irish people in the past, and not since restored in some manner to the actual tillers of the soil, ought at once to be confiscated and made the property of the Irish *State* . . . all factories and workshops owned by people who do not yield allegiance to the Irish Government immediately on its proclamation should at once be confiscated and their productive powers applied to the service of the community loyal to Ireland, and to the army at its service."

The final paragraph indicated the division of labour between the two main sections of the national movement. Each should aim at the Reconquest of Ireland, and "if the arms of the Irish Volunteers and Irish Citizen Army is the military weapon of, the economic conscription of its land and wealth is the material basis for that reconquest."

Such phrases as "the first stage of freedom" recall the approach of Lenin in *Two Tactics*. By using the expression "economic conscription" in a sense so different from that originally intended (conscription *of* economic resources, instead of military conscription *by* economic pressure) Connolly proclaimed his emancipation, not only from syndicalism, but from the social-democratic conception of the State which had dominated international working-class thought throughout his lifetime. Here was no state above classes, dependent solely on the "ballot box". Here was a people's state, pursuing a people's policy and supported by the people in arms.

But he was virtually alone in possession of this perspective. The I.L.P.(I.) had virtually disappeared. Partly it had been absorbed in the Labour Party. Partly also it was influenced by the pacifism of its English counterpart. The more radical Irish socialists had been, the more they tended to regard England as their international standard, as if to over-demonstrate their emancipation from prejudice against the "Auld enemy". Connolly castigated this tendency when, at home for Christmas, he addressed the Belfast North Branch of the British I.L.P. The tendency affected even Larkin in some measure. There is evidence that Sheehy-Skeffington when visiting the U.S.A. in the autumn of 1915 complained to Larkin about Connolly's increased bellicosity and brought back "orders" that "the boys were not to move". He was immediately embroiled in debate with Countess Markiewicz, whose mechanical mind read into Connolly's fear that war might end without revolution, a desire to protract the war long enough to provide the necessary opportunity. The theoretical confusion due to the absence of a unified scientific socialist centre cost the Irish movement dear, and has continued to be a weakness in the country's working-class life to the present day.

Connolly provided the perspective, the programme, the call to action and the appeal to the rank-and-file. He did so while managing the daily affairs of the union, even to arranging the auction of the cow and calf pasturing at Croydon Park. He found time to address the Trades Council demonstration in favour of improved housing in Dublin, in December, and the meeting of the Women's Franchise League on January 4, 1916.

Murmurings were now developing among the Volunteers, which the I.R.B. could not ignore, especially when the Government suddenly stopped the grants for the teaching of Gaelic. Sean MacDermott is said to have become convinced of the need for an alliance with Connolly, and of fighting irrespective of conscription or a German landing. Younger members began to follow his lead and letters supporting Connolly's position began to reach the *Workers' Republic*.

The I.R.B. had decided on a rising in principle and a military committee had been appointed, whose responsibility was to draw up plans and secure arms. The dissolution of the broad committees had not signified any halt in the preparations. Casement had been sent to Germany, suitable landing-places in Kerry had been surveyed. But Connolly could know nothing of this. The Irish Republican Brotherhood rested its power on a network throughout the Volunteer organisation. Thus Mellows in Galway, MacSwiney in Cork, acted publicly as Volunteer leaders responsible to MacNeill, but on vital matters were prepared to accept no instructions at variance with those of the I.R.B. Now that the rank-and-file were increasingly heeding Connolly, it was clear that the I.R.B. must meet and consult him. But the I.R.B. was a democratic body. In order to change the decision to organise an insurrection *in principle* to a decision to organise it *in fact*, a meeting of the Supreme Council, elected by all circles, was necessary and was indeed held on January 16, 1916 at Clontarf Town Hall. There could not be two revolutionary directories. The I.R.B. was applying the tactics of revolutionary Fenianism in an age when the working class had become an independent force. It was the greatness of the members of the military committee that they now recognised this. But to accept Connolly's conception of the revolution was another matter and *in any case* impossible because of their position within the Volunteers. They were imprisoned by previous decisions. To change now would be to jeopardise everything. It is said that attempts to reassure Connolly before January 16 were met with gruff scepticism. It was decided that the cards must be put on the table. All that was necessary was a decision to "prepare the insurrection as soon as possible". The military committee was then empowered to make all necessary arrangements and could co-opt those considered necessary for success.

Discussions with Connolly took place between January 19 and 22, but their surroundings are wrapped in mystery and embellished with romance. The *Workers' Republic* appeared each Thursday, though it bore Saturday's date. Hence Connolly must have written his defiant editorial, which appeared in the issue dated January 22, not later than Wednesday the nineteenth. This editorial, "What is our programme?" breathes through every line a sense that vital issues were about to be decided. But alongside it was a letter signed with the initials M.O'R. That Connolly published this letter simultaneously with the editorial is a coincidence and a clue. It indicates that for some reason Connolly was determined to state his case in public despite the prospect of discussions. The letter contained the passage:

> "The present leaders (i.e. of the Volunteers) do undoubtedly hold allegiance to Ireland as their most sacred duty, but what that really means has not been defined with absolute precision, and having close connection with many of them, both prior to and since the formation of the Volunteers, a private exchange of views would I believe lead to good results. If the Editor would arrange for a short conference with his two correspondents 'B.F.' and 'J.J.B.' and myself, the outlook may be more clearly defined. Our opportunity has arrived if we have but the will and the courage to use it."

The clumsy construction excludes the work of any leading committee. But Connolly must have known well who M.O'R. was. He left the office after lunch on Wednesday, and did not return. Nor was he at Surrey House that evening. He warned nobody of his impending absence, so presumably (since he was a trade union official) he did not expect to be away long. He was absent three days, and returned home late on Saturday night. Rumours began to buzz. A Volunteer is said to have told a Citizen Army man that Connolly had been "kidnapped", but the first definite assertion of this was not made until 1923, and was then categorically denied. The evidence of the disputants was at variance on so many points that Desmond Ryan, who made careful study of all the available evidence, was unable to draw a clear balance.

The editorial already referred to, which was published the day *after* Connolly disappeared, was a vigorous plea for working-class leadership in the Irish struggle. It was addressed to the revolutionary nationalist, who was asked to choose between Connolly's road and MacNeill's road. In words which at times distantly echo, as was Connolly's way, a famous passage in Marx's *Eighteenth Brumaire,* he contrasted the labour and petit-bourgeois revolutionaries. The "average non-labour patriot", who believed that "patriotism needs no foundation to rest upon other than the brainstorms of its poets, orators, journalists and leaders", was scathingly dismissed. "Ask such people for a programme and you are branded as a carping critic; refuse to accept their judgement as the last word in human wisdom and you become an enemy to be carefully watched; insist that in the crisis of your country's history your first allegiance is to your country and not to any leader, executive or committee, and you are forthwith a disturber, a factionist, a wrecker."

Connolly explained how the "power of the enemy to hurl his forces upon the forces of Ireland would lie at the mercy of the men who controlled the transport system of Ireland". But he warned that the end of the war would make his policy inoperable. Perhaps rumours of peace led him to suspect the possibility of a temporary armistice, while Britain crushed Irish resistance and imposed conscription to be followed by a resumption of hostilities. "We will be no party to leading out Irish patriots to meet the might of an England at peace," he declared. Then it would be a matter of trade union organisation, unless, he concluded with bitter irony, "we emigrate to some country where there are men".

This article could not of course be the cause of Connolly's disappearance. It did not appear till he had gone. Ryan thinks it shows evidence of a recent heated argument with the I.R.B. leaders. It could equally show a desire to rally support in an impending dispute. Two discussions are recorded. One was with MacNeill in the presence of Pearse. Le Roux, and after him Ryan, places it early in February. But it was just the type of conversation to evoke Connolly's tirade. MacNeill had argued that Irish independence could come gradually, and urged Connolly to talk less about aggressive action during the war. Connolly was nettled by Pearse's seeming toleration of MacNeill, and after sharply retorting, "I am glad to know where we all stand," went away and left Pearse and Mac-Neill together. It is probable that this interview has been mistakenly post-dated to February and was the occasion of Connolly's editorial demand that men like Pearse should choose their side.

The other recorded discussion may be that requested by "M.O'R.". According to Ryan, J. J. Burke, a Dublin Volunteer closely in touch with Connolly and the *Workers' Republic*, had some sharp words with Connolly in Liberty Hall in January 1916. Connolly told him the Citizen Army would move alone within a week. This is, of course unlikely, since there is no record of preparations having been made along the lines ultimately thought necessary, and Connolly's reliance on trade union participation in any rising has already been noted. But Connolly declared that the "bide your time" doctrine had frustrated every rising the Irish had ever tried. That Connolly willingly gave permission to Burke to do what he could not prevent, namely, to inform Ceannt of the conversation, indicates clearly that his aim was to force the Volunteer leaders to a choice. The following day, says Burke (who is presumably the J.J.B. referred to in M.O'R's letter), a conference was held in Liberty Hall, attended by Ceannt, Pearse and The O'Rahilly. It seems unlikely that Connolly would publish M.O'R's letter if the conference had already taken place, so that the most likely time for it is Wednesday January 19. Whether Burke was mistaken about the place, or whether Connolly then accompanied some of the others elsewhere, remains a matter for speculation. Burke cannot have been present throughout, since he recorded a subsequent conversation in which Connolly told him that agreement had been reached.

Pearse later gave Ryan a brief account of his interchange with Connolly. Lynch completely rejected it and accused Ryan of romancing. He argued that Pearse would never have disclosed particulars of the coming rising to one of his pupils at St. Enda's School. But Ryan did, in fact, take part in the rising. He may have mis-remembered the date of his discussion with Pearse, and Pearse may not have given the full story, but that does not dispose of its contents so easily.

According to Ryan, Pearse told him that Connolly had proposed to lead out the Citizen Army as a means of forcing the Volunteers to take action. Having learned of this, he and Sean MacDermott had gone to Connolly and urged him to hold his hand in order not to ruin well-laid plans. He could have the Volunteers as allies if he waited. After a terrible mental struggle, Connolly turned to Pearse and, with tears in his eyes, clasped his hand, warmly saying: "I agree; but God grant, Pearse, that you are right."

There was no mention of kidnapping. But in essentials this evidence tallies perfectly with Burke's. When Connolly received M.O'R's letter he decided to print it, along with his own statement of policy. But the proposed meeting must have started before the paper was on sale.

The allegations of kidnapping probably arose from events which took place during his absence. William O'Brien learned of Connolly's absence at lunchtime on Thursday. He recollects consulting with Foran, Mallin, the Countess Markiewicz and his brother Daniel. They could find no explanation. On the other hand they must have known, if they had time to read the *Workers' Republic* carefully, that there were some discussions afoot with the Republicans. But Countess Markiewicz urged that the Citizen Army should start an insurrection on its own. Mallin and O'Brien succeeded in calming her, but only on a promise from Mallin that he would approach the I.R.B., whose Supreme Council was believed to be in session at the time. Accounts of Mallin's appearance before the Council are likely to be as apocryphal as Lynch thinks them. The Supreme Council had been held the previous Sunday. Most probably their purpose was to satisfy the Countess.

Connolly returned to Surrey House very late on Saturday night, and it would seem that others also were interested in what those days were bringing forth. On the following night the police raided the house and searched it, while the Fianna boys and girls sang rebel songs. The police were probably looking for 1½ cwt. of gelignite which the Fianna boy Seamus Reader had brought to Dublin a week previously. The intention had been to land this consignment at the North Wall, but the ship was diverted to Belfast. Knowing that Connolly through his associates in Glasgow was assisting the I.R.B. in procuring arms (something which must have irked Connolly when he was kept ignorant of their possible use) he hired a jaunting car and took up his dangerous cargo to Glenalina Terrace. Made to realise the extremity of his folly, he apologised and drove to the G.N.R. station. He persuaded the porters that he was carrying steel machine parts urgently required for war work in Dublin. But on arrival at Amiens Street, he found he had forgotten the address of the Tobins in Rathmines to which the gelignite was to be delivered. He took it to Surrey House where another Fianna boy gave him the required information.

When Reader saw Connolly on the morning of January 17 Connolly commented, "I'd have had no rest if you'd told me that last night." It was therefore possibly the apprehension of possible arrest which led him to state his views so forcefully in the *Workers' Republic* despite impending negotiations with (as he believed) the Volunteers. Reader was arrested in Glasgow the following Thursday, but the gelignite was never traced.

It thus seems clear that Connolly's disappearance was connected with the I.R.B. Supreme Council's important policy decision. The fact that the date finally decided for the Rising did not reach America until February 5 and took Clan na Gael by surprise is strong evidence that what was at issue was precisely the policy changes attributed to MacDermott. The I.R.B. was to drop the conditions (German landing or conscription) which had previously been considered necessary before a rising could take place. But without taking Connolly's position into account nothing could be finalised. In this sense Sean T. O'Kelly was right in saying: "If it were not for Connolly the Rising might not have taken place exactly when it did." This did not mean Connolly spent three days haggling over a date. It means that he helped to create political conditions for the new decision.

For the I.R.B. to decide on unconditional insurrection was probably to relinquish the support of the most moderate Volunteers. This was Connolly's gain. He had won his argument. But on the other hand he must abandon his vision of a revolution led by the working class and involving the trade unions. The price he had to pay for finally detaching Pearse and his colleagues from Hobson and MacNeill was thus a heavy one. And at the same time he had to accept their assurances that the majority of the Volunteers would move on their instructions. Here was ample basis for a "terrible mental struggle", and a decision of this kind might well require three days.

On his return he declined to tell his friends where he had been, but declared that he had "been through hell" and had walked forty miles. It may be guessed that the forty miles may have been traversed within a room while he worked over the new situation in his mind and decided to accept the proposals of the I.R.B.

After his return Connolly wrote a very different editorial, for publication on January 29:

"The issue is clear, and we have done our part to clear it. Nothing we can say now can add point to the argument we have put before our readers in the past few months:

392

nor shall we continue to labour the point. In solemn acceptance of our duty and the great responsibilities attached thereto, we have planted the seed in the hope that ere many of us are much older, it will ripen into action. For the moment and hour of that ripening, that fruitful blessed day of days, we are ready. Will it find you ready too?"

It has been said that Connolly then joined the I.R.B. But his name was not given to the circles, possibly once more so as not to alert the party of procrastination, but possibly also on account of his political views. He certainly became a member of the military council which planned the rising. Everything was now centred on preparations for "the day". On Sunday January 23 Piaras Beaslai was despatched to Liverpool to contact those who would take the news to America.

THE DREAD ABYSS

Youth of Ireland, stand prepared,
Revolution's dread abyss
Burns beneath us, all but bared.

JAMES CLARENCE MANGAN

The January agreement decided the form of the rising. Thenceforth two forces worked together, representing respectively the most advanced sections of the workers and the petty-bourgeoisie. Connolly increasingly took the lead in military matters. Citizen Army training methods were adopted by the Volunteers, who now carried out a midnight exercise of their own.

The date for the proposed rising, April 23, was communicated to Clan na Gael on February 5 by Thomas O'Connor, a steward on an Atlantic liner. The news startled and surprised them, but tradition allowed Dublin the decision. The Germans were requested to prepare to land arms at Limerick, but preferred an alternative plan, already discussed, using Fenit. The change possibly implied some scaling down of the amount of aid they were prepared to give.

The conclusion of the alliance between Connolly and the I.R.B. improved the chances of military success. But its secrecy precluded any corresponding political advantage. Connolly was still in a dilemma. He had to depend on his colleagues' judgement that they could lead out the Volunteers in defiance of their official leaders, a position he had assented to only because he had no choice. "Perhaps Connolly was right," said Pearse to Desmond Ryan, probably with this crucial point in mind. In the actual event it was precisely on the obstacle presented by the official status of the compromisers that the undertaking foundered. Instead of politically defeating them and driving them out of the leadership, the I.R.B. decided on using them as a screen, which meant an edifice of deception. But by January 19 it was too late to change.

There were hesitations on the workers' side also, which Connolly sought to dispel, with more difficulty since the anti-Labour elements remained the figureheads of the volunteers. His editorial of February 5, "The Ties that Bind", showed how even a predatory and anti-national war can develop a temporary mass support.

"For long years we have carried on propaganda in Ireland pointing out how the strings of self-interest bound the capitalist and landlord classes to the Empire and how it thus became a waste of time to appeal to those classes in the name of Irish patriotism.

"We have said that the working class was the only class to whom the word Empire and the things of which it was the symbol did not appeal. ... Recently we have seen the spread of these ties of self-interest binding certain classes and individuals to the Empire ... we have seen it spread to a most astonishing degree until its manifestations cover the island like the spread of a foul disease. It would be almost impossible to name a single class or section of the population not partially affected by this social, political and moral leprosy."

He quoted examples of parliamentary representatives and Corporations engaged in recruiting propaganda. Journalists, professors and clergymen were all in it. "In all the grades of Irish society, the only section that has not furnished even one apostate to the cause it had worked for in times of peace is that of the ... militant Labour leaders." But the same could not be said of the working class as a whole. Granting all possible excuses, the facts were "horrible and shameful to the last degree".

"For the sake of a few paltry shillings, Irish workers have sold their country in the hour of their country's greatest need and greatest hope."

Wives had made the lives of their husbands unbearable

until they joined up. Girls had got married by the thousand to "Irish traitors". The British Government was "buying, buying, buying the souls of men".

But Connolly insisted: "The great heart of the nation remains true. Some day most of these deluded and misled brothers and sisters of ours will learn the truth, some day we will welcome them back to our arms purified and repentant of their errors."

The final paragraph is the most revealing. It gives Connolly's reason for urging that a rising should be attempted soon at all costs. It must be read in the light of his expectation of worsening prospects as the war progressed:

> "But deep in the heart of Ireland has sunk the sense of the degradation wrought upon its people—so deep and so humiliating that no agency less powerful than the red tide of war on Irish soil will ever be able to enable the Irish race to recover its self-respect, or establish its national dignity in the face of a world horrified and scandalised by what must seem to them our national apostasy."

So much has been attributed to Pearse's influence. Pearse's notion of a "blood sacrifice" was explained by T. A. Jackson as amounting to the doctrine that the Irish people themselves must generate the forces that would liberate them. Such was its "rational kernel". Connolly's concluding sentence bears out this interpretation. It ran:

> "Without the slightest trace of irreverence but in all due humility and awe, we recognise that of us, as of mankind before Calvary, it may truly be said 'without the shedding of Blood there is no Redemption'."

The form was scriptural. Connolly was so deeply moved that he drew upon the religious imagery of his childhood. The conceit was Pearse's and sealed the alliance between the two men. But Connolly had injected a profounder meaning into old words. It was the meaning given by the old Communard Meillet: "Without the shedding of blood there is no *social* salvation."

At this time Connolly was concerned to unify all forces making for the insurrection, to lose none, and to antagonise none. The young Capuchins of the Father Matthew Hall in Church Street had been brought into close touch with the un-skilled workers of Dublin in their work for temperance. They had stood aside from the general current of chauvinism which led the Bishop of Raphoe and others into recruiting prop-aganda. They gradually fell under the political influence of the men who chose them as spiritual advisers, and presented the Church authorities with a thorny problem. In Cork a sim-ilar situation was met by a form of Catholic Action, the call-ing in of lay experts like Professor Smiddy to propagate a species of Catholic Fabianism. In Dublin, despite Connolly's reprobations, then the most mature revolutionary centre in the western world, working-class consciousness was too strong to be satisfied with small concessions. The lock-out had changed things.

When on January 25[1] Father Lawrence addressed the Dublin Trades Council, Connolly was deputed by the Exec-utive to propose the vote of thanks. In the *Workers' Repub-lic* of January 29, he gave his impressions:

"Here we had a great meeting of working men and women, overwhelmingly Catholic in their religious faith, gather-ing together to discuss problems of social life and national aspirations with a priest whom they held in affectionate esteem, but insisting upon discussing these problems in the spirit of comradeship and equality ... the lesson of France has not been lost.... The Church recognises that if she does not move with the people, the people will move with-out her.

"It is generally recognised in Dublin that the editor of this paper represents the most militant, and what is called the most extreme, type of the labour movement. We are glad therefore to be able to say in all sincerity that we could see no fundamental difference between the views ex-

[1] The two dates in Desmond Ryan's collection are exactly ten days out.

pressed by Fr. Lawrence and those views which we ourselves never hesitate to express.... We accept the family
as the true type of human society.... Every man, woman
and child of the nation must be considered as an heir to all
the property of the nation ... to attain that end we seek
to organise every person who works for wages, that the
workers themselves may determine the conditions of labour. We hold that the sympathetic strike is the affirma-
tion of the Christian principle that we are all members one
of another."

He concluded with a simple statement of democratic policy:

"Recognising that the proper utilisation of the national resources requires control of political power, we propose to
conquer that political power through a working-class political party; and recognising that the full development of
national power requires complete national freedom, we are
frankly and unreservedly prepared for whatever struggle
may be necessary to conquer for Ireland her place among
the nations of the earth."

No more than a faint echo of syndicalism remained. "From
the organisation of labour as such, we propose to proceed to
organise upon the co-operative principle that we may control
the commodities we ourselves use and consume." Connolly
was practically back at the position of the *Communist Manifesto*: "Formation of the proletariat into a class, overthrow
of the bourgeois supremacy, conquest of political power by
the proletariat." Such were the political conclusions Connolly
read into the address by Father Lawrence.

February and March were full of feverish preparation. For
some time arms, ammunition and medical supplies had been
brought into Liberty Hall. Metal tubes and gelignite were
brought into an improvised bomb factory in the basement.
The armed guard had more than a printing press to protect.
Efforts were even made to manufacture a kind of machine-
gun. Connolly, too, was now protected. The decision to
provide him with a guard dates roughly from the time of his
disappearance. But if his daughter was correctly informed

during a visit to Liberty Hall, it arose not only from that episode but from a rumour that the authorities were considering having him assassinated. Most probably the Citizen Army feared that he might be arrested and deported to England. He was therefore provided with a whistle whose notes were several tones shriller than a police whistle; he must blow this if he apprehended any personal danger.

All this military preparation, an open secret that was never betrayed to the authorities, alarmed Sheehy-Skeffington more and more. The debate with Countess Markiewicz, held on February 18, hung on the issue of peaceful or violent resistance. Connolly spoke against the pacifists. Just as every polemic of Eastern Europe was paralleled in Ireland, so Connolly's conclusion was that of Lenin who wrote: "Whoever wishes a durable and democratic peace must be for civil war against the governments and the bourgeoisie." The pacifists could not understand that there could be no peace without war. All war was alike to them, irrespective of who waged it and what it was for.

Those who have written of the preparations for Easter 1916 seem invariably to expand the time scale. So much happened; feeling was so intense; even the rank-and-file who did not know the date shared the expectancy of the leaders. The dock strike dragged on, and S.F.U. seamen on sympathetic strike drew I.T.G.W.U. benefit. There was a proposal to organise a separate seamen's section for them. The T.U.C. and Labour Party Executive met, and Connolly seconded the resolution of protest against the administration of the Insurance Act. The agenda was concerned with economic issues. The national question was not even mentioned. In this the absence of a vanguard political party made itself felt; revolutionary thought was canalised into the military organisation only. Above ground Liberty Hall seemed the businesslike trade union headquarters. But members with nothing better to do were not encouraged to stray into its recesses. From time to time there were accidents which could have ended in catastrophe. Somebody lit a fire in the Citizen Army room. Behind the firebricks were thousands of live cartridges. That night there were burned fingers. John Haggerty had already peppered himself with shot which providentially missed the gelignite stuffing Sean McGlynn's pockets. A faulty detonator exploded, spattering Seamus McGowan and James O'Neill with fine shrapnel. Such incidents brought Connolly on the run from his room. Since the agreement with the I.R.B., I.C.A. bombs could be tested at St. Enda's. And still the authorities knew nothing.

Determined to utilise every spring of national feeling for the rising whose slogan was to be independence, Connolly organised a meeting to commemorate Robert Emmet on March 4, and the Fenians on March 6. All previous insurgents waited too long, was his theme. "To us a glorious opportunity has come." St. Patrick's day was celebrated with parades of Volunteers and the Citizen Army, public meetings and celebrations. "In this hour of travail, Ireland cannot afford to sacrifice any one of the things this world has accepted as peculiarly Irish." On March 26 the Dramatic Society performed in Liberty Hall a three-act play which Connolly had written. *Under Which Flag* tells the story of a young man torn between the seductions of the recruiting sergeant and his national sentiments. He joins the I.R.B. This was the second play Connolly wrote. The first was *The Agitator's Wife,* written in the U.S.A. Sheehy-Skeffington testified to its stage-worthiness. That Connolly could accomplish such a feat was remarkable. While he had devoured Shakespeare, he confessed to Mullery that he had never been in a financial position to see a single performance. No doubt his use of the soliloquy, which Skeffington criticised, arose from this circumstance.

Under Which Flag was produced under circumstances which made its message especially defiant. The authorities were beginning to show quick sensitivity to rebel activities. On March 25 Connolly received a letter from Liam Mellows telling of attempts to disarm Volunteers at Tullamore. Members of the Gaelic Athletic Association—a society for the encouragement of Irish national games—had been implicated, and Mellows was very concerned lest this national organisation should be seduced into imperialist hands, though the Volunteers had won the day with the aid of a few blank cartridges.

But this was as nothing to the tumult at Liberty Hall on the day the letter was written. The police raided the premises of the Gaelic Press, confiscating all copies of *The Gael* and removing formes of standing type. Connolly was brought from his office by the news that the shop attached to Liberty Hall was being searched.

He reached it in time to see a policeman with a bundle of papers in his hands. He drew his revolver. "Drop those or I'll drop you." The policeman put down the papers and explained that he had come to confiscate any copies of *The Gael, The Gaelic Athlete, Honesty,* or *The Spark,* which might be on the premises. He withdrew when Connolly explained that he could not search the shop without a warrant. Perhaps it was ignorance, perhaps the revolver decided him. Connolly's version of the law was his own—under D.O.R.A. a search could be made without a warrant, as nobody knew better than Connolly.

Countess Markiewicz then arrived with news of other raids. The men on duty at the hall ran out a line of pickets as far as the police barracks. Meanwhile Connolly, the Countess and Nora (on a visit from Belfast) signed two hundred and fifty mobilisation forms. By the time they were completed, Inspector Bannon, four plain-clothes men and two uniformed men had entered the shop. The neighbourhood was well populated with police of all ranks. A trusted Citizen Army man, James O'Shea, had called into the hall during his lunch hour. The forms were slipped down the back of his neck, and making off as if to return to the dockside, he was allowed to pass unchallenged. He then delivered the forms to Kane, the mobilisation officer, and to Michael Mallin.

The Inspector in the shop now produced a warrant to search for copies of *The Gael.* Connolly made him read it through and then, mounting guard at the interconnecting doorway, informed him that the warrant did not permit him to cross the threshold of Liberty Hall. There were no copies of *The Gael,* nor had there been; the police departed. Connolly and the Countess were busy congratulating each other when the results of the mobilisation order became apparent. From all over Dublin, from railway, factory, dockyard, the quays, and the holds of coal boats, poured in grimy men, some dripping wet from having swum the canal. They had downed tools on receipt of the notice. Within an hour one hundred and fifty had answered the summons. Connolly addressed them in the hall and declared that thenceforward Liberty Hall must be under armed guard day and night. Shortly afterwards he moved his bed into his office, and slept on the premises each night. The editorial of the *Workers' Republic* was headed with the pregnant double entendre: "We will rise again."

The events reawakened the alarm of the "pure and simple" trade unionists. Their fears were heightened when Connolly's next move was announced in the issue of April 8. On Sunday, the sixteenth, the "Green Flag of Ireland" would be hoisted over Liberty Hall. This act of defiance was more than trade union flesh could bear. On Wednesday, the twelfth, an Executive Committee meeting was held. It may have been that this was in reality the Committee of No. 1. branch which acted as a national Standing Committee. Connolly would not be a member of this body. By seven votes to five it decided to call a meeting the following day to "consider Connolly's action". This meant to repudiate him. Foran persuaded them to meet Connolly first. Accordingly on Thursday he told them that if any objection were raised he would sever his connection with the union. Permission was finally granted when Connolly gave a promise that the Citizen Army would shortly leave Liberty Hall, and "probably never return". Ten days before the insurrection this was not a difficult undertaking to observe.

Meanwhile the increasing vigilance of the authorities had created other difficulties. Liam Mellows, who was to lead the rising in the west, was suddenly arrested and deported to England. MacDermott consulted Connolly on how to secure his release. It was agreed that Herbert Mellows, Liam's brother, should travel to Belfast with a request to Nora Connolly to accompany him by a circuitous route to the address in Staffordshire where Mellows was staying. There Herbert and Liam changed clothes, and Liam returned to Ireland disguised as a priest. While he was away Connolly organised protest meetings against the deportation. Mellows was back in Ireland by April 15, and hiding in St. Enda's.

Next day was Palm Sunday. Connolly's ceremony took place amid scenes of great emotion. "On that day, the Irish Citizen Army, the armed forces of Labour, on the top of the Headquarters of the Irish Transport and General Workers' Union, hoisted and unfurled the Green flag of Ireland, emblazoned with the Harp without the crown, and as the sacred emblem of Ireland's unconquered soul fluttered to the breeze, the bugles pealed their defiant salute, and the battalion presented arms, strong men wept for joy, and women fainted with emotion." At the same time it was noted that, despite the "sunburstery", he raised the old green flag, not the new tricolour which would have given away his compact with the republicans, and made authority suspicious.

That evening he addressed the Citizen Army after a lecture on street fighting which was attended by Volunteer officers. "The odds are a thousand to one against us," he told them. "If we win, we'll be great heroes; but if we lose we'll be the greatest scoundrels the country ever produced. In the event of victory, hold on to your rifles, as those with whom we are fighting[1] may stop before our goal is reached. We are out for economic as well as political liberty." Here was the theory of "continuous revolution" put in a simple way. That night the Citizen Army were told that the rising was decided on. Those who wished to withdraw were offered the opportunity. There would be no recriminations. Not a man moved.

---

[1] It should be noted that "those with whom we are fighting" could at this time be a reference to MacNeill, etc. It would be mistaken to read here an attitude to Pearse and Clarke, with whom Connolly was in collusion.

Connolly had laughed at Hobson's "sunburstery". Now it was Hobson's turn to urge sobriety and caution. When an actual revolution was on the way, the roles were reversed. At the Cumann na mBan concert, where he took the place of another speaker who could not attend, Hobson urged the Volunteers to bide their time till after the war and hope to influence the peace conference. To leave behind a glorious tradition was not enough. He clearly suspected that insurrection was afoot. But as yet he had no certainty.

The very next day appeared a document the authenticity of which has been much disputed. It purported to be a Dublin Castle plan to arrest the Volunteer leaders, occupy Irish-Ireland premises and deport, imprison or restrict the movements of many leading citizens including, of all people, the Archbishop of Dublin. The last proposal credited the Castle with so little sagacity that it is usually taken to dispose of all claims to genuineness. The document was at once disowned by the authorities. But not only was it published, it was solemnly debated in the Corporation and caused much embarrassment. The author has been held to be the Machiavellian Joseph Plunkett, who revelled in romantic subterfuges which frequently met with success. Its political purpose would be to stampede MacNeill and Hobson into insurrection, or failing that to create a situation in which the Volunteers would pass them by and respond to the lead of the allies.

Unfortunately, after an initial burst of fear and indignation, MacNeill sat down to examine the document carefully. He was struck by the maladroit inclusion of the Archbishop, and decided that it was probably a forgery. The final preparations which Pearse described as a race against the government were also a race against MacNeill. A detailed study of the process by which MacNeill's suspicions were increased until at last the grisly truth burst in on him, has been made in Desmond Ryan's *The Rising*. Connolly busied himself with his own arrangements. He had never liked the position where MacNeill had to be deceived but had acceded to the common plan and was playing his part in it.

On Wednesday he invited the Citizen Army Officers to his room and informed them that the rising was timed for Easter Sunday evening at 6.30 p.m. in Dublin, and 7 p.m. in the provinces. A shipload of arms, including artillery, was expected from Germany. He assigned his men to their various positions and explained the parts they were to play, on the assumption that the I.R.B. would secure a full muster of Volunteers. He sent William Partridge to Tralee to supervise the distribution of arms to Limerick and Cork. With MacDonagh he toured the positions which were to be taken up in the various parts of the city.

On Palm Sunday the Executive had issued a warning to Volunteers to be on their guard against plans for their suppression. They must be prepared to take offensive action. Even then MacNeill drew no firm conclusion. Next day Hobson was visited by Liam Manahan, who had come from Limerick to enquire about the rumours of impending action. Hobson was now fully on the alert. A more practical man than MacNeill, he quickly guessed that the manœuvres arranged for Easter weekend were indeed the real thing. He went to Dundrum and told MacNeill. The professor insisted on going to St. Enda's, though it was after midnight, and knocking up Pearse. Was it true, he asked, that Pearse had given orders for seizing barracks, blowing up bridges and taking over railways? Pearse saw that it was useless to keep up pretences longer, and revealed the truth. "I will do everything I can to stop this," stormed MacNeill, "except to ring up the Castle."

Next day Pearse told MacDonagh and MacDermott the bad news. An approach was then made to MacNeill, who agreed to do nothing for the moment. If he could be immobilised until things were once started, all might yet be well. The crucial point lay in the mobilisation. There is evidence that his visitors tried to secure MacNeill's resignation, but whether he gave it or not remains uncertain. Hobson was tougher meat. There was no question of bamboozling him into inactivity. The I.R.B. had him kidnapped on Friday night. This news, of course, spread rapidly, and the split in the Volunteer leadership assumed serious proportions. But Pearse's instruction stood. The rising was still on.

Then came news of one of those mischances which impose a sad fatality on the pattern of Irish insurrections. The arms ship arrived off the coast of Kerry. But the party which was to have made contact with it and arranged the landing, racing for the rendezvous in a motor car, failed to make a right-angled turn in the darkness, and plunged over a quayside into deep water. The ship waited three days, was captured by the British, and scuttled by its crew in Cork Harbour. Monteith and Casement, arriving by submarine from Germany (not to prevent a rising but to take part in it[1]), struggled against wet, cold, fatigue and exposure to make contact with the local Volunteers. Casement was arrested. Monteith got through. He gave his message—that the rising should be called off *if* it was dependent on the landing of German arms—to a Volunteer who was detailed to take it to Dublin and deliver it to MacNeill or Hobson. Monteith had no notion of the dual leadership. But the I.T.G.W.U. had not organised in Kerry for nothing. The Volunteer delivered the despatch to James Connolly in Liberty Hall, and very late on the Friday night Pearse was summoned to a conference there. Leadership had passed to the working-class section.

Early next morning the opposing factions met again. Pearse and MacDermott saw MacNeill in the morning and believed they had convinced him that the die was cast. But the afternoon found him in conference with The O'Rahilly, Sean Fitzgibbon and Arthur Griffith, whose stand in this fatal matter has received curiously scant attention. From this conference came MacNeill's decision to countermand the orders for the weekend manœuvres. Plunkett and Mac-Donagh appeared to urge the inevitability of the rising. They intended to go ahead. The MacNeill faction was adamant at last. "These gentlemen are not my colleagues," declared MacDonagh as he swept out.

[1] T. A. Jackson was mistaken in thinking Casement communicated the plans of the Rising to the authorities. It was Eva Gore Booth who suggested he returned to prevent it, in her effort to have him reprieved.

The military council held an emergency meeting at a shop in Amiens Street. There was still uncertainty over MacNeill and nothing could be decided until his threat was put into execution. Early in the evening it was clear he had found decisiveness at last. His order ran:

> "Owing to the very critical position, all orders given to Irish Volunteers for tomorrow, Easter Sunday, are hereby rescinded, and no parades, marches, or other movements of Irish Volunteers will take place. Each individual Volunteer will obey this order in every particular."

The order was readily transmitted to the Dublin Brigade, but messengers must be found to take it down country. There were such difficulties in the way of this that for a while the I.R.B. leaders hoped that it might prove impossible. But there was no way of knowing. If Dublin mobilised without the country, all would be in chaos. Pearse therefore confirmed the order to the Dublin Brigade, which would not have obeyed without his signature. When the *Sunday Independent* came out, this proved to have been a wise decision. MacNeill had taken the precaution of cycling to its offices and inserting the countermand as an advertisement. Ceannt learned of these developments from Cathal Brugha, and went straight to Liberty Hall at 4 a.m. But the guard had received strict instructions not to waken Connolly. Plans might be in ruins, but he must wait till morning.

Nora Connolly, arriving on the night train from Tyrone, found her father awake, pale, tired and distressed. She described the arrival of MacNeill's order and the resulting confusion, but told him the Volunteers were still in the field. The military council was convened and met at Liberty Hall. Tom Clarke was for carrying out the original plan, relying on the Volunteers to respond spontaneously. His colleagues overruled him and it was decided to strike on the Monday.

> "If we don't fight now," said Connolly, "all that we have to hope and pray for is that an earthquake will come and swallow Ireland up."

Easter 1916 was the climacteric of the first world war. At that point the attempt to solve the crisis through war itself ran into crisis. Thereafter the popular forces throughout the world began to take the offensive. In this sense, as Lenin pointed out, the "misfortune of the Irish is that they rose prematurely, when the European revolt of the proletariat had *not yet* matured". In another sense the Easter rising was required for the maturing of that revolt. Unsuccessful revolts are a misfortune to those who take part in them, but are an inevitable part of historical development. Connolly's determination to fight now at all costs showed how completely he had identified himself with historical necessity.

While the military council deliberated in Dublin, two other meetings were in process. The British Cabinet was in the "peace or total war" crisis which led to the fall of Asquith, and the British Socialist Party was in conference in London. At the first, total war was decided upon. At the second, Hyndman was overthrown. The main force of British socialism broke with its opportunist past and resumed the revolutionary struggle. The war-clouds might now rain their heaviest, but it was for the end of the storm. A year later came the Russian Revolution; two years later the giant anti-conscription movement that heralded the collapse of British rule over the greater part of Ireland.

Connolly and his colleagues could act only upon what they knew. It was clear that, after the arrest of Casement, their days as free men were numbered. At that very moment, indeed, the authorities were preparing to swoop. The Cabinet crisis protracted the formalities, since peace was conceivable, and the countermanding order provided a temporary reassurance. There was thus just time. After the decision to strike next day, Connolly's deep chagrin changed to whistling high spirits. The die was cast and he sang to himself:

> "We've got another saviour now.
> That saviour is the sword."

Singing, he put on his uniform and fixed his equipment. Plans had to be revised. Dublin was to lead the way with such of the provincial centres as could be informed. The Citizen Army paraded lest its failure to do so should arouse suspicions, and the evening concert advertised to throw the authorities off the scent had to be improvised. Next morning the proclamation of the Republic was run off in the basement. It was drafted by Pearse and revised by Connolly and MacDonagh.

"Are these men sworn in?" asked MacDonagh as he watched Molloy and O'Brien setting the type. "They don't need to be," replied Connolly. Owing to the shortage of 24 pt. letters (such as were used for headlines in the *Workers' Republic*) the proclamation had to be printed in two operations, and even then type from another fount had to be used. Chris Brady ran off the copies on the Furnival machine that printed the *Workers' Republic*.

Lillie Connolly and the younger children arrived from Belfast, accommodation being found for them at Countess Markiewicz's cottage in the mountains. Thomas MacDonagh alerted the Dublin brigade. The new order was met with a mixture of relief and scepticism. Some Volunteers had already smashed their rifles and burned their uniforms. They laughed cynically and went off to the races. Others clung to the hope that the signal would now be given. The Citizen Army, with its firmer structure and democratic spirit, plus its long expectation of some such defection by MacNeill, was the stanchion to which all was fixed. But despite the split, as John Devoy proudly remarked, there was not one traitor or informer in 1916. The change of plans was accomplished with complete secrecy, and on Monday April 24 Connolly addressed the Citizen Army in Liberty Hall for the last time. He was now Commandant-General of all the insurgent forces in Dublin, and he told them there no longer existed a Citizen Army and a Volunteer force. There was now only the Irish Republican Army. There was no "keep your rifles" now.

As T. A. Jackson pointed out, the original plan to hold a circle roughly enclosing Dublin Castle and carry out two lines into the country to connect with provincial forces was sound enough in its original conception. It was a plan essentially offensive in purpose. The loss of the German arms, inadequate as they were, severely limited the first grand scope of the insurgent plan, which was intended as no local *putsch*. The defection of MacNeill struck a far harder blow; from the purely military standpoint it reduced the Dublin muster to one hundred and twenty Citizen Army men and seven hundred Volunteers. Among these was The O'Rahilly. As soon as he learned the issue was joined, despite his disagreements, he insisted on taking part even though Pearse and Connolly both sought to dissuade him. His magnanimity cost him his life. Twelve men of the (American) Hibernian Rifles and a few Volunteers joined in after the fighting commenced. All criticisms of the tactical conduct of operations must take into account the practical impossibility of adapting the first secret plans to the changed circumstances.

It is also clear that whereas Connolly had thought the original plan gave chances of success, he now had no hope of victory. He was concerned above all lest the authorities should move first and the revolution die whimpering amid arrests, ridicule and recrimination.

"We are going out to be slaughtered," he told William O'Brien as he passed down the stairs of Liberty Hall.

"Is there no chance of success?" asked O'Brien.

"None whatever."

The first Citizen Army men left at 11.35 a.m. They were to seize Harcourt Street station. Then followed Sean Connolly, not to seize the Castle, but to occupy buildings commanding it. It had been decided that, though the Castle itself could be taken, there were insufficient men to hold it. The presence of a hospital in the precincts precluded its being burned down. Mallin and Countess Markiewicz made for Stephen's Green, and finally Connolly, Pearse, Clarke, MacDermott and Plunkett made for O'Connell Street. At the first stroke of the Angelus the insurrection was to begin.[1]

[1] The following recapitulation is based mainly on Desmond Ryan's *The Rising*.

Connolly led his men through lower Abbey Street, and into the main thoroughfare. Scarcely a head turned. Then, as the bell sounded, he shouted, "Left turn. The G.P.O.–Charge!" Seventy soldiers rushed the portico, poured in through the doors, bustling out customers and staff, breaking all glass from the windows with rifle butts, and bringing in cart-loads of sandbags. The I.R.A. rapidly overpowered the guard on the upper stories. The interconnecting corridors were cleared, locks being blown off where necessary. Finally the roof was taken and the republican tricolour rose in the sunshine, together with a green banner embroidered *Poblacht na h'Eireann*.

While a handful of men toiled at fortifying the head-quarters, small groups seized all corner houses commanding the approaches. These were left manned by snipers. Very few shots had been fired, and at that mostly in the air, when Clarke, Pearse and Connolly stepped forward on the plinth, Pearse with a paper in his hand. This was the proclamation of the Republic which he now read, as it was posted up around the city beside the rising barricades. It ran:

POBLACHT NA H'EIREANÑ
THE PROVISIONAL GOVERNMENT
OF THE
IRISH REPUBLIC
to the people of Ireland

Irishmen and Irishwomen. In the name of God and of the dead generations from which she receives her old tradition of nationhood, Ireland through us, summons her children to her flag and strikes for her freedom.

Having organised and trained her manhood through her secret revolutionary organisation, the Irish Republican Brotherhood, and through her open military organisations, the Irish Volunteers and the Irish Citizen Army, having patiently perfected her discipline, having resolutely waited for the right moment to reveal itself, she now seizes that moment, and, supported by her exiled children in America and by gallant allies in Europe, but relying in the first on her own strength, she strikes in full confidence of victory.

We declare the right of the people of Ireland to the ownership of Ireland, and to the unfettered control of Irish destinies, to be sovereign and indefeasible. The long usurpation of that right by a foreign people and government has not extinguished the right, nor can it ever be extinguished except by the destruction of the Irish people. In every generation the Irish people have asserted their right to national freedom and sovereignty, six times during the past three hundred years they have asserted it in arms. Standing on that fundamental right and again asserting it in arms in the face of the world, we hereby proclaim the Irish Republic as a Sovereign Independent State, and we pledge our lives and the lives of our comrades-in-arms to the cause of its freedom, of its welfare, and of its exaltation among the nations.

The Irish Republic is entitled to, and hereby claims, the allegiance of every Irishman and Irishwoman. The Republic guarantees religious and civil liberty, equal rights and equal opportunities to all its citizens, and declares its resolve to pursue the happiness and prosperity of the whole nation and of all its parts, cherishing all the children of the nation equally, and oblivious of the differences carefully fostered by an alien government, which have divided a minority from the majority in the past.

Until our arms have brought the opportune moment for the establishment of a permanent National Government, representative of the whole people of Ireland and elected by the suffrages of all her men and women, the Provisional Government, hereby constituted, will administer the civil and military affairs of the Republic in trust for the people.

We place the cause of the Irish Republic under the protection of the Most High God, Whose blessing we invoke upon our arms, and we pray that no one who serves that cause will dishonour it by cowardice, inhumanity, or rapine. In this supreme hour the Irish nation must, by its valour and discipline and by the readiness of its children to sacrifice themselves for the common good, prove itself worthy of the august destiny to which it is called.

Signed on Behalf of the Provisional Government

THOMAS J. CLARKE

SEAN MACDIARMADA	THOMAS MACDONAGH
P. H. PEARSE	EAMONN CEANNT
JAMES CONNOLLY	JOSEPH PLUNKETT

The Proclamation was read "to an indifferent crowd and a few perfunctory cheers". The people did not yet understand. "Thank God," said Connolly to Pearse and Clarke, "that we have lived to see this day." In the Post Office, Plunkett had spread a large map. Despatch runners came and went. The main strong-points taken, the aim was now to extend the circle, relying on the accession of fresh volunteer forces who now knew the fight was on. Telegraph wires were cut, and Dublin was isolated. The railway stations could not be taken through lack of forces, but bridges and approaches were blown up. The expected reinforcements came, in a steady trickle. But they were insufficient to maintain the initiative. Once the initiative is lost an insurrection is doomed. Those who criticised the men of Easter Week for "shutting themselves up in rat-traps" forgot that they were not fighting as they had intended. Of perhaps more weight is Brian O'Neill's criticism that the possibility of taking over newspaper offices to print mass propaganda does not seem to have been considered. Yet who is to know that it was not considered? When printers were turned out of newspaper offices at the point of the gun, is there any certainty that they could have been induced to turn out a rebel newspaper? The operations had been pared to the bone. Forces were at a premium; a few strong points and no frills. Such were the realities of the situation.

The authorities were paralysed on Monday, despite the five thousand troops they were able to assemble at once. But by Tuesday morning reinforcements began to arrive from The Curragh and at Dun Laoghaire. The forces immobilised by Eoin Mac-Neill could have made all the difference on that first day.

Connolly seemed to draw new life from each moment of the struggle. He inspected barricades with seeming unconcern for his own safety, kicking them to see if they were sound, and berating poor workmanship in true army style. Inside the G.P.O., with the aid of his secretary, Winifred Carney, he kept up a continuous despatch correspondence with other insurrectionary centres. To those who enquired he replied that the British were beaten—hadn't the Citizen Army captured King George and Kitchener in the Henry Street waxworks?

Looting broke out and continued, despite the insurgents' efforts to stop it, till one by one the rifled shops went up in smoke and flames. Liberty Hall had been evacuated. But on the Monday night two eighteen-pounders were placed in Tara Street and began the reduction of "the centre of social anarchy in Ireland, the brain of every riot and disturbance". It has been said that Connolly believed that artillery would not be used since capitalists would never destroy capitalist property. But this is scarcely credible. He must have seen them do it. Class power is the condition of class property, and thus takes precedence over all standing structures. Connolly did believe, however, that the speedy introduction of artillery betokened haste, which might derive from the prospect of a German offensive or a development of the rising in the provinces. Writing, planning, inspecting, encouraging, Connolly was the soul of the revolt. But ever mindful of the independent claims of Labour, he sent the Plough and Stars across the road to be unfurled over William Martin Murphy's Imperial Hotel whence Larkin had thundered Labour's defiance less than three years before.

On Wednesday the Admiralty gunboat *Helga* sailed up the Liffey to help in the bombardment of Dublin. Constant reinforcements were enabling the British to compress the rebels. Connolly was forced to withdraw Traynor from Fairview; he succeeded in bringing back his stores and joined the garrison in the Hotel Metropole in Abbey Street. The leaders took turns to sleep and watch as the sound of the shells grew ever louder, and fire crept slowly down the East side of O'Connell Street. When the Imperial was engulfed the garrison made for the Post Office through a hail of bullets, often so thick that men thought it was raining.

It was on Thursday that Connolly numbered off his men, so that Pearse could address them. Despite a pensiveness which had grown over the past few days, he was full of quiet exaltation. Dublin had made its name splendid among cities. A few hundred republicans had defied thousands of trained troops for four glorious days.

But that afternoon the British succeeded in isolating the G.P.O. from the other rebel positions. Entire blocks were burned down so as to give a clear field for the artillery and field guns. It was in the effort to keep communications open that Connolly himself was seriously wounded. The Mendicity Institute higher up the Liffey on the far side had been cut off by British forces, which were crossing the intervening bridges and threatening the Post Office in the rear. Connolly had received a minor wound in the arm while inspecting a barricade, but had instructed the surgeon to keep it secret. When it was decided to take over the Irish Independent Building in Liffey Street, thus threatening the flank of the troops crossing the river, he accompanied the expedition to an alleyway in Princes Street. After seeing them on their way, he was returning to the G.P.O. when a dum-dum bullet shattered his ankle, and he fell on the cobblestones unconscious. There he lay for a while, unnoticed, till he recovered sufficiently to crawl back to headquarters, in terrible agony.

There behind a screen, Dr. O'Mahoney (a prisoner) performed an operation. Chloroform was available and so was morphine. He had lost much blood and scarcely slept, despite the sedative. But next morning he had himself wheeled on a bed into the front hall where, as Pearse wrote in his last despatch at 9.30 a.m. he lay "wounded . . . but still the guiding brain of our resistance". "Nothing could break the will of this man," said Dr. Ryan. For a while he rested and read a detective novel. Then he sent for Winifred Carney and dictated a defiant despatch aimed at sustaining the morale of the encircled garrison. Desmond Ryan notes that his summary of the situation was at variance with the known facts.

Even if Galway, Wicklow, Wexford, Cork and Kerry were on the move as he suggested, he could not have known of it. Perhaps, despite the power of his will, his sense of reality was beginning to weaken.

It was not long before reality beat hard on the rebel stones. It was decided to evacuate all women, except Winifred Carney who refused to leave Connolly, and two others. At one o'clock British artillery at last found its main target and a shell started a short-lived fire. Two hours later an incendiary shell set the building ablaze. The flames could not be quenched. From then on preparations for evacuation must be made. At 8 p.m. the prisoners were released. Connolly was carried out on a stretcher, down Henry Street and into Moore Street, a young Fianna boy interposing his body at every flash so as to protect the wounded leader. "We can't fail now," said Connolly, "such lads will never forget." A van was dragged across the road. Despite heavy casualties the withdrawal was made; the garrison burrowed into the small shops, tunnelling through the walls till at No. 16 they were held up by a pile of debris. The aim of reaching Williams and Woods factory in Parnell Street had to be given up. Connolly's stretcher was set down. This was the new headquarters of the Republic. While the I.R.A. men slowly burrowed on, passing wall after wall, the leaders deliberated. Connolly was exhausted and groaning with pain. His stretcher would not pass through the walls and he had been carried in a sheet.

There was still the sound of firing on Saturday morning. But Moore Street Headquarters was isolated. Escape was impossible. Tom Clarke urged fighting till the last bullet was spent. But his colleagues disagreed. To prolong the struggle now was to destroy life needlessly. What could be done had been done, and done with honour. For a time there was hesitation. Three men bearing white flags had been shot already. It was decided to send a woman, and the choice fell on Elizabeth O'Farrell. As she approached the Parnell Street barricade the firing stopped. She was sent to Tom Clarke's shop, of all places, where General Lowe interviewed her. At

3.30 p.m. she accompanied Pearse, who gave up his sword to the General. "In order to prevent further slaughter" Pearse agreed to unconditional surrender and sent instructions to all units in City and Country to lay down their arms. "I agree to these conditions for the men only under my own command in the Moore Street district and for the men in the Stephen's Green Command," Connolly added. Without his signature the Citizen Army would not give up.

Connolly was taken to the Castle. There he greatly impressed Surgeon Tobin, who gave him every attention. But, apart from one document, for the last fortnight of his life Connolly spoke to the world no more. His reflections on the struggle, his feelings for the future, must be reconstructed from the recollections, often recorded under terrible emotional stress, of those who visited him. Among these, perhaps the calmest would be Father Aloysius, one of the Church Street friars, who had put the Father Matthew Hall at the disposal of the insurgents as a hospital. On the other hand, he had never met Connolly and would scarcely understand his political philosophy. He visited him on Sunday, April 30, and at the suggestion of General Lowe asked him to confirm the genuineness of his signature. Connolly confirmed it at once. He had surrendered "to prevent needless slaughter".

According to the *aide-mémoire* which Father Aloysius prepared at the time but did not publish till 1942, Connolly sent for him on Monday, May 1. Gangrene had set in and he feared he would be unable to hold out. Pain precluded sleep even after morphine injections. He felt the things of this world slipping from his grasp, and the time coming to apply that other aspect of his teaching on socialism and religion which others so much misunderstood. He had said a Catholic could be a socialist. Then the converse must be true; a socialist could be a Catholic. There was no retraction, because such was unnecessary. His existing position provided exactly for what he was now to do. Father Aloysius' *aide-mémoire* is the only contemporary document, and contains no implication that Connolly revised his political opinions.

Attempts to interpolate evidence of such were not made till years afterwards, and are profoundly suspect.

At first, the military refused to remove the guard even while Father Aloysius was with Connolly. To fear that he might escape would clear even the British army from the charge of lack of imagination. But they may have distrusted the Capuchin, and feared Connolly's smuggling out some political document, possibly even instructions for continuing the struggle. He was, as the friar testified, in complete command of his faculties. After some discussion the guard was removed and Father Aloysius gave Connolly absolution.

After the surrender began the white terror. There had been no newspapers in Dublin during Easter week. A strict censorship withheld news of the rising from the provinces. Not till Thursday did the *Cork Examiner* report the shelling of Liberty Hall and the imposition of martial law. On Friday the "lamentable outbreak" was attributed to Connolly, Larkin and syndicalism, and described as a "Communistic disturbance". (It is worth noting again that at this time "communistic" meant what is now called "anarchist", since the anarchists were the only group describing themselves by the term.) It was not, they said, "a revolutionary movement". Only after the surrender was Cork allowed the details. Connolly was reported killed. Then, in the next weeks, came a steady retreat through grudging admiration to something near applause. Connolly's kindness to prisoners of war was favourably recalled. The reason for the change of front was that executions, deportations and arrests were in full swing and public opinion was revolted at official barbarity.

As Connolly lay in the Castle hospital, a special cage lifting the bedclothes from his shattered leg, the finest men in Ireland were murdered one after another. William Martin Murphy's *Irish Catholic* described the rising as criminal and insane. Cardinal Logue telegraphed the Pope: "Insurrection happily terminated. Insurgents have surrendered unconditionally. Hope peace soon re-established." The *Freeman's Journal* told the public how the Vatican "greatly praised" the Irish clergy for the zeal with which they supported the efforts of the government to restore order. But if the Bishop of Raphoe continued to demand action against the "new paganism" of Germany, the Bishop of Limerick took the opposite stand, denounced the executions and wrote pamphlets against recruiting. The crisis of opinion was reaching the higher clergy. A part of the big bourgeoisie was becoming convinced of the need for a national struggle.

Chief secretary Birrell resigned. His despotism had been softened by slovenliness. In the new reign of blood, Clarke, Pearse and MacDonagh were shot on May 3. Murphy's *Irish Catholic* described Pearse as a "crazy and insolent schoolmaster", and the insurgents as "an extra-ordinary combination of rogues and fools". Nothing was spared to whip up hatred. But the signs of the future were eagerly read. As prisoners were led forth to trial and deportation, the well-dressed philistines of Grafton Street rushed from the sidewalks to spit on them. The working class looked on silently, conveying the inextinguishable sympathy of the underdog though they lacked either the courage or the understanding for a faint cheer.

Plunkett the irrepressible was shot on May 4, with Edward Daly, Michael O'Hanrahan and William Pearse. The execution of Pearse's brother was an act of cold-blooded revenge, entirely without pretext or justification. Next day Major John MacBride paid the penalty for his part in the Boer War. Ceannt, Mallin, Heuston and Colbert went on the eighth, Thomas Kent of Cork on the ninth. It was rumoured that there were to be ninety executions. They were "becoming an atrocity", said the *Manchester Guardian*.

The first public figure in England to protest was George Bernard Shaw. "I am bound to contradict any implication that I can regard as a traitor any Irishman taken in a fight for Irish independence against the British Government, which was a fair fight in everything except the enormous odds my countrymen had to face." The Liberal press slowly began to pluck up courage. One solitary Nationalist M.P., Lawrence Ginnell, screamed "murder!" across the House as his fellow members (Redmondites included) *applauded* the announcement of the first executions. Meanwhile, as pressure in Dublin was kept up, William Martin Murphy achieved the crowning infamy of his life. He had declared his policy. Now he crossed to London while the fuse burned. The *Independent* published Connolly's photograph alongside a caption: "Still lies in Dublin Castle recovering from his wounds." The editorial declared: "Let the worst of the ringleaders be singled out and dealt with as they deserve." It has been given to few journals to achieve such wanton and tigerish cynicism.

These were days of torture for Lillie Connolly in the Countess's cottage. She knew, what was withheld from her husband, of the unprovoked murder of Sheehy-Skeffington. She had seen the casualty lists. Nora and Ina returned from the north to find her weeping over the false report of James's death. She was cheered by Roderick's reappearance. He had given the military the name of Robert Carney and they let him go. He was under sixteen. Then began the interplay of hope and fear, as the smoke of burning Dublin slowly cleared below the brilliant green of the mountain slopes. Always came the question, after every visit she was allowed, would they shoot a wounded man?

On Tuesday May 9 Connolly was propped up in bed and court martialled while unable to move. He rejected a line of defence which his Counsel suggested to him but which he considered unworthy, and contented himself with rebutting accusations of ill-treating prisoners. This incredible ceremony over, he was allowed a visit from Lillie and Nora. It was only with Nora he could talk politics, and one of his first questions showed how his thoughts were still on his own. "Have you seen any socialist papers?" he asked her. She had not. "They will never understand why I am here," he remarked. "They will all forget I am an Irishman."[1]

---

[1] *Voice of Labour*, May 10, 1919. This is the earliest account of this conversation, which was subsequently given an entirely different cast. The altered form was challenged by Cathal O'Shannon as improbable and mis-remembered through emotion. As given here it is perfectly comprehensible and in fact completely rebuts the claim that Connolly abandoned his socialism, which was based on the wrongly transcribed form.

Connolly knew that the cross-channel socialists did not understand the national question. In an imperialist country the criterion of a good socialist was his willingness to stand up against national prejudices for the brotherhood of man. It was easy to forget (and most had not even understood) that for an Irishman the freedom of his own country was a precondition of his taking such a stand.

Next day Dillon was interested enough to cross to London with the object of demanding a cessation of the executions. He withdrew a motion to this effect on receiving a solemn assurance that there would be no more shootings until there had been a full debate. Father Aloysius saw Connolly that day, but found him exhausted and feverish. On Thursday he was better. For the first time since he left Liberty Hall he fell into a natural sleep. His great recuperative powers were coming into play. It was then that his captors exercised that punctilious delicacy which graces the acts of high authority. They awoke him from his sleep at midnight with the information that he was to be shot at dawn. Lillie and Nora were summoned. To Nora he surreptitiously slipped his last statement made at the court martial, which was confined to justifying the rising and denying allegations of ill-treatment of prisoners. This point seems to have rankled with Connolly.

"I do not wish to make any defence except against charges of wanton cruelty to prisoners," he had told the court martial. . . . "We went out to break the connection between this country and the British Empire, and to establish an Irish Republic. We believed that the call we then issued to the people of Ireland, was a nobler call, in a holier cause, than any call issued to them during this war, having any connection with the war. We succeeded in proving that Irishmen are ready to die endeavouring to win for Ireland those national rights which the British Government has been asking them to die to win for Belgium. As long as that remains the case, the cause of Irish freedom is safe.

"Believing that the British Government has no right in

Ireland, never had any right in Ireland, and never can have any right in Ireland, the presence, in any one generation of Irishmen, of even a respectable minority, ready to die to affirm that truth, makes that Government for ever a usurpation and a crime against human progress.

"I personally thank God that I have lived to see the day when thousands of Irish men and boys, and hundreds of Irish women and girls, were ready to affirm that truth, and to attest it with their lives if need be."

This statement is not a political testament, as some have sought to make it, but an answer to specific charges brought by the prosecution at the court martial. It is therefore completely mistaken to complain that it makes no reference to socialism, and absurd to argue that such an omission indicates that during the last few days of his life, at the very point where its logic culminated in martyrdom, Connolly shed his socialist convictions. His demand for socialist newspapers just *after* the court martial is indeed a chronological refutation of any such claim based on the court martial statement.

When his wife and daughter left, little time remained to him. Father Aloysius arrived, heard his confession and administered the rites of the Catholic Church. The priest accompanied him to Kilmainham Jail. First they shot Sean MacDermott, crippled with arthritis and unable to walk. Connolly they carried in a stretcher and set in a chair. Would he say a prayer for his executioners, asked the priest. "I will say a prayer for all brave men who do their duty according to their lights," he replied. "He was the bravest man I have ever known," said surgeon Tobin. He gripped the sides of the chair to steady himself, and held his head high waiting for the volley.

His execution shocked the labour movement of the world, although Connolly was right in expecting little comprehension. In Glasgow, Tom Johnston remembered the mild gentlemanly lecturer and declared: "It remains a mystery." The Swiss Jeanneret, one of the S.D.F. men with whom Connolly used to lodge during visits to Edinburgh, expressed the rank-and-file opinion in similar words. How could the great socialist agitator have "got mixed up in that Sinn Fein business?" Leslie was prostrated with grief. A visitor from the U.S.A. found him weeping and bitterly reproaching himself for persuading Connolly to return to Ireland.

There was an attempt at a protest meeting in Birmingham. But the war was at its height. Gallacher and MacLean were in jail. Socialist morale was at its nadir. T. A. Jackson read the news in the evening paper and dazedly walked the streets of Leeds till it was time to hold a meeting on the Town Hall steps. It was the most fiery speech of his life. He was one of the very few who did understand.

In America too there was misunderstanding for a time. Berger could not see why Connolly should go down in a "skirmish". The De Leonites jumped in to damn the apostate to nationalism. Yet Lenin, whose party was to lead two great revolutions within the next eighteen months, rebuked all who belittled the rising. "Whoever expects a 'pure' social revolution will never live to see it. . . . The misfortune of the Irish was that they rose prematurely, when the European revolt of the proletariat had not yet matured." Lenin saw the rising as a natural consequence of the imperialist war against which he had launched his famous slogan. "Owing to the crisis of imperialism," he declared, "flames of national revolt have burst out in the colonies *and* in Europe." He brushed aside Radek's hesitations. Here was a great popular revolt of the petty-bourgeoisie and a part of the working-class—despite its lack of "economic content".

The rising transformed the situation in Ireland. In May, Bishop O'Dwyer denounced the government terror. Within two months the signatories of the proclamation had taken their places alongside Tone and Emmet. Their example shook the conscience of the Irish people, and the resurgent national movement merged with the democratic upsurge throughout Europe and culminated in the great anti-conscription general strike of April 1918. Had Connolly been able to leave behind him a scientific socialist party, it is possible that

1918–22 would have seen the completion of the struggle for Irish independence. The decimation of the movement in the south, however, handed the leadership and initiative to the I.L.P. socialists of the north, who acted honourably according to their lights, but lacked Connolly's vision in the national question. From this resulted a disorientation and a failure to utilise Labour's position as the *parti des fusillés*. But the set-backs which were later endured must never blind the eyes to the immensity of the transformation that was wrought, and the way in which Connolly engraved socialism indelibly on the national life of Ireland.

EPILOGUE

Throughout Ireland are streets, houses and here and there a fine hospital, called after James Connolly. Respect for his memory is universal. He is venerated as becomes a national martyr. But as a thinker he is little understood. The most diverse estimations exist side by side. Indeed, of all the leaders of 1916 he alone remains a figure of controversy as acute as in his lifetime.

How is his significance to be assessed? It has two related aspects, one for Ireland, the other for the international working-class movement.

The juxtaposition of two ideas, socialism and national independence, is at the heart of Connolly's contribution to Irish history. At the outset he advanced the view that "the two currents of revolutionary thought in Ireland, the socialist and the national, were not antagonistic but complementary". This had been Marx's opinion. But it was not the majority view among Irish Socialists, many of whom had been affected by the cosmopolitanising influences of British craft unionism.

It was Connolly's first great service to Ireland that he rallied the scattered Marxian elements and built a single organisation, the I.S.R.P., based on revolutionary social-democracy. Essential to this was the conception that Irish socialism was a *native* growth, arising from the necessities of the class struggle as it developed through Irish history.

Connolly held that the national revolution was a prerequisite of the socialist revolution. But he did not arrive easily at a clear conception of their mutual relationship. At first he was inclined to *identify* them. Later he distinguished them as the political and economic *aspects* of one process. Finally he reached the conclusion that they were two stages of one democratic reorganisation of society, each involving economic changes which it was the function of political change to promote. This is the significance of his phrase, "the first stage of freedom".

It is therefore not sufficient for a man to hold up a red banner, call himself a "socialist" and then claim the paternity of Connolly. Connolly distinguished three trends in Irish socialism. His own, socialist republicanism, regarded national independence as a primary goal. The other two, really varieties of one, he condemned as opportunist. Belfast socialists tended to capitulate to sectarian feeling, push the national question out of sight, and concentrate on "gas and water socialism" and the trade union movement. This made them respected "public figures" but left the working class substantially where it was. The same tendency in Dublin took the form of admitting the importance of the national liberation struggle, but trying to present socialist tasks separately, as if the two had no connection in actually existing conditions. This was to hand over leadership of the national struggle to the bourgeoisie.

The near half-century's controversy about Connolly has revolved round these points. How did it come about that an international socialist gave up his life and his prospect of seeing socialism in his lifetime for the sake of a national revolution? Until this question is answered he cannot be canonised and buried with the others. But it cannot be answered without obvious implications for future practice. The right pronounces, "He was an Irishman." The ultra-left rejoins, "He abandoned 'socialism'." Two contrary standpoints make a common assertion. The confusion is possible because Connolly is too often seen as an individual, not as the representative of a trend. That trend, despite its minority position in Ireland, in Connolly's day as in our own, corresponds to the world-historical mainstream of scientific socialist thought.

Until the epoch of imperialism the possibility of a socialist participating in a national revolution would never have been questioned. That Connolly held to the classical position is one of his claims to greatness. Non-republican socialism, of the right, or the ultra-left, is inspired from one common ideological source—British imperialism.

The history of Connolly's ideas in Ireland after his death

provides many examples of attempts to disconnect the two aspects of his teaching, to make him a "pure" nationalist, or a "pure" socialist. Aodh de Blacam and the Countess Markiewicz attempted the first. His own followers too, frequently tried the second, under the influence of the "great lie" of modern Irish history, namely, that the 1921 (partition) settlement completed the national revolution in Ireland and thus freed the workers to make their own revolution. Connolly had, indeed, already expressed himself on this subject. He believed that partition "as long as it lasted" would bar the way to working-class progress.

The same issue dominated the ill-fated Republican Congress during the thirties, almost evenly balanced between the demand for "The Republic" and "The Workers' Republic". Corpses can be revived no more in politics than in medicine, except perhaps when they have only just died. What was wanted, however, was certainly the *kind of republic*, a national democratic republic, that was fought for in 1916. But that being so, had the Republican Congress any justification at all? Both sides claimed Connolly. And what do we see? An economist labour movement claiming his socialism, and a paramilitary republican movement claiming his nationalism. Neither has got Connolly. If they understood him they would be striving for some approach to unity, in whatever form present conditions prescribe. And each would have to modify its practice for the sake of unity.

Attempts have been made to invoke Connolly's posthumous blessing on the treaty of 1921 and the Free State. What he foresaw of such developments he unconditionally condemned. What his tactics would have been to meet a *fait accompli* is pure guesswork. Similarly he has been described, by both friends and foes, as a "Communist". It was particularly unfortunate that during the thirties a reprint of his articles in *The Harp* appeared in a Dublin paper with the word "Communism" substituted for the original "Socialism". It should be said that the Communists were not responsible for this. But an error due to faulty editing became perpetuated by further quotation. It is a compliment to Connolly that every new socialist or republican development has seemed to require his *imprimatur*.

The issue of national independence (political and economic) is the crux of Irish politics. If, as was Connolly's mature and considered opinion, the national revolution takes precedence, then the working class is not the only revolutionary class. It may be the "only *incorruptible* inheritor" of the fight for Irish freedom, but it is not the sole legatee. It can expect allies, even if some of them are temporary, and the question arises of who they shall be. The evolution of Connolly's thought on this subject exactly corresponds to that on the relation between the two revolutions. While he identified them, he sought to make all republicans socialists. Then, during his syndicalist days, the conception of "seizing and holding" the means of production ran parallel with political Sinn Fein. His last writings, however, show that, especially after January 1916, he was adumbrating the conception of the National Front, or alliance of the forces making for liberation. Their victory would lead to the establishment of a national revolutionary government, resisting imperialism without, and suppressing its agents within the country. This was the "first stage of freedom". Before he died he had advanced far beyond the formulations in *Labour in Irish History*. During this period those capitalists who accepted the National State were to be left in possession of their capital. Connolly had recognised the existence of what would now be called a "national-bourgeoisie".

A further allied question was that of relations between the British and Irish labour movements. This he answered by advocating complete independence bridged by fraternal interchange. The Labour leaders in Britain could never understand why he advocated Irish independence but at the same time objected to their support for the Irish parliamentary party. They did not distinguish between its national and social aspects, still less appreciate that British working-class support for the national movements of oppressed countries has its *ultimate* foundation in *proletarian* internationalism. Their support for the Redmondites was a convenient parliamentary arrangement. Need they look more deeply than that? Their interest in Ireland evaporated with the departure of their parliamentary allies.

Connolly had many bitter things to say of chauvinism within the British working-class movement. Ireland is Britain's oldest colony. Therefore chauvinism in relation to Ireland is stronger, deeper, more subtle and *less conscious* than to any other occupied territory. The leaders of British Labour would acclaim the Irishman who mounted their platform to win them exiles' votes. That was international solidarity. That Irishman had shown he was "advanced". And indeed he had–far more than the leaders appreciated. But to them the Irishman's own struggles were for himself alone. Sinn Fein was invented in England not in Ireland. It was forced upon an island looking for co-operation. Least of all did Labour reformism tell the English workers the truth that they must be told, namely, that the separation of Ireland is required for the sake of *English* democracy.

Do traces of this chauvinism survive today? Certainly today the Irish question is still vital to the class struggle in Britain, and it is the *English* workers above all who need to understand it. Marx in his day believed that the decisive blow against the English ruling classes could not be struck in England, but only in Ireland. Connolly in 1916 endeavoured to put the same principle into action. In 1919–21 Irish resistance rocked the whole British social system, the prospect of a junction between the democratic forces of the two countries filling British reaction with terror. There may even now be more content in Marx's principle than is widely believed.

As has been indicated, Connolly went through three distinct phases of political thought; the first social-democratic, the second broadly syndicalist, and the third foreshadowing some of the most modern conceptions of scientific socialism. He wrote little about his own mental evolution. Consequently he has been held by some writers to have occupied a static position. He was not primarily a theoretician. He lacked the philosophical equipment for the fine analysis of concepts. He was a well-read and acute expositor rather than an innovator, except in his great last period when the sheer weight of responsibility evoked an entirely fresh development of his genius.

But there is another reason why he dwelt little on his own political history. It would seem superfluous, since it was common to others. He took it for granted. It was a part of the development of the world labour movement, against the backcloth of which it must be seen and understood.

The period from his joining the Socialist League in 1889 to his death before the imperial firing squad in 1916, corresponds almost exactly to the duration of the Second International. Nominally based on Marxism, the International developed a theoretical trend known as "revisionism" which expressed itself politically as "reformism". The central Marxist principle which was "revised" was that of the State as the organ of class power. The revisionist thesis that the State was above classes justified alike Millerand's coalitionism, Glasier's municipal socialism, and Hyndman's "strong navy". It was Lenin who exposed the essence of revisionism and related it to the existence in imperialist countries of a section of the working class who were supporting their capitalist States against the colonial peoples. The class struggle was, so to speak, exorcised by exportation.

As yet there existed no socialist parties in colonial countries. But the revisionists did not have it all their own way. Two trends developed in the International, the revolutionary and the reformist, the left and the right. But until Lenin's clarification of the theoretical issue, the left directed its fire against reformist policies without understanding their basis. The anti-reformist wing thus evolved through a process of ceaseless experimentation, with sectish breakaways and subsequent reamalgamations, ultra-revolutionism offset by conciliations, all arising from the constant search for the lost revolutionary principle, the class character of the State.

It is from this standpoint that Connolly's second, De Leonist or syndicalist, period must be understood. Connolly typified all that was best within the revolutionary wing of the

International. He displayed its splendid reckless militancy. He shared its frequent theoretical confusion. What marked him out as one of its greatest was his instant recognition of revolutionary *practice*. "Less theorising," he may have said, but he added: "more fighting." It was this intense practicality of Connolly which saved him from the inverted chauvinism of Rosa Luxemburg, and led him into conflict with De Leon on wages, marriage, the Church and the race-associations. Some of this was pure proletarian horse-sense. But there was also the solid political training of the old Socialist League.

James Connolly was one of the most important figures of what may be called the middle stage of the world labour movement. He was one of the first working-class intellectuals. He was one of the most tireless and dedicated socialist workers who ever lived. He is still the subject of controversy because the issues he raised are still alive. Revisionism and reformism still dominate the labour movement of the west, though many think the sands are now running out. In Ireland they take just those forms Connolly castigated. At the same time, nothing would be more foolish than to take his writings as a Bible for quotation and exegesis. To canonise is to kill. He must be understood, estimated, and advanced from. But it is to be hoped that the Irish labour movement will always honour its greatest leader, thinker, and hero. And perhaps England too, which has somewhat neglected him, may draw on his example in the times that lie ahead.

BIBLIOGRAPHY

No attempt has been made to compile an exhaustive bibliography, but the main sources for each chapter are indicated below.

BIOGRAPHIES OF CONNOLLY

1. Desmond Ryan, *James Connolly*, London 1924.
2. R. M. Fox, *Connolly the Forerunner*.
3. Nora Connolly O'Brien, *Portrait of a Rebel Father*, Dublin, 1935.
4. Noélle Davies, *Connolly of Ireland*, Caer yn Arfon, 1936.
5. P. Quinlan. Series of reminiscences of Connolly in the New York *Monitor*, 1932.
6. MS. Life of Connolly by H. Levinson, New York.

GENERAL HISTORICAL WORKS FOR THE PERIOD

1. T. A. Jackson, *Ireland Her Own*, London, 1947.
2. D. Macardle, *The Irish Republic*, London, 1938.
3. J. D. Clarkson, *Labour and Nationalism in Ireland*, London, 1925.
4. R. M. Henry, *The Evolution of Sinn Fein*, Dublin, n.d.
5. W. P. Ryan, *The Irish Labour Movement*, Dublin, n.d.
6. P. S. O'Hegarty, *Ireland under the Union*, London, 1952.

Numerous commemorative articles, of very various value, are to be found in the files of *An Poblacht, Irish Press, Voice of Labour, Irishman*, and other publications of the Labour and Republican movement. Some contain useful detail, but others are derived from unreliable secondary sources.

PRINCIPAL SOURCES FOR SEPARATE CHAPTERS
Chapter I

1. J. E. Handley, *The Irish in Scotland*, Cork, 1945.
2. —— *The Irish in Modern Scotland*, Cork, 1947.
3. H. M. Lee, *History of the Social Democratic Federation*, London.
4. Records in Registrar-General's Office, Edinburgh.
5. Edinburgh City Archives (Town Clerk's Office).
6. *The Blue Blanket* (magazine), Edinburgh.

7. Edinburgh Directories, etc., in Edinburgh Room, Public Library.
8. Files of *The Scotsman, Edinburgh Evening News, Weekly People*.
9. Recollections of John Mullery, J. Conlon and other associates of Connolly and Leslie.
10. For Monaghan: *Clogher Record*, 1954, Matheson's *Irish Names* and Hearth Money records in Irish National Library.
11. *Liberty*, March 1952, Dublin.

Chapter II

1. Military records in Public Record Office, London.
2. Edinburgh City Council Minutes (Town Clerk's Office).
3. Records in Registrar-General's Office, Edinburgh.
4. Letters of James Connolly to Lillie Reynolds.
5. Dundee Directory, Perth Directory.
6. Diocesan Records, Dunkeld.
7. Barry O'Brien, *Life of Parnell*, London, 1910.
8. Brian O'Neill, *War for the Land in Ireland*, London, 1934.
9. Files of *Irish Nation, Justice, Commonweal, Dundee Free Press*.
10. Recollections of J. Mullery.

Chapter III

1. Barry O'Brien, *Life of Parnell*.
2. Michael Davitt, *Fall of Feudalism in Ireland*, London, 1904.
3. John Leslie, *The Present Position of the Irish Question*, London, 1894.
4. Files of *Justice, Labour Leader, Scotsman, Labour World, Leith Pilot*.
5. Minutes of Edinburgh Trades Council.
6. Minutes Edinburgh City Council (Town Clerk's Office).
7. Recollections of Colon, Geddes.
8. John Leslie, *Proletarian Lays and Lyrics*, London, 1907.
9. MS. reminiscences of J. Gilray (Edinburgh I.L.P.).

Chapter IV

1. Files of *Justice, Labour Leader, Edinburgh Labour Chronicle, Scotsman, Leith Pilot.*
2. Minutes of Edinburgh Trades Council.
3. J. Connell in *Voice of Labour*, Dublin, June 7, 1924.
4. Recollections of Anna Munro.

Chapter V

1. Files of *Justice, Labour Leader, Evening Telegraph* (Dublin), *Waterford News, Shan Van Vocht, United Ireland.*
2. Maud Gonne, *Servant of the Queen*, London, 1932.
3. Desmond Ryan (Ed.), *Socialism and Nationalism* (reprints of Connolly's writings), Dublin, 1948 (I.S.R.P. Manifesto, etc.).
4. Minutes of Celtic Literary Society, Nat. Lib., Dublin.
5. E. Milligan, *Reminiscences of Connolly, Irish Freedom*, London, 1943.
6. Recollections of Mr. Justice Porter (S. Porter), J. Mullery, J. Carolan, Mrs. O'Farrell.
7. G. O'Connor (Sean MacGiollarnath, J. Forde), pamphlet *James Connolly*, based on Lyng's recollections, 1917.

Chapter VI

1. Maud Gonne, *Servant of the Queen.*
2. *Irlande Libre* (one copy of first number in Bibliothèque Nationale, Paris).
3. Files of *Weekly People* (N.Y.), *United Ireland, Freeman's Journal, Kerry Evening News, Justice, Labour Leader.*
4. Articles in *Irish Opinion,* (1918-20).

Chapter VII

1. Desmond Ryan (Ed.), *Socialism and Nationalism.*
2. —— (Ed.) *Labour and Easter Week.*
3. —— (Ed.) *The Workers' Republic.*
4. Maud Gonne, *Servant of the Queen.*

5. Records in Registrar-General's Office, Edinburgh.
6. Files of *Weekly People, United Irishman* (Dublin), *Cork Constitution, Evening Herald* (Dublin), *Freeman's Journal, Justice, Labour Leader, Clarion.*
7. Recollections of J. Mullery.

Chapter VIII

1. International Socialist Congress, Paris (Unofficial record, Brit. Mus.).
2. Reports of S.D.F. Conference (Marx Memorial Library, London).
3. J. Deighan, *Connolly in Salford, Irish Democrat*, London, June/August 1954.
4. Minutes of Dublin Trades Council.
5. Files of *Justice, Clarion, Labour Leader, Socialist* (Edinburgh), *United Irishman, Salford Reporter.*
6. Recollections of T. A. Jackson, L. Cotton, F. Newell.

Chapter IX

1. Symposium (Kuhn, Katz, Olive Johnson), *Daniel De Leon, the Man and His Work*, New York, 1934.
2. *Socialist Labour Party, 1890–1930*, New York, 1931.
3. Desmond Ryan (Ed.) Selections (V. Bibliog. Ch. 7).
4. Files of *Socialist, Justice, Labour Leader, Clarion, Weekly People, Evening Herald, United Irishman.*
5. Reports of S.D.F. Conferences.
6. Minutes of Dublin Trades Council.
7. Tom Bell, *Pioneering Days*, London, 1934.
8. Recollections of William Paul, G. Geddes, T. Drummond, J. Mullery, J. J. Lyng, T. A. Jackson, Frank Jackson, L. Cotton.

Chapter X

1. Symposium, *Daniel De Leon.*
2. Files of *Weekly People, Socialist.*

3. Recollections of T. Humes, J. Mullery, J. J. Lyng, J. Geddes.
4. Correspondence between Connolly and J. Mullery.

Chapter XI

1. E. Gurley Flynn, *I Speak My Own Piece*, New York, 1955.
2. Levinson manuscript.
3. De Leon Symposium.
4. Lozowsky, *Marx on Trade Unions*, London, 1935 (for Haman affair).
5. Files of *Weekly People, Daily People, Industrial Union Bulletin* (Chicago), *Il Proletario* (Philadelphia).
6. Recollections of E. G. Flynn, J. J. Lyng.

Chapter XII

1. E. G. Flynn, *I Speak My Own Piece.*
2. Files of *Weekly People, New York Evening Call, The Harp, Industrial Union Bulletin, Irish Peasant.*

Chapter XIII

1. James Connolly, *Labour, Nationality and Religion*, Dublin, 1910.
2. ——*Labour in Irish History*, Dublin, 1910.
3. ——*Socialism Made Easy*, Chicago, 1909.
4. E. G. Flynn, *I Speak My Own Piece.*
5. George O'Brien, *Economic History of Ireland in the 18th Century*, Dublin, 1918.
6. —— *Economic History of Ireland from the Union to the Famine*, Dublin, 1921.
7. *Watchford of Labour*, Dublin, January 17, 1920 (for Connolly's letter to W. O'Brien, May 24, 1909).
8. Recollections of O'Brien-Hishon.
9. Posthumous notes of J. Connolly on *Socialism and Religion* in *The Communist Review*, 1924.
10. Reports of Irish Trade Union Congress.

11. Files of *New York Evening Call, New Castle Free Press* (Pa.), *The Harp, The Nation, Weekly People.*
12. *Liberty* (Dublin), April/May 1950.

Chapter XIV

1. Files of *Justice, Forward* (Glasgow), *Irish Times, Irish Nation, Irish Independent, Evening Herald, Cork Free Press, Sinn Fein.*
2. Minutes of Dublin Trades Council.
3. Recollections of Tom Johnson (Belfast), W. Travers, Mrs. O'Shea, Seamus McGowan.

Chapter XV

1. Reports of Irish T.U.C.
2. Clarkson, *Labour and Nationalism in Ireland.*
3. Files of *Forward, Irish Worker* (Dublin), *Sinn Fein* (Dublin), *Belfast Telegraph, Irish News* (Belfast), *Dundalk Democrat, Wexford Free Press.*
4. *Report of Enquiry into Belfast Riots 1857*, S.P.R., Brit. Mus.
5. *Attempt to Smash the Transport Union*, I.T.G.W.U., Dublin, 1924.
6. Correspondence between Connolly and Mrs. T. Johnson.
7. Account Book of Textile Workers' Union.
8. Minutes of Dublin Trades Council.
9. C. O'Shannon, "Connolly in Belfast", in *Liberty*, December, 1954.
10. Recollections of S. Hazlett, A. Bell, S. Geddis, D. McDevitt, J. McConnell, T. Johnson, Mrs. T. Johnson.

Chapter XVI

1. Reports of Irish T.U.C.
2. Files of *Irish Worker, Forward, Belfast Telegraph, Northern Whig, Daily Herald, Catholic Times, Cork Examiner, Irish News, Sinn Fein, Justice.*
3. John Redmond, *Home Rule*, London, 1912.
4. Recollections of S. Geddis, T. Johnson, Mrs. T. Johnson.

5. *Attempt to smash the Transport Union,* (V. Bibliog. Ch. 15, 5).
6. James Connolly, *Reconquest of Ireland,* Dublin, 1915.

Chapter XVII

1. A. Wright, *Disturbed Dublin,* London, 1914.
2. Minutes of Dublin Trades Council.
3. Reports of Irish T.U.C.
4. Files of *Daily Herald, Irish Worker, Justice, Sinn Fein, Irish News, Irish Times, Daily Citizen.*
5. Sean O'Casey (P. O'Cathasaigh), *The Story of the Irish Citizen Army,* Dublin, 1919.
6. R. M. Fox, *History of the Irish Citizen Army,* Dublin, 1943.
7. —— *Jim Larkin,* London, 1957.
8. R. Monteith, *Casement's Last Adventure,* Dublin, 1953.

Chapter XVIII

1. Fox and O'Casey on Citizen Army (V. Bibliog. Ch. 17, 5 and 6).
2. Irish T.U.C. Reports.
3. D. Gwynn, *History of Partition,* Dublin, 1950.
4. F. Gallagher, *The Indivisible Island,* Dublin, 1957.
5. *Forward, Irish Worker, Daily Herald, Irish Freedom.*
6. Minutes of Dublin Trades Council.
7. Bulmer Hobson, *Short History of the Volunteers.*
8. Montgomery Hyde, *Carson,* London, 1953.

Chapter XIX

1. O'Shannon, *Connolly in Belfast* (V. Bibliog. Ch. 15, 9).
2. W. O'Brien, "Introduction" to *Labour and Easter Week,* D. Ryan, (Ed.).
3. Diarmuid Lynch, *The I.R.B. and the 1916 Insurrection,* Cork, 1957.
4. Reports of Irish T.U.C.
5. Minutes of Dublin Trades Council.
6. R. Monteith, *Casement's Last Adventure.*

7. Files of *Irish Worker, Daily Herald, Justice, Forward, Dublin Evening Mail, Sinn Fein, Irish Freedom.*
8. *The Attempt to smash the Transport Union* (V. Bibliog. Ch. 15,5).

Chapter XX

1. Desmond Ryan, *The Rising*, Dublin, 1949
2. Diarmuid Lynch, *The I.R.B. and the 1916 Insurrection.*
3. P. S. O'Hegarty, *The Victory of Sinn Fein*, Dublin, 1924.
4. Minutes of Dublin Trades Council.
5. Nora Connolly-O'Brien, *The Unbroken Tradition*, New York, 1918.
6. Files of *Fianna* (Dublin), *Cumann na mBan* (Dublin), *Evening Herald, Workers' Republic* (Dublin), *Evening Mail, The Spark* (Dublin), *Nationality* (Dublin), *Forward.*

Chapter XXI

1. Desmond Ryan, *The Rising.*
2. Diarmuid Lynch, *The I.R.B. and the 1916 Insurrection.*
3. R. Monteith, *Casement's Last Adventure.*
4. Brian O'Neill, *Easter Week*, London, 1936.
5. *Sinn Fein Rebellion Handbook, Weekly Irish Times*, Dublin, 1916.
6. D. Ryan, *The Man Called Pearse*, Dublin, 1923.
7. R. M. Fox, *History of the Irish Citizen Army.*
8. W. B. Wells and N. Marlowe, *History of the Irish Rebellion of 1916*, Dublin, 1918.
9. S. O'Faolain, *Constance Markiewicz*, London, 1934.
10. S. O'Casey, *Story of the Irish Citizen Army.*
11. Files of *Irish Nation, Freeman's Journal, Irish Catholic* (Dublin), *The Socialist* (Glasgow), *Scotsman, Cork Examiner, Workers' Republic, Forward, Justice.*
12. Nora Connolly-O'Brien, *The Unbroken Tradition.*
13. Report of Royal Commission on the Rebellion in Ireland, Cd. 8311 (1916), S.P.R. Brit. Mus.
14. Dr. Aloysius, *Capuchin Annual*, 1942.
15. Report of Conference of British Socialist Party, 1916.

INDEX

Aberdeen, 133, 315, 317
Agrarian Crisis, 33, 72, 101
Albert Hall Meeting, 327
All for Ireland Movement, 234, 257
Aloysius, Father, 417, 418, 421, 422
American Federation of Labour, 172, 173, 181, 186, 189, 193, 208, 209, 235
Anarchism, 47, 245
Ancient Order of Hibernians; Board of Erin; 234, 255, 256, 257, 290, 306, 310, 313, 319, 323, 324, 328, 329, 334, 336, 342; American Alliance, 361, 410
Anti-Semitism, 14, 108, 156
Anlore, 21
Argentina, 230
Arizona, 199
Armour, Rev. J. B., 286
Askwith, Sir G., 316, 317
Asquith, H. H., 336, 340, 341, 351, 362, 408
Atheism, 173, 195, 237
Australia, 229, 230, 330
Aveling, Edward and Eleanor, 36, 38, 68, 84, 101, 177
Axe to the Root, 218, 229

Bachelor's Walk, 73, 350
Bakunin, M., 72, 172, 173, 190, 207, 218, 222, 244
Balfour, J. A., 284
Ballybay, 22
Ballymena, 303
Bantry, Battle of, 254
Barnes, George, 344
Barry, Tadhg, 370
Bax, Belfort, 177, 181
Beaslai, Piaras, 393
Bebel, August, 169, 175, 179, 181
Belfast, 73, 87, 111, 125, 156, 246, 248, 249, 257, 258, 259, 260, 318, 321, 327, 336, 337, 342, 354, 355, 385; Connolly in, 264–283, 284–304, 328, 335, 340–350, 378; Falls Road, 267, 270, 290, 296, 297; history of, 266–271; Socialist pioneers, 73, 87, 113; Trades Council, 265, 270, 272; 289
Bell, Thomas, 160, 162, 166, 356, 368
Belloc, H., 294, 306
Bennett, Louie, 357, 374, 378
Berger, Louis, 233, 235, 423
Birmingham, 131, 312, 317, 326, 329, 423
Birrell, Augustine, 308, 419
Black Flags, 27, 90, 261

Blane, Alexander, 79
Blatchford, Robert, 120, 121, 331, 355
Bodenstown, 106, 348, 373
Boer War, 20, 113–118, 121–125
Bohn, F., 189, 201, 205, 222, 239
Boston, Mass., 149, 227, 230
Bower, Fred, 321, 369
Boyle, Bridget, 16, 151
Boyle, Owen, 16, 29
Bradshawe, W. H., 111, 113, 157, 254
Brady, Alice, 335
Brady, Chris, 409
Brann, Monsignor, 212
Brennan, J., 263
Brewers' Union, U.S.A.; 189, 194
British Socialist Party, 278, 308, 331, 337, 356, 408
Bronx, 205
Brugha, Cathal, 407
Buffalo, N.Y., 150, 227
Builder's Labourer's Union (*see* United Labourers' Union),
Bulley, W. S., 350
"Bummery", the, 228, 229
Burke, J. J., 387, 389
Burns Laird Line, 266, 379
Byrne, James, Dublin, 309, 310, 311, 323, 358
Byrne, James, Dun Laoghaire, 323

Cahirciveen, 102, 235
California, 140, 203
Campbell, D. R., 249, 265, 282, 296, 316, 321
Carlin, Thomas, 169
Carney, Jack, 296
Carney, Winifred, 290, 292, 296, 297, 414, 415
Carolan, J., 24, 80, 113, 254
Carpenter, W., 234, 262
Carrickmacross, 235
Carson, Edward, 285, 293, 297, 305, 308, 340, 350
Cartels, 126
Casement, Sir Roger, 328, 386, 406, 408
Castlebar, 26, 235
Castledawson, 290
Catholic Times, 294
Ceannt, Eamonn, 231, 257, 274, 359, 360, 389, 407, 413, 419
Celtic literary societies, 73
Chamberlain, Joseph, 117, 248
Chartism, 244, 270
Chatterton, Joseph, 86

Chicago, 177, 189, 210, 227, 229, 230, 233, 237

Childers, Erskine, 350

Christian Socialism, 226, 237

Churchill, Winston, 286

Clann na Gael, 365, 373, 392, 394

Clarion, 57, 120, 144, 331, 355

Clarion Scouts, 250

Clarke, Tom, 327, 329, 358, 360, 362, 376, 407, 410, 413, 416, 419

"Clear-cuts", 134, 142, 160

Clones, 21

Clonmel, 282, 288

Clydebank, 166

Cobh (temporarily known as Queenstown), 24, 102, 249, 254, 282, 301

Colbert, Con, 419

Colorado, 151, 193

Communism, 244, 245, 427

Communist Manifesto, 1848, 101, 218, 220, 236, 244, 245, 398

Conlon, J., 160

Connell, James, author of "The Red Flag", 49, 54, 163

Connolly, Aideen, 71, 183

Connolly, Fiona, 205

Connolly, Ina, 86, 183, 312, 420

Connolly, James, Askwith Enquiry, 316; anti-conscription meeting, 383; Belfast, 258, 264-283, 284-304, 312; Belloc debate, 294; birth, 17; Chile, 69; closes port of Dublin, 326; cobbler, 64-67; controversy with De Leon, 173-182, 209; disappearance, 387; departure for U.S.A., 145, 166; departure from U.S.A., 238; Dublin lock-out, 305-339; Dublin lock-out trial, 309; Dublin Trades Council, 137, 369, 372, 375, 382, 385, 397; elected to N.E.C. American S.L.P., 197; enlistment, 20; *Erin's Hope*, 87; execution, 422; first writings, 45, 46; hunger strike, 312; I.C.A. mobilisation, 401; *Ireland for the Irish*, 81; Irish Labour Party, 282, 301; Irish Socialist Unity, 233; Italian language, 185; Italians in U.S., 196; I.W.W. organiser, 204; I.W.W. propaganda leagues, 218; Kerry, 101-102; *Labour in Irish History*, 240-245; *Labour, Nationality and Religion*, 240; *linen slaves of Belfast*, 293; marriage, 27, 31; Mellows, Liam, 368; mill-girls organised, 272; Monaghan legend, 22-25; Municipal elections: St. Giles, 58-64; Wood Quay, 137, 154-156; Dock, 295-296; *Nationalism and Socialism*, 84; New Castle Free Speech campaign, 238; *New Evangel*, 129; *Old Wine in New Bottles*, 338;

parentage, 16; Partition, 343; physical force, 115; playwright, 400; polemic with Walker, 259-261; poet, 162-163; Proclamation of Republic, 111-113; public speaking, 48, 56, 164, 166; rents protest, 95; resignation from I.S.R.P. leadership, 158; resignation from American S.L.P., 204; return to Ireland, 248; Secretary of S.S.F., 46; sickness, 336; *Socialism Made Easy*, 229; Socialist Labour Party, 166; Socialist Party Organiser, 233; South African War, 113-114; *The Harp*, 214-228; unemployed, 67-69, 79, 183-188; war, 361-364; *What is Our Programme?*, 380; *Workers' Republic*, 106, 372; wounded, 415; Yonkers Tramway Strike, 208

Connolly, John, Jr., 16, 17, 18, 28, 32, 46, 70, 301, 320; victimisation, 47

Connolly, John, Sr., 15, 28, 32, 107, 123

Connolly, Maire, 183

Connolly, Mary, *née* McGinn, 15, 33

Connolly, Mona, 43

Connolly, Mrs. Lillie, *see* Reynolds

Connolly, Nora, 22, 43, 183, 202, 230, 234, 258, 267, 318, 360, 376, 401, 403, 407, 420, 421

Connolly, Ruaidhre, 183, 420

Connolly, Sean, 410

Connolly, Thomas, 17

Cooney, Patrick, 226

Cooper Square, 209, 214, 229

Cooper Union, 147

Cork, 20, 87, 112, 123, 235, 249, 254, 301, 334, 370, 386, 397, 405, 406, 419; A.O.H., 310; *Free Press*, 257; National Society, 90; Trades Council, 138; Trade Union Congress, 299; Wolfe Tone Literary Society, 100

Cotton, Len, 108, 134, 136, 161

Coulter, George, 254

Coveney, Daniel, 250

Craigavon, 285

Crawford, Gerald, 158, 162

Crawford, Lindsay, 231

Crawford, Sean, 249

Criddle, Mrs., 321

Croydon Park, 309, 329, 335, 348, 350, 364, 372, 373, 377, 385

Cunningham-Grahame, 66, 355

Cumann na nGaedheal, 124

Cumann na mBan, 404

Curragh, Kildare, 26, 340, 343, 413

Curran, Peter, 68, 121

Daily Citizen, 313, 329, 355

Daily Herald, 248, 294, 308, 313, 318,

322, 325, 331, 337, 355
Daily Herald League, 319
Daily People, 198
Dalton, Edward, 372, 377
Daly, Edward, 419
Daly, John, 81, 88, 90, 121
Daly, P. T., 108, 138, 232, 235, 250, 258, 274, 275, 305, 347, 362, 363, 365, 367
Davitt, Michael, 19, 49, 51, 88, 274
Debs, Eugene, 189, 226
Deering, Mark, 20, 147
Defence of Realm Act (D.O.R.A.), 373, 401
De Leon, Daniel, 101; 107, 141, 142, 144, 145, 147, 149, 150, 156, 163, 168, 170, 173, 174–182, 189–192, 197, 199–207, 210–218, 223, 225–228, 242, 278, 337, 339, 357
De Leonism, 130, 133, 137, 140
  see Syndicalism
Democratic Party, U.S.A., 225
Denver, Col., 193
Derry, 156, 248, 254, 302, 327
Derrynane, 104
Despard, Mrs. C., 234
Detroit, 148
Devlin, Joe, 99, 254, 271, 303, 306, 323, 329, 340, 341, 361, 371, 372
Devoy, John, 373, 409
Dewsbury, 39, 161
Diamond Jubilee, 88, 89, 90
Dillon, John, 91, 98, 131, 421
Dogmatism, 156, 170, 174, 181, 215, 224, 236
Donnelly, J. E. C., 226, 233
Dorman, 73, 113, 121
Dowling, John, 249, 254, 255, 282, 301
Drummond, J., 160, 162, 165
Dublin, 26, 27, 142, 143, 154, 163, 165 to 167; 182, 183, 184, 231, 233, 246, 248, 250, 262, 264, 267, 287, 288, 289, 304, 355, 358, 408; Castle, 85, 90, 124, 308, 404, 405; Great Lock-out; 305–339; socialist pioneers, 27, 70, 72, 73, 236; Trades Council, 80, 87, 128, 137, 138, 232, 236; 249, 253, 264; 274, 305, 306, 308, 310, 315, 318, 323, 361, 364, 369, 372, 375, 379, 382, 385, 397
Dundalk, 113, 239, 273
Dundee, 16, 29, 30–32, 34, 71, 134, 164 to 165, 320
Dunkeld Diocese, 31, 40
Dun Laoghaire, 27, 249, 308, 325, 335, 413
Dyson, Will, 328

Easter Rising, 242, 352, 392, 399
Ebert, Justus, 190, 198, 205, 222, 238, 239
Economic determinism, 221, 225

Edinburgh, 36, 158, 159, 160; 164, 177, 301, 319, 320, 329; Anti-Irish feeling, 14; *and Leith Labour Chronicle*, 57, 58, 65, 68; *Catholic Herald*, 59; Connolly in, 11–21, 43–71, 107, 123; 140, 159, 164, 258, 423; East Meadows; 38, 44, 65, 165, 320; Flanagan Case, 40; Irish in, 11–15, 37, 39; socialist pioneers, 37, 133, 231; Trades Council, 46, 47, 66, 140
Elizabeth, N. J.; 188, 197, 204
Ellis Island, 182
Emmett, Robert, 99; 244, 400
Employers' Association, 305, 310
Engels, F.; 35, 55, 172; 173, 178, 220, 241, 244; *Origin of the Family*, 177, 241
Enniscorthy, 274
Erfurt Programme, 178; 191
Essex County; N. J.; 188, 192, 204
Evening Call, 222, 230
Evening Herald (Dublin); 307, 381

Fabians, 80, 99, 120, 142
"Fakirs", 134, 160
Falkirk, 70, 134; 142
Family, socialists and, 175
Famine, 23, 39, 101–105
Faneuil Hall, 149, 230
Farrell, William, 95
Farrell, Mrs. W.; 321
Farren, Thomas, 361; 372, 382
Fenians, 20, 52, 53, 72, 81, 89, 156, 244, 365; 375, 400
Fenit, 379
Fianna na h'Eireann, 368, 391
Figgis, Darrell, 328
Fitzgerald, M. D.; 168, 199
Fitzpatrick; T.; 73; 87
Flynn, Elizabeth Gurley, 194, 199; 227, 230
Flynn; Kathleen; 230
Flynn; Thomas, 199
Foodships, 313, 315, 317; 322
Foundrymen's Union, 277
Foran, J.; 349; 390
Forward (Glasgow); 46, 251, 259, 301, 318, 336, 337; 344; 347
Foster, W. Z.; 218, 221
Fox, R. M.; 24; 206
Freiligrath, F.; 55, 163
Friedberg, J.; 161
Fullerton, Father, 294

Gaelic; 110; 111; 225; 231, 241
Gaelic American, 226, 373
Gaelic Athletic Association, 275, 400
Gaelic League, 72, 86, 110, 318, 360
Gallacher, W.; 356, 423

Galway, 258, 386
Galway, Miss M.; 272
Geddes, Charles; 162, 163, 165, 182
General Post Office, Dublin; 411, 413, 414, 415
Germany, 352; 405
Ginnell, Lawrence, 419
Gladstone, W. E., 41
Glasier, Bruce, 51; 66; 120; 121; 126, 146
Glasgow; 133; 134; 144; 160; 162, 164; 236, 250, 317, 320; 327; 329; 333, 336, 337, 344, 356, 368, 391
Glasnevin, 287; 376
Glasse, Rev. W., 37; 55
Gompers, Samuel; 172
Gonne, Maud, 81; 88; 90; 98; 100, 103; 116–123; 231, 253
Good, J. W., 87
Gordon, Ellen; 296, 297; 301
Gore-Booth, Constance, see Markiewicz
Gosling, H.; 316, 321; 332
Grattan, H.; 243
Grayson; Victor, 278
Green, Alice Stopford; 240
Griffith, Arthur, 116, 123; 127; 157; 167; 224; 231; 232; 234; 257; 274; 277; 281; 319; 360; 361; 378; 380; 382; 406
Griffith; Teasdale, 285
Grimley; James; 296, 298
Gwynn, R. M.; 328
Guesde; Jules; 127

Haggerty, Father, 189; 236
Hardie, Keir, 27; 39; 49; 56; 66; 73; 88, 106, 120; 131; 134; 139; 310
Harland and Wolff's; 291
Harp, The, U.S.A., 214–228, 233; 234; 240; Dublin, 234; 235, 239–240
Harrington, Tim, 80; 89; 98; 109; 112
Haslett, Sam, 261
Haulbowline, 26
Haywood, W. D.; 189; 194; 212, 238
Head Line; 265; 329; 334; 337; 342
Healy; T. M.; 24, 316
Hearsey, J.; 250
Henderson; Arthur, 330, 332
Heriot-Watt Technical College; 159
Heuston; Sean; 419
Hickey; Dr.; 234
Hishon, see O'Brien-Hishon
Hoboken; N. J.; 204; 207; 210
Hobson, Bulmer, 350, 376, 382, 392, 404; 405
Hobson, J. A.; 143
Home Rule, 34, 41; 83; 246, 248, 286, 288, 293, 303, 305
Home Rule Bill, third, 235; 277; 279;

280; 282; 284; 296; 300; 340; 350
Home Rule Party; see Nationalist Party and United Irish League
House of Lords, 78; 285, 296, 298, 340
Hull, 317; 329
Humes, Thomas and Helen, 169
Hyde, Dr. Douglas, 110, 231
Hyndman, H. M.; 68; 78; 108; 134; 160; 164, 247; 261; 278, 408

Idaho, 193
Il Proletario, 194–196
Imperial Hotel, Dublin; 309, 414
Imperialism, 34; 143
Independent Labour Party, British; 27; 39; 45–46; 49; 59, 62; 66; 67; 96; 121, 135; 140; 142; 144; 248, 259, 278; 282, 295; 296; 385; 424
Independent Labour Party of Ireland, 279–283; 292; 296; 301; 323; 336; 354, 355; 357, 361, 385
India, 17; 135, 225
Inghinidhe na h'Eireann; 116; 121; 231; 253
Industrial Union Bulletin; 207; 208; 210–213; 215; 217; 218; 228
Industrial Workers of the World; 172; 189, 192–195; 205–213; 216; 222; 224; 226–228; 231; 232; 238; 242; 265; 338; propaganda leagues, 216
Insurance Act; 261; 282; 295; 301; 399
International (First), see International Workingmen's Association; Second; 430
Internationale, 37; 54; 215
International Socialist Review, 229; 235; 353
International Workingmen's Association; 72; 74; 172; 244; 253; Geneva Manifesto; 217
Irlande libre; 93
Irish Citizen Army, 324; 329; 330; 334; 341; 346; 348; 354; 362; 365; 369; 370; 372; 376; 377; 388; 390; 394; 399; 401; 403; 405; 409; 410
Irish Freedom, 274; 280; 281; 351; 367
Irish Independent; 307; 420
Irish Labour Party; 236, 258, 282, 287; 288, 346
Irish National League, 42; 50; 61
Irish Neutrality League; 361; 363; 364
Irish News, 303
Irish Peasant, 226
Irish Press, 21
Irish Republican Army, 409; 411, 416
Irish Republican Brotherhood, 116; 351; 358; 359; 362; 365–368; 377; 380; 386; 389; 391–393; 405; 407; see also Fenians

Irish Socialist Federation, 198, 202, 207, 209, 222, 230, 233, 238, 253
Irish Socialist Party, 232
Irish Socialist Republican Party, 72 to 92; 93–101; 111, 112–113, 118, 134–135, 138–139, 143, 147, 152, 157, 159, 161, 165–167, 199, 211, 212, 230, 248, 357, 425; foundation, 74; manifesto, 262 to 263; programme, 75–77
Irish Trades Union Congress, 50, 75, 138, 239, 258, 282, 299, 300, 301, 341, 342, 346, 347, 355, 357, 358, 359, 370, 372, 399; inaugural meeting, 50; Clonmel meeting, 381–382; Cork meetings, 138, 299; Dublin meeting, 346; Dundalk meeting, 239
Irish Transport and General Workers Union, 249, 258, 264, 265, 272–276, 282, 292, 294, 297, 299, 303, 341, 358, 361, 367, 370, 376, 382, 399, 403, 406
Irish Transvaal Committee, 117, 121, 122
Irish Volunteers, 330, 334, 346, 351, 359, 361, 365, 366, 373, 376, 377, 386, 387, 389–392, 400, 403–407
Irish Volunteers, U.S.A., 199
Irish Work, 367
Irish Worker, 280, 286, 305, 334, 341, 350, 362, 367
Irving, Dan, 68, 131, 133, 140
Italian Socialist Federation, 194, 196

Jackson, T. A., 22, 108, 380, 396, 406, 409, 423
Jacobs (biscuit manufacturers), 306, 325, 337
Jaurès, J., 127, 279
Jesuits, 211, 215, 225, 236, 255
Johnson, Olive, 203
Johnson, Tom, 249, 254, 281, 282, 296, 301, 316, 318, 344
Johnson, Mrs. T., 272, 290, 292, 296
Johnston, T., 251, 261, 422
Jones, J., 112
Jones, Jack, 332
Joyce, Myles, 26
Judge, M., 362
Justice, 35, 45, 47, 54, 69, 70, 107, 108, 111, 120, 131–132, 134, 139–141, 144, 161, 164, 177, 313

Kane, Father, 236, 237, 255, 336
"Kangaroos", 150, 174, 180, 189, 197
Katz, Rudolf, 168, 201, 210, 212
Kautsky, K., 127, 131, 132, 133, 144, 178, 237
Keady, 22
Keighley by-election, 323
Kenny, Patrick, 226

Kent, Thomas, 419
Kerr, C. H., 229
Kettle, Lawrence, 330
Killarney, 131
Kilmainham, 19, 51, 53, 422
Kiltimagh, 102
King's Liverpool Regiment, 20, 25, 26
Kinneally, J. J., 147
Knights of Labour, 173
"Know-nothing" movement, 225

Labour candidates, 44, 49, 80
Labour Electoral Association, 112, 114; 119
Labour in Irish History, 35, 42, 53, 146; 157, 158, 216, 233, 240, 245, 349, 428
Labour Leader, 56, 81, 101, 106, 111
Labour, Nationality and Religion, 40; 42, 237, 240, 248, 250, 294
Labour Party, British, 42, 95, 259, 303; 344, 347
Labour World, 49
Lafargue, Jules, 127
Lalor, Fintan, 51, 81, 260
Lancaster, Pa., 211
Lanchester, Edith, 177
Land Acts, 34, 260, 277
Land League, 19, 27, 35, 37, 51, 87, 224; 242
Lansbury, Geo., 248, 328, 337
Lansdowne, Lord, 284, 286
Larkin, Delia, 337, 377
Larkin, James, 24, 231, 234, 236, 238 to 240, 247–248, 253, 258, 264, 274, 282; 288–289, 299, 301, 342, 347–350, 362; 372, 385, 414, 418: Great Lock-out; 305–339; O'Connell Street baton-charge, 309; Release Committees, 249
Larne, 301, 350
Lassalle, Ferdinand, 170, 172, 173, 177; 206, 215, 218, 222, 242, 319
Law, Bonar, 286, 293
Lawrence, Mass., 150, 180
Lawrence, Father, 294, 397, 398
Leather *v.* Craig case, 125
Leeds, 38, 236, 326, 329, 423
Leith, 36, 48, 66, 107, 133, 320
Lenin, V. I., 178, 215, 297, 338, 352, 353, 384, 399, 408, 423
Leslie, John, 18, 30, 38, 39, 43, 45, 48, 50, 56, 69, 70, 73, 107, 109, 134, 163, 165, 240, 258, on Ireland, 49–55
Liberal Party, 41, 42, 44, 49, 246, 257, 286
Liberty Hall, 306, 309, 321, 336, 338, 364, 365, 369, 372, 378, 389, 398, 399 to 402, 406, 418, 420
Limerick, 90, 112, 113, 121, 255, 349, 405
Linen, 267